ENLIGHTENED SEXISM

ENLIGHTENED
SEXISM

THE SEDUCTIVE MESSAGE THAT
FEMINISM'S WORK IS DONE

SUSAN J. DOUGLAS

TIMES BOOKS
HENRY HOLT AND COMPANY   NEW YORK

Times Books
Henry Holt and Company, LLC
Publishers since 1866
175 Fifth Avenue
New York, New York 10010

Library of Congress Cataloging-in-Publication Data

Douglas, Susan J. (Susan Jeanne)
    Enlightened sexism : the seductive message that feminism's
work is done / Susan J. Douglas.—1st ed.
        p. cm.
    Includes bibliographical references and index.
    ISBN 978-0-8050-8326-2
    1. Women in popular culture—United States.   2. Mass media and
women—United States.   3. Feminism—United States.   I. Title.
    HQ1233.D68 2010
    302.23082'0973—dc22   2009032358

First Edition 2010

Designed by Kelly Too

Printed in the United States of America
1 3 5 7 9 10 8 6 4 2

For Paul Golob

and for Ella and her generation

CONTENTS

ENLIGHTENED SEXISM

FANTASIES OF POWER

Spring 1997. It is 8:12 A.M. Saturday. The feminist mom, who looks like she just got shot out of a wind turbine and has a cheap chardonnay hangover, is making pancakes for four eight-year-old girls who have had a sleepover party. Let's just say that she's not in the most festive mood. Then, blasting from the other room, she hears what had become the faux-rap anthem of that spring: "I'll tell ya what I want, what I really really want . . ." She peeks around the corner to see the four girls singing and dancing with abandon, sucking in "girl power" with every breath. At that instant, she saw the postfeminist zeitgeist that would envelop her daughter's generation and wondered: Should she be happy that they're listening to *bustier* feminism instead of watching Barbie commercials on Saturday morning TV? Or should she run in, rip the CD out of the player, and insist that they listen to Mary Chapin Carpenter or Ani DiFranco instead?

This was the Spice Girls moment, and debate: Were these girly, frosted cupcakes really a vehicle for feminism? And how much reversion back to the glory days of prefeminism should girls and women accept—even celebrate—given that we now allegedly "had it all." Despite their Wonderbras, bare thighs, pouty lips, and top-of-the-head ponytails (of the sort favored by Pebbles on *The Flintstones*), the Spice Girls nonetheless advocated "girl power." They demanded, in their colossal, intercontinental hit "Wannabe," that boys treat them with respect or take a hike. Their boldfaced liner notes claimed that "The Future Is Female" and suggested that they and their fans were "Freedom Fighters." They made Margaret Thatcher an honorary Spice Girl. "We're freshening up feminism for the nineties," they told the *Guardian*. "Feminism has become a dirty word. Girl Power is just a 90s way of saying it." They proclaimed that New Age feminism meant "you have a brain, a voice and an opinion." And hot pants. Hmmm.

Fast-forward to 2008. Talk about girl power! One woman ran for president and another for vice president. Millions of women and men voted for each of them. The one who ran for vice president had five children, one of them a four-month-old infant, yet it was verboten to even ask whether she could handle the job while also tending to a baby. (Other issues, like whether she ever read a newspaper or really could see Vladivostok from her window seemed a tad more pressing.) At the same time we had a female secretary of state, and the woman who had run for president became her high-profile successor. There were female CEOs, a woman anchoring the *CBS Evening News*, and female attorneys, surgeons, police chiefs, and judges all over dramatic TV. On reality TV shows like *Survivor*, female contestants battled fire ants and iguanas the size of golf carts right alongside the men. Remember when Ellen DeGeneres came out in 1997, supposedly scandalizing a nation and then having her sitcom canceled? By 2008 she and Rachel Maddow hosted their own talk shows and it was no big deal at all; in fact, millions of us loved them, and De-Generes's wedding to her girlfriend was splashed all over the cover of *People* just like that of any straight celeb.

Feminism? Who needs feminism anymore? Aren't we, like, so done here? Okay, so some women moaned about the sexist coverage of Hillary Clinton, but picky, picky, picky.

Indeed, eight years earlier, career antifeminist Christina Hoff Sommers huffed in her book, *The War Against Boys: How Misguided Feminism Is Harming Our Young Men*, that girls were getting way too much attention and, as a result, were going to college in greater numbers and much more likely to succeed while boys were getting sent to detention, dropping out of high school, destined for careers behind the counter at

Arby's, and so beaten down they were about to become the nation's new "second sex."[1] Other books like *The Myth of Male Power* and *The Decline of Males* followed suit, with annual panics about the new "crisis" for boys. Girl power? Gone way too far.

So wait a minute—in 1999, one year before Sommers's book came out, the top five jobs for women were not attorney, surgeon, or CEO. They were, in order, secretaries, retail and personal sales workers (including cashiers), managers and administrators, elementary school teachers, and registered nurses. Farther down among the top twenty were bookkeepers, receptionists, cooks, and waitresses. Eight years later, in 2007, when presumably some of the privileged, pampered girls whose advantages over boys Sommers had kvetched about had entered the workforce, the top five jobs for women were, still, secretaries in first place, followed by registered nurses, elementary and middle school teachers, cashiers, and retail salespersons. Farther down the line? Maids, child care workers, office clerks, and hairdressers. Not a CEO or hedge fund manager in sight. And, in the end, not a president or vice president either. But what about all those career-driven girls going to college and leaving the guys in the dust? A year out of college, they earn 80 percent of what men make. And ten years out? Sixty-nine percent.[2] And if girls and women really have come so far, and full equality has truly been achieved, why is it that K-Mart sells outfits for four-year-old girls that look like something out of Fredericks of Hollywood? Why did the Ladies Professional Golf Association (of all groups!) in 2002 feel compelled to call in hairstylists and makeup artists to enhance the players' sex appeal? And why is it that pundits felt free to comment on Hillary Clinton's cleavage but not John McCain's—well, let's *so* not go there.

How do we square the persistence of female inequality with all those images of female power we have seen in the media—the hands-on-her-hips, don't-even-think-about-messing-with-me Dr. Bailey on *Grey's Anatomy*, or S. Epatha Merkerson as the take-no-prisoners Lieutenant Anita Van Buren on *Law & Order*, Agent Scully on *The X-Files*, Brenda Leigh Johnson as "the chief" on *The Closer*, C. C. H. Pounder on *The Shield*, or even Geena Davis as the first female president in the short-lived series *Commander in Chief*? Advertisements tell women that they have achieved so much they should celebrate by buying themselves their own diamond ring for their right hand and urge their poor, flaccid husbands, crippled by an epidemic of emasculation and erectile dysfunction, to start mainlining Viagra or Cialis. Indeed, in films from *Dumb and Dumber* (1994) to *Superbad* (2007), guys are hopeless losers. In *Sex and the City*, with its characters who were successful professionals by day and Kama Sutra masters by night, there was no such thing as the double standard: women had as much sexual freedom, and maybe even more kinky sex, than men. *Cosmo* isn't for passive girls waiting for the right guy to find them; it's the magazine for the "Fun, Fearless Female" who is also proud to be, as one cover put it, a "Sex Genius." Have a look at *O!* The magazine is one giant, all-encompassing, throbbing zone of self-fulfillment for women where everything from pillows to celadon-colored notebooks (but only if purchased and used properly) are empowering and everything is possible. And why not? One of the most influential and successful moguls in the entertainment industry is none other than Oprah Winfrey herself.

Something's out of whack here. If you immerse yourself in the media fare of the past ten to fifteen years, what you see is a rather large gap between how the vast majority of girls and women live their lives, the choices they are forced to make, and what they see—and *don't* see—in the media. Ironically, it is just the opposite of the gap in the 1950s and '60s, when images of women as Watusi-dancing bimbettes on the beach or stay-at-home housewives who needed advice from Mr. Clean about how to wash a floor obscured the exploding number of women entering the workforce, joining the Peace Corps, and becoming involved in politics. Back then the media illusion was that the aspirations of girls and women weren't changing at all when they were. Now, the media illusion is that equality for girls and women is an accomplished fact when it isn't. Then the media were behind the curve; now, ironically, they're ahead. Have girls and women made a lot of progress since the 1970s? You bet. Women's college basketball, for example—its existence completely unimaginable when I was in school—is now nationally televised, and vulgar, boneheaded remarks about the players can get even a money machine like Don Imus fired, if only temporarily. But now we're all district attorneys, medical residents, chiefs of police, or rich, blond, So-Cal heiresses? Not so much.

Since the early 1990s, much of the media have come to overrepresent women as having made it—completely—in the professions, as having gained sexual equality with men, and having achieved a level of financial success and comfort enjoyed primarily by the Tiffany's-encrusted doyennes of Laguna Beach. At the same time, there has been a resurgence of retrograde dreck clogging our cultural arteries—*The Man Show, Maxim, Girls Gone Wild.*[3] But even this fare, which insists that young women should dress like strippers and have the mental capacities of a vole, was presented as empowering, because while the scantily clad or bare-breasted women may have *seemed* to be objectified, they were really on top, because now they had chosen to be sex objects and men were supposedly nothing more than their helpless, ogling, crotch-driven slaves.

What the media have been giving us, then, are little more than fantasies of power. They assure girls and women, repeatedly, that women's liberation is a fait accompli and that we are stronger, more successful, more sexually in control, more fearless, and more held in awe than we actually are. We can believe that any woman can become a CEO (or president), that women have achieved economic, professional, and political parity with men, and we can expunge any suggestions that there might be some of us who actually have to live on the national median income, which for women in 2008 was $36,000 a year, 23 percent less than that of their male counterparts. Yet the images we see on television, in the movies, and in advertising also insist that purchasing power and sexual power are much more gratifying than political or economic power. Buying stuff—the right stuff, a lot of stuff—emerged as the dominant way to empower ourselves.[4] Of course women in fictional TV shows can be in the highest positions of authority, but in real life—maybe not such a good idea. Instead, the wheedling, seductive message to young women is that being decorative is the highest form of power—when, of course, if it were, Dick Cheney would have gone to work every day in a sequined tutu.

And not that some of these fantasies haven't been delectable. I mean, Xena single-handedly trashing, on a regular basis, battalions of stubble-faced, leather-clad, murdering-and-raping barbarian hordes? Or *Buffy the Vampire Slayer* letting us pretend, if just for an hour, that only a teenage girl (and a former cheerleader to boot) can save the world from fang-toothed evil? What about an underdog law student, dismissed by her fellow classmates as an airheaded bimbo, winning a high-profile murder case because she understood how permanents work, as Elle did in *Legally Blonde*? Or let's say you've had an especially stupid day at work and as you collapse on the sofa desperately clutching a martini (hold the vermouth), you see a man on TV tell his female boss that the way she does things is "just not the way we play ball," and she responds drolly, "Well, if you don't like the way I'm doing things, you're free to take your balls and go straight home"? (Yes, *The Closer*.) Oooo-weeee.

So what's the matter with fantasies of female power? Haven't the media always provided escapist fantasies; isn't that, like, their job? And aren't many in the media—however belatedly—simply addressing women's demands for more representations of female achievement and control? Well, yes. But here's the odd, somewhat unintended consequence: under the guise of escapism and pleasure, we are getting images of imagined power that mask, and even erase, how much still remains to be done for girls and women, images that make sexism seem fine, even fun, and insist that feminism is now utterly pointless—even bad for you. And if we look at what is often being said about girls and women in these fantasies—what we can and should do, what we can and can't be—we will see that slithering just below the shiny mirage of power is the dark, sneaky serpent of sexism.

There has been a bit of a generational divide in how these fantasies are presented. Older women—I prefer the term "Vintage Females"—like myself have been given all those iron-clad women in the 10:00 P.M. strip: the lawyers, cops, and district attorneys on the entire *Law & Order* franchise; the senior partner Shirley Schmidt on *Boston Legal*; the steely (and busty) forensic scientists on the various *CSIs*; the ubiquitous female judges; and Brenda Leigh Johnson who, with her big hair and southern drawl, whipped her male chauvinist colleagues into shape ASAP on *The Closer*.

But many of us, especially mothers, have been less thrilled about the fantasies on offer for girls and younger women. For "millennials"—those young women and girls born in the late 1980s and 1990s who are the most attractive demographic for advertisers—the fantasies and appeals have been much more commercial and, not surprisingly, more retrograde. While they are the "girl power" generation, the bill of goods they are repeatedly sold is that true power comes from shopping, having the right logos, and being "hot." Power also comes from judging, dissing, and competing with other girls, especially over guys. I have watched these fantasies—often the opposite of the "role model" imagery presented to me—swirl around my daughter and, well, I have not been amused.

Things seemed okay back in the 1990s when she could watch shows like *Alex Mack*, featuring a girl with superhuman powers who morphed into something that looked like a blob of mercury and conducted industrial espionage, or *Shelby Wu*, a girl detective. But then she graduated to MTV: by this time, the network had stopped showing Talking Heads videos and, instead, offered up fare like *Sorority Life*. Here viewers got to track the progress of college girls pledging to a sorority, and to see which traits, behaviors, and hairdos got them in ("nice," "pretty," ponytails) and which ones kept them out ("like so bossy," "like so phony," any hairstyle that resembled a mullet). Even though the show was allegedly about college life, no books, newspapers, novels, debates about the existence of God, or discussion of any recent classroom lectures cluttered the scene or troubled the dialogue. These college girls were way too shallow for any of that. My sympathetic response to my teenage daughter on the sofa, wrapped in a quilt, escaping for a bit into this drivel-filled world? A simple bellow: "Shut that crap off!"

Now I ask you, what teenager wouldn't love to have a feminist mother standing over her shoulder while she watches TV, pointing out how the show perpetuates stereotypes about girls being narcissistic twits obsessed only with personal relationships? Then, warming to my task as I basked in my daughter's obvious gratitude, I moved on to what I regarded as a quite entertaining critique of the ads for Cover Girl, Victoria's Secret, and MTV's upcoming *Ultimate Spring Break Orgy Blow-Out*. My daughter, eager to convey her appreciation, gave me a look that could melt a meteor.

Things were not much better between us when I was periodically dragged into that electronica-thumping haberdashery from hell, Abercrombie & Fitch. Talk about paralyzing your pleasure in retail. The firm that once sold men fishing rods and helped outfit Teddy Roosevelt for safari (and had a twelve-story shop in midtown Manhattan with a log cabin on the roof), Abercrombie & Fitch in the early 1990s changed its focus to sell overpriced wifebeaters and half-naked Aryan men to the youth of America. The blown-up black-and-white shots of muscular, self-satisfied blond pretty boys in low-slung boxer shorts may have been attractive to my daughter, but all I kept thinking was "Hitler youth." And "statutory rape." The deafening boom-boom dance-floor music was supposed to convey that, dude, we were in a totally cool zone, but I always felt like I was trapped in Godzilla's left ventricle. When the Homeric excursion was mercifully over, my daughter would be in possession of various items that would turn her into a walking billboard for Abercrombie & Fitch, and carrying shopping bags with bare-naked, sushi-grade torsos that proclaimed that nothing—nothing—was more important than turning yourself into a sexual commodity.

It kept getting worse: entire TV specials based on Victoria's Secret bras, or those MTV or BET "spring break" programs in which young women are routinely expected to flash their breasts for any zit-studded male in baggy shorts who asks, or have whipped cream licked off their thighs by a guy named Trek and his best bud Diesel. All too many rap videos require thong-clad women to shake their booties while climbing all over the strutting, self-satisfied men. Television also hurled forth such media vomit as *Age of Love*, which pitted "kittens" (size two women in their twenties) against "cougars" (astoundingly well-preserved size two women in their forties) for the affections of a thirty-year-old tennis player none of them knew anything about. (Guess who won.)

As I stewed about the fantasies of power laid before my daughter and those laid before me, I was, of course, most struck at first by their generational differences, and how they pitted us against each other, especially around the issues of sexual display and rampant consumerism as alleged sources of power and control. But if you think about it, they simply buy us off in different ways, because both approaches contribute to the false assumption that for women, all has been won. The notion that there might, indeed, still be an urgency to feminist politics? You have totally got to be kidding.

This book is about the rise and evolution of these media-created fantasies, from the early 1990s to the present: their origins, their manifestations, their contradictory mixed messages, and their consequences. While these fantasies have been driven in part by girls' and women's desires, and have often provided a great deal of vicarious pleasure, they have also been driven by marketing—especially niche, target marketing—and the use of that heady mix of flattery and denigration to sell us everything from skin cream to running shoes. So it's time to take these fantasies to the interrogation room and shine a little light on them. Because what the media giveth with one hand (which is why we love them), they taketh away with the other hand (which is why they endlessly piss us off). So we need to understand, and unravel, the various forces that have given us, say, the fearless computer geek Chloe on *24*, without whom Jack Bauer would have been toast twenty-five times over, versus Jessica Simpson on *Newlyweds*, who didn't know how to turn on a stove (ha! ha! get it?).

One force is embedded feminism: the way in which women's achievements, or their desire for achievement, are simply part of the cultural landscape. Feminism is no longer "outside" of the media as it was in 1970, when women staged a sit-in at the stereotype-perpetuating *Ladies' Home Journal* or gave awards for the most sexist, offensive ads like those of National Airlines, which featured stewardesses purring, "I'm Cheryl. Fly Me" (and required flight attendants to wear "Fly Me" buttons). Today, feminist gains, attitudes, and achievements are woven into our cultural fabric.[5] So the female characters created by Shonda Rhimes for *Grey's Anatomy*, to choose just one example, reflect a genuine desire to show women as skilled professionals in jobs previously reserved for men. Joss Whedon created *Buffy the Vampire Slayer* because he embraced feminism and was tired of seeing all the girls in horror films as victims, instead of possible heroes. But women whose kung fu skills are more awesome than Jackie Chan's? Or who tell a male coworker (or boss) to his face that he's less evolved than a junior in high school? This is a level of command-and-control barely enjoyed by four-star generals, let alone the nation's actual female population.

But the media's fantasies of power are also the product of another force that has gained considerable momentum since the early and mid-1990s: enlightened sexism.[6] Enlightened sexism is a response, deliberate or not, to the perceived threat of a new gender regime. It insists that women have made plenty of progress because of feminism—indeed, full equality has allegedly been achieved—so now it's okay, even amusing, to resurrect sexist stereotypes of girls and women.[7] After all, these images (think Pussycat Dolls, *The Bachelor*, *Are You Hot?*, the hour-and-a-half catfight in *Bride Wars*) can't possibly undermine women's equality at this late date, right? More to the point, enlightened sexism sells the line that it is precisely through women's calculated deployment of their faces, bodies, attire, and sexuality that they gain and enjoy true power—power that is fun, that men will not resent, and indeed will embrace. True power here has nothing to do with economic independence or professional achievement (that's a given): it has to do with getting men to lust after you and other women to envy you. Enlightened sexism is especially targeted to girls and young women and emphasizes that now that they "have it all," they should focus the bulk of their time and energy on their appearance, pleasing men, being hot, competing with other women, and shopping.

Enlightened sexism is a manufacturing process that is produced, week in and week out, by the media. Its components—anxiety about female achievement; a renewed and amplified objectification of young women's bodies and faces; the dual exploitation and punishment of female sexuality; the dividing of women against each other by age, race, and class; rampant branding and consumerism—began to swirl around in the early 1990s, consolidating as the dark star it has become in the early twenty-first century. Some, myself included, have referred to this state of affairs and this kind of media mix as "postfeminist."[8] But I am rejecting this term. It has gotten gummed up by too many conflicting definitions. And besides, this term suggests that somehow feminism is at the root of this when it isn't—it's good, old-fashioned, grade-A sexism that reinforces good, old-fashioned, grade-A patriarchy. It's just much better disguised, in seductive Manolo Blahniks and an Ipex bra.

Enlightened sexism is feminist in its outward appearance (of course you can be or do anything you want) but sexist in its intent (hold on, girls, only up to a certain point, and not in any way that discomfits men or pushes feminist goals one more centimeter forward). While enlightened sexism seems to support women's equality, it is dedicated to the undoing of feminism.[9] In fact, because this equality might lead to "sameness"—way too scary—girls and women need to be reminded that they are still fundamentally female, and so must be emphatically feminine. Thus enlightened sexism takes the gains of the women's movement as a given, and then uses them as permission to resurrect retrograde images of girls and women as sex objects, bimbos, and hootchie mamas still defined by their appearance and their biological destiny. So in the age of enlightened sexism there has been an explosion in makeover, matchmaking, and modeling shows, a renewed emphasis on women's breasts (and a massive surge in the promotion of breast augmentation), an obsession with babies and motherhood in celebrity journalism (the rise of the creepy "bump patrol"), and a celebration of stay-at-home moms and "opting out" of the workforce.

Lurking in this media fare is the *Men Are from Mars, Women Are from Venus* principle that women are fundamentally different from men and can never be equal to them. (In the first two seasons of *The Apprentice*, for example, it was a given that young career women would compete with men for The Donald's top prize—to be mentored by him, oy!—yet it was made clear that no woman could win because they're too backstabbing and emotional.) And enlightened sexism rests crucially on ageism, on severing young women from their elders. Because of its insistence that women now "have it all" (whatever "it" is), enlightened sexism ignores girls and women who are not middle class, upper middle class, or rich and, for the most part, not white. It is emphatically heterosexist. Enlightened sexism thus seeks to become the updated, hip, prevailing common sense about what girls and women can be and do in today's world.

In this way enlightened sexism is more nuanced and much more insidious than out-and-out backlash.[10] As Susan Faludi amply demonstrated, backlash involves a direct, explicit refutation of feminism as misguided and bad for women. Enlightened sexism is subtler. Male pundits couldn't very well call Hillary Clinton a bitch on TV (although the knuckle-dragger Glenn Beck did on his radio show), but they could say that when men hear her voice, they hear, "Take out the garbage," and everyone knows what *that* means.

Feminism thus must remain a dirty word, with feminists (particularly older ones) stereotyped as man-hating, child-loathing, hairy, shrill, humorless, deliberately unattractive Ninjas from Hades.[11] (So we get books like Kate O'Beirne's screed *Women Who Make the World Worse: And How Their Radical Feminist Assault Is Ruining Our Schools, Families, Military, and Sports*, in which Eleanor Smeal, the former president of the National Organization for Women, is suddenly more powerful than the secretary of defense, Halliburton, or the entire doping industry in baseball and the Tour de France.) More to the point, feminism must be emphatically rejected because it supposedly prohibits women from having any fun, listening to the Rolling Stones or Shaggy, and condemns spending the equivalent of a car payment at Sephora, buying high heels, or wearing spandex hip-huggers. As this logic goes, feminism is so 1970s—grim, dowdy, aggrieved, and passé—that it is now an impediment to female happiness and fulfillment.[12] Thus, an amnesia about the women's movement, and the rampant, now illegal discrimination that produced it, is essential, so we'll forget that politics matters.

Because women are now "equal" and the battle is over and won, we are now free to embrace things we used to see as sexist, including hypergirliness. In fact, this is supposed to be a relief. Thank God girls and women can turn their backs on stick-in-the-mud, curdled feminism and now act dumb in string bikinis to attract guys. In fact, now that women allegedly have the same sexual freedom as men, they actually prefer to be sex objects because it's liberating.[13] According to enlightened sexism, women today have a choice between feminism and antifeminism, and they just naturally and happily choose the latter because, well, antifeminism has become cool, even hip. Rejecting feminism and buying into enlightened sexism allows young women in particular to be "one of the guys."[14] Indeed, enlightened sexism is meant to make patriarchy pleasurable for women.[15]

Enlightened sexism emerged, in part, from the fact that young women were coming of age in an era of expanding opportunities. It came into full bloom under the Bush administration, and especially after 9/11. Coincidence? I think not. Before he and his ilk trashed the economy, Bush presided over the perfect enlightened sexism presidency. And talk about the illusion of power! There were the poster women of female achievement: Condoleezza Rice, Karen Hughes, Christine Todd Whitman. But they were beards for the silverbacks Bush, Cheney, and Rumsfeld, who chest-thumped their way through one of the most macho-posturing administrations in recent history while working behind the scenes to curtail women's rights. The real female role model was supposed to be retro-mom Laura Bush. This was a political environment that positively suckled enlightened sexism, Bush's frat boy persona resonating well with the guys-will-be-guys ethos of *Maxim*. And as Susan Faludi reminds us in her book

The Terror Dream: Fear and Fantasy in Post-9/11 America, feminism came in for a sound thrashing after 9/11 because it had supposedly made the country all girly and weak, unable to protect itself, and thus it provided a double dog dare to al-Qaeda to show America what happens when women are not kept in their place.[16] The 9/11 attacks were, as Faludi recounts, cast as "a blow to feminism" that had "met its Waterloo." Now it was time, as the conservative columnist Mona Charen put it, to simply yell, "Hooray for Men."[17]

So enlightened sexism also includes in-your-face sexism, in which the attitudes about women that infuriated feminists in the 1960s and '70s are pushed to new, even more degrading levels, except that it's all done with a wink—or, even better, for the girls' own good. *The Man Show,* in which barely clad young women jumped on trampolines so men could watch their boobs bounce, would, in 1972, have prompted the studio that produced it to be torched to the ground. Not today.

As the British feminist scholar Angela McRobbie has brilliantly argued, it is essential that feminism be repudiated as something young women should shun as old-fashioned, withered, humorless, repulsive. To do this, the media must explicitly acknowledge feminism, point to it, and "take it into account" in order to argue that it is no longer needed, a "spent force."[18] On *The Man Show,* for example, it was understood that it *is* sexist and ridiculous to have bikini-clad women jumping on trampolines and, furthermore, that the guys who wanted them to do this were morons. This is the knowing wink: guys are so dumb, such helpless slaves to big breasts, and the female display is, in the end, so harmless, that a feminist critique is not necessary. Therefore, the objectification of women is now fine; why, it's actually a joke on the guys. It's silly to be sexist; therefore, it's funny to be sexist.[19] This is the same strategy used by *Maxim,* the *Cosmo* for guys. *Maxim's* objectification of women is so over the top, and constantly wedded to suggestions that most guys are so totally under women's thumbs, that its sexism is meant to be seen as pathetic. Indeed, as the feminist scholar Rosalind Gill puts it, "The extremeness of the sexism is evidence that there's no sexism!"[20] If there is no more sexism, then there is no longer a need for sexual politics, and sexual politics can be mocked and attacked.

Enlightened sexism has cranked out media fare geared to girls and young women in which they compete over men, many of them knuckleheads (*Next, The Bachelor, Joe Millionaire, The Flavor of Love*); compete with each other (*America's Next Top Model*); obsess about relationships and status (*Laguna Beach, The Hills*) or about pleasing men sexually (*Cosmo*, most music videos); and are fixated by conspicuous consumption (*Rich Girls, My Super Sweet Sixteen, Laguna Beach, The O.C.*, and that wonderful little serpent of a show *Gossip Girl*). Yet I can assure you that my female students at the University of Michigan—academically accomplished, smart, and ambitious—have flocked to these shows. Why?

This is the final key component to enlightened sexism: irony, the cultivation of the ironic, knowing viewer and the deployment of ironic sexism.[21] Irony offers the following fantasy of power: the people on the screen may be rich, spoiled, or beautiful, but you, O superior viewer, get to judge and mock them, and thus are above them. With a show like MTV's *My Super Sweet Sixteen*, in which, typically, a spoiled-brat rich girl has her parents buy her everything from a new Mercedes to multiple evening gowns to a Vegas-style floor show to make sure her Sweet Sixteen party is like the most totally awesome ever, viewers are not merely (or primarily) meant to envy the girl. Animated stars superimposed on the scenes accompanied by a tinkling sound effect signal that we are also meant to see the whole exercise as over-the-top, ridiculous, exaggerated, the girl way too shallow and narcissistic. The show—indeed many MTV shows—elbow the viewer in the ribs, saying, "We know that you know that we know that you know that this is excessive and kitschy, that you're too smart to read this straight and not laugh at it."

For media-savvy youth, bombarded their entire lives by almost every marketing ploy in the book, irony means that you can look as if you are absolutely not seduced by the mass media, while then being seduced by the media, while wearing a knowing smirk. Viewers are flattered that they are sophisticated, can see through the craven self-absorption, wouldn't be so vacuous and featherbrained as to get so completely caught up in something so trivial. MTV offers this irony as a shield; you can convince yourself that you are seeing a parody of girls as party-obsessed airheads only capable of thinking about popularity and conspicuous consumption while, of course, *My Super Sweet Sixteen* repeatedly shows girls as party-obsessed airheads only capable of thinking about popularity and conspicuous consumption. This kind of irony allows for the representation of something sexist—most girls, and especially rich girls, are self-centered bimbos—while being able to claim that that's not really what you meant at all, it's just for fun.[22]

Girls often watch shows like this or *Laguna Beach* or *The Real World* in groups (as they did *Beverly Hills 90210* in the '90s) and part of the fun here is collectively performing your outrage at how empty-headed and materialistic the girls on the screen are while still becoming enmeshed in their stories. This public, group ridicule says, "We are not dupes"; it is an emphatic performance of media sophistication. It affirms viewers' power, both over the media and over the representation of girls as shallow and frivolous. The pleasure comes from feeling that you *are* reading against the grain, seeing through and deconstructing this media sludge. But the bacteria that comes in with this inoculation is girls policing one another and themselves, reinforcing norms about being "nice" and "hot." And this ridicule-as-power also gives girls permission to look forward to noxious girl-on-girl violence—the catfight—and to watch shows that, in the end, are about female competition and consumerism as the ultimate privilege and delight.[23] It's not that many young women don't see through this. But it's precisely because so much media fare geared to young women incorporates their own ironic, self-reflexive critique that sorting out their effects—what creeps in through that shield of irony?—is much harder to discern.

Despite the successful onward trudge of enlightened sexism—How can *The Bachelor* have survived to a thirteenth edition? How is Hooters still in business?—there is a war in the media between it and embedded feminism. As a result, we are bombarded by overlapping and often colliding streams of progressive and regressive imagery, both of which offer us very different fantasies of female power. Yet, in the end, embedded feminism and enlightened sexism serve to reinforce each other: they both overstate women's gains and accomplishments, and they both render feminism obsolete. One click of the remote gives us tough-talking female police lieutenants, surgeons, and attorneys, or cocksure female cable news anchors and pundits; another click gives us spoiled bubbleheads in hot tubs whose only thought is their next themed party. Indeed, the proliferation of the former is meant to excuse, even justify the latter. Thus, the success of enlightened sexism rests on representations of accomplished, sexually liberated women. After all, girls and women would hardly read and watch all this stuff if it were relentlessly sexist, which it isn't. In fact, enlightened sexism and embedded feminism often celebrate female-centered knowledge—about fashion, makeup, babies, relationships—that used to be derided as trivial, and insist that such knowledge matters. In this way, enlightened sexism is powerfully seductive, just the way the Spice Girls were: it claims you can have independence, power, and respect *and* male love and approval *and* girly, consumerist indulgences all at once, all without costs. And images of ever more empowered, confident, independent women are seamlessly accompanied by incessant harangues that we're still not thin enough, busty enough, gorgeous enough, or wearing the most enviable logo.

Because of these powerful crosscurrents—both appealing, both profitable, both tapping into our ever-contradictory cultural zeitgeist—girls and women are pulled in opposite directions, between wanting serious success and respect, and wanting acceptance, approval, and love; between wanting power and dreading power. The fantasies laid before us, in their various forms, school us in how to forge a perfect and allegedly empowering compromise between feminism and femininity. And that compromise insists that women strike a bargain. We can play sports, excel at school, go to college, aspire to—and get—jobs previously reserved for men, be working mothers, and so forth. But in exchange, we must obsess about our faces, weight, breast size, clothing brands, decorating, perfectly calibrated child-rearing, about pleasing men and being envied by other women. And we should expect no support from the government or our workplaces when it comes to juggling work and family because that's just a personal "choice" we made, and should live with. So this ersatz, "can do" feminism substitutes our own individual efforts, and our own responsibility to succeed, for what used to be a more collective sensibility about pushing for changes that would help all women.

What so much of this media (especially advertising) emphasizes is that women are defined by our bodies, our identities located *in* our bodies, and those must be sexually alluring (now, even when we're pregnant—thanks a lot, Demi Moore!) and conform to a very narrow fashion-model ideal of beauty.[24] This is nothing new, of course, but it was something millions of women hoped to deep-six back in the 1970s. Indeed, it is precisely because women no longer have to exhibit traditionally "feminine" *personality* traits—like being passive, helpless, docile, overly emotional, dumb, and deferential to men—that they must exhibit hyperfeminine *physical* traits—large boobs and cleavage, short skirts, pouty lips—and the proper logos linking this femininity to upper-class ranking. The war between embedded feminism and enlightened sexism gives with one hand and takes away with the other. It's a powerful choke leash, letting women venture out, offering us fantasies of power, control, and love, and then pulling us back in. The only way women today can straddle all of this is to be superwomen.

This, then, is the mission at hand: to pull back the curtain and to note how these fantasies distract us from our ongoing status—still, despite everything—as second-class citizens. A Vintage Female such as myself is not supposed to be so rude, or to have any credibility to do so because I am—at least according to Jurassic life-forms like Rush Limbaugh—three really bad things: an academic, an aging woman, and, lowest of the low, a feminist. Feminists supposedly don't enjoy movies, television, music, or shopping and seek to take all the pleasure out of these for everyone else. (This is why I go to the MAC counter in a ski mask—can't undermine my image.) Young women should see us as out-of-touch has-beens in bad shoes who have nothing in common with them. Limbaugh has summed it up well: "Feminism was established to allow unattractive women easier access to the mainstream of society." (Fortunately, no social movement was needed to allow pudgy, unattractive men access to the top.) Pat Robertson asserted that feminism "encourages women to leave their husbands, kill their children and practice witchcraft." (I really wish I had known this a lot earlier.) Jerry Falwell blamed "pagans," "gays and lesbians," and "feminists" for the 9/11 attacks on the World Trade Center and the Pentagon. He later apologized to gays and lesbians, but not to the feminists, let alone the poor pagans.

You get the idea—stale, white-bread, lard-butts like this get to utter such idiocies to audiences of millions (and not get laughed into oblivion) while girls and women are not supposed to offer a few choice words about how or why a TV show like *Are You Hot?*, in which Lorenzo

Lamas directs a red laser light onto women's offending body parts, ever got on the air. But while the media do all they can to divide my daughter's generation from mine, and to make the voices of older women illegitimate, I say girls, we're still all in this together. When I see the young women of America urged to devote even one nanosecond to anything said or done by Paris Hilton (well, except for her priceless "see you at the debates, bitches" response to John McCain's suggestion that she and Barack Obama were just alike) or to school themselves on "The Sex He'll Die For" (*Cosmo*, as opposed to the sex *you'll* die for), I feel like Julia Child forced to sample the cuisine at Hooters.

It goes without saying that there is not a cabal of six white guys in Hollywood saying, "Women are getting too much power; before they get too far let's buy them off with fantasies that will make them think they've already made it and will get them to focus on shopping and breast implants instead of eying the glass ceiling." (Although now that I think about it, maybe they *did* say that!) On the contrary, what we see and hear from the media comes from the most noble intentions of certain writers and producers to offer girls and women strong role models and from the most crass commercial calculations to use illusions of power to sell us, well, pretty much everything. And we are surrounded by and enmeshed in the media as never before. Spending on entertainment as a proportion of family income has increased sevenfold between the late 1960s and the mid-2000s.[25] To my students, a home with only three television networks and no cable, no Internet, and no cell phones sounds like a medieval Albanian outhouse. So while the media are hardly hypodermic needles injecting a passive and unsuspecting culture with powerful alien images and messages that we all say "yes" to, they play a potent role in shaping our identities, our dreams, our hopes, our ambitions, and our fears.

Many producers insist that the mass media are simply mirrors, reflecting reality, whatever that is, back to the public. Whenever you hear this mirror metaphor, I urge you to smash it. Because if the media are mirrors, they are fun house mirrors. You know, the wavy kind, where your body becomes completely distorted and certain parts—typically your butt and thighs—become huge while other parts, like your knees, nearly disappear. This is the mass media—exaggerating certain kinds of stories, certain kinds of people, certain kinds of values and attitudes, while minimizing others or rendering them invisible.[26] This is even more true today than it was thirty years ago because specific media outlets targeted to specific audiences traffic in an ever narrower range of representations. These media also set the agenda for what we are to think about, what kinds of people deserve our admiration, respect, and envy, and what kinds don't. We know, just to pick one example, that the media's relentless parading of hyperthin women corrodes many girls' and women's self-esteem, makes them very dissatisfied with their own bodies, and contributes to the prevalence of eating disorders in the country. This doesn't mean that we don't talk back to these images, hurling Krispy Kremes at Tyra Banks or "Body by Victoria" commercials. There's plenty of defiance and sass out there. And acquiescence. At the very same time.

So girls and women are not dupes, simply saying "whatever" to the sexism of *The Real World* or *The Swan* (in which contestants underwent up to fourteen often heroic cosmetic surgeries so they could compete in a beauty contest), as we could see in the outpouring of fury against the media coverage of Hillary Clinton's campaign, or as the ridicule my students heap on most MTV fare suggests. We enter into TV shows, movies, magazines, or Web sites and chat rooms to escape, to transport ourselves into another realm, yet we don't want to feel like we're totally suckered in either. This is where most of us are, in the complicated and contradictory terrain of negotiation.[27]

Negotiation was what the Spice Girls were all about: between sexual objectification and feminist politics, between female bonding and pursuing male approval, between self-respect and self-display. They tried to look like Barbie and sound like Gloria Steinem. They insisted that girls could have it both ways, to capitulate to—and even embrace—male fantasies about how young women should look and dress and, at the same time, defy and even conquer the dismissal of women as serious, independent beings that the Wonderbra–short shorts look typically evokes. They were the Roman candles of girl power, their message that feminism was necessary *and* fun sparkling through the culture before fizzling out. In their wake, young women are still struggling to finesse how to have respect and love, achievement and relationships, work and family, and the media continue to give them contradictory answers.

Thus, despite my own love of escaping into worlds in which women solve crimes, are good bosses, live in huge houses, can buy whatever they want, perform lifesaving surgeries, and find love, I am here to argue, forcefully, for the importance of Wariness, with a capital W. The media have played an important role in enabling us to have female cabinet members, in raising awareness about and condemning domestic violence, in helping Americans accept very different family formations than the one on *Leave It to Beaver*, even in imagining a woman president. But let's not forget that in the United States, we have the flimsiest support network for mothers and children of any industrialized country, an estimated 1.9 million women are assaulted each year by a husband or boyfriend, and nearly 18 percent of women have been the victim of a completed or attempted rape.[28] White women still make 75 cents to a man's dollar, and it's 62 cents for African American women and only 53 cents for Latina women.[29] The majority of families with children in poverty are headed by single women. African American and Latina women, still vastly underrepresented or stereotyped in the media, endure more poverty, brutality, crappy health care, and disease than their white counterparts.

The disasters around the wars in Iraq and Afghanistan and the crumbling U.S. economy have made so-called women's issues seem trivial by comparison. These wars also directed our attention away from the fact that the Bush administration throughout its two terms worked assiduously to erode women's rights, especially their reproductive rights, sought to slash health care for poor women and children, and closed the White House Office for Women's Initiatives and Outreach. Information about issues like pay equity and child care were removed from the Department of Labor's Web site; twenty-five such publications vanished from the Women's Bureau Web site alone. Instead, new bogus information, such as the claim that there was a link between having an abortion and getting breast cancer, appeared on the National Cancer Institute's Web site. And in 2005 the Bush administration weakened the standards for compliance with Title IX, making it easier for schools to avoid providing equal athletic opportunities for women and men.[30] With *The Closer*, the surgeons on *Grey's Anatomy*, Dr. House's female boss, and all those technically savvy forensic scientists on the various *CSIs*, might we be tempted to think such political rollbacks are irrelevant and can't really touch us? Or, conversely, do the female obsessions with extreme makeovers and being the one to get the bachelor suggest that, at the end of the day, women really are best confined to the kitchen and bedroom? A 2009 poll revealed that 60 percent of men and 50 percent of women "are convinced that there are no longer any barriers to women's advancement in the workplace."[31] The media may convey this, but data about the real jobs most women hold, and the persistence of discrimination against them, belie this happy illusion.

So how did we get here, to this ironic pass, where the media have both exaggerated female achievements and, at the same time, resurrected misogynistic stereotypes of yore? To answer that we'll need to go down memory lane, starting in the early and mid-1990s, when Riot Grrrl, *Sassy*, Janet Reno, Hillary Clinton, and Buffy all seemed to augur a new era of gender equality and a general unease that girls and women were getting too big for their britches. Indeed, it is striking to go back to this period and see how much feminist ferment there was.

We typically look back on the 1970s, with the eruption of the women's movement and its attacks on women's second-class citizenship—and its condemnation of images of women as too dumb, hysterical, or erratic at "that time of month" to be a doctor, or a cop, let alone a presidential candidate—as the high-water mark of feminism. In its wake the media had to make some adjustments. So there was some progress, although it was still hard for Hollywood to give up on wet T-shirts and bikinis (*Charlie's Angels*), bustier superhero outfits (*Wonder Woman*), and depictions of powerful women as rapacious bitches from Hades (Joan Collins as Alexis on *Dynasty*—be still, my heart!—Ursula the sea witch in *The Little Mermaid*, Sigourney Weaver as the conniving she-boss in *Working Girl*).

But it was really in the early and mid-1990s that we started to see more significant change, both in real life and in the nation's imagery of women. The news media tagged 1992 "The Year of the Woman" because so many ran for office, in no small part because we felt our jugulars pop out of our necks as we watched how Anita Hill was treated by the fossils on the Senate Judiciary Committee during Clarence Thomas's confirmation hearings in 1991. But in the early 1990s girls were discovered, too—both as a group still victimized by sexism and, more important of course, as a market, one even bigger than their mothers had been. They became a booming demographic: indeed, by 2005, there were more teenagers than any other age group, and by 2010 the teen market will have hit 34 million. And when you are a market in America, you really matter, culturally and economically (if not politically). Thus girls—white middle-class girls, white rich girls—became a media fixation, inspiring cultural panics, federal uplift programs, best-selling books, and a spate of new magazines, TV programs, chick flicks, chick lit, Web sites, and pop stars, not to mention an entire new generation of paparazzi dedicated to catching Lindsay Lohan, Paris Hilton, and Britney Spears in compromising positions. Girls themselves, especially in the early and mid-1990s, claimed their own voices, and a Do-It-Yourself subculture (quickly coopted, of course) that produced zines, Web sites, independent films, videos, and music flourished.[32]

It is only through tracing the origins of these images of female power that we can begin to untangle how they have offered empowerment at the cost of eroding our self-esteem, and keeping millions in their place. Because still, despite everything, what courses through our culture is the belief—and fear—that once women have power, they turn into Cruella De Vil or Miranda Priestly in *The Devil Wears Prada*—evil, tyrannical, hated, unloved. And the great irony is that if some media fare is actually ahead of where most women are in society, it may be thwarting the very advances for women that it seeks to achieve.

But still we watch. There is plenty here to love, and even more to talk back to and make fun of. Because, while it's only a start, laughter—especially derisive laughter—may be the most empowering act of all. This is part of the ongoing, never-ending project of consciousness-raising. Then we can get down to business. And girls, there is plenty of unfinished business at hand.

1

GET THE GIRLS

In October 1990, while most of America was watching *Roseanne, Coach, L.A. Law, America's Funniest Home Videos,* and the buildup to Operation Desert Storm on CNN, the still fledging Fox network debuted a show on Thursday nights opposite *Cheers,* the top-rated program in the country. In December the new show was ranked eighty-seventh out of eighty-nine. The reviews were not kind either. A "new experiment in comatose television," was the verdict of Tom Shales at the *Washington Post*: "You keep checking your pulse to make sure you haven't died."[1] Matt Roush in *USA Today* used words like "tired" and "stock characters" and predicted "few will leave *Cheers* for this."[2] Jay Sharbutt of the Associated Press said the premiere "is so stultifying it would get an F even in film school."[3] Ouch.

None of these guys, however, was a teenage girl. Within six months, *Beverly Hills 90210* was the top show among teenagers in the Thursday 9:00 P.M. time slot, and 60 percent of them were girls, that delectable demographic. Instead of running reruns during the summer of 1991, Fox aired new episodes, which built the audience even more. In August, heartthrob Luke Perry—deliberately modeled after James Dean right down to his pompadoured hairdo (which presided over his forehead like

Diamond Head)—visited a Florida shopping mall to promote the show. Ten thousand fans, most of them screaming girls, rushed toward him, injuring twenty-one people and prompting the mall to be closed for three hours.[4]

By the fall *90210* was the top show, period, among American teenagers and especially teenage girls.[5] Within a year, a whopping 69 percent of teenage girls reportedly watched it. By 1993, it was airing in thirty countries.[6] Calendars, T-shirts, lunch boxes, backpacks, pillows, and *90210* Barbie dolls followed. Most fans were utterly devoted, especially in the beginning, arranging their homework, showering, and social schedules around the show and insisting that friends not call them, at all, while it was on (unless girls called each other and watched together while on the phone).[7] The show lasted for ten years.

To understand the ascendency of enlightened sexism in the twenty-first century, its early scrimmages with embedded feminism, and the way it sought to transform girls' desires for power and change into consumerism and profits, we need to revisit the riptides of the early 1990s. One could be forgiven for forgetting that this was, in fact, a time of considerable feminist ferment among women *and* girls. For while *90210* addressed teen girls as if their primary concern was where to get the coolest stonewashed jeans (and a blond, tousle-haired hunk to go with), many real-life girls, and their mothers, were expressing a desire for what would eventually come to be known as girl power.

Girls and women may not have been in the streets the way they were in 1970, but there was an intense level of feminist agitation and aspiration, especially in the face of what Susan Faludi's best-selling 1991 book labeled, simply enough, *Backlash*. On the one hand, First Lady Barbara Bush famously warned women, "At the end of your life, you will never regret not having passed one more test, not winning one more verdict or not closing one more deal. You will regret time not spent with a husband, a friend, a child, or a parent." And the *Sports Illustrated* swimsuit issue was selling more copies than ever. On the other hand, in the song "Don't Need You," the Riot Grrrl band Bikini Kill advised men, "Don't need your atti-fuckin-tude boy . . . Us girls, we don't need you . . . Does it scare you that we don't need you?" coupled with Bratmobile's full-bore assault on patriarchy in its song "Brat Girl," "I'm gonna throw this knife right thru yr chest."

There was plenty for women to be enraged about in the early 1990s. When Thurgood Marshall, the first African American Supreme Court justice and a pioneer against school desegregation, decided to retire in 1991, President George H. W. Bush nominated Clarence Thomas, a deeply conservative, anti–affirmative action African American bureaucrat who had only been a federal judge for two years, to replace him. Many civil rights and women's groups denounced the nomination, and it barely squeaked out of the Senate Judiciary Committee with a 7-to-7 vote. Then, in October, all hell broke loose when the allegations of Anita Hill, a University of Oklahoma law professor who had told the FBI during the background checks on Thomas that he had sexually harassed her, got leaked to the press. Hill had to provide testimony before a riveted national television audience about how Thomas, at work, would start talking to her about "acts he had seen in pornographic films involving such matters as women having sex with animals, and films showing group sex or rape scenes." Hill stated that Thomas kept asking her out despite her refusals, kept commenting on her clothes and appearance, and also boasted to Hill "graphically of his own sexual prowess," which included references to "the size of his own penis being larger than normal." In a truly weird workplace comment, Thomas allegedly asked Hill, "Who has put a pubic hair on my Coke?"[8] This last event struck most women as particularly hard to make up. Yet various of the all-white male Judiciary Committee members—in a Senate that was 98 percent male—treated Hill dismissively, implying that she may have been delusional. The spectacle of a lone woman, and a black one to boot, sitting across from a patronizing tribunal of rich white guys who seemed to think that sexual harassment was a figment of the female imagination got women's blood boiling.

Their wrath was further fanned by the outrageous Tailhook scandal, which exploded in the spring of 1992. The news emerged that the navy had covered up an incident at the Tailhook Association convention in Las Vegas the previous September, when naval aviators formed a gauntlet on the third floor of the Hilton and trapped women in it, pawing and molesting them, stripping off their clothes. The first reports—whitewashes—identified only two suspects from approximately five thousand Tailhook attendees. Because twenty-six women, fourteen of them officers, claimed to have been assaulted, these findings, you might say, defied credulity. By June the secretary of the navy, H. Lawrence Garrett, faced a full-blown scandal about the cover-up, including the fact that—oops—fifty-five pages of interviews had been omitted from the final report, including one that placed Garrett himself in at least one of the Tailhook party suites. Time for that pink slip. Garrett quickly resigned, shortly after Paula Coughlin, a helicopter pilot and admiral's aide, appeared on *ABC News* to describe the ordeal that she and the other women had suffered. That women in the *military*, no less, could be assaulted in this way only added to the public fury.

Energized by Anita Hill, Tailhook, and *Backlash*, women emerged as a political force in 1992, which the press dubbed "The Year of the Woman." In November four women won election to the male-dominated U.S. Senate for the first time in American history: Dianne Feinstein, the former mayor of San Francisco, and Representative Barbara Boxer in California; Patty Murray, a state senator from Washington who described herself as "a mom in tennis shoes," and Carol Moseley Braun of Illinois, the first black woman to serve in the Senate. Arlen Specter nearly lost his Senate seat to Lynn Yeakel, a first-time candidate who ran specifically because of her fury over how Specter had questioned Anita Hill during the Thomas hearings.[9] A record number of women—108—ran for Congress, and twenty-four were elected to the House, the largest number ever in any single election.[10] Bill Clinton's election as president brought change as well. He made a point of supporting equal rights for women, and in addition to his brainy and accomplished wife who, unlike Barbara Bush, actually had a professional career, he named three women to his first cabinet, a woman to head the Environmental Protection Agency, and the first African American woman to become surgeon general.

So the early 1990s indeed seemed a turning point for women starting to achieve political power. Nonetheless, there was also considerable concern about girls not achieving their full potential because of ongoing discrimination in the classroom, and issues like sexual harassment, date rape, and domestic violence were getting more widespread attention.

Naomi Wolf's bestseller *The Beauty Myth* (1991) attacked the impossible standards of physical perfection imposed on us all, and Mary Pipher's *Reviving Ophelia* (1994), on the bestseller list longer than most of my daughter's hamsters lived, decried the hostile media environment surrounding girls and the decline in self-esteem it produced. So girls and women, after the dormant years of George H. W. Bush, were insisting on new political and social visibility in the early 1990s. At the same time girls, in particular, were emerging as a very important niche market.

The war between enlightened sexism and embedded feminism was on. It was in this swirling, contradictory milieu of a renewed press for women's rights, a backlash against these efforts, and the increased cultural, political, and commercial attention to girls that *Beverly Hills 90210* premiered and flourished along with other media fare that couldn't have been more different, like *Murphy Brown* or the music of Bratmobile.

So why did a seeming piece of fluff like *90210* matter? And what made the show such a phenomenon with young women? Because *90210* hailed teenagers as important. In addition to giving us great male and female eye candy (even though it was all vanilla), *90210* took teenagers and their dilemmas seriously. The show was one of the essential early building blocks of enlightened sexism because it was at the vanguard of targeting teenage girls with an intensity that made the 1960s efforts, like *Gidget* and *The Patty Duke Show*, seem puny. It stood at the beginning of what some would come to see as "the rampant juvenilization" of American popular culture, which would lead to increased teenpics, teen girl magazines, and boy bands.[11] Industry observers had doubted whether the novice network Fox could compete against the big three, even though their share of the viewing audience had dropped from 92 percent in 1977 to 62 percent in 1991. Given the competition, Fox chose to go after the kids. It was a strategy that worked and was widely imitated. *90210* was followed by *Melrose Place*, MTV's *The Real World*, *Party of Five*, *Dawson's Creek*, the rise of "chick flicks" and "chick lit," boy bands, Britney Spears, and all those new teen girl magazines like *Cosmo Girl*, *Teen Vogue*, and *Teen Elle*. The foundational pillars of this marketing juggernaut were sex and merchandising.

So this was the beginning of the media wedge that would divide many mothers and daughters around the issues of sexuality and consumerism.

90210 was at odds with other shows in the early 1990s that were increasingly showcasing strong, sometimes counterstereotypical, often mouthy women: *Murphy Brown*, *Who's the Boss?*, *L.A. Law*, *Northern Exposure*, *Law & Order*, *The Simpsons*, and, of course, *Roseanne*. These shows were obviously informed by feminism and spoke to its goals and values. Not *90210*. So despite—indeed, because of—its sun-splashed pleasures, and the fact that, for the most part, it threw the sexual double standard out the window, *Beverly Hills 90210* was a crucial first step in exploring what enlightened sexism might entail.

The fish-out-of-water premise of *90210* was that an apple pie, midwestern family with the moral rectitude of *The Waltons* moves to that den of carnality, dissolution, and merchandising, Beverly Hills, and finds every fiber of their Minneapolis-bred saintliness challenged, week in and week out. We know that the nearly perfect mom, Cindy Walsh (played by Jane Fonda look-alike Carol Potter), will not be corrupted because her blue denim dirndl skirt and truly heinous plaid or paisley shirts—indeed, her entire *Plow & Hearth* couture—scream, "I'm a square and I'm really, really grounded." But things will be more challenging for her gorgeous twin kids Brandon (Jason Priestly), with his soft, souffléed hair poised over his left eye like a wave, and especially for Brenda (the dreaded Shannen Doherty) because, well, she's the girl.

The opening sequence with its shots of Cartier, Armani, and Polo storefronts accompanied by the wailing electric guitars and pulsing drums brings together "teens" and "conspicuous consumption" like a perfect ice-cream sandwich. And this is high school unlike anything the rest of us poor schlumps suffered through. There's valet parking. Surfboards stick out of the kids' convertibles and everyone drives a Mercedes, a Porsche, or a Beemer. When the kids' car alarms go off on remote signalers in class, it's perfectly okay with the teachers for them to run out and check on their vehicles. It's also okay with the teachers to have flowers delivered to students during class. The Hacienda mansion of a school looks like a presidential palace in a Mediterranean country, not like the prison-issue boxes most viewers were forced to attend. The sun always shines; everything is brightly colored and brightly lit; no one, except the benighted Walsh twins, has a curfew and everyone, except the benighted Walsh twins, has a wallet exploding with gold and platinum credit cards. There are pool parties with white-jacketed waiters serving the dancing, throbbing teens; there are hot tubs; no one's parents (except the benighted Walsh twins') are ever, ever home. Dylan (Luke Perry) actually gets to live, alone, in a five-star hotel suite with room service whenever he wants it. Let's not forget that the country was in the middle of a recession with a serious spike in unemployment in 1990–91; many kids, and their parents, were happy to pretend they were in 90210 for an hour.

Of course, under this gilded veneer of bottomless wealth and ceaseless indulgence lurks the dark, disappointed other side: the rich, negligent, selfish, carousing parents who don't care; the kids who have everything except love and self-esteem; the punishing rules for fitting into rigid social hierarchies; and the corrupting temptations that must be resisted. In the first season alone, various of the teens confronted alcoholic parents, date rape, cheating on exams, parents doing lines of coke, drinking, drinking while driving, shoplifting, eating disorders, teenage pregnancy, parents getting indicted, breast cancer, losing their virginity, and, of course, having their parents come home to a trashed house after an unauthorized party. All of this—except losing your virginity—was very, very wrong. (In what was a gutsy move for the show, Brenda lost her virginity to Dylan on prom night and was not wracked with remorse but was, instead, positively glowing as a result. Many of the network's affiliates, fielding calls from irate parents, were not quite so blissful.)

This formula—offer the fantasy of being able to buy whatever you wanted, yet flatter viewers that such unrestricted consumerism is corrupting and empty—had worked for *Dallas* and *Dynasty*. Now it was tailored for teens, and subsequent shows down the road for young women (*My Super Sweet Sixteen, Laguna Beach, Gossip Girl*) would further inflate the levels and rates of conspicuous consumption. And unlike teens in most sitcoms, those in *90210* had sex and emphatically asked each other if they had condoms: there were actually lines like "Thank God for safe sex." (As the series spiraled ever downward into a soap opera after the characters' high school years, pretty soon everyone had slept with everyone else, with the possible exception of their own family members.) In its early years the show offered this delicious suspension between vicariously indulging in the excesses of the leisure class while—when reminded of your own more shabby surroundings during the commercial breaks—feeling superior to, even emotionally better off than, the hollow denizens of Rodeo Drive.

The women's movement seems to have bypassed this zip code, or at least its female inhabitants. Indeed, Cindy—always there with her pot-holders and apron to listen, advise, understand, and feed all the other teens whose lacquered, pool boy–chasing mothers are too self-absorbed to cook—is a living primer on the importance of being a stay-at-home mom. (The non-stay-at-home mothers come in for serial, routine bashing, with lines like, "You'd never see my mom with a cleaning utensil—you'd never see my mom at all.") The message is clear that the nuclear family with a solid, male breadwinner is the only unit that can help teens weather the vicissitudes of growing up. And Brenda (before she becomes the queen bitch of the show) is much more impressionable, more susceptible to the temptations of Beverly Hills than her more rational, anchored brother. He works for the school newspaper and gets a job; she colors her hair and shops. He drives himself and his sister to school because—ha, ha, ha—Brenda the girl can't pass driver's ed. Early plot lines for Brandon involve struggling over academic ethics, trying out for the basketball team, exposing the exploitation of immigrant workers in a restaurant, and serving as a coach to younger boys. Early plot lines for Brenda keep her in the ladies' room: shoplifting clothes, having a sleepover party, finding a lump in her breast. No school newspaper or soccer for her. And the one academically ambitious girl Andrea (Gabrielle Carteris) is, yes, Jewish, wears glasses, and is poor. Oy gevalt.

The show's producer, the prolific and savvy Aaron Spelling (*Charlie's Angels, The Love Boat, Dynasty*), consistently offered up what he called "mind candy"—which his legion of critics called "mindless candy." But what is "mind candy," and what made a bonbon like *90210* so delectable? *90210*'s look, locale, and teenage characters transported young women to a financially untroubled universe in which they could leave their lives behind and try on identities quite different from their own. Some of these identities, like "the bitch" or "the spoiled rich girl" were in fact forbidden or not possible for most girls in real life. Accounts of girls' emotionally powerful connection to the show and its characters—especially when viewing in groups, they talked back to them on the screen as if they were actual friends or acquaintances—capture how gripping the fantasy world of *90210* was.[12]

But the voyeuristic pleasures that made the show as fun as settling into a beach chair in Malibu also drummed in the rewards of acquiescing to patriarchal norms of femininity. So *90210* was an important early building block of enlightened sexism because it insisted that the true, gratifying pleasures for girls, and their real source of power, came from consumerism, girliness, and the approval of guys. How yummy to sit back and watch the ever-changing parade of clothes and accessories, hairstyles, scantily clad nubile bodies, and relationships and to be invited, each week, to comment on them, to feel that you could be the expert on whether Donna's new hat was a fashion disaster or whether Brenda was really getting bitchier. (Eventually there was a national "I Hate Brenda" fan club and Doherty was kicked off the show.) *90210* encouraged viewers to feel like active, engaged experts, but exclusively about "female" things.[13]

What was really retrograde about *90210*, then—aside from the fact that there were no people of color except for African American athletes who, duh, needed tutoring (and, briefly, Andrea's Latino husband)—was how it magnified the absolute centrality of thinness, beauty, fashion, sexual objectification, and boyfriends to teen girl happiness. Admirable, truly enviable girls were also "nice." And it got worse as the show wore on. The girls conformed to a very narrow *Cosmo* ideal of beauty, and by the seventh season, when they were in college—where, in my experience, women often come to class in jeans and sweatshirts—their wardrobe alternated between miniskirts, halter tops, and bikinis.[14] Whatever the plot lines, these young women were, first and foremost, sexual objects on display who maintained their attractiveness by buying things. Their main task—in other words, the status quo for girls—was to construct and maintain a great appearance. They also competed with one another over men, and as the show developed there was much more emphasis on the importance of heterosexual romance. Even college women who were avid viewers became exasperated by the fact that you rarely saw the characters in class or studying, and they complained about the skimpy outfits and unrealistic body images on the show.[15]

And then, of course, there was *90210*'s flirtation with feminism, in which, not surprisingly, feminism was "taken into account" so it could be trashed as hypocritical and a danger to guys. In the fourth season (1993–94), there is a "Take Back the Night" week at the fictional California University they all attend. Meant to raise awareness about sexual violence against women, the event prompts a student to come forward and claim she was date-raped by Steve (Ian Ziering), one of the ongoing characters. Except it turns out that she is making it up, reinforcing the myth that Katie Roiphe would popularize in her 1994 book *The Morning After* that those claiming date rape are often exaggerating or deluded. (Roiphe's main argument was that since neither she nor any of her Ivy League friends had been date-raped, well, shit, the statistics must be wrong.)[16] Then there was the anthropology professor Lucinda (Dina Meyer), who spouts feminist rhetoric in class, but whose brand of liberation means cheating on her husband, seducing her students (Brandon and Dylan), and trying to steal these boys from their girlfriends.

Having said all this, girls don't embrace shows that consistently put them down. What made the show especially irresistible was that while feminism may have bypassed the girls, it had very much touched the heartthrob boys, especially Brandon. The usually evil jocks in the show are bullying, date-raping louts. But unlike the other guys who are basically governed by their crotches, Brandon and Luke do not constantly objectify the girls around them. In the pilot, for example, Brandon meets ultra-wealthy Mary Ann and in short order they are in a hot tub, sipping champagne. After one of those steamy, openmouthed, lip-sucking kisses she proposes, "Let's take off all our clothes," to which Brandon responds, "Whoa, wait a second." He assures her that's not all he wants, there's no need to rush, they should get to know each other first. (He also doesn't like what he sees as a "role reversal," with Mary Ann as the sexual aggressor.) And Brandon isn't so much handsome as he is pretty, with his great pouf of a hairdo that seemed to have been modeled after Princess Diana's.

Meanwhile, Dylan, the Luke Perry heartthrob, was a closet fan of Lord Byron (although we do want to know what we are to make of his wearing denim overalls with one strap undone and hanging down). He sleeps with Brenda only after confessing his love for her; indeed, when

Brandon warns Dylan not to use his sister Dylan responds, "What kind of a jerk do you think I am?" And these guys are vulnerable. After a nasty encounter with his father, the rebel-hero Dylan breaks down to Brenda, sobbing, "He gets to me, he always gets to me," and she consoles him. As one viewer said of Dylan, "He needs someone to take care of him."[17] More emotionally available and open than most boys are supposed to be, Dylan and Brandon offer the fantasy of a teen world humanized by girls and feminine values, a world where nurturing and treating girls with sensitivity matters—and is rewarded. Who needs feminism anymore if teen guys are like this?

Having hit the jackpot with *90210*, Aaron Spelling joined forces with writer-producer Darren Star and came up with *Melrose Place*, which premiered in 1992 and aired on Wednesdays at 9:00, just after *90210*, giving viewers two full hours of California dreamin'.[18] Now this show really allowed us to imagine being a young woman with power (while being reassured that such power corrupts). Summarizing the hookups, breakups, illnesses, attempted suicides, car crashes, attempted murders, successful murders, kidnappings, bomb explosions, brain tumors, office politics, ruthless plots, and counterplots during the show's seven-year run requires more space—and an organizational chart from hell—than is available here. But the purpose of the show was to expand the teen audience Fox had captured to a broader swath of Gen-Xers, college students, twentysomethings and beyond.

As someone teaching at the college level in the 1990s—whose students were often media-savvy, feminist, antiestablishment types—I knew better than to schedule a night class that conflicted with this. *Melrose Place* was another show that people loved watching together, so they could prove to themselves how resistant they were to such campy fare while still succumbing to its powerful appeal. And the show itself, with its over-the-top villainy and surreal plots, came to invite such ironic viewing, where you knew everything about the characters and plots but then made fun of them (and yourself, for clogging your temporal lobes with such cultural lint). By the show's end it had become so farcical it was like a parody of a soap. But in its heyday it had nights when it beat

90210 in the ratings, and its 1994 two-hour season finale, with a much-hyped gay kiss scene, catapulted Fox to number one that night. By the end of the year, Fox had increased its audience among the eighteen to forty-nine demographic by 10 percent.[19]

The apartment complex at Melrose Place was another Hacienda-style building with a vine- and flower-draped courtyard—complete with pool—onto which a variety of apartments faced. Only people in their twenties with bodies sculpted like Greek statuary lived there. Every male character had to be seen bare-chested multiple times—when striding across the courtyard, improbably wrapped in a towel from the waist down to complain about the water pressure, when hanging out in the apartment, when answering his door—and they were all ripped or semi-ripped. The women were all beautiful and size two.

When the show first premiered in the summer of 1992, George H. W. Bush was still president, the country was in a recession, and college graduates wondered if they could get a job anywhere except Burger King. So the initial episodes followed, in part, the financial struggles of Allison (the deeply dimpled Courtney Thorne-Smith), Jake (Grant Show), Billy (Andrew Shue, also deeply dimpled), Jane and her husband, Michael (Josie Bissett and Thomas Calabro), Matt, the token gay guy (Doug Savant), and Rhonda, the token African American woman (Vanessa Williams, not the Miss America one), as they sought to find work, pay the rent, and the like. Allison confronted sexual harassment at work. Matt, who worked in a teen shelter/halfway house, got fired for being gay. Jane and Michael struggled with how his demanding work schedule as a medical resident left little time for them to be together.

By the fall, the ratings had slipped. There were scenes like the one in which Jane woke Michael by kissing his big toe and then slithering up his body, and plenty of scantily clad splashing in the pool, but the producers deemed the show "too serious." Enter fantasies of power in the form of the scheming, platinum blond, power-hungry sex machine Amanda (Heather Locklear); then have the characters hook up with each other with the speed and randomness of pinballs. By 1994 the show was a sensation, "the *Dynasty* of Generation X."[20] And it was all about sex and female power, in the workplace and the bedroom.

To make a really long, convoluted story short, Allison began the show working in D&D Advertising as a receptionist aspiring to move up the ranks. Her problem was that she was too nice, kind of a whiner, and cared about romantic love. Not Amanda. Amanda wanted Billy, Allison's (at first) platonic roommate. So she bought the Melrose Place apartment complex to be near him. (How's that for a dating move power play?) But in short order Amanda was sleeping with the equally ruthless Peter Burns (Jack Wagner), who helped her organize a takeover of D&D that made Amanda president. (Amanda's former boss killed himself, reminding us of the consequences of such blond ambition.) There were other men along the way—Jake, Reed, Bobby, Kyle, one kinda lost track—but the most important thing was getting the account. After a bout with Hodgkin's disease, which, as you can imagine, made staying on as president of D&D difficult, Amanda came back to the firm, this time reporting to Allison, and clawed her way back to the top. Under these circumstances, Allison had to toughen up, and she also became an alcoholic. Believe me, this account barely scratches the surface of the intertwined Möbius strips of plots that kept people coming back for more.

Melrose Place premiered just a few months after the April 1992 Los Angeles uprising, in which thousands of African Americans took to the streets to protest the acquittal by a predominantly white jury of four cops who had been caught on videotape beating Rodney King into submission. So at first it appeared socially conscious that *Melrose Place*—set in Los Angeles, after all—included a black character, Rhonda. Unfortunately, the show's depiction of a black woman was totally jive. Rhonda was an aerobics instructor (she had rhythm and could dance, don't ja know) and was reduced to uttering dialogue like "he really has it goin' on" and "hey girl." When one of her black male students borrows her towel, he smells it and says, "I'm takin' this home and I ain't never gonna wash it." Her best friend in the complex was the other outsider to white heterosexuality, Matt. And except for some dates and a fiancé, we didn't see Rhonda as part of any black community when Los Angeles, in fact, as the news had just shown us, had some. So the Rhonda character was simultaneously stereotyped as a yuppie fly girl meant to bring some color to the show, while also cast as insulated from any racism that might affect her life (unlike Matt, who was beat up for being gay). Rhonda was eliminated as a character after the first season. This did finesse the problem of what to do about the possibility of interracial relationships once the show became a musical chairs of sex partners.

In explaining the appeal of the show to women, Heather Locklear told *Playboy*, "They like it because the women hold all the power—which is as it should be—and the men have no balls." She had wanted Amanda to be "an intelligent, aggressive businesswoman in her 30s" to which the producers added "the sluttiness."[21] (And being cutthroat, ball-busting, and vindictive.) The show allowed viewers to be transported to a fantasy world in which women could have sex with any Nautilus-crafted hunk they wanted, while also allowing women to vicariously try on the exercise of heartless power at work and in relationships, something still prohibited in real life. In one of many classic scenes, Dr. Kimberly Shaw (Marcia Cross), now married to Michael (who, yes, used to be married to Jane), walks in on him and Amanda making out in a sudsy hot tub. With the speed of a curare dart, she grabs a plugged-in lamp and threatens to throw it into the tub. (Talk about quick thinking!) When Michael says it's not what it looks like (right), Amanda storms out of the tub, denouncing him as a "spineless fraud." Kimberly smashes the lamp on the floor and laughs derisively at Michael. "Look at you," she sneers, "you're a selfish, philandering, dripping wet bastard. That I'd want you at all is amazing." A cheating doctor dissed by two tough-talking vixens within seconds! What young female wouldn't want to see that? And there was always more where that came from.

With the various female characters on the show, there was a range of traits and personas to sample, even though what was on offer was about as varied as the display cases at Sephora. Many viewers identified with Allison because she was both "nice" and ambitious and struggled with her weakness, alcohol. But how much fun to slip into Amanda, a real transgressor of the feminine behavioral playbook, a woman unencumbered by the pressure to be "nice." Amanda looked at "nice" and just said no. The show got you both ways—it let you imagine how much fun it would be to break the rules (except for being blond and having buns of steel, of course) while also reaffirming that people (including, or especially, you and your friends in the audience) really liked and admired women who were the antithesis of Amanda—a woman, like, say, you in real life.

And when female power is this exaggerated, there will inevitably be small craft advisories about its costs. The lying, cheating, backstabbing, promiscuous Amanda was a caricature of feminism run amok, a fantasy and a warning about what would happen if women became more like Ivan Boesky or Michael Milken. She was the career-at-all-costs woman you were supposed to love to hate. What made her rapacity even acceptable to watch was that she was slim, blond, and beautiful, so at least she was an exemplar of the physical, if not the behavioral, ideals of femininity. Even though she was successful and ruthless, men still lusted after her. Place another woman with a few wrinkles or an extra thirty pounds in the same role, and she would have been vehemently loathed for not making one gesture toward the demands of proper gender roles.

So while *Melrose Place*'s great seduction was its weekly offering of fantasies of power, it also made perfectly clear that power turned women into, well, something akin to the Marquis de Sade. Women could not "have it all." The role of Amanda made it clear, week in and week out, that successful, driven career women could not have real love. The fact that she herself preferred power sex to romance hardly undercut this message. It was no accident that she and Kimberly, the two major bitches of the show, also had considerable wealth. It was almost as if "success" and "bitch" just went together.[22] If you had the former, you would automatically become the latter. Don't think this warning was missed by young women.

So there was enlightened sexism in one corner, developing its jabs. In the other corner was embedded feminism, delivering more than one right cross to male privilege, especially in prime time. Shows for the older set, admired then and now for a feminist sensibility (and great writing) utterly absent from *90210* and *Melrose Place*, contained a very explicit recognition of feminism. And these shows, especially those in the 10 P.M. strip, had little truck with conspicuous consumption and only occasionally with steamy sex (*NYPD Blue* and its bare-butted cops in the shower comes to mind). These were indeed different media universes, and show just how contested feminism was on television in the early 1990s. A look at two of the most popular and critically acclaimed shows from this era, *Murphy Brown* and *Northern Exposure*, reminds us of what existed before—and may have evoked—the emergence of enlightened sexism.

Murphy Brown premiered on CBS in 1988 and ran for ten years, primarily opposite *Monday Night Football*. By 1990 it was the network's highest-rated entertainment series. Aggressive, outspoken, acid-tongued, feared by her colleagues—especially the men—and totally driven by her hugely successful career, Murphy Brown the character (Candice Bergen) has been described as "a male persona in a female body."[23] The humor in the show, driven by excellent scripts, lay in the contrast between how women, even successful career women, were supposed to act and Murphy's utter violation of and often outright hostility to those norms. She is antimaternal, and reportedly advocated that all children on planes be required to sit in the cargo hold. She has no idea how to cook. Whatever the antonym to "nurturing" is, she's it. When firing one of her many hapless secretaries, she says simply, "Take everything of yours out of this desk, put it in your car and drive away."

After the former beauty queen ditz Corky (Faith Ford) reports a story on-air that Murphy was meant to deliver, she warns Corky, "Do anything like this again and you're dead." In case Corky took this metaphorically, Murphy adds, "It's not just an idle threat or a colorful exaggeration, I *know* people, it *would* happen. It could be fast, or painful and lingering, water, cement, without a trace, or well-placed bits and pieces. All my choice." Even the most ruthless male CEO is not supposed to issue mob-style death threats to his coworkers. Her toughness is further magnified in juxtaposition to weak sniveling men, like her producer Miles (Grant Shaud), who cowers when he has to go into her office. At the same time, this is Candice Bergen, after all, beautiful, perfectly coiffed (by early '90s standards), and a great clotheshorse.

The show simultaneously offered women depictions of the consequences and joys of female liberation, and it was this ambivalence that we snuggled into. Single-minded attention to getting to the top of her field meant, for Murphy, no personal life, no network of female friends, and regrets, expressed as early as the first season, about not having children.[24] Because the jokes, and often the resolution of each episode, rested on making fun of the excesses of feminism, Murphy was often disciplined in some way, and she even expressed fleeting remorse for taking competitiveness and selfishness to extremes many men would not have. So being really independent and really competitive was so ridiculous for a woman that it had to be laughed at.

But if a subtext of the show was that feminists were brittle, unlovable, and would pay for success with their personal lives, another was that being a mouthy, independent broad who didn't care what others thought of her was wonderfully freeing. For women over thirty in particular, Murphy validated their own experiences and concerns rarely seen elsewhere at the time. Viewer letters sent to the show affirmed that many women embraced Murphy as a role model; they were sick of stereotypical depictions and loved seeing a successful working woman whose conundrums were about her job and only rarely about a relationship with a man. How great that she couldn't cook, supported herself quite comfortably, and got to expose political and corporate corruption on TV.

What women especially loved about Murphy was that she wasn't afraid to use her voice. She was not embarrassed to sing Motown hits really loud and off-key, and she had no compunctions about calling things as she saw them, personally and politically. In a culture where women were, twenty years after the women's movement, still urged to be soft-spoken and to censor themselves, Murphy embodied the sheer joy of talking back, of committing verbal transgression, of revolting against such self-silencing. Viewers wrote in with comments like "I enjoy Murphy ranting on and on. She says what many of us have always wanted to say to someone or *about* someone"; or "I am 39 and I need a couple of Murphy-like lines to say back to people." The 1992 "Send in the Clowns" episode, a satire of how Congress had handled the Clarence Thomas–Anita Hill hearings, drew tons of appreciative mail. "Thank you for hearing all women and letting our message out," wrote one. "Ridicule like that in your ... show is the best weapon against these miserable little midgets," wrote another. They loved that Murphy—a woman—was "the perfect adversary" for white men in power.[25]

The series' greatest impact on the wider culture came during the 1991–92 season, in which Murphy became pregnant after a fling with her ex-husband and decided to have the baby and raise him on her own. In May 1992, the day after the episode in which Murphy gave birth, Vice President Dan Quayle delivered a speech denouncing the show for "mocking the importance of fathers," "glamorizing illegitimacy," and turning the decision to bear a child alone into "another lifestyle choice." While Quayle was instantly and widely ridiculed for attacking a fictional character for her actions, having Murphy become a mother was controversial, and not just for social conservatives. Many women, including some mothers, wanted the show to resist having Murphy succumb, stereotypically, to her "biological clock." They wrote letters to the show's creator Diane English imploring, "I would be disappointed if Murphy had to prove her 'total womanhood' by being pregnant and caring for an infant. . . . Let Murphy represent the childless professional woman who doesn't need a baby to round out her identity."[26] But the show betrayed these hopes, and after Murphy gave birth—in an episode watched by 38 million people—she sang to her newborn, "You make me feel like a natural woman," implying that she had been "unnatural" before. The feminist media scholar Bonnie Dow saw this capitulation as "the ultimate postfeminist moment" in the series, "giving credence to the claims about . . . the emptiness of childless career women, and women's 'natural' destiny to mother."[27]

The show's depiction of single motherhood offered the same fantasies and alarm bells as its depiction of feminism. Given that Quayle's comments—which turned him into an even bigger laughingstock than he already was—had made the 1992 season premiere "must-see TV," Murphy got what was billed as her "revenge" by responding to the vice president. The episode showed Murphy and her colleague Frank (Joe Regalbuto) watching Quayle's comments on TV. She turns to Frank in shock, as she has been unable to even take a shower. "Glamorized single motherhood? What planet is he on? Look at me Frank, am I glamorous?" To which he responds, "Of course not—you look disgusting." She then launched into one of the famous soliloquies of the episode. "What was that crack about 'just another lifestyle choice'? I agonized over that decision. I didn't know if I could raise a child by myself. . . . I didn't just wake up one morning and say, 'Oh gee, I can't get in for a facial; I might as well have a baby.'" This episode provided both a ringing defense of single-motherhood and a depiction of how hard it was. And despite the "natural woman" moment at the birth, Murphy did not morph into June Cleaver. Frank had to show her how to hold the baby. There were many jokes about her total absence of maternal capabilities and she was not fazed by the prevailing (and escalating) demands of the times to indulge in intensive, perfect mothering. This, too, was a gift to the women of America—a recognition that you could keep working, not know what you were doing when it came to child rearing, and still be a good mother. Of course it helped if you had Murphy's salary.

Yet, as any sitcom writer knows, baby jokes are only good for so long, and portraying the relentlessness of mothering an infant and toddler can be more depressing than funny. So in short order, Murphy's son Avery made little difference in her life and we didn't see all that much of him. Because Murphy was rich, there were no structural issues—no national day care system, no national health care system, crappy maternity leaves, minimal flex time—that she, unlike real mothers, had to confront. So, on the other side of the coin the show *did* make working motherhood seem much easier than it was and thus legitimated leaving motherhood the unfinished business of the women's movement.

Another mainstay of CBS's Monday lineup in the early 1990s was *Northern Exposure* where we were clearly not in sunny southern California with its bimbettes, himbos, and bitches. We were in the fictional town of Cicely, Alaska, where moose walk down the street—already signifying that little is normal here—and people of various ethnicities and worldviews mingle easily. This was the opposite of *90210* territory; here consumerism was impossible and irrelevant. Most important, in Cicely the women were utterly unintimidated by male privilege, and indeed had much of the power. One woman is the local bush pilot who fixes her own plane and knows how to hunt, while another—in her seventies no less—runs the local general store and is not played for laughs. It was also a place where a heavyset and impossibly taciturn Native American woman could be a love object.

Here was another fish-out-of-water premise, this one featuring the semineurotic Jewish New York doctor Joel Fleischman (Rob Morrow) stuck in the Alaskan interior and pining for Zabar's, the Second Avenue Deli, and someone who's read Kafka. Throughout its four-year run the show featured eccentric, even surreal, plotlines, like the one in which Mike Monroe (Anthony Edwards), allergic to everything, moved to Cicely to live in a large plastic bubble. But it was the battle of the sexes that was often front and center.

In an award-winning episode about Cicely's early history, we learn that two women, Rosalind and Cicely, lesbian lovers, were the real founders of the town. When the beautiful Rosalind confronts a bar bully who tells her to sit down before she gets hurt, she hauls off and decks him, saying she despises those who abuse power. A female missionary played by Maggie (Janine Turner) confesses to Rosalind that she can't seem to attract men and doesn't know what they want. Rosalind tells her that men are confused because they want a woman who is their intellectual equal but they're also afraid of women like that, that they want a woman they can dominate but then hate her for being weak. Rosalind asks Maggie, "Do you really want a man?" and then assures her that "fortunately there are alternatives." In another episode Maurice (Barry Corbin)—the gung ho flag-wearing hypermacho, elk-hunting ex-astronaut—falls in love with equally macho Barbara (Diane Delano), a state trooper, because she shoots a gun even better than he does. "I can't tell you what seeing you handle that sidearm means to me, Barbara," he pants and then kisses her passionately. Only in the alternate universe of Cicely could conventional gender roles for women be abandoned, and lesbianism seem utterly natural.

Maggie, the assertive, even confrontational bush pilot whose hair, in many episodes, was shorter than Brandon's on *90210*, has a love-hate relationship with Fleischman, whom she constantly makes look like a wimp by fixing his roof and defending him from bears. But even in Cicely, a woman like this is unlucky in love: the standing joke is that all five of her previous boyfriends died in accidents, as if divine retribution was required for loving a woman like that. Like Murphy Brown, Maggie is a caricature of feminism who also gives expression to feelings real women actually have. Maggie complains to the childlike and asexual Ed (Darren E. Burrows) that men never listen, they pretend to but they don't, because they're only thinking of one thing, "the joy stick, is it big enough and where can they put it." She continues, "You know what I feel when I look at a man, Ed? Pity. Loathing. Genuine revulsion." Ed points out that he is, in fact, a man, but of course he's not the kind she's talking about. "Men have been running things for thousands of years. What do we have to show for it? War. Pollution. The S&L thing. And do they ever put a toilet seat down? No. So what do we need them for?" She acknowledges that they're good for sex, but that's about it. In another episode Maggie asks Ruth Ann, the seventysomething store owner, "Why are all men such swine?" "They're not all swine, dear. Most of them, perhaps," responds Ruth Ann. "The problem is they don't know us and we don't know them," echoing a theme that would make John Gray's *Men Are from Mars, Women Are from Venus* a runaway best-seller in 1993.

This was the contradictory terrain of television in the early 1990s, in which shows with strong female leads—*Roseanne*; *Designing Women*; *Murphy Brown*; *Murder, She Wrote*; *Grace Under Fire*—varyingly informed by feminism, were often among the top five most highly rated shows. And the leads were not all necessarily young, gorgeous, or skinny. But as Fox went after the younger demographic, a reversion began to archetypes of bitches, nice girls, and bimbos, with an underlining of the importance of physical appearance. How were young women making sense of all this?

Despite its popularity, the young women of the early 1990s weren't all watching *90210*, and if they were, many had a more rebellious take. Millions of them were reading *Sassy*, others were starting zines, and a smaller but highly influential group started a radical female counterculture and a type of music known as Riot Grrrl. This was as different from Aaron Spelling as you could get: an indie culture dedicated to defying the "Where to Spy on Guys" and "A Better Butt in 10 Days" catechism of *Seventeen* magazine. Riot Grrrl sprang from two foundational desires. As Allison Wolfe, one of the movement's early pioneers, put it, "One thing is to put a fresh punk face on feminism; but the other thing is to put the feminism back into punk . . . how can we make this kind of stodgy . . . feminism have a fresh face that speaks to us, to a younger generation? And, at the same time, how can we make the punk that we're involved in less macho, less violent?"[28] (We would hear this notion of "putting a fresh face on feminism" co-opted by the Spice Girls just a few years later.) Most important, Riot Grrrl sought to bring forth and legitimize a less compliant and much more defiant emotional identity for girls.[29]

Now for a Vintage Female such as myself, Riot Grrrl music wasn't what I felt like putting on when driving to the supermarket back in 1994. I was too old for its raw, pounding sound and screaming vocals. But Riot

Grrrl was not meant for me; it was for girls and young women who were in their teens, twenties, and early thirties, who saw plenty to be pissed about in a culture that fed them Mötley Crüe and Whitesnake videos and *Teen* magazine, and silenced their experiences about sexual abuse, harassment, and assault. And the lyrics, the performance styles, and the feminist sensibilities of the movement—these a fortysomething feminist could applaud.

Riot Grrrl emerged in Washington, D.C., in the summer of 1991, when members of two bands based in Olympia, Washington, Bikini Kill and Bratmobile, began circulating with media producers in the D.C. punk community. The story is that in the wake of a race riot, Erin Smith of Bratmobile said the male-dominated punk community could use a "girl riot."[30] Two other members of the band started a zine—for the over-forty set, a zine is a do-it-yourself handmade, homemade magazine produced by an individual or small group—and called it *Riot Grrrl*. They especially liked the evocation of growling produced by the three *r*'s as they wanted a "vehicle where your anger is validated."[31]

They also wanted to reclaim the term "girl" as positive and politicized.[32] Their message was "Revolution Girl Style Now," and before long similar-minded young women were getting together for '90s-style consciousness-raising meetings. When the mainstream media learned about the Bratmobile zine, they labeled the movement Riot Grrrl and it stuck. In August 1991 various Riot Grrrl bands joined up with Bikini Kill and Bratmobile in Olympia for a "Grrrl Night" collective performance. These young women's lyrics—bold, unruly—took on sexual violence, domestic abuse, homophobia, misogyny, HIV/AIDS, the narrow body image forced on girls, patriarchal control of the music industry, and the overall containment of young women. They urged girls to stand up for themselves and to become more politically and culturally active. By 1992 there was a national Riot Grrrl convention in Washington, D.C., with an estimated two hundred attendees.[33]

Deeply anticommercial and especially hostile to how the mainstream media addressed and portrayed young women, Riot Grrrl urged girls to produce their own media—zines, music, videos, Web sites. And they had fabulous titles: *Satan Wears a Bra, Quit Whining, Not Your Bitch, Wrecking Ball,* and *Girl Germs*. Take that, *Cosmo*. Riot Grrrl celebrated the necessarily and often deliberately amateur look of all these, as that encouraged more girls to feel that they, too, could be makers and not just consumers of media fare.

As a subculture of iconoclastic and teed-off girls, Riot Grrrl faced that paradox so many youth movements confront: it was at once deeply threatening to the mainstream media and attractive to them as the source of "the next new thing." The media responded much as it had when radical feminism emerged in the late 1960s and early 1970s: attack, ignore, trivialize the political substance of the movement, decapitate the look or style of the movement from its substance, and use this new style to marginalize the movement and to create new stuff to sell. While the immediate press response to Riot Grrrl was hostile, the movement's energy and its members' insistence on a new empowerment for girls was not ignored: within a few years we had "girl power" lipstick and an entire federal initiative, headed by Health and Human Services secretary Donna Shalala, labeled "girl power."

In the summer of 1992, just a few weeks before the Riot Grrrl convention, the mainstream news media discovered Riot Grrrl and did not like what it saw. L.A. Weekly profiled the movement in an article that was reprinted in newspapers around the country. So reporters showed up at the convention and, as one participant recalled, "It did surprise us how quickly and how negative the reaction was. . . . And the ways the media, especially the male journalists, tried to discredit the ideas was also very shocking."[34] Riot Grrrl faced the nearly identical fate of the women's movement twenty years earlier. The mainstream press helped spread the word about the movement. But it also framed Riot Grrrl as frivolous, self-indulgent, and not relevant to the broader female experience—yet, at the same time, as man-hating and threatening.

One reporter for USA Today, without identifying herself as a journalist, snuck into a workshop on rape and then published the stories told there about the girls' and women's experiences in a way that utterly misrepresented and trivialized them. The dismissive headline read "Feminist Riot Grrrls Don't Just Wanna Have Fun" and its opening line warned, "Better watch out, boys," as if this was about them and not the girls. Riot Grrrls, the reporter wrote, are "strident," "self-absorbed," and mostly "anti-male."[35] In an adjacent story titled "Anti-Fashion Statements" we read that "the Riot Grrrls' punk feminist look is pure in-your-face fashion: unshaven armpits and legs, heavy, black Doc Marten boots, fishnet stockings and garter belts under baggy army shorts. Among their tribal tokens: painstakingly pierced lips, cheeks and noses; ears ringed with a dozen hoops; big, bold tattoos decorating ankles, backs and arms." But their politics? Forget it. This article ridiculed the fact that Riot Grrrls thought that the body image promoted by Barbie was harmful, even though they were trying to combat girls' self-hatred and the high rates of bulimia and anorexia.[36]

A *Newsweek* profile kept emphasizing the group's "anger" (girls are not supposed to be so unladylike, you know), accentuating that they "apply a kind of linguistic jujitsu against their enemies" and that they are "dressed to kill but ready to fight." They were also dismissed as "sanctimonious," yet as having "a mushy warm spot for cute skater boys." The singer Courtney Love was invoked as "the patron saint of Riot Grrrls," and the magazine mocked her by saying she "wears vintage little-girl dresses that barely make it past her hips—all the better to sing songs about rape and exploitation." Thus the Riot Grrrls were hypocrites and weren't real feminists. "Riot Grrrl is feminism with a loud happy face dotting the 'i,'" *Newsweek* concluded. "For people accustomed to more august models of feminism, the Riot Grrrls might seem a bit of a stretch."[37]

After this kind of press coverage, many in Riot Grrrl refused to talk to the media at all. But Riot Grrrl continued to evolve and helped set the stage for the massive success of *Jagged Little Pill*, Alanis Morissette's 1995 breakout album filled with songs about female rage and coming-of-age. "You Oughta Know," a wailing chant of betrayal by an ex-boyfriend, became a national anthem of fury for young women. *Jagged Little Pill* was the second best-selling album of the entire decade and the best-selling debut album of all time by a female artist.[38] Morissette especially captured the contradictions young women felt—"I'm hard, but I'm friendly . . . I'm brave but I'm chicken shit"—their fierce desires for strength and agency in the world, and their fear of the possible consequences of achieving these very desires.

Riot Grrrl was a threat to the conventional notions of girls as compliant and passive, and as primarily obsessed with boys and shopping. It was also too radical and defiant for many young women. And the press coverage showed how swiftly and vehemently deviations against the norm of teen girl femininity would be demonized. However unconscious or unacknowledged, enlightened sexism began to coalesce as a direct response to the danger that Riot Grrrl, and comparable feminist initiatives in the early 1990s, embodied. And the task was obvious—how to domesticate girls' rebellion and longing for power into something a bit safer, and much more profitable.

From time to time a magazine captures the spirit of its era, burning brightly for a brief interval and then disappearing for good. For teenage girls and young women in the early 1990s, this magazine was *Sassy*, described by its fans, correctly, as "the greatest teen magazine of all time."[39] Nothing less than "an insurrection" (in the words of the cultural critic Alex Ross)[40] against all of the media telling girls they had to be makeup-obsessed, boy-centered, marriage-aspiring airheads, *Sassy* premiered in February 1988 under the editorship of Jane Pratt, with a core writing staff who quickly (and deservedly) came to be idolized: Karen Catchpole, Christina Kelly, and Catherine Gysin, known to their readers primarily by their first names. These women were united in their hatred of *Seventeen*, with its incessant dating and dieting advice and its "parade of Nordic-looking models," whose purpose was "to tear you down, but then tell you how they can help you fix yourself."[41] They and the magazine's first publisher, Sandra Yates, wanted to speak to the millions of girls who also "felt like they were outsiders, but who could still pass for normal in the high-school cafeteria. Girls who didn't want to completely reject mainstream culture, but didn't want to completely embrace it either."[42] And they wanted to speak to them not in the phony-hip, condescending tones of *Seventeen*, but in an intimate and mouthy tone that was how real teenagers talked. Within six months of its launch, *Sassy*'s circulation soared from 250,000 to 500,000. A few years later, *Sassy* guaranteed its advertisers a circulation of 800,000, and *Newsweek* reported it had 3 million readers.[43] The magazine instantly started getting sacks of mail from grateful girls all over the country.

Like other teen girl magazines, *Sassy* had fashion spreads and articles about makeup, but it also covered topics that would have given *Seventeen* hives: gay teens, teen suicide, incest, eating disorders, racism, and (a recurring specialty) exposés on how impossible standards of beauty and thinness were sold to girls by the mainstream media. And it was obvious from the sheer rebellion of these articles that the writers were having a blast, a gratification they passed on to their readers. An early piece by Catherine Gysin, "Backstage at Miss America," revealed the codes that judges used to rank the contestants' bodies: WC for weak chin, H for heavy, and "my personal favorite . . . BB, which stands for big butt. Ah the wisdom of the judges."[44] A cover story, "Why We Don't Like Our Bodies," ranted against the thinness ideal for girls, tracked how the ideal had gotten thinner and thinner over the years, called this "brainwashing," and also noted that it was racist.[45] Karen Catchpole sent away for various products claiming to help you lose weight, get bigger breasts, thicker hair, and the like, and trashed their claims with joyful derision. She reported that one breast enhancer product, which she sent off to a lab for testing, was made of ground-up cow's brains and should never be consumed by anyone.[46] Now this was fun!

The magazine's beauty advice column was the utterly straightforward "Zits and Stuff." In an article titled "Why You Liked Yourself Better When You Were 11," Christina Kelly cited the research by Carol Gilligan and Lyn Mikel Brown about girls losing their self-esteem as they moved from girlhood to adolescence.[47] In "What Now," she cast celebrity exercise videos as "Another Way to Keep the People Down": "It is in these videos that the twin demons of celebrity worship and body obsessiveness intersect and become ever more powerful. The American people need to stop emulating these dorks to the point where they wish to follow their fitness routines. The idea that some of our readers might spend their money on this crap and waste their time imitating Cindy's lunges truly makes me sad. I'm serious."[48]

In a 1989 article, "The Dirty, Scummy Truth About Spring Break (Or, Where the Jerks Are)," Christina lacerated this supposedly fun initiation rite for girls, and chronicled the parade of drunken, vomiting guys who said they were at Daytona "'to check out the tasty morsels' (a direct quote)." She added, "Bikini contests I will never understand. Even if I did have an amazing bod, I could not stand in front of hundreds of drunk, sweaty, hairy dudes and simply, by my very presence on the stage, drive them into a frenzy. Yet some girls delight in this." She concluded that the trip to Daytona was "hellish."[49] "How to Make Him Want You... Bad," from 1993, lampooned advice offered by *Cosmo* and *YM*, some of it astoundingly creepy, like "Brush up against someone in the elevator, in a restaurant, on the street" (*Cosmo*) or "Kick off your shoes so he can see your lovely feet—lots of men have foot fetishes!" (Eeewww.) The two authors Margie and Mary Ann (again, with just their chummy first names in the byline) then went out and tried the advice and recounted, hilariously, how guys either ran away from them or thought they were cruising for sex.[50]

Rather than promoting conformity and popularity, *Sassy* ran articles like "Ways to Fit in Without Even Trying," "Five Types of Guys to Avoid at All Costs," "How, When and Where and Why to Dump That Dude; Get Your Worthy Butt Out of That Nowhere Relationship," and "9 Things About America That Make Us Want to Scream and Throw Stuff," which included, "It rots to be female." In "6 Reasons You Don't Want to Be Popular," *Sassy* insisted that being popular is overrated because, secretly, popular people are "As Insecure As You," they're "Forced to Conform," "Play Dumb," and "Buy Useless Status Symbols." Most gratifying of all? "Your Chance of Being Cool Later Is Inversely Related to Your Popularity Level in High School."[51] In its holiday party issue, the magazine instructed, "Tell your boyfriend what you think of those dumb blond jokes he's been throwing around. Then dump him and go party with your best friend."[52] Even the starring systems for reviews were sassy: five stars for a film meant, "See this or die," while one star meant, "A kick in the head is a better way to see stars"; a five-star record review meant, "I've seen God and this is the soundtrack," versus one star, which meant, "I'd rather work for Clarence Thomas."[53]

In *Sassy* there was a near-perfect blend of a love for and validation of girl culture, with a deep commitment to feminism. Baby boom feminists, having seen fifty-year-old women referred to dismissively as "girls," and the trappings of femininity used to justify discrimination against women, had long rejected most things "girly" as trivializing. But by the early 1990s, many girls wanted to reclaim girl culture as just as legitimate as boy culture: why was getting a pedicure any dumber than lifting weights? *Sassy* insisted—despite the fact that being female still "rots"—that being a girl was great and that girls should love themselves. Once a year there was an issue produced by readers, and the magazine ran an annual "Sassiest Girl in America" contest, whose winners and runners-up were accomplished students or musicians, social activists, white and girls of color, and the opposite of "the skinny girl from L.A."[54]

In articles like "How to Fight Sexism" and "Do You Need Armpit Hair to Be a Feminist?" *Sassy* insisted on the importance of feminism to girls, laid out how it had changed since the 1970s and challenged the stereotypes about feminists: "These days you might as well say you eat dirt as admit to being a feminist. Well phooey. We're not embarrassed to admit in print that we all be feminists because, hot news flash, in terms of fairness, being female in America still stinks big time and needs all the muscles we can give it. It stinks economically: In 1955, women made 64 cents for every dollar a man earned. In 1987 . . . they made—are you ready?—65 big cents. Whoopee. And the average woman college grad earns less than the average white male high school grad."[55] "Okay, okay—so probably no one has ever told you to your face that you're inferior because you're a woman," wrote Jodie Hargus in 1991. "But it gets implied constantly in subtle ways, which makes it even more powerful. So what do you do? Get bummed and rag on guys? Or start taking action to change things? I pick choice B."[56] In "I Am Woman, Hear Me Roar," Christina reported, "It's summer, that lovely time of year when women everywhere can't even walk down the street without hearing some idiot make gross comments about their body parts. Street harassers used to intimidate me because I was afraid they'd hurt me. But then I took this amazing self-defense course, and now they'd better be scared of me." The article got tons of fan mail for bearing witness to all of the daily, obnoxious come-ons millions of young woman were subjected to every day, twenty years after the women's movement.[57] What *Sassy* did was make feminism relevant and cool to an entirely new generation of young women, no mean feat in an era of "I'm not a feminist, but . . ."

Sassy addressed its readers by assuming that they were smart. "How's That Drug War Going, Guys? Why the Government's Drug-Fighting Strategy Is a Colossal and Misguided Waste of Our Money" in September 1992 could have appeared in the *Village Voice* or *Mother Jones* (and probably did), just with a slightly different tone. "The Iraq Thing," in February

1991 opened with this disarming line: "I hate current events; they bore and depress me." But then the author added, "However, when American troops were sent over to Iraq last summer, all of a sudden the US was dangerously close to war and I didn't have a clue what the fight would be about. So I found out and I thought you'd like to know too. . . . Reading quotes from George's advisers is kind of like listening to a football coach talking about how his team will destroy the opponent. Has everyone forgotten the lessons of Vietnam?" She asserted her opposition to the probable war, and the justifications for it. "I almost puked when I saw George Bush having Thanksgiving dinner with the troops, telling them they were fighting for freedom." Taking on this conceit of the war being a fight for freedom, she pointed out that the leaders of Kuwait were autocrats and that women there did not have the right to vote.[58] This article received more reader mail than any story in the magazine's history.[59]

Just like most women and girls, *Sassy* had a love-hate relationship with American popular culture, and especially with *Beverly Hills 90210*. The writers loved to ridicule the show and also apparently never missed an episode. In "What a Bunch of Thespians," they asked an acting coach to watch several episodes and then offer his assessment of the stars' acting abilities, which was less than kind, especially to Shannen Doherty. Christina Kelly authored a *"Beverly Hills 90210* Indecently Exposed" paper doll layout. "They're such typical teenagers, aren't they? Brenda and Kelly always in those fashion-correct little bodysuits and minis, not a hair out of place. . . . Your high school is chock full of people exactly like the characters in 'Bev Hills,' right?" Next to each paper doll was a profile with categories like "Hobbies," "Friends," and the like. For the Kelly doll the response under "Job" was "You must be kidding" and under "Hobbies" it was "Likes to shop and apply make-up." Dylan's "Distinguishing qualities: Is supposed to be sincere and sexy but comes off as phony and slimy"; "Morals: Ha"; "Job: Not"; and "Hobbies: Surfing, reading, driving his upscale convertible, doing it." Brenda's hobbies were "Hangs out with Kelly and Donna. Makes out with Dylan."[60] This was more fun than watching the show itself!

"Shannen Doherty, Pathetic Loser" was how *Sassy* headlined its January 1993 cover story on its annual entertainment poll among its readers. Inside we learned that *90210* was voted "the show that most often depicts women in a demeaning way," second only to *Married with Children*.[61] Though teen girls were not the target audience, *Northern Exposure* was nonetheless the second favorite show for *Sassy* readers, who also regarded *Murphy Brown* as the TV show that "most often shows women as fully developed people."

Sassy had an especial affinity for indie and underground culture, and showcased bands and actors outside the mainstream. It also started a "Zine of the Month" feature that brought these do-it-yourself publications—and their defiant sensibilities—to a much wider audience. Erin Smith of Bratmobile became a *Sassy* intern in 1991, and shortly the magazine began covering Riot Grrrl bands and zines.

So what happened to derail a magazine this fabulous, one still pined for by its fans fifteen years later, one we wish we still had? (And for more age groups—where's the mouthy magazine like this for the over-forty set instead of all that empowerment stuff we get?) You will not be surprised to hear that the first villain—the villain of so many infuriating stories about thwarting women's aspirations—was the religious right. In its view, *Sassy* did two really bad things: it spoke honestly to teens about sex and featured sympathetic stories about gay teens. All of this made Jan Dawes, a woman from Wabash, Indiana, clearly with a lot of spare time on her hands, and member of a right-wing group called Women Aglow, crazed. She started a petition campaign in 1988 against the magazine through its advertisers and convinced her local Kmart and Hook's Drug Store to stop carrying the magazine. In short order James Dobson's Focus on the Family, Donald Wildmon's American Family Association, and Jerry Falwell's Moral Majority joined in, bombarding advertisers like Revlon, Cover Girl, Maybelline, and Tampax with threats of a boycott if they didn't yank their ads. The publisher and editor had to embark on a major counteroffensive, and gradually the advertisers came back, in no small part because of *Sassy*'s robust circulation. But the magazine had to scale back on its features and advice about sex. And some advertisers decided it was best to avoid the publication.

In 1989 *Sassy* was acquired by Lang Communications, a relatively small and mismanaged firm that did not have the deep pockets or the inclination to push circulation higher through tactics like preferential newsstand placement, direct-mail campaigns, or promotional tours.[62]

Five years later, in October 1994, Lang sold *Sassy* to the Los Angeles–based Petersen Publishing—the belly of the beast itself that published *Teen*. The New York staff was fired, and instantly a new, obviously fake teen jargon entered the magazine with references to one's "fave actor." By 1996, *Sassy* trafficked in dating dos and don'ts and bad celebrity hair days. Readers were beside themselves and wrote in to say they had burned the new issue or torn it into tiny pieces. That same year, the magazine folded.

Adolescents in America are expected to be restless, rebellious, defiant of adult society and strictures. But girls are supposed to conform to preexisting (mostly male) standards of beauty and behavior, to comply, to obey. Thus, if they behave like true adolescents, they can't be feminine, and if they adopt the mantle of femininity, they aren't really adolescents.[63] How is that for an impossible place to stand? The fluorescence of feminism in the early 1990s created an environment encouraging girls to claim their sassy selves. At the same time, with the media trashing of Riot Grrrl, the demise of *Sassy*, and the success of *90210* and *Melrose Place*, girls saw which kinds of women got rewarded and which kinds didn't. Meanwhile, TV and film producers understood that girls and women liked seeing women with power in entertainment programming, and that advertisers would be satisfied as long as such fare sold mascara, Oil of Olay, Ultra Slim-Fast, and push-up bras. But it wasn't only entertainment media that discovered the frisson generated by teen girl sexuality, or the need to discipline women's desires for power. So did that august institution, the news media.

2

CASTRATION ANXIETY

On June 24, 1993, when the men of America read their morning news-paper, their hands instinctively snapped to their crotches, protectively cupping their privates. They read of a Virginia woman who, claiming her husband had raped her, went to the kitchen after he had dozed off, got what the *Washington Post* described as "a 12-inch filet knife," and cut off his penis while he slept. The man, soon identified as John Wayne Bobbitt—named after John Wayne and a former marine no less—showed up at Prince William Hospital at 5:00 A.M. in what can only be described as serious distress. "Police officers were dispatched to his nearby apart-ment to search for the missing penis, but couldn't find it," the *Post* was compelled to report with a straight face.

It turned out that his wife, Lorena Bobbitt, had "unknowingly taken the penis with her, and had thrown the penis out the window of her car at Old Centreville Road and Maplewood Drive." Fortunately for John Wayne, Lorena dropped a dime and gave the cops the location of the defenestrated member. They rushed to the scene, packed the orphaned penis in ice, and raced it to the hospital where, after a nine-and-a-half-hour surgery, it was reattached.[1] Said one surgeon about previous efforts at penile reattachment (at least for white guys), "You put the penis back on and if it didn't turn black, it was a success."[2] Doctors hoped for a better outcome here. Even women felt their sphincters shrivel, and crossed their legs real hard, although some did whisper, under their breath, "You go, girl."

This display of female aggression was book-ended by two other stories in the news. Just a year before, of a spring morning in May 1992, a teenage girl rang the doorbell of a suburban home in Merrick, Long Island, and when the lady of the house answered, the girl—packing a .25-caliber Titan semiautomatic pistol—shot the woman, Mary Jo, in the face and fled the scene in a red Thunderbird.[3] The girl, Amy Fisher, said she had been having an affair—since the age of sixteen—with Mary Jo's thirty-six-year-old husband Joey, a beefy auto mechanic who favored snakeskin boots. The last name of the couple—Buttafuoco—evoking as it did some unholy combination of Italian desserts exploding with cream stuffing and rough lovemaking between mountain goats—only added to the delight of the tabloid press as they followed the case of the pistol-packin' "Long Island Lolita."

And then, just over six months after the Bobbitt incident, in January 1994, a refrigerator-sized assailant approached Nancy Kerrigan, the Olympic figure skater, at the end of her practice session, and whacked her in the knee with a metal baton. Within days, Shawn Eric Eckardt, a 350-pound bodyguard to Kerrigan's skating rival, Tonya Harding, was arrested along with another man.[4] Harding, described in the *New York Times* as "a woman who drives a pickup truck, shoots pool with a cigarette hanging from her mouth and has compared herself to Charles Barkley, the bad boy of basketball," quickly came under suspicion, especially when it emerged that her ex-husband, Jeff Gillooly, an "unemployed former warehouse worker," had also been arrested and had sought to cop a plea.[5] In early February, Gillooly asserted that Harding had been in on the scheme from the beginning, and in March Harding pled guilty—not to planning the attack but to hindering its investigation. Most people assumed she was the mastermind of the whole plot. After all, Kerrigan was the princess, feminine, all-American-girl, while Harding was hard-edged, tough, working class, apparently ruthless. The news was getting juicier than *Knots Landing*, *L.A. Law*, or *Melrose Place*.

Finally, we need to add to this mix of high-profile news stories the revolutionary figure of Janet Reno, the six-foot-one-inch Florida "crime fighter" who, according to the press, supposedly wrestled alligators in her spare time. Just one month after taking office as Bill Clinton's attorney general, she approved a raid on the Branch Davidians' compound in Waco, Texas, that led to the deaths of more than eighty people.

What, exactly, was going on here? Had girls truly gone wild? How much power did they want—as much as Dirty Harry? "The Year of the Woman" was one thing, but was *this* what feminism had really wrought: girls and women being just as violent as men, having no compunctions about wielding weapons in the name of revenge or justice or, worst of all, sex? The spectacle of women with power interacting with the spectacle of women deploying guns, filet knives, lead pipes, and tanks gave the news media chills—and plenty to churn through, and sell, as they both managed and inflamed what, in retrospect, seems like a national bout of castration anxiety. Here was a cultural brew about gender in which female achievement—and transgression—heightened ever-present nervousness about gender roles, the dangers of female power, and the pathos of emasculated men. It may seem bizarre to evoke the memories of Amy Fisher, Lorena Bobbitt, and Janet Reno in adjacent sentences—not to mention in the same thought!—but with the advantage of hindsight we see that the cultural response to them was of a piece, and reveals how in these years the news media became a key site where jitters about the potential powers of girls and women got expressed and worked through. And it offered this admonition: look out, guys, they're striking back. Women's fantasies of power would become, for men, nightmares of power, if left unchecked.

The news was hardly operating in a vacuum. The top-grossing films of 1992 featured a tough-as-nails female cop added to the previously all-male *Lethal Weapon* team; a stern, epaulet-enhanced Demi Moore as a navy lieutenant commander (with, at first, more balls than Tom Cruise) in *A Few Good Men*; and the murderous Sharon Stone in *Basic Instinct*, whose m.o. was killing men in bed with an ice pick just after sex. *Single White Female* starred Jennifer Jason Leigh as a psychopath who throws her roommate's dog out the window and then kills her boyfriend. In Hollywood films of yore, women received libidinous stares from men when they ran along the beach in bikinis or were draped across a piano singing in a husky voice. In *Lethal Weapon 3* (a truly egregious film whose script reduced Joe Pesci to hyperventilating "u-kay, u-kay, u-kay" like a squeak toy for 118 minutes), Riggs (Mel Gibson) has witnessed Lorna Cole (Rene Russo) single-handedly kickbox about eight bad guys into submission. The next time the cops confront more bad guys who require interrogation, Lorna says she'll handle it and starts to approach them. Murtaugh (Danny Glover) asks Riggs if he shouldn't go with her. "No," Riggs insists admiringly. "No, I want you to see something, she has a gift; watch this." Lorna then punches and kickboxes about eight more bad guys while Riggs stares lovingly on; when she's done, he applauds and brags, "That's my girl." So now, in some films, women with black belts in karate were sexy—or at least to the crazy Riggs. But they were also way scary.

Of course, women wielding sharp instruments or karate chops were not the only icons of feminism—or femininity—circulating through the media fun house. One distorted set of mirrors gave us the cartoon of the female predator; another, the figure of the female victim; and yet another, the triumphal career woman with power. Women and girls could be forgiven for feeling one minute like feminism really had made so much possible, and the next minute like they were really, really going to pay for that.

So another stream that began feeding the emergence of enlightened sexism was this sense of threat to male dominance. But as the Anita Hill–Clarence Thomas hearings demonstrated, and the huge success of Faludi's *Backlash* affirmed, a full frontal assault on female assertiveness wasn't always the most effective tactic. But sensationalism, titillation, and ridicule, all reminding girls and women that they will always be defined by and reduced to their sexual attractiveness (or lack thereof) and their sexual behaviors—now that's an effective form of social control. Enlightened sexism rests on that ever-quaking and shifting fault line about female sexuality: it should be exploited and stoked (especially to sell products) but it should be policed and punished (to keep girls and women in their place). And that's exactly how the news media played it.

With the cold war over, Desert Storm concluded, and news organizations slashing their budgets, especially for international news, Americans were treated to new levels of mayhem and sex scandals. Shows like *A Current Affair* (1986–96), a piece of televisual black-lace-and-garter-belts from Rupert Murdoch that aired on most Fox TV stations; *Hard Copy* (1989–99); and *Inside Edition* (1989–present), whose host until

1995, let us not forget, was Bill O'Reilly, competed with one another as well as with the network news and helped import a slavering sensationalism and celebrity journalism into television's more staid precincts. To cite just one example of the contamination process, the same edition of ABC's *World News Tonight* with Peter Jennings that announced the nomination of Janet Reno as attorney general ended with a story about the color of Michael Jackson's skin.[6]

The nightly news, at least the version offered by *Hard Copy* and *Inside Edition*, consisted of murders (preferably gruesome), acrimonious palimony suits, celebrity divorces gone postal (and any other juicy celebrity gossip), and as much gratuitous sex as could fit into a half hour. And television news and tabloid TV became deeply invested in and reliant upon melodramas about gender. The girl-scandals of the early 1990s became the bread and butter of tabloid TV (and later, with the Clinton–Lewinsky scandal, of the nightly news). They also served as another Rorschach test of the media psyche about how far feminism could, and could not, go. All over, there were incessant reminders that female sexuality—especially in young women—was dangerous, and that women with power were a threat or, well, not real women. Angst about the wages of feminism got swept up and refashioned by an increasingly scandal-addicted news media as sexual melodramas and morality tales of girls—and sometimes guys—gone wild. When the guys went wild (yes, think O.J.), it was, in the end, because they couldn't help it: they were driven to it by the promise, or threat, of female carnality.

Ironically, in the real world, girls and women were achieving more than ever; it just wasn't terribly sexy, or, therefore, newsworthy. More women than men were attending and graduating from college—67 percent of female high school graduates in 1991 went to college, whereas only 57 percent of males did—and a survey in 1993 found 123 women enrolled in college for every 100 men.[7] The proportion of doctors who were women had risen to 17 percent by 1990, up from 11.6 percent a decade earlier, and 43 percent of those graduating from law school in 1992 were female.[8] But if young women watched the news, such accomplishment was nowhere to be seen, except in the occasional story about girls' sports. Instead, young women were either victims or delinquents of some sort. Sex crimes against girls, rape, murders, harassment, eating disorders, teenage pregnancies, girls in gangs, girls failing in math and science—these were the staple of the news. And what primarily made them newsworthy was their sexuality, which was always fraught with peril—but great for ratings.

Amy Fisher was the poster girl for such young women, perfect because she could be seen as both a villain and a victim. The Fisher–Buttafuoco story was huge, a yearlong media hootchy-kootchy show, and not just for the *New York Post* or *Daily News*. It was also raw meat for *A Current Affair* and *Inside Edition*; it spawned three TV movies (one worse than the next), two books (including *Amy Fisher: My Story*, in which she revealed that she didn't wear underpants), the Amy Fisher–Joey Buttofuoco comic book (which sold out its first run of sixty thousand copies in one week), and *Amy Fisher: The Musical*, which became a cult hit in Greenwich Village.[9]

Initially reported under the staid headline "Girl, 17, Arraigned in Shooting of Woman" and buried on page 40 of the Metro section of the *New York Times*, the story went like this.[10] Fisher, a senior at John F. Kennedy High School, had been having an affair with Buttafuoco, the owner of Complete Auto Body and Fender Company. The affair began when Fisher was sixteen, after her parents brought a car there for repair. When Buttafuoco reportedly tried to break off the relationship, Fisher went into a jealous rage and on May 19, 1992, shot his wife, Mary Jo, in the face, leaving her for dead on her doorstep. When Mary Jo came out of her coma she was able to describe her assailant, and Fisher was arrested several days later. Immediately one of the homicide detectives, who cast the case as "one of the most bizarre in years," likened it to the 1987 film all feminists love to hate, *Fatal Attraction*.[11] The judge set Fisher's bail at a whopping $2 million. And for his part, the gallant Buttafuoco vehemently denied the affair.

A news story–cum–sex thriller that was a real-life *Fatal Attraction*, except with a teenage girl? You could almost hear them screaming "woo hoo!" from the offices of *A Current Affair* and *People*. The highly publicized rape trials in 1991 and 1992 of William Kennedy Smith and Mike Tyson, as well as the case of Carolyn Warmus—another "real-life *Fatal*

Attraction" in which a blond schoolteacher killed her married lover's wife—had greased the skids well. And this story had the Hemi-engined New York tabloids in the driver's seat. And it wasn't just tabloid TV that fed on such scandals. The broadcast TV networks, seeking to save money on high-priced writers and name actors, had been turning increasingly to made-for-TV movies that were "ripped from the headlines." Made-for-TV movies cost "only" about $3 million to $5 million to make—much cheaper than a theatrical film or a series—and they were popular and thus profitable.[12] Interest in the shows would have been stoked already by the news (in industry parlance, the audience was "presold"), you didn't need to hire A-list actors to play the likes of Joey Buttafuoco, and the story wrote itself.

Within days this little appendix of a story had blown up to its Macy's Day Parade proportions, where it remained for nearly a year. The story ran on the front page of the New York *Daily News* for more than ten days straight, and the paper's circulation director claimed that by itself the story boosted sales by 2 to 3 percent.[13] *Newsday* revealed that Fisher worked for an "escort service" in her spare time.[14] In early June, *A Current Affair* aired a home video purportedly of Fisher having sex with someone who was "a client"; *Hard Copy* ripped it off of *A Current Affair*'s satellite feed and aired it, too. In it Fisher says, "I'm wild. I don't care. I love sex."[15]

Wow! Now it was the case that Fisher was also a prostitute and wore a beeper to high school to take calls from johns: schoolgirl by day, hooker by night. It was at once fascinating and threatening to consider that a white, middle-class, suburban teenage girl (as opposed to Madonna in any of her music videos) could be a horny sexual agent. Immediately a paperback by *People* magazine reporter Maria Eftimiades was in the works, published in October 1992 with the title *Lethal Lolita*. The *New York Post* columnist who landed an exclusive interview with Mary Jo was reportedly bombarded with feelers for a book or screen deal as soon as the story appeared. Amy Fisher's lawyer, Eric Naiburg, announced in early June that he was looking for offers for Fisher's story so she could make the bail that her parents, the proprietors of the Stitch-N-Sew discount fabric store, could not pay. Naiburg—a former vibrating bed salesman (you could not make this stuff up)—claimed he fielded twenty panting offers within forty-eight hours and narrowed them down to ten. This was immediately pegged the "tale-for-bail" scheme. (Butta-fuoco's lawyer sniffed that such a deal would transform Fisher "from a $180-a-night prostitute to a $2 million prostitute.")[16] Studios and pub-lishers hit up everyone—both Buttafuocos, all the attorneys involved, the journalists covering the story, even members of the district attor-ney's office—exploring possible movie and book deals.

Epithets, charges, and countercharges flew. Naiburg said it was Buttafuoco who got Fisher into the escort service business, called him a lecher and a pimp, and accused him of statutory rape. Buttafuoco's lawyers threatened to sue for libel, which certainly would have been a stretch. Naiburg sought to cast Fisher as the victim, claiming she had been raped repeatedly by Joey, a line somewhat harder to sustain once people saw her turning tricks on *Hard Copy*. Fisher had allegedly at first asked a friend to off Mary Jo in exchange for sexual favors; the *New York Post* dubbed him "Amy's Horny Hitman."[17] The *Daily News*, somehow sensing the story was not juicy enough, felt the need to add drugs to the mix, alleging that Joey had a little problem there.[18] (His coke-selling handle? "Joey Coco Pops.")[19] The *Post*, not to be outdone, asked readers to vote about who was really to blame here, Amy or Joey.[20] All summer, talk radio fulminated with debate about who was the real predator and the real victim.

Fisher sat in jail for two months before her attorney—who had not had as much luck peddling her story as he once claimed—was able to post bond. A small independent film company, KLM Productions, had offered $80,000 for Amy's story, which helped Naiburg put a deal together. (KLM later sold the rights to NBC.) By now, Mary Jo also had a movie deal. In September Fisher copped a plea, agreeing to the lesser charge of reckless assault, thereby depriving the media of a lurid trial. Then another tabloid bombshell: the "sex nymph" had a new boyfriend, thirty-year-old Paul Makely. He owned a gym, and also, it turned out, a hidden video camera. With the camera rolling, Fisher, on the night before her plea no less, and in between making sexual overtures to Makely, suggested they get married so she could have conjugal visits in jail. She said she liked all the publicity "because I can make a lot of money. I figure if I have to go through all the pain and suffering, I'm getting a Ferrari."[21] After Makely sold the tape to *Hard Copy*, Fisher made two suicide attempts. Now she

wasn't just a sexual whore, she was a media whore to boot, the two prosti-
tutions reinforcing each other.[22] In December she was sentenced to up to
fifteen years in prison.

Fisher and Buttafuoco were boffo box office. Producers at *Hard Copy*
claimed their ratings tripled when they broadcast the videotapes of
Fisher.[23] When *Dateline NBC* aired its interview with Fisher, it scored its
highest ratings in the show's history; in fact, the interview catapulted the
show from 45 to 7 in the weekly Nielsens.[24] Then came the movies, and
each network had one. NBC's Christmas card to America, *The Amy Fisher
Story* (her side of it, Joey in heat), aired on December 28 and raked in a
19.1 rating, making it one of the highest-rated TV movies of the season.[25]
(The average rating for a network show at the time was about 12.) Six days
later, on a Sunday night, CBS's *Casualties of Love: The "Long Island Lolita"
Story* (Mary Jo's side of it, "Amy Fisher was a customer. First she wrecked
her car. Then she wrecked his life.") went head-to-head with ABC's *The
Amy Fisher Story* (multiple points of view, "Drew Barrymore is Amy
Fisher").[26] Dialogue snippet from the Barrymore film: Joey gives Amy one
of his shirts to wear. Joey: "It may be too big for you." Amy: "I can handle
your size." Joey "Extra large?"[27] Possibly because of this excellent writing,
and the fact that it had the most sex, the ABC version brought in 19.4 in
the overnights, with CBS's trailing with only a 15.8 rating. What this
meant was that nearly 18 million households tuned in to the first movie,
and a minimum of 16.2 million tuned into one of the others.[28] Survey
researchers later found that 40 percent of Americans had seen at least one
of the movies.[29] Network executives were flabbergasted that three made-
for-TV movies about exactly the same scandal—including two that aired
opposite each other—would do so well.

Then the spotlight shifted to Joey. Could he be busted for statutory
rape? Was he in on the shooting? What about Amy's allegations that
they had sex nearly every day, in his office, in seedy motels, on his power
boat *Double Trouble*? Her best-selling book, *Amy Fisher: My Story*, which
came out in April 1993, described all this and more. That month a grand
jury indicted Joey on nineteen counts of statutory rape, sodomy, and
endangering the welfare of a child. Mary Jo continued to stand by her
man, telling the *Daily News* (and anticipating Lorena Bobbitt), "If I
really believed Joey Buttafuoco had an affair with Amy Fisher, I'd cut

his testicles off."[30] After nearly eighteen months of swearing something to the effect of "I never had sexual relations with that woman," Buttafuoco changed his tune and pled guilty to one count of statutory rape, for which he served six months in prison. By this time he was a laughingstock. As David Letterman said, "For months the punch line to every joke we told was 'Joey Buttafuoco.' Kaboom."[31]

Why was this story so huge? Aside from the fact that the media kept churning so it would produce the maximum amount of cheese every day, the scandal called everything into question: the myth of suburban normalcy; the taboo against older men having sex with underage girls; the taboos against teenage girls being sexually aggressive, enraged, and physically violent; the understanding that men should be rational and in control, especially of their women. Everything here was rendered unstable. But most important were the questions it raised about teenage girls and power, especially their sexual power, how much they had, how much they should have, and what should be done about it. Were women and girls always the victims of older or more powerful men? Not if the scheming, lewd, murderous Fisher was Exhibit A. Girls were now capable of anything, even of being predators. But what about Buttafuoco? Hadn't he both cheated on his wife and taken advantage of an impressionable teenage girl, possibly turning her into a call girl? Wasn't it the same as it ever was with men—they seduce you and then deny you when you become inconvenient?

The coverage of the scandal seductively insisted that we take sides, invited us to be the morally superior judge, while asserting that the whole mess was much too tawdry—beneath us—to follow.[32] There were other pleasures—viewers could be shameful voyeurs, titillated by the videotapes, and then upright moral guardians, condemning either Joey or Amy or both. While Buttafuoco became a joke, it was Amy who was the female and thus more dangerous, and so it was Amy who had to be, and was, serially debased by the media gaze. This is what happens if teen girl power is unleashed. America, beware.

The Fisher–Buttafuoco peep show was just starting to spiral down when Lorena Bobbitt provided the media with a story equally thermonuclear.

This, too, started out as a Metro story, this one in the *Washington Post*, and it, too, quickly became a national sensation. Headline writers, whetting their rhetorical razor strops, slapped out banners like "Slice of Life," "The Unkindest Cut," "Painful Separation," "Severance Pay." There were jokes about "getting even with a Ginsu."[33] Both parties were charged with crimes and in July 1993 Lorena filed for divorce. John Wayne Bobbitt went on trial first, that fall, for marital sexual assault, and was found not guilty. Outside the Virginia courthouse, hawkers sold T-shirts that read, "Manassas—A Cut Above the Rest."[34] By November, a radio station in Los Angeles had organized a "Lorena Bobbitt Weenie Toss," which involved motorists hurling hot dogs at a target. David Letterman featured Bobbitt top ten lists—"best Lorena Bobbitt excuses: (7) that's what he gets for hoggin' the remote and (5) I was trying to cut the price tag off his new pajamas and he sneezed."[35]

Lorena went on trial next. His trial was not televised; hers was a media orgy: sixteen satellite uplink trucks and more than two hundred reporters descended on Manassas. Again the women in these scandals, because they were so shockingly transgressive, were much more fascinating to— and thus violated by—the media cameras. Outside, vendors sold his-and-hers T-shirts: "Revenge—How Sweet It Is" and "Love Hurts," the latter autographed by John Wayne himself. CNN, along with Court TV, carried the trial live and saw its ratings double.[36] (The Associated Press transmitted the photos shown in court of the severed penis, which one can now see on Wikipedia; unlike tapes of Amy Fisher having sex, this image found zero takers.)[37] A *Newsweek* poll reported that 60 percent of the country followed the trial, men and women in equal numbers.[38] After expert testimony that Lorena was suffering from posttraumatic stress disorder as a result of years of physical and sexual abuse during her marriage, she was acquitted of malicious wounding in January 1994. Lorena had emigrated to the United States from Ecuador at the age of seventeen and had married Bobbitt, the only guy she had ever dated, at age twenty. Rush Limbaugh asked why she didn't "leave the jerk," no doubt unaware that at the time there were three times as many animal shelters in the country as there were shelters for battered women.[39]

Despite repeated boasts by their attorneys that both Bobbitts were being bombarded with offers of book and movie deals, no "true crime"

TV movie came out of this story. The reason remains unclear, but it is hard to imagine the women of America wanting to sit through two hours of a woman serially abused and raped by her husband, or to imagine the men of America wanting to watch the scene where Bobbitt was separated from his manhood. John Wayne did go on to star in porn films, including *John Wayne Bobbitt... Uncut* and one with possibly the best title ever, *Frankenpenis* (in which, yes, his penis falls off during sex).

The Bobbitt case became a national joke. The guy had been mutilated; the story was beyond gruesome. So why were people laughing their asses off? Endless movies and TV shows had, for decades, featured men with machine guns, bazookas, canons, submarines, swords, switchblades, billy clubs, and choppers, which reassured male viewers about the unconscious fear of no longer having one. The Bobbitt case dispatched these metaphorical phallic comforts and brought the real thing—castration—smack into the national consciousness. It is precisely when something is so scary (especially to men) that it must be made fun of to exorcise the fear. Laughter is also about asserting power over terrible threats. And castration—physical and metaphorical—is the ultimate threat women pose.

The Bobbitt jokes were mostly about the act itself and about what John Wayne—pathetic, passed out drunk—let happen to him. Jay Leno, David Letterman, the headline writers, the radio talk show hosts had to humiliate Bobbitt, to make it clear that they and the rest of the real men in America were superior to him and thus would never suffer his fate. These jokes were, of course, about catharsis, about transforming the agony of castration into the pleasure of laughter and release. But they were also abusive, and they had to emphasize that Bobbitt was ridiculous and impotent because he embodied emasculation, and that men had to aggressively attack that specter of losing power. However much men had had to give up or compromise because of the women's movement, at least they were not like Bobbitt, a real wretch now because he had, well, fucked with a woman (and one half his size) and paid the ultimate price.

The case also became a morality tale about the wages of feminism. The media sought to cast the Bobbitt case, with great exaggeration, as a defining moment in the ongoing battle of the sexes. More to the point, they were keen to set up Lorena as a hero to all feminists because she had

struck back—where it hurt—against male abuse of women. Camille
Paglia's typically theatrical pronouncement that Lorena's knife work was
"a wake-up call," a "revolutionary act," and a "Boston Tea Party" for feminism hardly helped. The Virginia chapter of the National Organization
for Women did establish a Lorena Bobbitt support line. If most women,
and especially feminists, applauded John Wayne's near castration, wasn't
that prima facie evidence that feminists were vengeful, man-hating Medu-
sas and that the quest by women for power had gone too far?

What many women did commend was how Lorena's trial, with her
tearful, graphic account of her abuse (including forced anal sex and a
forced abortion), raised awareness about domestic violence. Feminists
like Kim Gandy, executive vice president of NOW, emphasized that
every day women were beaten, mutilated, and killed by their partners
and this never made the news, but one guy loses his penis and the country goes ballistic.[40] And as interviews with ordinary women suggested, a
not insignificant number of them thought "Right on!" when they first
read the news. But prominent feminists hardly celebrated the mutilation
itself; for them there was a real distinction between empathizing with an
abused woman and endorsing how she responded. As Barbara Ehrenreich noted in *Time*, "I admire the male body and prefer to find the penis
attached to it rather than having to root around in vacant lots with Zip-
loc bag in hand."[41]

Nonetheless, looking back at the way Amy Fisher and Lorena Bobbitt
were framed by the media, it is noteworthy that both were linked to
feminism—Fisher, in being likened to Glenn Close's quasi-feminist-
rhetoric-spouting career bitch in *Fatal Attraction*, and Bobbitt, through
a new awareness about sexual harassment and domestic abuse—even
though neither woman made any feminist claims herself. Both cases
garnered so much attention because, in addition to being lurid, they
raised primal anxieties about maintaining the existing hierarchies in
which men remained on top.[42] As women's entry into previously male-
dominated realms continued apace, the contradictions about women's
roles, and especially female sexuality, intensified even more. And the
takeaway from these two melodramas? Feminism was getting out of
hand.

This is why it was just as important to ridicule Joey Buttafuoco and John Wayne Bobbitt as it was to pinion Amy and Lorena under a disciplining national gaze. Both men were caricatures of masculinity, preening body builders (Bobbitt actually signed into his gym as action star Jean-Claude Van Damme) too concerned with their appearance for their own good, who could not control their women. As one writer put it, "Bobbitt has become an emblem for the hapless state of North American masculinity."[43] Both Bobbitt and Buttafuoco were victims of female violence yet both were also dumb brutes who had evoked that violence. Their helplessness on the one hand and their macho complicity on the other had to be ridiculed so that "normal" masculinity could be reinforced as still deserving to reign supreme. The media circuses were, in the end, morality tales about the absolute necessity of containing female sexuality, female rage, and their threats to masculine authority and prerogatives. Whatever fantasies of power girls and women harbored, they had to be herded up, corralled, tamed.

Intersecting with these scandals was the ascension of the presidency of Bill Clinton. (Only later would we appreciate the historical irony of this.) Between the prominence of his wife in public affairs and his unprecedented number of female cabinet appointments (plus appointing a second woman to the Supreme Court), Clinton did seek to further embed feminism in the federal government. And no woman captured the country's ambivalence about whether there were or were not real distinctions between men and women than Janet Reno. After Bill Clinton's first two disastrous nominations for attorney general—Zoë Baird and Kimba Wood, both of whom had illegal nanny problems—Reno, childless, was a relief. A state prosecutor in Miami with a reputation for getting stiff sentences against drug traffickers and other criminals, the media described her repeatedly with the male monicker "crime fighter," who was "plainspoken" and/or "outspoken," and "tough."[44] Nominated the day before Lincoln's birthday in 1993, Reno "at 6 feet, one inches tall . . . stood eye-to-eye with the president in the Rose Garden"; she "still lives in the bungalow house built by her parents with their bare hands," a house that had "no central air conditioning, peacocks in the yard and a rocking chair on the porch."[45] She was "scrupulously honest," we were told, a public servant of "unquestioned integrity"[46] and an "avid out-doors woman" who paddled the Everglades.[47] She seemed like Lincoln himself; in fact, maybe a little too much like Honest Abe. Reno had to dispel suspicions that she was a lesbian with statements like, "I am just an awkward old maid who has a very great attraction to men."[48] (One can see Will Ferrell hearing this and jotting "Note to Self" . . .)

Within ten days *Newsweek* was reporting that Reno's Everglades home was "right out of *Tobacco Road*," and that her mother had been "an alligator-wrestler and an honorary princess of the Mikasuki Indi-ans." The *Economist*, with this description—"She is a 54-year-old, six-foot-two-inch pipe-smoking spinster who lives in a log-and-stone house built by her mother (a tough bird herself who was famous for wrestling alligators)"—made Reno sound like Popeye in a skirt. Pretty soon, cour-tesy of *People*, we were in Dogpatch with Reno as Li'l Abner. Reportedly one of Reno's young nieces once tried to feed a hog when the swine grabbed her by the coat. Reno "ran out and punched that hog right between the eyes." Now she herself was the one who "wrestled alligators with Miccosukee Indians" and presided over her family's "East Ever-glades Wild Hog Hunting and Drama Society."[49] By late June, in an address before the National Press Club, Reno bemoaned this media cre-ation of the "myth of this lady from the swamps."[50]

Reno was confirmed by the Senate on March 11, 1993; just over a month later she approved the raid on the Branch Davidian compound in Waco, Texas. David Koresh, the thirty-three-year-old self-proclaimed Messiah, was holed up with his followers (including, allegedly, nineteen wives), and he was wanted on weapons charges after neighbors com-plained about the sounds of gunfire coming from the Waco compound.[51] On February 28, before Reno had even been confirmed, more than one hundred agents of the Bureau of Alcohol, Tobacco and Firearms launched a surprise raid on the place, except it wasn't a surprise. Someone had tipped off the heavily armed Branch Davidians and they fired back, kill-ing four agents and injuring others. The ATF agents withdrew after forty-five minutes, and the standoff began. There were negotiations; Koresh released some of the children; Koresh promised to surrender but didn't;

the Feds cut off the electricity to the compound; and still the standoff persisted. By the end of March, the Feds began blasting the Davidians with the sounds of dentist's drills and rabbits being slaughtered.[52] (Where does one even *get* such audio?) When that didn't work they resorted to Nancy Sinatra's "These Boots Are Made for Walking," chanting by Tibetan monks, and, best of all, a Sing-Along-with-Mitch-Miller Christmas album, which would certainly have broken all but the most determined group. (Although as Peter Di Vasto, a psychologist for the Albuquerque police, told the *New York Times*, "If they go Barry Manilow, it's excessive force.")[53]

So here was Reno, with a history as a ferocious child advocate, stuck with this mess she didn't make, being told by ATF and FBI officials that seventeen children were being abused or held against their will in unsafe conditions in the compound. The FBI proposed battering holes in the walls of the compound and spraying in tear gas to force the Davidians to leave. Reno approved the plan. Shortly after the attack, on April 19, the compound erupted in flames in what the FBI claimed was a mass suicide, killing eighty-six people, including more than twenty children. It was a disaster.

Unlike 99.7 percent of American politicians, Reno immediately admitted that the decision to go in was "obviously wrong." Moreover, she said, simply, "I'm responsible," and added, "The buck stops with me." Visibly shaken, she did not hide from the press or retreat to an undisclosed location; she appeared on CNN and *Nightline*, and told Ted Koppel, "I think it's one of the great tragedies of this time." On national television, she offered to resign. As Laura Blumenfeld wrote for the *Washington Post*, "It is clear that a different kind of bird has nested at Justice. . . . The attorney general's candor may surprise those used to politicians who duck and cover when things go wrong."[54]

Janet Reno instantly became a national folk hero. According to *USA Today*, more than two thousand people called the Justice Department the day after the assault on the Branch Davidians, and these calls were 80 percent in support of the attorney general.[55] Public opinion polls confirmed this report. When Reno appeared before Congress two days later, Senator Fritz Hollings of South Carolina proclaimed, "I think you acted in an outstanding fashion. I commend you for it," a sentiment echoed on both sides of the aisle—even the Republicans did not go after her.[56] Several months later Reno's approval ratings were higher than the president's, and soon she was on the cover of *Time*, profiled in *Vanity Fair*, and named one of *Glamour* magazine's "Women of the Year" and one of *People*'s "25 Most Intriguing People." She would also be one of the few cabinet members to stay in office during the entirety of Bill Clinton's two terms.

Nonetheless, within no time it was almost impossible to make it through a late night talk show monologue without hearing a joke about her. In a David Letterman "Current Events" quiz, as viewers saw a photo of a giant Christmas tree, the question read, "What's eighteen-and-a-half feet tall and can currently be seen at the White House?" Correct answer? Janet Reno. Or, high on Letterman's top ten list of the most dangerous toys for kids? Rock 'em, Sock 'em Janet Reno. In another joke, at first seeming to comment on Reno's decision not to appoint a special prosecutor to investigate campaign fund-raising abuses, the question went, "Clinton was relieved when Janet Reno decided not to do what?" Punch line? "Corner him under the mistletoe."

Jay Leno, commenting on the Clinton family's Christmas shopping trip in New York, noted that the president bought a pair of size 13EE running shoes at Foot Locker. "I guess we know what Janet Reno's getting for Christmas," he quipped. In Leno's joke about Reno not appointing a special prosecutor, Leno said it was "Janet Reno's toughest decision since boxers or briefs." The jokes were incessant. And Will Ferrell's ongoing drag impersonation "Janet Reno's Dance Party" on *Saturday Night Live* featured the nation's first female attorney general as a pathetic, love-starved nerd who threw herself at men and danced like a robot on angel dust. A giant; too butch; unloved; a freak.

Even the news media got in on the gag. Picking up on a story apparently first floated in that august publication, the *Weekly World News*, CNN, *Time*, the *Boston Globe*, and others reported that 78 percent of Japanese men surveyed allegedly said they'd rather be shipwrecked on a desert island with Janet Reno than with any other woman on the planet. Well—what do you expect? Japanese men aren't *real* men anyway; they're just as freaky, just as asexual as Reno in the eyes of Americans. These guys must have had to be "wacky" if they reported, as fashion photographer Kazutaka Itosu reportedly did to the *Weekly World News*, that Reno was "a vision of beauty—and by far the sexiest woman in the world."

I'm going to go out on a limb here, but my guess is that prior to this, the network news organizations had never cited the black-and-white tabloid as a source. But unlike the *Weekly World News*'s other stories about public figures, such as its famous photo of Ross Perot shaking hands with an alien, the mainstream press did not dismiss this curio. In a Web site about the story, Reno's head was superimposed on a woman's body wearing a black leather strapless bathing suit doing a bump and grind. In a related story, a 1998 report in the *New Yorker* noted that Clinton staffers referred to Reno simply as "The Martian."

Why was Reno the butt of all these jokes, especially jokes designed to make middle-aged male talk show hosts seem funny and hip? Why did this ridiculing of Reno take on such a regular, ritualistic, almost cathartic quality?

Janet Reno had looked at the masquerade of femininity that women are supposed to don and just said no. Why, Bill Clinton—with his trademark line "I feel your pain"—wore the masquerade of femininity better than she did. This was deeply, deeply threatening. Sure, Reno was a far cry from the Estée Lauder standard of beauty: the poreless, thick-haired, slim-hipped, big-busted, pouty-lipped sylph. But so was Madeleine Albright, the country's first female secretary of state, and she was not a regular in Letterman's nightly monologue. Albright reportedly knew how to flirt with Jesse Helms (which must have required a great deal of Maalox—or Xanax).

No, the really unsettling thing about Reno was that she simply refused to conform to all the ways that women were—and are—supposed to perform femininity, especially in America's craven consumer culture where billions rest on all the products women need for this performance. With a few exceptions, most prominent public women in America in the early 1990s remained in the entertainment industry: actresses, models, TV hosts, and newscasters for whom beauty was—and is—part of the job description. They may be smart, they may be talented, but the industry of which they are part continues to insist that women are, first and foremost, to be looked at. They are also supposed to be empathetic, to make others feel comfy. Even women like Oprah Winfrey or Katie Couric, who could put people on the spot, still smiled enough, teased enough, sympathized enough to be thought of as "feminine." Not Reno.

She apparently could not care less what anybody thought about her appearance. The sort of facile approval that comes from wearing the right clothes, having the right haircut, and putting people at ease seemed utterly irrelevant to her. And that made people extremely uncomfortable. The fact that she was a *woman*—a straight woman at that—and didn't care was even more alarming. A man whose attire and coiffure seemed an after-thought would have been fine; after all, the sourpuss Warren Christopher, Bill Clinton's first secretary of state, was no matinee idol, and he didn't become a national joke.

Despite the 1992 election year having been proclaimed "The Year of the Woman," or maybe because of it, the performance of gender, the daily, emphatic, and obligatory marking of ourselves as male or female, so ingrained in American culture, seemed under threat in the wake of the violent femmes and Janet Reno. From the minutest things—how girls and women greet each other versus how they greet men, how we hold our bodies and use our hands, how we speak, our clothes, accessories, hair, cosmetics—it is supposed to become second nature for straight men and women to constantly make sure that we are marked as a member of one sex and not the other. This insistence that everything we say and do announces and re-announces our gender is strenuous; it is a minute-by-minute series of actions that adds up to an entire repertoire.[57]

By these standards, Reno generated a crisis of intelligibility.[58] Was she asexual? Was she really a woman? Yes, she wore skirts and even lipstick, but only in the most obligatory fashion. She rarely smiled, never canted her head in the way even Bill Clinton did to make himself look more accessible. In fact, she had none of the body language women learn to adopt as we present ourselves to others in everyday life. Her voice was low-pitched and often monotone, and she did not use the usual higher-note inflections that women do to convey interest, surprise, vulnerability. Her sins were multiple: she was androgynous and didn't care about sexual display; she refused to follow all the rules of public performance;

she would not ingratiate herself and seemed oblivious to the pressures to fit in. As Liza Mundy of the *Washington Post* noted, "She doesn't feel the need to help, conversationally." How come *she* got to evade all the psychic angst about fitting in and succeeding and we didn't?

The jokes about Reno usually came in the guise of political humor. But the jokes weren't about politics at all; they were deeply uneasy, nervous outbursts against a woman who personified what it might be like if most women just got up one day, looked in the mirror, and said "Okay, I'll take it." If Reno could say no to Revlon, *Glamour* magazine, Oil of Olay, Victoria's Secret, and to being deferential to or flirtatious with men, and *still* be professionally successful, what was to stop other women from following suit? She was a constant reminder that gender is not embedded in biology, but is an arbitrary cultural construct. The adamant insistence that women constantly perform femininity suggests that somehow the world as we know it would come crashing down if we all stopped marking and announcing these sex distinctions between men and women.[59] A woman who—not deliberately or defiantly, but just because of who she was—challenged the very foundations of patriarchy and consumerism gave men, in particular, the heebie-jeebies. Was it possible that there weren't two diametrically opposed sexes, as Reno in her padded shoulder suits and Mr. Magoo eyeglasses implied? She had to be disciplined.

And so the jokes, which sought to tame her in three basic ways. The first, of course, was to suggest that she was more mannish than any man, that she was such a far cry from a woman that she was laughable, ridiculous. The second was to undermine her power by sexualizing her, degrading her with Web images of her in a bustier or, as *The Tonight Show* did, put her head on the body of the mythic TV character Xena. Such images simultaneously mocked the fact that she was not sexy, implied that despite her denials she was really a lesbian, and reminded women that *any* woman can be reduced to her anatomy and thus degraded and objectified.[60] The third—this was Will Ferrell's tack—was to fantasize that her refusal to "just say yes" to femininity left her hopelessly lonely, desperate for love, and desperate for sex. Just as our culture's marking of gender differences through costuming, hair, tone of voice, and so forth is filled with redundancy so the marking cannot be missed, so, too, did it then seem important to repeatedly tell jokes about Reno so that the challenge she posed to the blurring of these boundaries would be incessantly rebuffed.

If we take Janet Reno as one point on the spectrum of female success in the 1990s, and the supermodel Cindy Crawford as on the near-opposite end of that spectrum, we see how the media reminded Americans which of these women deserved to be envied and which one did not. Yes, Reno remained in office for eight years. And many people admired her, despite the fair share of criticism, some of it deserved, that her decisions and actions provoked. But the media made it clear who would be rewarded with big contracts, television shows and appearances, the admiring looks from men, the envy of other women, and who would not. They made it clear who was a joke and who was not. Women who refused to take on the masquerade of contemporary femininity had to pay a price, and the price here was ostracism, a lesson not lost on most of us.[61]

The early 1990s was an era of fits and starts for the emerging common sense we'd eventually know as enlightened sexism. Despite Amy Fisher, girls were not being sexualized the way they are today; feminism—explicit, out-there feminism—still sold TV shows, books, and even politics. *Maxim* didn't exist, and there were not yet multiple reality TV shows in which women presented as bimbos got in catfights over men. Nonetheless, for a new ideological understanding to take hold, it often needs to identify a threat to which it is responding, and from which it offers protection and escape. This the media began to do—however inadvertently and unconsciously—in their obsession with deviant teen girls and its marginalizing of Janet Reno. For enlightened sexism to convince most women, especially girls and young women, that feminism is unnecessary, irrelevant, or horrid, the media had to make clear what would happen if the advance of feminism were not halted. They had to make it clear that feminism, if taken too far, would turn girls and women into monsters or ridiculous, unlovable freaks. This kind of feminism—that just says no to femininity—had to be repudiated. This crucial plank in the platform of enlightened sexism got laid down during these years and especially (although hardly solely) through these stories.

The moral from the media, then, was that it was now accepted that some women could have power—witness Janet Reno, Madeleine Albright, Donna Shalala, Sandra Day O'Connor, Ruth Bader Ginsburg, Hillary Clinton, and others—as long as they did not threaten existing regimes about the marking and performance of femininity. Another lesson was that the media had a greater interest than ever in capitalizing on while also moralizing about teen girl sexuality. (Far be it from me to label this as hypocritical exploitation.) So, what if you took these contradictory edicts about female power and female sexuality to heart? That was the next challenge for popular culture to answer.

3

WARRIOR WOMEN IN THONGS

So, what might you get if you combined the six-foot, fearless, alligator-wrestling, unsmiling crime fighter Janet Reno with the statuesque, gorgeous, dark-haired supermodel Cindy Crawford? One delicious outcome just might be *Xena: Warrior Princess*. Another—if you were going for a more Valley Girl look—might be *Buffy the Vampire Slayer*. "Pow! Slam! Thank You, Ma'am," observed the *New York Times*; "Fierce Femmes Storming Pop Culture," proclaimed *TV Guide*. Referring to kickboxing heroines like Lara Croft, Buffy, the Powerpuff Girls, and the updated sock-'em-up version of *Charlie's Angels*, the article continued, "They may be physically adept and emotionally resilient but they also know their way around a make-up counter."[1] No namby-pamby Cinderella types here: these babes could make you swoon *and* kick your butt if you messed with them.

Xena and *Buffy* became major hits in the mid- and late-1990s in part because they spoke to many girls and women oscillating between the Reno and Crawford icons of female success. The Reno icon affirmed that it was important to be tough and accomplished, femininity be damned; the Crawford icon said no, it was more important to be thin, beautiful, and busty. Together, they embodied how the scripts for female achievement were changing, yet they were the same as they ever were. The resolution of this tension? Possibly the most satisfying yet unrealistic fantasies of power ever: action chick superheroes, warrior women in thongs. They were accomplished and powerful, but always, always, slim and beautiful. If the more regressive tendrils of enlightened sexism were beginning to sprout in *90210* (girls are defined by shopping and boys), or *Melrose Place* (women who seek power are lethal vixens), or tabloid sex scandals (young women plus sexual agency equals serious trouble, especially for men), the more progressive response, the one that gave full, metaphorical expression to girl power, was the warrior woman.

In the olden days of Hollywood films and TV shows, women were primarily to be looked at while men, through their actions, advanced the narrative. But for a decade beginning with the premiere of *Xena* in 1995, we saw the proliferation of a new kind of heroine, a sexy, mouthy, physically violent ass-kicker whose duty it was to save the entire world from really monstrous evildoers. Only she—a female—could do it. In addition to *Xena* and *Buffy*, we got *La Femme Nikita*, *Dark Angel*, and *Alias* on TV, along with the wildly successful films *Crouching Tiger, Hidden Dragon*; *The Matrix*; and *Charlie's Angels* (and the sequels) and the *Lara Croft: Tomb Raider* video games and films. They all showcased gorgeous women who could somehow make their bodies go horizontal so they could kick guys' teeth down their throats. Most didn't need help from any man, nor did they need to have a man to define them. Not only were they *not* victims, they typically had to rescue others, including men. In other words, the old gender hierarchies were turned totally upside down. These were girls and women who defied feminine norms about being nice, passive, and deferential to others and who, instead, took on the male prerogatives once reserved for the likes of James Bond, Rambo, Jackie Chan, and Chuck Norris.[2] Traits and skills—like hand-to-hand combat—previously taboo for girls and women turned these action chicks into instant cult heroes.

Most of these women were not just formidable physically, they were tough verbally as well, armed with sarcastic comebacks and cutting putdowns. These were not catty remarks; this was muscular verbal jousting. And they wielded with total confidence, and deadly accuracy, the various phallic emblems—swords, stakes, knives, spears, and guns—typically reserved for the male of the species. They turned the tables on female victimization, especially targeting men who preyed on women and children. Male bashing, such as this line from Buffy's male "watcher"— "Testosterone is a great equalizer; it turns all men into morons"—was often de rigueur. Women weren't the only ones trapped by out-of-date gender roles; men were, too.

These women weren't simply more like men, they inhabited *the* most dominant form of masculinity: extremely aggressive, fully able to master guns, helicopters, tanks, and other technological instruments of death (or rescue), and able to kill efficiently and to withstand torture. Indeed, their beat-up bodies recovered almost instantly from brutal assault, just like Wile E. Coyote and Bruce Willis. Some had androgynous or male names, like Max, Alex, Nikita, and Sydney. And they didn't just fight strong, they fought smart, thinking instantly on their feet about just which move to use when. Tougher and more lethal than any man, more beautiful (and more scantily clad) than most women, warrior women in thongs fused feminism and femininity in a fantasy reconciliation between the fury of Riot Grrrl and the body politics of *Cosmo*. This wasn't girl power; this was girl supremacy. At the same time, for most of the warrior women, this power was a burden. Some had been forced to be heroines, against their will. There were very real personal costs to being a leader, especially if you were female.[3] And with one or two fleeting exceptions, they were all white.

Almost instantly there were debates about whether these characters were feminist role models because they were so powerful, or retrograde because they conformed to, and thus advanced, very narrow fashion magazine standards of beauty and thinness while exposing vast acreages of flesh. But it's obvious that warrior women in thongs had both feminist and antifeminist elements to them. The more interesting question than the either/or one posed at the time is this: Why did our culture, at this millennial moment, produce so many jujitsu supergirls in miniskirts whose fate was to thwart primarily powerful, monstrous men? Also, these shows and films were often very, very violent. What were girls and women to make of that as a way to resolve conflict? Was brute force less objectionable if exerted by beautiful women?

Now, as far as we know, no TV executive made this pitch: "Hey, let's splice together Janet Reno and Cindy Crawford and see what kind of recombinant female we get—and if she'll sell." (Although who knows what industry types come up with after a few martinis—just look at *Manimal*, a short-lived series in which an NYU professor of "animal behavioral sciences" by day turned himself into a pussycat or wild boar at night to fight crimes.) It is rarely the case that male producers of television shows witness phenomena like the blockbuster sales of *Reviving Ophelia* (about the loss of self-esteem among adolescent girls and the hostile media environment surrounding them and on the *New York Times* bestseller list for a whopping 154 weeks), or the proliferation of "Take Back the Night" rallies, and then sit around a bar and say, "Hey, let's make a show that responds to girls and women being pissed off about being victims."

But in this case, that's partially what happened. Joss Whedon, the male creator of *Buffy the Vampire Slayer* and a self-identified feminist, said he had begun feeling sorry for the female victims of all those slasher films. "I started feeling bad for her. I thought, you know, it's time she had a chance to take back the night."[4] And Jordan Levin, an executive at the WB network and the father of two daughters who helped bring *Buffy* to the small screen, had in fact read *Reviving Ophelia*, and vowed to bring "empowered, intelligent" women to prime time.[5] Indeed, TV programmers succeed by tapping into current anxieties and desires and packaging them in such a way that the program on offer confronts and resolves these concerns. And the concerns of many women and feminists in the 1990s were different from what they had been in the 1970s. Back then, women fought explicit discrimination in education, the workplace, and the legal system that had made women second-class citizens. They fought for, and won (however incompletely), women's rights to enter the professions, to control their own reproductive lives, to be entitled to equal pay for equal work, and the like.

In the early and mid-1990s, with some of these gains achieved, girls and women focused on how sexual politics, subtle cultural practices, and violence against women—actual and feared—still kept us in our place.[6] Women who sought abortions in many places had to endure the vicious gauntlet of Operation Rescue bullies as they walked into their local clinic. The horrific and widely publicized Central Park Jogger case in 1989, the William Kennedy Smith date rape case in 1991 (in which he was acquitted despite other women coming forward with similar allegations), the Mike Tyson rape case of 1991–92 (not acquitted), and, most infamous of all, the brutal murder of Nicole Brown Simpson in June 1994, which revealed a history of domestic abuse at the hands of the football star O. J. Simpson (as we all know, the husband gets off), had a cumulative impact. You could be an athlete and run fast, you could be out on a date with someone you thought was a nice guy, or you could be married to someone and in your own home, and you were not safe—indeed you were in lethal danger. Equal pay for equal work, access to law school or medical school—none of that mattered in these situations. Between 1992 and 1996, the number of sexual harassment charges filed with the Equal Employment Opportunity Commission increased by 50 percent; that doesn't necessarily mean the harassment itself increased so dramatically during this period, but it does show a huge new awareness that such complaints could and should be reported.[7] Rape rates spiked in 1991 and 1992 after seven years of decline, bringing them back to levels not seen since 1984.[8] And women were very, very sick of it.

It was in this milieu that we began to see the rise of kick-butt women. Their power was justified, in fact necessary, because the worlds they lived in—over a Hellmouth, among roving hordes of barbarians, in a world threatened by terrorists—were dangerous, especially for females.[9] A recurring scene in warrior women fare was the sight and sound of menacing footsteps coming up behind our heroine; but this did not signal, as it had in endless crime and horror tales, her demise. Au contraire. Before the stalking predator knew what hit him, he was splattered on the ground. And even as these shows and movies deliberately inverted decades of cowering, screaming, swooning women-as-victims, they also tapped into the very real cultural apprehensions about changing gender scripts for men and for women.[10]

Something else made these shows so successful, especially with women: they were a new hybrid genre of TV and film. With few exceptions, television of yore was divided up into formulaic genres, such as sitcoms, where there was no action, or cop dramas, where there was little comedy, or soap operas, where there was no science fiction. Ditto for most films. Until the *Scream* movies, horror films with vampires and monsters were rarely *intentionally* funny. As the television scholar

Amanda Lotz astutely points out, these 1990s shows broke the mold by fusing the male-oriented action-adventure genre with elements of serial dramas, romance novels, comedy, and sci-fi.[11] While typically there was resolution of the danger at hand by the end of each episode, story lines often carried over from one episode to the next, and revelations about the characters' past were rationed out gradually, much like the soaps. Thus, we wanted to tune in as much to see what was going to be disclosed that we didn't know before about the heroine's past, or about changes in people's feelings and relationships, as we did for the action. There were more points of entry for viewers, male and female, young and old, and more creative opportunities for the writers and directors to push different elements of the shows at different times. Having a less straitjacketed approach was especially fruitful in dealing with what was, after all, comic book material.

The first of these shows, *Xena: Warrior Princess*, grew out of the cheesy but successful syndicated show *Hercules: The Legendary Journeys*. Xena (played by the pitch-perfect Lucy Lawless) was originally a villain, but she was so popular that the show's creators, Rob Tapert, John Schulian, and Sam Raimi, proposed a spin-off based on her adventures. TV executives initially believed no one would watch a female superhero.[12] But Tapert, Schulian, and Raimi turned Xena into a good warrior who had seen the error of her bad old ways and was now dedicating herself to battling evil and injustice. *Xena*, too, was a syndicated show—meaning it was sold to individual stations around the country rather than being broadcast on a network—and within four months of its premiere in September 1995, it was on the air in 196 markets and surpassing *Hercules* in the ratings.

By the end of December it was the number one syndicated show in the country.[13] Just over a year later, in February 1997, the show's ratings had increased by 36 percent from the previous year, and there were cities like New York and Los Angeles where *Xena* was beating the competition on the networks, including the considerably more wimpy *Dr. Quinn, Medicine Woman*.[14] With each successive week in the spring of 1997, *Xena* gained viewers, and it was especially popular among teens, kids, and women, although it had plenty of male viewers, too.[15] It also had a devoted following among lesbians, and enterprising gay bars featured *Xena* nights. The inevitable action figures, posters, T-shirts, beer mugs, trading cards, faux weapons, and jewelry followed. Secretary of State Madeleine Albright declared on CNN that Xena was her hero.[16] It was also an international hit, and multiple Web sites stoked its cult following. Lucy Lawless's fans were "Xenites," her realm the "Xenaverse," and by 1997 there was the first Xena convention, which drew twenty-five hundred fans, many outfitted in Xena regalia.[17] The Web site Whoosh! became the home of the *Journal of the International Association of Xena Studies.* The show lasted for six seasons.

Here is the basic premise. Set in ancient Greece by way of New Zealand at an indeterminate time somewhere between, say, 700 B.C. and A.D. 1200 (or as Scott Simon of NPR put it, "some imprecise all-inclusive antiquity"), *Xena: Warrior Princess* follows the efforts of the title character to redeem herself after having been an evil and destructive warrior. She does not have a home or a family, although this would change as the series progressed. The notion of Xena having a boyfriend would be like Arnold Schwarzenegger having a crinoline. As she quests through the land on her heavily armed Palomino horse looking for trouble with her blazing aquamarine eyes, she is joined by the initially insufferably perky little blonde Gabrielle (Renée O'Conner), who is fleeing from an arranged marriage to a guy she considers a dolt. "I'm not the little girl my parents wanted me to be," she tells Xena, adding that she does not fit into her village at all. She wants adventure, not marriage and kids. At first, Xena really, really does not want Gabrielle to join her, but Gabrielle persists, and although she's annoying at first, she and Xena develop a deep friendship that is at the heart of the show.

So what made *Xena* such a hit? First of all, the show strutted its campiness like a Mae West smirk. In the opening sequence (cue the bagpipe music so we know we're in a mythic place), a stentorian male voice proclaimed—over a scene of Xena talking to a giant animated Poseidon—"in a time of ancient gods, warlords, and kings, a land in turmoil cried out for a hero . . . she was Xena, a mighty princess, forged in the heat of battle." The narrator then intoned, with increased throat-warbling drama, "The power . . . the passion . . . the danger—her courage changed the world." Then the inevitable raping and pillaging would begin, which Xena would have to take care of. The soundtrack was pure, self-knowing kitsch: pounding music for the fight scenes, oboe or bassoon solos, or plucked violin strings to mark when a scene was supposed to be funny.

Another thing that made the show so popular was its utterly spectacular fight scenes, of which there were at least three in every episode. This was not some girl slapping her boyfriend in the face. This was Bruce Lee crossed with Mary Lou Retton on steroids. (Indeed, Rob Tapert was heavily influenced by the female action stars of Hong Kong kung fu cinema.)[18] Xena could punch, kickbox, and whip her sword around with the best of any ninja. Individual louts, as well as entire armies, would get hurled twenty feet and stomped into the ground. But she could also vault into trees, somersault backward onto her horse, and hurl spears with pinpoint accuracy into guys' chests. She could catch arrows in mid-flight. She was completely ferocious and ululated like the women in *The Battle of Algiers* yelling "Iy-yi-yi-yi-yi" as she galloped toward her enemies. Every sword movement, punch, and the like was accompanied by overheated sound effects of whooshes, smacks, thuds. In one typically over-the-top fight scene in the first episode, "Sins of the Past," a spear is staked straight up into the ground with a mob of bad guys circled around it and our heroine. Looks like curtains for Xena. But then she jumps up, grabs the stake halfway up, and positions her body parallel to the ground like a human pinwheel. She then rotates furiously around the spear, serially knocking down all the bad guys with her feet and legs. Game over. Xena also knew how to pinch a guy in the carotid artery so the circulation would be cut to his brain within thirty seconds unless he told her what she wanted to know. If enemy thugs crept up on her while she was sleeping, she could instantly grab a frying pan and twirl it in the air with delight before the inevitable smackdowns, noting, "I like to be creative in a fight, it gets my juices going." In fact, Xena loved to fight; little seemed to give her as much sheer pleasure as totally creaming a horde of dirtbags. On top of all this, Xena had her "chakra," the lethal, oval disc she hurled that could slice and dice anyone or anything in its path. You did not—not—mess with Xena.

Then, of course, there were the outfits. Xena was about six feet tall, gorgeous, and had some meat on her bones—this was no runway waif.

Her "armor," as it were, consisted of knee-high leather boots, a leather miniskirt, and a form-fitting, D-cup leather bustier with metal finials swirling around and defining her impressive, New Zealand breasts. One critic, who wrote that the outfit "doesn't emphasize her breasts," must have had glaucoma. For as Debbie Stoller of *Bust* magazine put it (and who would know better?), the bustier was "a molded breast-plate contraption that would make Madonna's mouth water."[19] So here we could take pleasure both in what Xena was doing and in what she and her adversaries were wearing. One of Xena's recurring archrivals was Callisto, a busty blonde in a metal-studded black leather number straight out of an S&M catalog. In addition to a navel- and thigh-baring miniskirt, Callisto's outfit included a bustier with what looked like black leather flying buttresses arching over and showcasing her not inconsiderable endowments. Then there were episodes like the one where Xena and Gabrielle enter Amazon country, and the most defining feature of their hosts is their cleavage.

This costuming seemed to make almost everyone happy. For men, there were a lot more heaving breasts and bare thighs than anything on *Law & Order*. Ditto for lesbians. For many feminists, whether lesbian or straight, it was thrilling to see a sexualized woman who, rather than getting blamed or punished for strutting her stuff, was powerful and could actually kick butt in her miniskirt. If you made the mistake of thinking that Xena even remotely wanted your attentions because of what she wore, you would be Hamburger Helper, instantly. What woman doesn't want to pretend for an hour that the world is like this?

But Xena wasn't just stronger than the Terminator and more scantily clad than the Bionic Woman. She also had a mouth on her. So did Gabrielle. Tough-talking and sarcastic, Xena seemed modeled very closely after Bruce Willis's John McClane in the *Die Hard* movies. (Rob Tapert told an interviewer that the writers for the show actually modeled the dialogue on the repartee in the film *Butch Cassidy and the Sundance Kid*.)[20] In an encounter with a blind but nonetheless scary Cyclops who is trying to squash her with a sledgehammer, Xena dodges and quips, "You've lost some weight since I saw you last," while laughing at him. Then she hurls her chakra at him, which makes his pants fall to his ankles, prompting him to trip, fall, and start to cry. She would ask sarcastically of a foe she's about to destroy, "Are we having fun yet?" When Xena and Gabrielle are staying with the Amazons, Gabrielle is summoned for some training by a woman who demands curtly, "Come, now," to which Gabrielle responds, "You must have me mistaken for a pet." This kind of arch dialogue added to the self-knowing style of the show, and to its pleasure. As one fan said with envy, "Xena says things everybody would like to say. She's tough, she's funny and she kicks butt. Everybody wants to do that sometimes."[21] Xena also didn't smile much and had she walked into a bar and been told by some random guy sitting there—as happens to so many women—"Hey, honey, smile"—well, he'd be splattered all over the walls.

So, what about the men in *Xena*? Completely unreconstructed dirt- and stubble-covered barbarians with matted hair and really bad teeth who traveled in packs torching everything in their path. If Xena was a feminist icon, she routinely battled the apotheosis of brute patriarchy run amok. Here, most men were just awful, with the few exceptional good guys, like Hercules. Their hallmark was savage physical violence against women, children, and families. Their vicious assaults on defenseless villages felt like a metaphor for gang rape, which Xena always thwarted. The warlords couldn't get along, either, and often Xena had to deliver the feminist message about the importance of cooperation and compromise. Then there was Joxer, the dorky warlord wannabe who even Gabrielle could beat the crap out of, at the other end of the spectrum: the embodiment of failed, flaccid masculinity.

On a narrative level, two things drove the show: Xena's struggle against her past and against her own dark and vengeful inner demons, and the deepening relationship between Xena and Gabrielle. As the series progressed, Gabrielle became more endearing, served as a moral and temperamental counterpoint to Xena, and got to fight more. And the show—produced by Liz Friedman, an out lesbian—maintained a "don't ask, don't tell" stance toward whether the two were indeed lovers.[22] The same evangelicals who threw a hissy fit over *Sassy* and would later hallucinate that the Teletubbies and Sponge Bob Square Pants were gay icons were always poised for action, and the show aired in some markets at 8:00 P.M., so the writers had to be cagey. Thus, straight women and men could choose to see the relationship as a deep bond of friendship, especially as there were those occasional episodes when Xena would get physical with, say, Hercules (prompting women in gay bars around the country to scream in unison, "No, Xena, don't do it!"). Lesbian viewers could see Hercules as "just a phase," and regard Gabrielle as Xena's true love, a view supported by scenes of hugging and kissing, and dialogue like "You are a gift to me" and "I love you."[23]

In "A Day in the Life," a fan favorite episode from the second season, it is hard not to read the two women as a couple. Bickering over Xena's destruction of their only frying pan, they spar like an old married couple, punctuated by playful kicks in the butt and culminating with an infamous candlelit hot tub scene. As thick steam rises from the tub, Gabrielle washes Xena's back and hair and then Xena returns the favor. And then the dialogue: Xena: "Are you sitting on the soap?" Gabrielle: "I was wondering what that was," followed by a splashing match. Later, Gabrielle tries to jump Xena from behind and falls, and then uses Xena's body to pull herself up, one hand firmly on Xena's left breast as if it were a piton. At the end of the episode they have made up and are lying side by side when Gabrielle kisses Xena—yes, demurely, on the cheek.

The show also took opportunities to expose and make fun of the masquerade of femininity most women felt they had to put on every day. In the episode "Miss Amphipolis," Xena gets an emergency plea to go undercover in a beauty pageant, an event celebrating a new but fragile peace among various warlords. While Gabrielle refers to such pageants as "meat markets" and "a feeble excuse for men to exploit and degrade women," Xena snaps, "You sent urgent word for us to come and see some underdressed overdeveloped bimbos in a beauty contest?" But Xena wants to help them avert war, so she agrees to become a contestant. Out she comes disguised as Miss Amphipolis, with all the accoutrements of exaggerated femininity. In a big blond wig, nearly exploding out of a gold lamé bustier atop a gold chiffon gown trimmed with fringe and coins, Xena, of all people, shimmies in front of the audience and throws kisses as she bends, ever so coyly, at the knees. We know that for Xena this is her parody of how men ask women to perform; she looks ridiculous (and feels it, too), and thus makes the ritualized way in which femininity is performed seem really strange and utterly arbitrary. Later in the episode we learn that all the contestants think the pageant is "a crock." One tells Xena she entered because her boyfriend wanted her to, and she didn't want to hurt his feelings. Xena asks, "What about your feelings; don't they count?" "They never have before," she replies. "He loves me, but he's so hung up on the way I look . . . that it's hard for him to see past that to the person underneath . . . and I guess a lot of people make that mistake." Xena urges her to tell him how she feels. Gradually all the contestants quit the competition rather than surrender their pride. In a perfect *Xena* finish, Miss Artifice, the one drag queen contestant, wins, and rightly so, as dressing like a woman actually made him feel like his true self.

Eighteen months after the premiere of *Xena* came the next female butt-kicking phenomenon. From the opening sequence of the first show we knew that we were not in the land of *Highway to Heaven* or *Walker, Texas Ranger* anymore. A cute, dark-haired, leather-jacketed boy, accompanied by a sweet young thing, breaks into his old high school at night and, deploying his best bedroom eyes, seeks to lure her into having sex with him "on top of the gym." She is the classic jittery scared blonde from every teen horror show you've ever seen. She jumps at every sound, and resists going to the gym because she is not sure who or what may be up there and, anyway, they'd get in trouble. But he really wants to get laid and assures her, "There's nobody here." "Are you sure?" she asks skittishly, still thinking she hears noises. He is sure. She turns to him as if to finally give in and kiss him, and instead morphs into a simian-browed vampire with fangs the size of a picket fence that she sinks hungrily into his neck. Cut to opening sequence. The driving rock music tells us this show may not be for the *Murder, She Wrote* crowd.

Welcome to *Buffy the Vampire Slayer. TV Guide* critics included the show as one of the fifty greatest TV shows of all time,[24] and there actually emerged a group of professors and intellectuals known as "Buffy scholars." You can learn about the postmodern politics of *Buffy*, do queer readings of *Buffy* or a postcolonial analysis of *Buffy*, consider mimetic excess in *Buffy* (don't ask), or contemplate the connections between *Buffy* and Plato. A journal, *Slayage*, emerged to serve as the *Online International Journal of Buffy Studies.* You can learn that in the second season, when Buffy's love interest Angel turns into a fully restored and very evil vampire after sleeping with her (giving new meaning to the term "bad sex"), his transformation "mirrors the pronounced split between the good mother and the bad mother . . . and calls to mind the trauma of infantile weaning."[25] Excuse me while I torch all my psychoanalytic theory books.

Buffy premiered on the WB network in March 1997 and built on the success of *Xena* and *The X-Files*, whose premise was that various things supernatural were in fact very real. Its creator, Joss Whedon, affirmed that the mission of the show was to celebrate "the joy of female power: having it, using it, sharing it."[26] The WB, learning from the experience of Fox, also staked out the teen market—and especially the teen girl market. As with *90210*, *Buffy*'s initial ratings were dismal, but by the winter of 1998 (when it was the lead-in to another WB hit, *Dawson's Creek*), it had become a hit with teenagers in particular. *Buffy* had everything: suspense, danger, the supernatural, humor, and romance.

Sixteen-year-old Buffy (Sarah Michelle Gellar), a former cheerleader who had to relocate because she had burned down the gym at her previous high school, learned two unpleasant things: her new school, Sunnydale High, sat atop the Hellmouth, a direct portal to a ghoul-infested Hades, and she was predestined to be "the slayer," the Chosen One, the only one who can save the earth from the bloodsuckers below. She was assisted by her "watcher" Giles (Anthony Stewart Head, who some older folks may remember from those Taster's Choice coffee commercials as the sexy neighbor seductively exchanging coffee and double entendres with the woman down the hall), and her friends Xander (Nicholas Brendon) and Willow (Alyson Hannigan), one of TV's first female computer whizzes. She was also helped, at first, by the hunky, brooding Angel (David Boreanaz), a vampire who, having been cursed by gypsies, had a soul and so couldn't be evil anymore.

Joss Whedon made clear that the show was, indeed, a metaphor for the multiple horrors of high school that typically scar a person for life. So in addition to the vampires that sought to feast on the high school kids and take over the world, there were the Hitleresque principals, the hard-ass teachers, dating disasters, romantic heartbreaks, and the inevitable clique of really mean girls (whom Buffy referred to at one point as "the winged monkeys"). As with most high schoolers in the media, Buffy's mother, Joyce (who, yes, worked outside the home), was at first completely clueless about her: she was unaware of Buffy's closeted iden-tity, her destiny, her special powers, and why she roamed the streets at all hours of the night with a stake tucked inside her hoodie. Unlike her male "watcher" Giles, Buffy's mother was completely incapable of train-ing or advising her. Instead, Buffy typically had to protect her, as Joyce was so gullible that she once took up with a cyborg serial killer, whom Buffy had to dispatch.[27]

Like Xena, Buffy was physically formidable. (Gellar reportedly had studied tae kwon do since the age of eight, which helped with the stunts.) And she, too, really relished fighting. Despite the hulking size, serrated fangs, and bulging, bas-relief foreheads of the vampires, they were no match for the kickboxing, punching, crossbow-wielding Buffy. In one fight scene, she did a handstand on a bar and as a vampire walked under her she swung down and kicked him to the ground with her feet. She could also take a punch herself, get hurled against walls, and spring back just in time to drive her wooden stake into their hearts. If a guy had her pinned down cold on the floor (a scary worry for a girl), Buffy could throw him off. Nonetheless, she still had to train with Giles, with sparring scenes reminiscent of *Rocky*, but in a library. Yet also like Xena, Buffy was easy on the eyes, and her diaper-sized miniskirts, knee-high boots, and skintight cardigans or other tops straining to contain her breasts and failing to cover her midriff distinguished her from many of the other female stu-dents who wore slacks or knee-length skirts to school.

While Buffy was not as emotionally intimidating or stern as Xena, her verbal bravado and smart-ass remarks were a trademark. When she con-fronts two vampires about to attack Willow, she disses one by telling him his outfit is so dated he "looks like DeBarge" (a Google image search of one of their album covers will confirm why this was such a put-down) and then warns them that things are going to get pretty rough—"we're talking violence, strong language, adult content." When another tells Buffy he wants her blood, and only hers, she wisecracks, "Works for me," before kicking him to the ground and hurling a cymbal like a discus to behead another. When another vampire threatens to kill her, she taunts, "So, are you going to kill me, or are we just making small talk?" In the first season Angel keeps showing up to warn her about various incipient dangers, and she regards him as crying wolf or trying to scare her. So when he cautions that the latest beast on the block is really dangerous and will rip her throat out she quips back, "Okay . . . I'll give you improved marks for that one, 'rip your throat out,' strong visual, not cryptic." Buffy and Giles verbally spar like Tracy and Hepburn and she gives as good as she gets. When Giles takes too long to explain something, Buffy interjects, "Giles, while we're young." In another exchange Buffy advises Giles, "Okay, you're abusing sarcasm." In a culture that for decades had told young women to be soft-spoken, always tactful, deferential to men, and thus to self-censor their feelings and desires, hearing an adolescent girl mouth off like this to powerful males was, yes, liberating.

As with many of the warrior women offerings, the threats to our heroine became more challenging, dangerous, and daunting. Thus Buffy and her friends (the "Scooby Gang") had to research, plan, and strategize differently each week and each season in order to survive, and Willow eventually acquired witchcraft skills to help fight the outpouring from the Hellmouth. So the series (and the others like it) established that one part of being a successful heroine was the ability to develop and transform your approaches, an ongoing active process, that showed that these women were not only constantly active physically, but mentally and strategically as well.[28] This, too, was a fresh, alternative view of girls and women.

The show also took special delight in skewering the popular girls as shallow, vain, mean-spirited, selfish, and mindless slaves to the fashion and beauty industries, especially as embodied in Cordelia (Charisma Carpenter). This was, of course, satisfying, but it also added to the emerging archetype of the rich, spoiled teenage bitch. Cordelia was one of the original Mean Girls. She ridicules Willow's dress by observing witheringly that Willow has embraced "the softer side of Sears" and brags that when she goes shopping she has to have the most expensive thing simply because it costs more. She wins the election for May Queen and in her acceptance speech oozes entitlement when she thanks everyone "for making the right choice and for showing me how much you all love me. Being this popular is not just my right, but my responsibility." When a teacher's decapitated body is found in the cafeteria walk-in freezer (a typical day at Sunnydale High), all those who witnessed the scene have to talk to a counselor. Cordelia reports that she hasn't been able to eat anything since she saw the body and has lost seven and a half ounces in two days, much more than the diet her "quack doctor" put her on. As she tells the counselor, it isn't that she is recommending that a teacher be killed every day so she can lose weight or anything, but "when tragedy strikes, you have to look on the bright side." Such unself-conscious dialogue was one way the show reminded viewers that popular girls were assholes. Another was to sic Buffy on them. When Buffy becomes somewhat antisocial as she has to kill an especially powerful vampire, Cordelia asks, "You're really campaigning for Bitch of the Year, aren't you?" Buffy shoots back, "As defending champion, you nervous?"

Buffy also had an episode, like the *Xena* beauty pageant, in which our heroine donned the masquerade of prefeminist femininity to demonstrate how ridiculous and dysfunctional it now was. In "Halloween," from the second season, Buffy dresses up as an eighteenth-century lady in part because she thinks that Angel, for whom she is developing the hots, will find that attractive, as he was alive back then. (This after we have seen her strong-arm an alpha male who was about to hit the distinctly non-macho Xander.) A warlock then puts a curse on everyone, including Buffy, turning them into the characters they are dressed up as. Thus Buffy morphs into the stereotype of the totally helpless damsel in distress just when various vampires and bad guys are out to get them all. As Willow goes for help, she instructs Xander, Cordelia, and Buffy that if anyone comes to the door, fight them off. Buffy is astounded: "It's not our place to fight, surely some men will protect us," and then demands of Xander, "You would take orders from a woman? Are you feeble in some way?" Her coda is, "I was brought up a proper lady. I wasn't meant to understand things. I'm just meant to look pretty. And then someone will marry me." Quips Willow, "She couldn't have dressed up like Xena?" Putting words like this into Buffy's mouth makes clear that male-dependent femininity is outmoded, ridiculous, and artificial, as Buffy is now a danger to herself and impedes the efforts of the others to protect themselves and her. The show is emphatic that the female empowerment brought about by feminism is liberating to women and necessary for their well-being and the well-being of others. It is even attractive to men: Angel confesses to Buffy that he hated the girls back in the eighteenth century, because they were really dull, simpering morons, and he always wanted to meet someone exciting and interesting, like her. By having someone as powerful as Buffy perform the role of passive ditz, the show mocks traditional gender roles and emphasizes that Buffy's true identity (and that of most girls) is as a tough and independent person. By having Angel confirm that Buffy is desirable, the show also asserts that despite feminism, male approval still matters.[29]

By the same token, alpha male masculinity was also retrograde and dangerous. In various episodes, frat boys, jocks, and, of course, power-hungry vampires who wanted to rule the world were all evil. Giles, the father figure, gained his power through research and knowledge and only rarely through physical force, although he, too, had a dark, violent past, as "the Ripper." And a running joke, especially in the earlier episodes, was how impossible and undesirable it was for Xander—the quintessential sensitive New Age guy—to don the mantle of tough guy masculinity.[30] But what could drive home more how dangerous, hurtful, and unreliable men can be than the story of the guy who seduces a virgin and then dumps her? This is what Angel did to Buffy, and while he really did love her, the sex broke the curse on him and made him monstrous once again. She wakes up to an empty bed and when she finds Angel to get an explanation he sneers, "Like I really wanted to stick around after that. You've got a lot to learn about men, kiddo, although I guess you proved that last night." She asks imploringly, "Was it me? Was I not good?" He laughs and responds condescendingly, "I thought you were a pro," a smear on her alleged innocence. In this and various subsequent episodes (especially when she takes up with the Billy Idol look-alike vampire Spike), male sexuality is a threat to women. But just as important, a woman's own sexual desires are a threat to herself and others. They distract you from the task at hand, make your friends vulnerable to attack, and prompt you to get involved with bad boys who will dump you or stalk you.

Xena and *Buffy* were not isolated phenomena: their huge success and cult followings helped inaugurate a spate of warrior women films and TV shows. The campy, comic book–like approach to women with power was taken up in the *Charlie's Angels* remakes and the wildly successful *Lara*

Croft video games and films. The first *Charlie's Angels* kicked butt at the box office in November 2000, raking in $40.5 million in its first weekend, the biggest non-summer opening at the time.[31] The new and still semiclad Angels—played by Cameron Diaz, Lucy Liu, and Drew Barrymore—were masters of everything, from computer hacking to archery to race car driving, and their martial arts leaps, kicks, and levitations were shot in slo-mo so we could relish the gravity-defying acrobatics. (Thank you, *The Matrix*.) They decimated thugs while the soundtrack played Prodigy's "Smack My Bitch Up," as if to say, "Hey, guys, who's smacking who? Who's the bitch now?" And Dylan (Barrymore), threatened with rape by five thugs, pummels them all. Their endless parade of girly outfits and disguises—geisha robes, lederhosen, microminis—made fun of the hyper-feminized regalia women were supposed to wear, and of the contrast between the image of female vulnerability and the reality of female power.[32]

But unlike Xena and Buffy, who did not use their sexuality as weapons to seduce, ambush, or hoodwink their opponents, their successors used their barely clothed bodies to entrap the villains, thereby adding back into the warrior woman scripts the message that true killer power comes from hyperfemininity. The sequel *Charlie's Angels: Full Throttle* (2003), which seemed designed, primarily, to let us see that forty-year-old Demi Moore still looked awesome in a bikini, was also the number one film in its open-ing weekend, although it quickly ran out of gas.[33] The movie opens in a bar in "Northern Mongolia" filled with savage, filthy, unruly men yell-ing, drinking, and fighting, while below the bar men are torturing a U.S. marshal. To distract the Mongolian hordes so Alex (Liu) can spring the marshal, Natalie (Diaz) flounces into the bar-cum–frat party run amok wearing a white miniskirt, thigh-high white stockings, and a white fur jacket and asks her double-entendre question in a fake Swedish accent, "This is hostel, yeah?" The Mongolians, clearly anticipating a gang bang, cheer for her to come in while they pour beers on each other in celebra-tion. (I presume an aside about the racism of this scene would be stating the obvious.)

Natalie walks in and mounts the giant mechanical Mongolian ox at the center of the bar, screaming and giggling in delight, lying back on the ox and kicking her legs up like a cross between a little girl and a stripper. Turned into slavering animals by such a display of female sexuality, the louts don't detect that Alex has kickboxed the captors and rescued the marshal. She then assures the lawman that she has "two girlfriends" in the bar, to which he responds with concern that the Mongolians have fifty armed men there. "I know, it hardly seems fair," Alex says with a smile. Of course they escape in a truck-off-a-bridge, jumping-onto-a-helicopter stunt that even James Bond could not have pulled off. Here, again, men who thought that pretty, sexy women were also powerless and vulnerable were in for a big surprise. It was those kinds of men in particular who would find themselves tricked by women who knew how to use the guise of femininity to dupe and dominate men.

Given that *Lara Croft: Tomb Raider*—able to leap tall buildings in a single bound and sporting breasts the size of watermelons—had conquered the land of video games, why not make a film as well? Especially if Angelina Jolie was available. Premiering in May 2001, just seven months after the first *Charlie's Angels*, *Lara Croft* was another box office bonanza, bringing in $48.2 million in its first weekend.[34] By this time the computer game—"a tale of world domination and raw sex appeal"—had reportedly sold 26 million copies. Although her creator said "everything about Lara was to exaggerate her female-ness," her black spandex shorts with the trademark giant phalli strapped to each thigh suggested a more complicated appeal.[35] In addition to beating up or shooting down giant, insect-like metal robots, Lara's specialty was swinging up, down, and around on large black ropes, bungee cords, and vines as she sought supercharged antiquities in ancient temples and ruins before the bad guys got hold of them. The film made clear that she couldn't cook, handled large machines with ease (including her big black motorcycle), and was not only stronger but also smarter than most men. There wasn't any very large, cylindrical *objet*—from handheld canons to giant battering rams—that Lara couldn't master.

Other warrior women would come to inhabit less mythic realms than Buffy and Xena, fighting terrorists or criminals, and doing so reluctantly. This darker, more fatalistic genre of warrior women did not feature hordes of beefed-up bloodsuckers or vandals, but instead included a cold-blooded father figure whose ethos and worldview were completely opposite, and dangerous, to the heroine's. *La Femme Nikita*, which aired on the USA network from 1997 to 2001, starred the lanky platinum blonde Peta Wilson as "the fatal femme you can't take your eyes from." Falsely accused of murder while she was living as a disheveled, dirty street person with a nose ring, Nikita was forced to join the top-secret antiterrorist group Section One run by the ruthless patriarch "Operations." She bemoans that "I'm only guilty of not taking charge of my own destiny," reminding girls that failing to take control of your life means that others (men) might do it for you in a way you don't like very much. Nikita did not take pleasure in fighting the way that Buffy and Xena did, nor was she as invincible. She did not want or relish the power she had; it was a curse. And unlike Buffy and Xena, Nikita did not call the shots; Operations did. Section One trained her to shoot and master kung fu, and they also taught her how to put on black stockings, walk in black patent leather stilettos, and cross her legs seductively, because, as they told her, "You can learn to shoot, you can learn to fight, but there's no weapon as powerful as your femininity." I repeat: "no weapon as powerful as your femininity." This was a turn for the worse.

Dark Angel (2000–2002), James Cameron's entry into the genre on Fox, had more mixed messages about girls and power. There was some new handwriting on the wall: our heroine had superpowers, but implanted by others (not inhering from within), an ongoing male love interest and partner, and the sexual desires of a nymphomaniac during certain cycles of the calendar. *Dark Angel* featured the pouty-lipped Max (Jessica Alba), a "genetically enhanced human prototype hunted by her former military handlers" from the top-secret compound Manticore run by a covert government agency in Wyoming (Dick Cheney territory). Manticore had impregnated women with a genetic cocktail designed to produce a superior human, a warrior, an "advanced infantry soldier." Max had escaped from the compound and, ten years later, was living in postapocalyptic Seattle, a broken-down, dirty, litter-strewn city with people huddled around fires in garbage cans. She worked as a bike messenger at a place called Jam Pony.

Like *Xena* and *Buffy*, *Dark Angel* was a fun fantasy because of Max's particular array of powers, her deep care for and friendships with women, and her mouthy repartee. Max could hear a phone call speed-dialed and instantly convert the tones into the correct phone number. She had telescopic vision, could swing from one skyscraper to the next on a rope (all in a black skintight body suit), did cartwheels that propelled her over tall fences, and, of course, drop-kicked bad guys across various tracts of real estate. She did wheelies on her motorcycle the way the Lone Ranger used to rear up on the two hind legs of Silver. Verbal aggression was also part of the package. To one bad guy's bodyguard Bruno, she jeers, "Jeez, you're so stupid the word 'special' comes to mind." After he tries to shoot her, she dodges the bullets, knocks him to the ground, and then taunts, "Come on, you're not even trying."

At first Max was out for herself and her close friends, which included Original Cindy (Valarie Rae Miller), an out, African American lesbian and possibly one of the most fun female characters ever on TV. But Max met the hunky, sensitive Logan Cale (Michael Weatherly), also known as "Eyes Only," who hacked into the news and brought viewers "Streaming Freedom Video" reports about corporate criminality and government corruption, which of course worked hand in hand. Logan gradually persuaded her to help him in his battles against evil, and of course, sexual sparks eventually flew between them. Except for Logan, most men were cruel, evil predators or unreliable, horny bastards governed by their libidos. Thus, feminist sensibilities often dominated the show. When Sketchy, Max's coworker and friend, tells her that he has been cheating on his girlfriend Natalie even though he doesn't like the other woman, Max demands, "Do you guys actually believe these lame, self-serving excuses? Or do you think we're so grateful to have one of you idiots we'll look the other way, which is condescending and arrogant?" Max told Original Cindy that guys were prisoners of their genes, to which Cindy replies, "So are dogs." A guy Max brings home one night passes out before they have sex, but is so dumb he insists the next morning that it was amazing.

In spite of moments such as these, *Dark Angel* also made clear that female sexual desire, when out of control and unregulated, was dangerous. It turned out that Manticore (how's *this* for a plot element?) had added some feline DNA to their science project kids so they could jump really far. The downside was that Max went into heat a couple of times a year, meaning any man—including the revolting boss at Jam Pony, named Normal—appealed to her. Or, as Cindy said, "You run around acting like the average male?" She lusted after nearly every guy she saw, but also knew it was freaky and didn't want to act on her urges because they were exaggerated, at least for a woman; this level and intensity of sexual agency was scary, even for a warrior woman.

One of the last entries into the warrior women category was Jennifer Garner as the CIA undercover double agent Sydney Bristow in *Alias* (2001–2006), which premiered a few weeks after 9/11. This was a family melodrama with martial arts and innumerable costume changes thrown in. Sydney worked with her father, Jack Bristow (Victor Garber), also a double agent, and what had by now become a stock figure of this genre, the hunky, sensitive "handler" Michael Vaughn (Michael Vartan). Her mission was "to infiltrate and destroy SD-6, a secret organization dealing in espionage, extortion, weapons sales, posing as the CIA." Thus, she also had to work with the paternal and dangerous Arvin Sloan (Ron Rifkin), the director of SD-6. Later in the series she would battle other terrorist organizations.

The basic plot of each episode required that Sydney go undercover in some often outlandish and sexualized disguise and typically in an exotic locale, which included places as diverse as Barcelona, Taipei, Rabat, and Siberia. Virtually every shot of her in disguise started with her feet and tilted up her body to reveal the latest leg-baring, breast-propelling outfit as she strode forward, as if on a fashion show runway, with the electronica music thumping in the background. Wigs of various styles and colors were also crucial. We saw her in a black fishnet top, black push-up bra, and black patent leather pants, evening gowns slit up to her crotch, a zebra striped cocktail dress with a plunging neckline, and full décolletage; in all of these, she could punch, kick, karate chop, and thwack bad guys into pancakes. Sydney, too, could endure considerable corporeal discomfort, as when her mother (yes, her own mother, an evil spy on the other side) shot her while she was handcuffed to a chair, and yet Sydney managed to bust out of the chair and escape, bullet wound and all. Her mother—sigh, an older woman with power—had been so corrupted by it that she turned against her own daughter. How's that for a warning?

It was the campier, earlier versions of warrior women—*Xena, Buffy, Charlie's Angels*—that had emphasized the importance of female friendship and group cooperation to the successful exercise of female power.[36] The heroines in *La Femme Nikita, Dark Angel*, and *Alias* were partnered with a man and, except for *Dark Angel*, were part of a male-dominated ensemble that had to execute, at times, unwelcome orders from the alpha male at the top with ice in his veins. But in all this fare, patriarchy, whether represented by red-eyed, white-faced vampires, marauding Huns in breastplates, or steely-eyed, pitiless heads of secret government organizations, was destructive, inhumane, heartless. It was the sensitive New Age guys like Xander, or Eyes Only, or even Hercules, the men touched by feminism, who held out hope for a new, improved masculinity. Just as the warrior women took on masculine traits, these guys took on feminine traits like caring for others that moved them beyond stereotypes about "real men" being defined by some essential, tough-guy persona.

Having said this, our heroines' leadership came at a price. Most had to hide their true identity and their powers from others, often including close friends. Because of their leadership position and their mission, they posed a threat to their loved ones who could be targeted or hurt by their enemies. They couldn't "have it all," a "normal" woman's life of dating, relationships, domesticity, because these were incompatible with female power. Sound familiar? Their destiny was typically not of their choosing, but imposed on them, often against their will; they had no choice but to use their extraordinary abilities, as ordained by others. Xena, Charlie's Angels, and Lara Croft may have relished their power, but Nikita and Max did not, or at least not completely. So while women had power, they didn't all want it or like it. As the genre evolved, power for women became a most unwelcome burden, its price just way too high.

The fantasies here often hit the spot: women no longer victims but champions, no longer muted but mouthy, not tied to one man but to other women or a group, no longer trapped by patriarchy but challenging it. And at least some of these creations stemmed from the genuine desire to invert the woman-as-prey conventions in the media and provide images (and role models) of strength. The warrior women in thongs insisted that females could, and should, combine force and aggression with femininity and sexual display. On the one hand, this was welcome, given how often our culture emphasizes that female sexuality is dangerous and shameful. On the other hand, they also reaffirmed the sexual objectification of women and girls, and suggested that women could be as strong as any man as long as they were poreless, stacked, and a size two. No matter how strong we got, it was more important to be slim and beautiful and to know how to deploy femininity as a weapon. And for most of the warrior women, their sexuality got them into trouble with the wrong men and even endangered those closest to them.

Finally, and obviously, these female heroes could only be kick-butt strong in fantastical otherworlds either in some mythic past, in a place over a Hellmouth, or in a netherworld or parallel universe of spying. In the real world, there's the question of whether it's all that great for girls to feel empowered primarily through the use of physical violence against others. But it was precisely because the settings of warrior women fare were mythological that they provided ideal metaphorical realms for exploring the increased fluidity and uncertainty of gender roles in the 1990s and beyond.

Warrior women were both transgressive and conformist. They fought like Jackie Chan but cried over romantic betrayal or injury done to others; they were physically dominating yet caring. While they suggested, on the one hand, that with enough tae kwon do lessons women could reduce the differences between the sexes even further, their form-fitting, skin-baring outfits made clear that emphatically marked gender differences were here to stay. In addressing, however campily, our culture's anxieties about changing gender scripts at the turn of the century, the warrior women in thongs asserted that to exert power, women had to be a lot more like men (hardly the feminist hope of the 1970s) and, at the same time, true to their socialized female selves that were not like men at all. They insisted that women were and could be comprised of a complicated, daunting bundle of roles, skills, and emotions that drew from both sides of the old gender divide. In particular, increased physical strength matched by a defiant rhetorical toughness might be necessary now for women, but the traditional male emotional repertoires of aloofness and insensitivity were not. This was a very different and more complicated and ambiguous kind of female persona from those on *Dallas*, *thirtysomething*, or *Touched by an Angel*. So while some of us wish that the genre had not so relentlessly reinforced a standard of beauty to which only .0035 percent of the population can conform, even with Ultra Slim-Fast, we welcomed women who were heroic rescuers and even, at times, victims. The warrior women were the switchboards between conventional male and female traits where the wires got crossed, begging the question of why they got wired that way in the first place, and by whom. They said the old boy-equals-strong, girl-equals-weak binary divisions were ridiculous and passé.[37] And for that, we yelled "Iy-yi-yi-yi-yi," right along with Xena.

4

THE NEW GIRLINESS

It has long been an article of faith in Hollywood that girls will go see films that boys like, but that boys will never go to a film made for girls. Then, in the summer of 1995, while steroid-packed movies like *Species*, *Judge Dredd* (starring Sylvester Stallone's biceps), and *First Night* (Sean Connery *is* King Arthur) bombed at the box office, audiences—including males—flocked to a movie with the following opening line: "Okay, you're probably going, is this like a Noxzema commercial or what?"

Clueless, Amy Heckerling's send-up of, and valentine to, a rich, pampered teenage girl in Los Angeles became the surprise hit of the summer and made "as if" the phrase of the year. Heckerling had initially offered the film to Twentieth Century Fox, which felt it was too "female-oriented"; Fox wanted to change the script to make it more about boys. Paramount, headed by Sherry Lansing, allowed Heckerling to make the film she wanted, and the studio laughed all the way to the bank.[1] Made for the bargain price of $13 million, *Clueless* grossed $56.6 million, taking in $20 million its first weekend. All of a sudden, "chick flicks" were big business, and the old conventional wisdom evaporated.

Clueless—a film impossible not to love—launched not only the everyday use of "whatever," but also marked a turning point in the depiction of girls and women in film and TV. A new girliness—girl power in a mini-skirt and pink boa—beckoned to the girls and women of America as a rediscovered pleasure and acceptable persona. True empowerment came from buying the right things and using the right products to look irre-sistibly attractive. Girliness was both celebrated and mocked, and thus had to be calibrated very carefully, as subsequent hit films about girliness like *Legally Blonde* and *Miss Congeniality* made clear. In this world there were typically two kinds of men: predatory, clueless clods untouched by feminism (for Cher, high schools boys were "like dogs . . . like these ner-vous creatures who jump and slobber all over you"); and men who totally got it. Feminism was, like, so yesterday—hostile to the fun of the new girliness and unnecessary because equality had, like, so totally been achieved.

Most important, *Clueless* ushered in the use of the female voice-over: the story was told from Cher's point of view. She addressed the audience directly, telling us how she saw the world and laying out her central preoc-cupations. Thus began a trend of films and TV shows with female voice-overs—girls and women thinking to themselves or speaking to us—that were meant to represent, *finally*, not how men viewed women, but how women themselves felt. After years in which feminists had itemized all the ways that girls' and women's first-person voices had been silenced in TV, films, even books and music, now we were going to go spelunking into the deep interiority of the female psyche. Previously we had seen girls and women primarily from the outside, as objects to look at. Now we would hear them from within, and enter their very subjectivities. This technique was picked up by *Ally McBeal, Bridget Jones's Diary, Dark Angel, What a Girl Wants, Sex and the City, Grey's Anatomy, Gossip Girl,* and even *What Women Want*, in which Mel Gibson heard women's allegedly innermost fears and desires. These interior monologues were meant to represent the true, authentic female: what women and girls really thought, really hoped for, really wanted. So what did these voices say?

They said that women were obsessed with dieting, shopping, men, and having babies. Were these the silenced voices yearning to be heard? Indeed, these voice-overs seemed to promise empowerment, but what we got was a powerful justification for enlightened sexism, and from women themselves. With equal opportunity allegedly achieved and the women's movement presumed successful, the female of the species could now be preoccupied with what she allegedly cared about most: herself, and finding Mr. Right. In *Backlash*, Susan Faludi had debunked the infamous 1986 *Newsweek* report on "the spinster boom" in which single women were "more likely to be killed by a terrorist than marry"; *Newsweek* itself eventually had to recant.[2] But by 1997, Ally McBeal, Bridget Jones, and others were desperate to marry, and in their world decent men were very, very, very hard to find.

Under these circumstances, women could be legally equal but they had better be visually feminine.[3] If feminism came into the picture, it was something typically embraced by has-been women in their fifties and sixties—that older generation—who still had no sense of humor. Indeed, feminism, which had made all this possible, was now outdated, and, in fact, a threat to women's happiness. Its real achievement was to give young women the right to choose what they wanted, and what they always and truly wanted, it seemed, was to be feminine and loved by a man. This new freedom to be feminine was a "postfeminist triumph" that set apart the young women of the 1990s from those old feminists who cared too much about boring (and irrelevant) old politics.[4] Young women were not supposed to identify with feminism; instead, they were supposed to actively *dis*-identify with it.

By 1997 and 1998, the new girliness was everywhere, and it offered a fleeting fantasy that girls could have it both ways: they could be sex objects in fuck-me pumps and microminis while simultaneously critiquing patriarchal ways of looking at and thinking about young women. The Spice Girls conquered the worldwide pop charts with the speed of an Exocet missile. Their biggest fans were girls between the ages of eight and fourteen; their first single, "Wannabe," hit number two on Billboard's Top 10 about fourteen minutes after its American debut in January 1997, and soon hit number one. In a five-month period, they sold 10 million albums worldwide, grossing an estimated $165 million for Virgin Records. Their liner notes read "She Who Dares Wins" and "Silence Is Golden But Shouting Is Fun," and their advice to girls included, "Don't rely on your sexuality, but don't be afraid of it," and "Don't wait around for him to call. . . . You believe in yourself."

In this pop culture brew, the celebration of girls coexisted with a denunciation of retrograde, hypermasculinity among young male per-formers. Boy bands like the Backstreet Boys, Savage Garden, and 'N Sync, with their earnest, I'm-singing-to-you-girl, soul-eyed perfor-mances, respected and exploited the girl market; *Millennium* (1999), the Backstreet Boys' quadruple platinum CD, sold 75 million copies world-wide and 'N Sync's *No Strings Attached* (2000) sold 2.4 million copies in just one week. It was the repeated viewing of *Titanic* (1997) by teenage girls that made the movie such a blockbuster. They didn't go for the disaster footage: they went to see the pretty, smooth-faced Leonardo DiCaprio insist that the full-bodied, independent Kate Winslet reject her controlling, domineering fiancé and instead fulfill her own dreams. And on television there was *Ally McBeal*, which brought girliness into the courtroom. "Girl Power" became the name of a 1997 campaign launched by Health and Human Services secretary Donna Shalala and the Girl Scouts to empower girls; it also became a massive marketing campaign that sold T-shirts, body glitter, lip gloss, and thongs.

The contradictions of the moment could hardly have been greater. The new girliness emerged at the same time (and even on the same net-works) that the warrior women were flattening any hulk who dared to get in their way. And while pop culture may have been celebrating girls' new voices, a series of highly publicized school shootings involved teen boys with guns most frequently aimed at ex-girlfriends or females in general. In Pearl, Mississippi, in October 1997, it was an ex-girlfriend; in West Paducah, Kentucky, two months later, Michael Carneal killed three girls and wounded three others. In Jonesboro, Arkansas, in March 1998, the twelve-year-old and fourteen-year-old gunmen killed four mid-dle school girls and one female teacher, and nine of the eleven wounded were also female. This wasn't, as was often reported in the press, students killing students; it was boys killing girls. No wonder girls may have wanted to take solace in the caring harmonies of boy bands or watch the self-sacrificing DiCaprio urging Winslet to take charge of her own destiny.

As if all this wasn't enough to make girls wonder whether they were empowered agents in the world or, still, objectified and vulnerable vic-tims, the very office of the presidency got into the act (literally). In Janu-ary 1998, the nation was confronted with the following question. Was

Monica Lewinsky, the twenty-four-year-old intern who couldn't wait to flash her thong for the president of the United States, a consenting adult or the victim of sexual harassment?

Despite the boy bands, who successfully sold androgyny and an imagined sympathy between boys and girls, there was also a growing sense in these years that men and women have a basic, innate essence that is utterly distinct and unchangeable.[5] Well, except that men can't and won't change, so women must accept this and accommodate to it—another building block of enlightened sexism. This throwback credo was most effectively popularized in the 1992 book *Men Are from Mars, Women Are from Venus* by John Gray of Uranus. On the bestseller list years longer than the Ice Age, and just as numbing, *Men Are from Mars* asserted that men and women are completely and inherently different. Martians (a.k.a. men) value "power, competency, efficiency and achievement," are "concerned with outdoor activities" and less concerned with "people and feelings." Venusians (a.k.a. women) value "love, communication, beauty and relationships" (just like Ann Coulter?); "to share their personal feelings is much more important than achieving goals and success" (just like Martha Stewart, Nancy Pelosi, or Condoleezza Rice?). "Instead of being goal oriented, women are relationship oriented." It is a really big mistake to expect a woman who is upset to "make complete sense" or to expect her feelings "to always be rational and logical," like a man's. (I'll remember that the next time I hear about another man, gun in hand, who has gone postal.) Men are "hard" (Jack Black? John Candy?) and women are "soft" (the Williams sisters?). You get the idea.[6]

Then there was *The Rules*, the 1995 guidebook for "capturing the heart of Mr. Right." Here, too, we learned right away that "men are different from women." Women had to play hard to get and turn themselves into "a product" in order to snare a man. *Cosmo, Vogue,* and *Glamour* would be helpful on this point, the authors advised. "Men like women who are neat and clean" (ever seen a guy's dorm room?), and these neat freaks "make better mothers." "Don't act like a man," say the authors. "Let him open the door. Be feminine. Don't tell sarcastic jokes." (Jeez, how did I ever manage to get married?) The chapter "Don't Tell Him What to Do" insisted, "Don't push your interests on him," and "Let Him Take the Lead" instructed, "He picks most of the movies, the restaurants, and the concerts the two of you go to."[7] In the used copy of this book I bought from Amazon for a penny plus shipping, the previous owner had written "What the fuck?" in the margins. Amen.

No one took *Clueless*, in which Cher (Alicia Silverstone) devoted her time to dropping the GDP of Luxembourg at the mall and fixing people up, as anything other than a carbonated comedy of Valley Girl manners. *Ally McBeal* was different. She was the first major female lead in a show who was not a baby boomer. Thus she was, as Cher might have put it, like, way dissimilar from Murphy Brown or Roseanne.[8] And whether David E. Kelley, the show's creator and frequent writer, was a John Gray fan remains dubious, but the Venus/Mars blather was pervasive. (To wit, in the second episode, Ally's former boyfriend points to his crotch and says, "This makes men stupid" and then points to his heart and said, "This makes women stupid.") And it was the quest for the perfect relationship, pursued by the flighty lead character, which drove and dominated the show.

Ally McBeal premiered in September 1997, on Monday nights right after *Melrose Place*, as Fox continued to try to consolidate its hold on young women. It was an instant hit, and got even bigger once *Monday Night Football* ended. The show's ratings were especially strong among the college educated and households with incomes above $75,000; women of all ages watched it, although it was particularly popular with younger women, and *Variety* reported that after pigskin season it attracted men "in hordes."[9] In January 1998, on the highest-rated Golden Globes show ever, *Ally McBeal* won the awards for best comedy series and best comedy actress, for the series' star, Calista Flockhart. By the next fall, the show was actually beating *Monday Night Football* among the prized demographic, adults eighteen to forty-nine.

The show took place in a totally unrealistic, bizzaro Boston law firm run by the crass, greedy Richard Fish (Greg Germann) and his neurotic, tic-ridden, pet-frog-owning partner John Cage (Peter MacNicol). The other male attorney was Billy (Gil Bellows), Ally's former boyfriend, now married to another associate, Georgia (yes, again, the deeply dimpled Courtney Thorne-Smith, fresh off her role as Allison on *Melrose Place*).

Ally joined the firm after a lecherous walrus of a partner at her previous firm kept grabbing her ass. The firm's staff also included Ally's ambitious, intrusively nosy, know-it-all secretary Elaine (Jane Krakowski) and, in time, two other female lawyers, Nelle (Portia de Rossi) and Ling (Lucy Liu). Ally's African American roommate, Renee (Lisa Nicole Carson), was a public defender. The cases the firm took routinely centered on the battle of the sexes and, in particular, various forms of alleged sexual harassment. One of the many hallmarks of the show was its blurring of the boundaries between public and private, as embodied by the unisex bathroom where men and women peed and commiserated side by side.[10] Here the sexes were equal, and the impossibility of compartmentalizing personal from professional concerns—a central struggle for women—was made clear.

Watching *Ally McBeal* was like jumping on a roller coaster; it shot up and delighted you with its narrative innovation, depictions of female confidence, and attacks on patriarchal oafishness, and the very next second it hurtled down, plunging you into a sea of female incompetence, insecurity, and stammering. The show was instantly controversial and prompted major debates about whether it was the worst thing to happen to women since Clarence Thomas and Howard Stern, or offered an updated incarnation of feminism in which women's struggles to reconcile the professional with the personal was finally and honestly acknowledged. Part of the shock of the show, as the media scholar Amanda Lotz notes, was the stark disjuncture between Ally and the stronger, self-assured characters of *Designing Women* and *Murphy Brown* who preceded her.[11] Many older women, who knew firsthand how tough the fight had been against gender discrimination in education and the workplace, felt that this skittish gerbil of a woman would only help restore every piece of sexist drivel they had heard in 1970 about females not being fit for the professions. And it didn't help that Flockhart was vermicelli-thin, stoking charges that she was anorexic and that the show promoted retrograde standards of thinness as beauty.

The hairpin turns from feminism to antifeminism gave viewers options for how to view the show: progressive, regressive, both? Just when you wanted to cheer Ally for her courtroom victories, you then wanted to smack her upside the head and tell her to stop being such an embarrassing whiner. It was precisely because *Ally McBeal* almost always cut both ways, between empowerment and self-abnegation, that women embraced it and damned it. The show wasn't feminist or antifeminist: it was both. Women, especially younger women, appreciated this, because navigating between the achievements of feminism and the demands of femininity was the story of their lives. So, too, was their desire to combine their professional aspirations with romantic love, and to have their quest for love validated as compatible with being independent and successful.[12] So *Ally McBeal* gave women a new postfeminist subjectivity to try on and inhabit, accomplished yet insecure, riddled with ambivalence and contradiction. In fact, it took a swipe at women who seemed unvexed by these tensions and who seemed to have finessed professional work as well as most men. When the unflappable Nelle—nicknamed "Sub Zero"—began practicing with the firm, Ally hated her instantly. "She's good [in court], she's poised, she doesn't pull at her hair, nothing comes out of her mouth that she doesn't want to come out, she doesn't over-gesticulate . . . that bitch."

There was much to love. It was simply a given in the show that women were, and could be, accomplished, successful lawyers who frequently won their cases. And they didn't have to wear those dumpy "managerial woman" navy blue 1980s power suits (with those awful white bow-tie blouses) to fit in. In the show's first episode, Ally forcefully argues a First Amendment case and wins; in later episodes she is a very tough negotiator in divorce settlements, she lands clients, and she gives smart, passionate closings that seal the success of a case. At the same time, women's ongoing struggles with sexual harassment, with being judged at times entirely on the basis of their appearance, all got their due (sometimes to excess) on the show. We were exposed to deep and complicated female friendships, and the variety of female characters offered different women's takes on the same legal or interpersonal issue.[13] So unlike *Murphy Brown*, in which the hardened career woman was constantly juxtaposed against her opposite, the beauty queen airhead, the women of *Ally McBeal* offered a more nuanced range of attitudes and opinions about women's place. David Kelley also deftly and effortlessly moved back and forth between comedy and drama, inspiring critics to hail it as an exemplar of a new genre, the "dramedy."

Visually and conceptually, the show broke new ground by literally showing us how Ally saw people and situations, picturing her unspoken and sometimes even subconscious desires and fears. This was one of the techniques designed to encourage viewers to identify with her. When her know-it-all secretary, Elaine, offers yet more condescending advice, we see her head, through Ally's eyes, swell up like a balloon as Ally thinks to herself, "There she goes again, me, me, me." When Ally gets dumped by a boyfriend, we literally see her body being hurled into a giant dumpster. And then, of course, there was the ooga-chacka-ooga-ooga, "Hooked on a Feeling" dancing baby, a visual manifestation of Ally's fear that pursuing her career would preclude her from having a family of her own. Such fantastical, graphic filigree gave expression to how people—not just women—navigated between the public selves they presented to others and the inner imaginings that helped, or interfered with, getting through the day. Some of these imaginings were at the expense of others with whom Ally had to interact. But most, it seems, were at Ally's own expense, especially when we see her as a little girl in a big chair during a deposition, or her heart pierced with arrows, or hurling herself inappropriately at some man. Female insecurities and sexual desires dominated Ally's visual inner life, externalized for the audience to see.

But even as the show trivialized women's concerns, it was equally harsh on male chauvinism. In one episode, Ally and Georgia represent an anchorwoman (played by Kate Jackson) who has been fired because the station managers feel she is getting too old for the job. The station is represented by the same lecherous walrus who had harassed Ally. As he asserts that the function of an anchorwoman is to be "physically arresting," Ally says to herself, "There's only one word to describe this guy," and the camera cuts to a shot of a horse's ass. "As for the stuff he's saying?" and here we see a shot of the horse shitting on the courtroom floor. How many women happily took that image with them the next time they were stuck in a meeting with some Neanderthal colleague?

In another episode, a judge cites Ally for contempt for wearing a micro-mini in his courtroom. Nelle attacks this as bias, arguing that every billboard tells women they have to look like models, and yet when they comply, they face the assumption that "if she's beautiful she must be stupid." In a particularly cringe-worthy installment, because Ally is brought before the bar for possibly being too unstable to practice law, the sixtyish Judge Whipper (Dyan Cannon) attacks the double standard for women: "A man acts passionate we call him impassioned; a woman, she's emotional . . . she stands most guilty of being female, young, and attractive and how dare she be aggressive on top of that!" There were many moments like this throughout the series, in which sexism and the objectification of women got exposed as posing ongoing hurdles for women, even for accomplished, professional women.

Nonetheless, there was also a whole lot to hate. David Kelley was not always kind to his creation, having Ally do completely mortifying, unprofessional things like deliberately tripping a woman in the supermarket in order to get the last package of Pringles, smacking passersby in the street, or getting knocked down by elevator doors. Although Ally was financially comfortable, had a good job and great friends, and got to go to a bar after work where Vonda Shepard was singing, being single was akin to a death sentence. She was frequently pathetic. She was so desperate to find a man that she read *The Rules*, until her roommate Renee threw it out. We often saw her walking home at night, alone, weeping or on the verge of tears, as some chanteuse (usually Shepard) sang about lost love. And then there were the stereotypes: Why, in the overwhelmingly white universe of the show, did the Asian lawyer Ling have to be a dragon lady? Why did Renee have to be an oversexualized, aggressive black woman?[14]

So much has been made of the visuals in the show—the whimsical fantasy inserts, the dancing baby, the skirts the size of a washcloth—that the importance of Ally's voice has been neglected. But it was precisely her voice, forceful one minute, halting the next, that both captured women's own ambivalence about success and romantic love and made us wince, or reach for the remote. Her stammering—"and, and, and, and," "but, but, but, but," "Wh-wh-wh-what is it"—signified that she was often so emotionally overwrought at work that she could barely do her job. And Ally's voice-overs of her innermost thoughts—again, designed to have us bond with her—were almost exclusively about men, relationships, dating, and performance anxieties at work even though, as an attorney, she would presumably also be having extended inner dialogues about the substance and strategies of her cases. "Here I am, the victim of my own choices," she tells us in the pilot, in which she also looks in the mirror and says she really wishes her breasts were bigger. The implication was that women—even Harvard-educated women—don't enjoy (or bother to think about) ideas. They think about girly things and their own failures.

As David Kelley told *Time* reporter Gina Bellafante, Ally was not "a hard, strident feminist out of the '60s and '70s." And, indeed, old-bag feminists on the show were portrayed as too doctrinaire, too humorless, and too inflexible for modern times. This was most vividly brought to life in an episode where Ally and the firm defend the male editor of *La Femme* magazine, who was fired when the magazine's female editor in chief discovered that he was a Baptist. As her attorney demands in court, "How can you have an editor of a feminist magazine who believes a woman's place is in the home?" The editor herself, a woman in her late fifties, says she doesn't care if it's a religious tenet, if it says, "Men dominate, women submit," it's untenable. "It's not a religious view, it's a chauvinistic view. . . . You can't just say women are weaker and then hide behind 'God says so.'" The problem here is that the audience has met the male editor, George (the inherently likable John Ritter), and has never heard him say that women should be submissive. Plus, he is really nice to Ally. Nor do we meet the feminist editor outside the courtroom setting, in which she, like George, would have been more humanized and less caricatured. The judge rules against the bigoted feminist editor; this occurs in the same episode in which Ally fights for her right to appear in court in a miniskirt so short it doesn't even reach the hem of her suit jacket. Desiccated middle-aged feminists no longer had the right to set the terms of discussion, and what younger women had really won was the right to expose themselves.

On Sunday, January 18, 1998, the dramedy that focused on sexual harassment, date rape, hostile work environments, litigious relationships, and gender discrimination won a Golden Globe for best comedy. Three days later came the biggest political bombshell of the decade: that President Bill Clinton had allegedly had an affair with the White House intern Monica Lewinsky and then told her to lie about it. The story broke just two days after Clinton was deposed in the sexual harassment case brought against him by Paula Jones, dating to his time as governor of Arkansas. Under these circumstances, the plot lines of *Ally McBeal* could hardly have been more timely. So what did the show contribute to what had become an urgent national discussion?

Most of the harassment cases Fish & Cage took on were increasingly absurd, over-the-top, frivolous, even surreal, and bore little resemblance to the come-ons, threats, ogling, gropings, name-calling, and assaults that constitute harassment cases in the real world.[15] In short, the show simultaneously raised further awareness about sexual harassment while also trivializing it. In the first season, Elaine threatens to sue Fish & Cage because the male lawyers have been caught eying an attractive office worker. But Elaine's real motivation for the suit is to get more attention, and ultimately none of the other women workers actually joins the suit. In the second season, Ling, represented by Nelle, sues Harold Wick (Wayne Newton), a Howard Stern–type radio host, for sexual harassment, alleging that his broadcast creates a hostile work environment in her client's factory because of its explicit sexual objectification of women. Most middle school civics students would have been able to point out that the shock jock's speech is protected by the First Amendment and the charges are a total stretch. In another episode an employer (possibly mainlining margaritas?) institutes "Beach Day," in which employees can come to work in bathing suits (as if!) and is sued for sexual harassment. Farrah Fawcett makes a cameo appearance as a magazine editor in a somewhat infamous episode in which she sues her male employees who got her fired by calling in sick and undermining her authority. After she loses the case, she seduces Billy in his office, again showing how hypocritical such women are in playing the gender card in court. As Billy sums it up, sexual harassment law does not "make sense." He continues, "We just have to assume that if any woman anywhere at anytime feels the slightest twinge of hypersensitivity, and she can link it to anything remotely sexual, she has a cause of action."[16]

As if Ally McBeal were not controversial enough on its own terms, it became more so after Time magazine's notorious cover story in June 1998. Lined up against a pitch-black background like the ghosts of Christmas past were grim disembodied black-and-white head shots of Susan B. Anthony, Betty Friedan, and Gloria Steinem. The fourth image in the row was a color head shot of Calista Flockhart, labeled "Ally McBeal," with the huge, capitalized, bloodred headline underneath demanding

"Is Feminism Dead?" You were meant to know the answer, especially if McBeal (as opposed to real-life feminist activists) was where feminism had ended up. While exact counts vary, my estimate is that this was the 117th time the media had loudly proclaimed feminism dead. The black-and-white images of Anthony, Friedan, and Steinem signified their antique status. The color image of Ally McBeal, by contrast, conveyed that she was the new, up-to-date exemplar of American womanhood—leaving aside the fact that this exemplar was not to be found in everyday life, but in a fictional character created by a man.

The article inside, titled, "It's All About Me," claimed that "feminism today is wed to the culture of celebrity and self-obsession" and that "the flightiness of contemporary feminism is a problem." The author, Gina Bellafante, never mentioned any real-life younger feminists who were anything but flighty, or the ongoing breaking down of barriers by their mothers. The opening of the article trivialized the very feminism that Bellafante wanted to resuscitate ("paparazzi-jammed galas, mindless sex talk"), implying that feminists didn't really mean what they say about social change but just wanted a good party and publicity. Thus, even though Bellafante herself clearly hated what *Ally McBeal* represented and argued for a renewed focus on issues like pay equity and universal day care, the article (mainly because of the sensational cover) was part of the media drumbeat announcing that enlightened sexism had over-taken feminism. And in a larger sense, this was an accurate depiction of the changing media landscape. In hindsight the question is not whether Ally McBeal was the next phase of feminism, which she wasn't. The question, knowing what we know now, is how far was it, really, from *Ally McBeal* to *The Bachelor*?

"Ugh. Cannot face thought of going to work. Only thing which makes it tolerable is thought of seeing Daniel again, but even that is unadvisable since am fat, have spot on chin, and desire only to sit on cushion eating chocolate and watching Xmas specials."

Welcome to the inner thoughts of another single, professional woman, whom the New York *Daily News* would describe as "Ally McBeal with a British accent." Bridget Jones, the protagonist of Helen Fielding's

1996 novel and the two movies it spawned, was not musing about the substance of her work, the existence of God, or world peace. Her confessional mode of address, like the voice-overs in *Ally McBeal*, laid bare Bridget's vulnerabilities and asked us to sympathize and identify with her—while also adding more reinforcing struts to the edifice of enlightened sexism. *Bridget Jones's Diary* gave us another female protagonist whose self-esteem rested solely on the approval of men and how many calories she had consumed. Her monitoring of herself was incessant.

While the book was an exaggerated farce about the extent to which women's confidence had been corroded by the relentless bilge in magazines like *Cosmopolitan*, many in the press also hailed it as telling the hidden truth about what really dominated women's interior monologues. "Fielding . . . has rummaged all too knowingly through the bedrooms, closets, hearts and minds of women everywhere," wrote *Glamour.* "Bridget Jones is channeling something so universal and (horrifyingly) familiar that readers will giggle and sigh with collective delight," added *Elle.*

Bridget, to be blunt, is a mess. Her assessment of herself? "I'm no good at anything." This seems to be true, as she can't even manage to throw a dinner party for friends because she puts trays of food on the floor and proceeds to step in them, neglects to buy key ingredients, and then forgets various of her shopping bags at the store. She is an embarrassing failure at work. She is self-absorbed beyond belief. She wastes "two days glaring psychopathically at the phone, and eating things. Why hasn't he rung? Why? What's wrong with me?"[17] The call she waits in vain for would have been from her boss, Daniel, who had sent her an e-mail at work saying, "I like your tits in that top." Hello, sexual harassment division of Fish & Cage.

Now, it would be a flat-out lie to assert that women do not think about their weight or their relationships or long, sometimes, to lie in front of the TV with a box of Godivas and a pitcher of sangria. But because the book became a bestseller (and why not? a quick read, at times funny, a send-up of the tyranny of beauty culture), Bridget became another icon of the allegedly new postfeminist woman, a new "'90s heroine." This hailing of the pitiable, hapless, self-absorbed, marriage-obsessed Bridget Jones as the epitome of millennial womanhood pissed off a lot of females, and not just war-horse feminists. Of course women have their insecurities, but these are intermixed with accomplishment, confidence, successes, talent, self-control, poise, and even the ability to make dinner without grinding their high heels in the mashed potatoes. Anyone who has worked with female publicists in their twenties and thirties (which Bridget was at first) knows that their job is to understand and promote the work of others. So they talk and think about politics, cultural trends, novels, art, terrorism, the environment, and religion in addition to guys and pantyhose, and not just reluctantly.

As a BBC radio presenter e-mailed the movie critic Joel Siegel, "I HATE BRIDGET JONES. . . . Women do NOT count calories/fags/drinks every-day, and that victim/ditsy rubbish MAKES MY BLOOD BOIL. . . . It puts women back at least 50 FUCKING YEARS."[18] Siegel himself tried to imagine the outraged reaction that actresses like Katharine Hepburn or Bette Davis would have produced if asked to play such a demeaning role. Andi Zeisler, writing in *Bitch* magazine, observed pithily, "It's hard not to loathe this book," and added, "The story is retrograde, and its attempts to be a universal comment on single womanhood . . . serve to make carica-tures out of all women." What was particularly offensive, she rightly noted, was that the media continued to "seize upon endless variations on insecu-rity and incompetence" as emblematic of the new '90s young woman, and then praised them as being the truly honest representations of women's inner lives and identities.[19]

The gender stereotypes were right out of the 1950s—or right out of *Men Are from Mars, Women Are from Venus*, which constitutes Bridget's reading material. All men are either lying, cheating cads, or commitment-phobic. London is filled with "single girls over thirty . . . who can't get a chap."[20] And feminism is to romantic, heterosexual love what Raid is to ants. Bridget's feminist friend Sharon constantly, and publicly, fumes and rants about men to the point where she has to be silenced by her friends: "After all, there is nothing so unattractive to a man as strident feminism," notes Bridget, which may indeed be true, but that doesn't mean they all want doormats either.[21] Through Sharon we see that feminism does ren-der women to be humorless, shrill man haters. And, as the feminist scholar Angela McRobbie sharply observed, by having Bridget think and care about what feminists allegedly told her not to, the book (and the movie) casts feminism as a grumpy, censoring, out-of-touch ideology. Bridget wallows in prefeminist preoccupations about men and marriage that women are not supposed to obsess about anymore. But the diary mode "reveals" that real women are not, in their secret selves, constrained by the feminist thought police; they naturally, even inherently, rebel against feminism and are genuinely pathetic slaves to the desires for men and marriage. While we are supposed to laugh at how pitiful Bridget is, we are also supposed to say to ourselves, "Yes, this may be a bit exaggerated, but this *is* me." In the diary, then, Bridget and we escape—whew—from the feminist censors who know nothing about what women really want and have in fact only rendered them lonely and miserable.[22]

The interior monologues of women were also at the center of the 2000 box office hit *What Women Want*, a film that soured my feelings about Mel Gibson long before his gruesome *Passion of the Christ*, or his anti-Semitic rant after being picked up for drunk driving, or even the silly and religiously pedantic *Signs*, in which the only way an attack by aliens can be foiled is for Gibson's character to re-don his ministerial collar. The premise of *What Women Want* is that Nick Marshall (Gibson), a prime cut of male chauvinist pig, gets electrocuted in his bathtub by a hair dryer, and rather than killing Nick (which was the desired outcome), this allows him to hear what women are thinking. So what does he hear from women as he walks through the park on the way to work? "Did I turn the coffee maker off?" "One kiss doesn't make me a lesbian, does it?" (No, but being forced into contact with Nick would.) Another woman (just like Bridget) is overheard counting the calories she has consumed so far, and another wonders about the benefits of estrogen. Later, in a department store, one woman wonders whether to buy more lipstick while another says to herself, "If he doesn't answer the phone in the next two rings, I swear to God . . ." Later, while passing a female jogger, Nick hears her think, "I'm thirty-four and I want a kid," just like Ally McBeal. When he goes to see his former shrink, she wonders to herself why she answered the door when she was about to buy a lamp on eBay. Not one of the thoughts of the women on the street is about the substance of her work, a social or political issue, finances, or even one of those concerts *The Rules* said you should let "him" take you to. Yeah, yeah, I know, it was a comedy: but by now all the interior monologues of all these comedies were leaving their stereotypical residue.

The redemption of Nick, and the movie, is supposed to rest on the fact that he hears what a pig the women in his life secretly think he is. He comes to understand that women worry about how they were going to accomplish everything (duh), and he appreciates the consequences of his own sexism. The moral of the story is that women want men who have been reconstructed by feminism. But the other revelation here, à la Bridget Jones, is that what women really (and only) think about is dieting, shopping, men, relationships, and babies. And if a swine like Nick can see the error of his ways, feminism is no longer needed: men get it, and those who don't pay the price. Right.

Now that embracing feminism was, for young women, about as alluring as using Limburger cheese as a cologne, other romantic comedies also dramatized the pleasures of the new girliness as first laid out in *Clueless*. And they, too, took feminism into account so as to reveal how, well, out of style it was. *Miss Congeniality* and *Legally Blonde* (two movies I have probably eagerly watched at least seventeen times each) took women at utterly opposite ends of the antifeminine/feminine spectrum and showed how important it was to move toward the happy and perfect median between the two. In *Miss Congeniality* (2000), Sandra Bullock plays the asexual FBI agent Gracie Hart, who carries herself like a teamster and dresses like one of the Beastie Boys. Everything about her screams "antifeminine"; the stringy strands of hair hanging in her face, her unruly eyebrows, her equally disheveled apartment with its unmade bed and, the centerpiece of the décor, an Everlast punching bag hanging in the living room, which she regularly pounds the crap out of. She snorts when she laughs and, even worse, eats like a guy, chewing with her mouth open and chomping down a huge hamburger for lunch instead of a ladylike salad. She is completely devoted to her work and has no personal life. Her colleagues refer to her as Hart, not Gracie. This is the inevitable outcome of feminism if taken to its logical conclusions: deliberately unattractive women who repel men.

Because of a threat to disrupt the Miss United States pageant, Hart has to go undercover as one of the contestants: this requires a major, major makeover, not least of Hart's own attitudes toward beauty pageants. She refers to the contestants as "bikini stuffers" and objects to having to parade around "like some airhead bimbo . . . and all she wants is world peace." Hart tells her coworker Eric Matthews (Benjamin Bratt), "What could possibly motivate anyone to enter a beauty pageant is beyond me. . . . It's like feminism never even happened . . . to think any woman could do this is catering to some misogynistic Neanderthal mentality." In other words, Hart could have been right there on the front lines of the 1968 demonstrations against the Miss America pageant, when feminists hurled hair curlers, steno pads, and bras into "Freedom Trash Cans."

Victor Melling (Michael Caine) is the unlucky bastard who has to turn Hart into a lady. As soon as he lays eyes on her he announces, "If you are Gracie Hart I quit here and now . . . there's no way on earth I can make this woman ready in two days." Nonetheless, he begins his instructions, telling her, "Miss United States is always polite and well-spoken" and that ladies don't walk, they glide. (When Victor sees Hart stomp down the street he moans, "Oh my God, I haven't seen a walk like that since *Jurassic Park*.") As Hart and the FBI, accompanied by a SWAT team of makeover artists, fly to the airport hangar where she will be transformed, she watches footage of previous pageants and mimics the contestants' exaggerated crying when they win. "Oh look, she's going to cry again," she tells Victor, " 'If I only had a brain.' "

After an all-night procedure in which Hart is subjected to multiple facials, hair treatments, and the waxing of almost every part of her body, she emerges from the hangar. As "Mustang Sally" plays on the soundtrack, and the camera grinds down to a slight slow motion, out she comes in a skintight pale blue minidress, spike heels she can barely walk in, and gorgeous hair flowing as perfectly as in any Pantene commercial. Even though the makeover sequence parodies the ridiculous lengths to which women had to go to become beautiful, this shot, and Eric's incredulous and admiring reaction to the transformation, make it clear that she has become gorgeous—and whatever it took, it was worth it.

As Victor continues to train her to compete in the pageant, Hart—renamed the more girly Gracie Lou—resists. "I am an FBI agent, I'm not a performing monkey in heels," she insists. But Victor has a critique of her life: "You're also a person and an incomplete one at that. In place of friends and relationships, you have sarcasm and a gun." Victor has clearly hit a nerve, and Gracie responds defensively, "I don't have relationships because I don't want them and I don't have friends because I work 24/7, and you have no idea why I am the way that I am." She later insists to Eric, "I am the job," and admits that she has had, like, two dates in ten years.

Nonetheless, one of the great pleasures of the movie is watching Gracie Lou bring some distinctly nongirly elements into the pageant. Gracie is juxtaposed with Miss Rhode Island, a stereotypical giggly blond airhead with a high-pitched voice—a real ditz. When asked what her idea of a perfect date is, she responds, "I'd have to say April twenty-fifth." In contrast to all the other contestants who say that the most important thing our society needs is world peace, Gracie says that the most important thing is "harsher punishment for parole violators." (Confronted by the audience's stunned silence, Gracie hastily adds, "And world peace.") In defiance of the self-starvation ethos of the competition, Gracie gets the women to indulge in pizza and beer. Her talent—possibly the high point in the film—comes when she demonstrates self-defense techniques women can use against assaulters. So Gracie is not merely dragged kicking and screaming into the zone of femininity; the girly world also gets a solid injection of feminism.

In the end, though (this is Hollywood, after all), the film abandons its critique of the beauty pageant as a retrograde objectification of women. It also abandons feminism and instead repudiates it. In the interview part of competition, the pageant's founder, Miss Morningside (Candice Bergen), asks Gracie, "There are many who consider the Miss United States pageant to be outdated and antifeminist. What would you say to that?"

"Well, I would have to say I used to be one of them," Gracie responds. "And then I came here and I realized that these women are smart, terrific people who are just trying to make a difference in the world. And we've become really good friends. . . . And for me this experience has been one of the most rewarding and liberating experiences of my life." What is odd about this assertion is that we have already seen some catty, competitive remarks among the contestants and we've seen Gracie having fun with them in a bar; but we've not heard any of them talk to her about exactly how they hope to make a difference in the world or what their other interests, besides makeup, are.

At the end of the film, Gracie is named "Miss Congeniality" for being the "nicest, sweetest, coolest girl at the pageant," and she acknowledges how honored she is, adding, "And, I really do want world peace." So "world peace" is not some packaged, calculated cliché, one of the few safe social goals for hyperfeminized women to articulate, but rather a genuine, lofty ideal that the pageant contestants truly share. Gracie has seen the error of her old, bigoted, narrow-minded feminist ways, which dismissed beauty pageants as objectifying meat markets and their contestants as shallow bimbos. In the end, then, feminism itself is sexist, because it stereotypes certain women and denies them their full range of choices. And girliness is also essential to heterosexual love—Gracie, having found that she could have Pantene-style hair and still be an FBI agent, gets her guy, Eric.

Poles apart from FBI agent Gracie Hart is Elle Woods (Reese Witherspoon), the ultimate girly-girl president of her sorority Delta Nu in the 2001 hit *Legally Blonde*. Here the markers of hyperfemininity are everywhere: the room painted pink and filled with cosmetics and hair care products, the stacks of *Cosmo*, the wedgies with glittery hearts across the toes. The only way Elle and her sorority sisters know how to interact is to squeal, giggle, and jump up and down a lot. Their ultimate goal is to get married. Then, boom: Elle's Harvard Law School–bound boyfriend Warner (Matthew Davis) dumps her precisely because she's too girly; he needs "a Jackie," he says, not "a Marilyn."

Determined to win Warner back, Elle crams for the LSATs (which her sorority sisters think is the name of a venereal disease), submits a video admissions essay featuring her in various bikinis, and gets accepted to Harvard Law. Not the way you usually get in, but hey, it's a movie. She arrives in Cambridge in a neon pink, faux-fur-trimmed satin suit and sunglasses with pink lenses; the other law students, in their gray shirts and brown sweaters, eye her incredulously and call her Malibu Barbie. In her first class, when all the other students open their laptops, she pulls out a heart-shaped pad and a pen topped with a pink feather. The fiftysomething female law teacher Professor Stromwell (Holland Taylor), a feminist from central casting, regards Elle with barely concealed amusement and condescension and throws her out of class for not being prepared. Hyper-girliness is vapid, superficial, a dead giveaway that someone should not be taken seriously.

But feminism is worse. The face of feminism here is Enid Wexler (Meredith Scott Lynn), another first-year student with a Ph.D. in women's studies from Berkeley and an out lesbian. Enid stereotypes and ridicules Elle from the start. After Elle tries unsuccessfully to join Warner's study group, Enid mocks, "Hey, maybe, there's like a sorority you could like join, like." Elle responds that if Enid had come to a rush party, Elle would have at least been nice to her. Enid counters that Elle would then have voted against her and called her a dyke behind her back. Elle insists she doesn't use that word, and the audience believes her; Enid (typical feminist) has anticipated slurs and slights where none existed. Later, at a party, we see Enid lecturing Warner about the built-in sexism of the English language. Her example is the word "semester," which she claims is derived from a supposed patriarchal bias in favor of semen over ovaries. (It's not.) Enid is thus petitioning to have next term called an "ovester." Once again, feminists are silly, humorless, and obsessed with trivial, utterly symbolic issues and political correctness.

Elle, meanwhile, realizes that she will actually have to study if she is going to be good enough for Warner and survive law school. The pink outfits give way to darker hues; her overly curly hair becomes straighter. She starts interning at a law firm that is defending Brooke Windham, the creator of "Brooke's Butt Buster Workout," who has been accused of killing her husband. As she thinks through the case, Elle does not rely on the law; she relies on girly logic. She believes that Brooke—a former Delta Nu sister—is innocent because "exercise gives you endorphins, endorphins make you happy, happy people just don't shoot their husbands." Elle infers that Brooke's pool boy, who claimed to have had an affair with her in order to frame her, was gay because he knew designer shoes—and Elle was correct.

Callahan, the head of the law firm, hits on Elle, prompting her to quit. She retreats to the beauty parlor that has become her psychic oasis and tells her friend Paulette (the fabulous, nonpareil Jennifer Coolidge), "All people see when they look at me is blond hair and big boobs" and that no one takes her seriously. She was just kidding herself that a girly girl like her could be a lawyer; "turns out I am a joke," she moans. But who should happen to be at the salon but Professor Stromwell, who gives Elle a feminist-inspired pep talk. "If you're going to let one stupid prick ruin your life," she says, "you're not the girl I thought you were." The key here is that Stromwell calls her a girl, not a woman.

Back at the firm, once Brooke finds out about the sexual harassment, she fires Callahan. Next, the camera reveals her new representation, starting with the feet in red strapped patent leather heels with rhine-stone buckles, and tilting up to her pink dress and her recurled hair: Elle has reclaimed her girliness. The judge, Callahan, and the district attorney regard Elle as a laughingstock, and at first she is at sea, as she doesn't really know how to try a case. She tentatively begins question-ing Chutney Windham, Brooke's stepdaughter, who has testified that she saw Brooke standing over her husband's body, "drenched in blood." Chutney repeatedly testifies that she had been in the shower when the shooting occurred, and Elle keeps repeating that she was in the shower, to the amusement of the assembled court. But then Chutney adds that she had washed her hair in the shower and that she had gotten a perma-nent earlier that morning.

The lightbulbs in Elle's head go off. She knows all about perms. Her confidence soaring, she tells the courtroom about a friend who had got-ten a perm but lost her curls because she had gotten hosed down in a wet T-shirt contest. She then moves in for the kill. "Isn't it the first cardinal rule of perm maintenance," she demands, "that you're forbidden to wet your hair for at least twenty-four hours after getting the perm at the risk of deactivating the ammonium thioglycolate?" Elle then accuses Chut-ney of not having washed her hair because her curls were still intact, and then goes on to assert that she had the time, however, to hide the gun after shooting her father. At this point Chutney breaks down and con-fesses to the murder, to the utter amazement of the courtroom. Brooke is acquitted. Hordes of reporters descend on Elle afterward, but she is modest. "Any *Cosmo* girl," she says, would have known the perm rules.

Here the fantasy is that girly knowledge matters, and not just in soror-ities. Girls and women are still socialized to understand that detailed information about fashion, hair, and makeup are essential to master, and yet they also see it ridiculed as a frivolous and useless knowledge base. But surrounded by doubt and ridicule in that sanctum sanctorum of male knowledge, the courtroom, Elle wins her case because she knows how the chemicals in permanents work. Most of us would like to think that such information is no more or less significant than who won the Super Bowl in 1992. At the end of the film, when Elle has been elected the student speaker at her class's graduation (and we learn she has an offer from a prestigious Boston law firm), she advises her audience that first impressions may not always be correct, and "you must always have faith in yourself." Hyperfemininity should not be stereotyped as dumbness. Even Enid the feminist applauds. Still, just as Gracie Hart in *Miss Congeniality* has to move from her antifeminine terminus to a middle ground that balances career accomplishments with getting a bikini wax, so, too, does Elle have to moderate her girliness with achievement in a previously male-dominated profession.

In both films, feminism is equated with being deliberately unattractive, out of touch with, and indeed antagonistic toward other women. It is hostile to femininity. (It is noteworthy that Professor Stromwell gives Elle her little pep talk at the beauty parlor; Stromwell is a professional, but still feminine, so Elle can take her advice.) And *Legally Blonde* explicitly reduces feminism to something only lesbians espouse or support. So however ridiculous hypergirliness may be—we know that Elle cannot possibly walk into her new job as an attorney with her pink feathered pen—femininity is still essential for women, not only to find love but also to be taken seriously.

Especially pernicious was *Down with Love* (2003), a movie that purported to take us back to the founding days of the women's movement itself. An homage to the Rock Hudson–Doris Day romantic comedies of the late 1950s and early 1960s, this film asserted that whatever motivated feminists, the dirty little truth was that they never meant any of what they said. Renée Zellweger plays Barbara Novak, a hypergirly single girl in 1962 who has written an international bestseller, *Down with Love*. In it, she argues that women are oppressed by romantic love and thus should repudiate it. They should treat sex the way men do—as a physical pleasure divorced from love. They don't need men and they don't need marriage, and they deserve the same rights and opportunities as men.

In comes Catcher Block (Ewan McGregor), a playboy journalist who doesn't believe Novak's line and sets out to get her to fall in love with him. By the middle of the film, Catcher has succeeded, and Barbara must admit that really she is not a "down with love" girl at all. Her feminist editor Vikki (Sarah Paulson) confesses that she just wants to get married, too. So the biggest message of this movie is that feminism itself (even at the height of sexism in America) was and is a masquerade, a pose. Women who spout feminist positions don't really mean it; they are just trying to make money off other women by selling their feminist tracts, and trying to make other women miserable by telling them to abandon men, marriage, and family while they secretly covet the same things. "You didn't just fool me," Catcher marvels when he discovers Barbara's hypocrisy, "you fooled the whole world." Meanwhile, the aspirations Barbara inspires in other women are held up as laughable. In one scene a fashion-model-gorgeous stewardess says she is training to be an airline pilot because of Barbara's book. The audience is supposed to find this preposterous and funny.

By the end of the film, Catcher has fallen in love and become a "new man." The beautiful faux feminist has domesticated the playboy and has converted the previously unreconstructed exploiter of women into a New Age guy, finally in touch with his feelings, no longer a woman-hurting cad, a man who wants marriage and domesticity just like a woman. Since the film was set in 1962, it suggested that this is what happened to so many men as a result of the women's movement, and thus they, too, have been reformed by feminism—another reason we don't need it anymore.

The turn of the millennium, then, was a watershed era for enlightened sexism. All of these TV shows, films, and books offered a compelling fusion of female accomplishment, girliness, and antifeminism. Indeed, the specter of feminism past was raised to show that it was a musty, petrified ideology that didn't represent women's innermost desires, but rather made women shrill, silly, and intolerant, and it repelled men. Women may be Harvard-educated lawyers, or publicists, or FBI agents, but such professions offered precious little satisfaction or fulfillment compared to the love of a man. And this wasn't some sexist man or reactionary right-wing woman asserting this, it was women's allegedly genuine inner voices saying so, mercifully hidden from and uncensored by those scary feminists. Girl power may have emerged in the mid-1990s to enhance girls' self-esteem and validate girl culture (and, yes, to sell records, makeup, and bras), but the "power" part had now shriveled and the "girl" part inflated as the new girliness took hold. Girls and women, to be happy, had to be supergirls who, with the precision of surveyors, located the perfect coordinates between Janet Reno on one end and Cindy Crawford on the other so they could have love and success. That these coordinates had to move even further away from the Reno model and snuggle ever more closely to the Crawford model was the undisputed moral of the new girliness.

5

YOU GO, GIRL

I am sitting here laughing my ass off at Wanda Sykes's 2006 concert film *Sick & Tired*. Letting her gravelly voice soar up to a screech, strutting across the stage full of confidence and attitude, Sykes milks the talk-to-the-hand, sassy black woman archetype for all it's worth. Her topics range widely, from racial profiling to abortion to the battle of the sexes. "I hate when women compare men to dogs," Sykes tells the audience. "We gotta stop doing that ladies, sayin', 'Men are dogs, men are dogs.' . . . Men are not dogs, nuh uh. . . . Dogs are *loyal*"—punching the final word to howls from the women in the audience. "Dogs never leave you and they can lick their own balls."

Later she emphasizes that women face so much pressure to be beautiful and are constantly objectified, which in turn makes women furious and want to lash out at men. "We're judged so harshly, about looks and everything . . . and we end up snappin'," she explains. "We think about killing men two, three times a day." When a man says something particularly awful, Sykes says, women think, "I wish I could just snatch his eyeballs right out of his head and shove 'em up his butt so he could see how big an asshole he is." According to Sykes, God had a reason for not giving women big muscles: "Guys, if we were physically stronger than y'all we would whup your ass every day . . . just unprovoked ass-whuppin'." And then in the part of her routine that has become especially famous on You-Tube, Sykes fantasizes that one way women could be released from all the pressure to service men and yet protect themselves and their honor would be to have detachable vaginas (although she uses a more vulgar term). How great it would be to just leave it home sometimes: "Think of the freedom that you'd have," she proclaims. Women could go for a jog at night without fear, because if a potential rapist accosted them, all you'd have to say is, "Sorry, I left it home." If only Sykes were God.

Sykes delivers her routine mostly in standard white English, but often drops her *g*'s and peppers her commentary with Black Speak locutions and terms like "ain't nobody," "I need me some," and, of course, "girl."[1] We all instantly recognize Black Speak for what it is: way cool insider talk. It instantly signifies that a truth is being spoken, one that requires a solid "amen" from listeners and a truth that standardized white-bread English can't quite convey because it's too official, too straight, too establishment.[2] And by code switching between these two ways of talking, Sykes defines the situation and her intentions: she's in *and* out, a black woman who has been positioned to see all of white society, and certainly male society, as a voyeur, and thus with a much keener view.

I want this view; it's like a secret peephole I want her to share with me. This view has power because of its certainty and fearlessness. When Sykes struts across the stage, she is in command, of the space and of her audience. So when I watch her and laugh with her, I can fantasize about having that fearless power, too, and instead of being punished or hated for it, being applauded and admired. Here, female verbal power is cool!

Why do so many of us love the sassy black woman? And why has she become such a fixture in pop culture? What kind of work does she do for us? There are tricky pleasures women take in watching Wanda Sykes do her stand-up, Queen Latifah steal every one of her scenes in *Chicago*, and Dr. Bailey—more on her later—dress down her interns on *Grey's Anatomy*. African American women get some affirmation of their hard-won ability to even have a voice in mainstream culture. For middle-class and upper-middle-class white women, it's a bit different: we are (still) supposed to be diplomatic, conciliatory, and nurturing, at home and at work. We are not supposed to be too tough, have sharp tongues, point out sexism, or express anger—if we slip, you know what that makes us. To quote Barbara Bush, it rhymes with "witch." So Wanda Sykes letting Larry David have it on *Curb Your Enthusiasm*—well, I want to steal it, the pose, the attitude, the confidence, the language, the pronunciation, the whole damn package.

From the early 1990s, with the premiere and popularity of the sitcom *Living Single*, to the rise of Wanda Sykes and the ongoing, staggering success of Oprah Winfrey, African American women have offered the delicious performance of the code-switching woman, who one minute passes as fully assimilated into (and comfortable with) professional, middle-class norms, and the next minute uses Black Speak to expose how phony and hypocritical those norms are, especially for women. Code switching serves as a deeply gratifying verbal performance about the turnstile all women spin through day in and day out, putting on the compliant, cooperative front in what is still a male-dominated world, and then, behind the scenes, telling the truth about the wages of patriarchy. What Black Speak does is make feminism hip, cool, and funny.

When I watch Wanda Sykes, then, I don't see her expressing only black women's exasperation with sexism and injustice, I see her expressing it for all women. But she's out there and we get to hide behind her. She is our surrogate, the cocksure woman we want to be but usually can't be without getting into some pretty serious trouble. So am I maybe a little too happy to have a black woman express my rage for me, especially when it's really funny to boot? I know that what the journalist Joan Morgan has called the "talk-to-the-hand superwoman" is yet another stereotypical media cliché, one in which a snappy style masks the painful substance of life, but she also offers a fantasy of power and transgression.[3]

The daydream is pretty savory: be able to speak (with your hands on your hips, and your eyes rolling, oh yes) the unvarnished truth about sexism, the ongoing subjugation of women, and cloddish male behavior and be seen as totally cool for doing so. Yes! Sykes's kind of verbal aggression would get me nowhere in real life, but it's great to inhabit for a while on my sofa. (Not that it gets black women far in real life either, but on TV the message is you don't mess with them; wouldn't it be nice to think no one would mess with you?) For decades white people have projected onto black culture, through our embrace of jazz to rock 'n' roll to hip-hop, romanticized notions about freedom from middle-class constraints that many whites crave, however vicariously. The talk-to-the-hand African American woman represents such an escape, and she is a fantasy offering liberating delights, a jailbreak from demure femininity. But she also has perils, especially for black women themselves. Because while sassy may be cool, sassy also always has to be tamed.

The same year that Sykes got her own short-lived comedy on TV, another African American woman commanded the small screen, Chandra Wilson as Dr. Miranda Bailey on the instant hit *Grey's Anatomy*. Along with Cristina (the flawless Sandra Oh), Dr. Bailey was instantly my favorite character. She was a professional woman totally uninterested in being nice or liked, and completely unafraid to tell the truth or hurt people's feelings if that's what the work required. Referred to as "the Nazi" before we even met her, we quickly saw why she struck terror into the hearts of all the surgical interns she supervised. "I have five rules, memorize them," she commanded through her pursed lips. "Rule number one, don't bother suckin' up. I already hate cha. That's not gonna change.... You're interns, grunts, nobodies, bottom of the surgical food chain.... Rule number three, if I'm sleeping don't wake me unless your patient is actually dying. Number four, the dying patient better not be dead when I get there, not only would you 'av' killed someone you woulda woke me for no good reason. Are we clear?" When one of the interns, Izzie (Katherine Heigl) failed to follow rule three, Bailey snapped, "Next time you wake me he better be so close to dead there's a tag on his toe." As the interns hope to get to scrub into a surgery, Bailey decreed, "Your job is to make your resident happy. Do I look happy? No. Why? Because my interns are whiney.... No one holds a scalpel 'til I'm so happy I'm Mary Freakin' Poppins.... Why y'all standin' there? Move!" She warned them, "If you make your resident look bad, she'll torture you until you beg for your mama." Standard English and Black Speak in delicious suspension, making female power awesome, intimate, with it.

Bailey was equally fearless when taking on her superiors; she told her boss Dr. Burke (Isaiah Washington), "I think you're cocky, arrogant, bossy, and pushy, and you also have a God complex, you never think about anybody but your damn self." Boy, I've worked with men I would have loved to say that to, but never had the nerve. And when a Wall

Street attorney for some incredibly spoiled undergraduate calls the dean's office because I've given the kid a C (which was probably a gift), I'd like to say to him what Bailey said to some reckless bikers who nearly got their friend killed: "You little snivelin' no good snot rags." Amen, sister. But I am not allowed to say such things and, despite my desires, cannot really be part of this insider call-and-response choir. But I love that Bailey says them for me.

Now, if black women—certainly one of the most oppressed, abused groups in American history—can speak truth to power in front of millions, doesn't that *really* dramatize how unnecessary feminism is today? If they are *this* freely outspoken, *this* liberated, and surgeons to boot, don't all women have it made in the shade? So here's the quicksand we sink into as we cheer them on from our sofas: at the same time that the smart-mouthed black woman gives so many of us vicarious pleasure and access to core truths about women's ongoing fury with sexism, her presence serves as absolute evidence that women's equality has been achieved. She can also mask the ongoing invisibility of more realistic women of color in the media, and certainly those who are not surgeons or successful entertainers.

So let's begin by asking how millions of actual African American girls and women are doing in the United States, the ones not on our TV and movie screens. It is true that more African American women than ever are going to college and have entered the ranks of college professors, journalists, lawyers, and owners of their own businesses. Nonetheless, they earn considerably less than white and Asian American women, and only 62.5 cents to every white man's dollar (in Louisiana it's 48.9 cents to his dollar). They have some of the highest poverty rates in the country; this is especially true in states like Louisiana, Mississippi, and Arkansas. They continue to experience "persistent discrimination in hiring and promotion, occupational segregation by race and gender, and differences in access to higher education," according to the Institute for Women's Policy Research.[4] They are more likely to get breast cancer before the age of forty and more likely to die from it. Their rates for other cancers—colon, pancreatic, lung—are also higher, and they are more likely to die from the disease than people of any other racial or ethnic group. They are more likely to get and die from heart disease. Young African

American women and girls do not have the same access to sex education and birth control as white girls; rates of HIV/AIDS have been soaring for black women; they have 25 times the AIDS rate as white women. Here's another underreported tragedy: many of these women get delayed or no prenatal care at all, and their infant mortality rate is 2.4 times that of whites. Their babies are 2 to 3 times as likely to die from sudden infant death syndrome. How many oceans of tears is that?[5] African American women are disproportionately victims of rape and assault (which never get the attention that assaults on white women do). They are 4.5 times more likely than white women to be incarcerated, typically for offenses like drug possession, theft, or drunk driving.[6]

The contradictions between visibility and invisibility abound for African American women. In the media mirrors around us, with a few exceptions, we see neither the middle-class black women who have made it nor the lower-middle-class or poor ones who are struggling. Sykes and Dr. Bailey stand out, still, in a mediascape that remains overwhelmingly Wonder Bread. Recent female ensemble shows—*Desperate Housewives, Lipstick Jungle, Cashmere Mafia, Gossip Girl*—have had no ongoing cast members who were African American. Other dramas—*CSI Miami, ER*—have the token black female forensic scientist or doctor. To make up for this there are all those endless, anonymous black female judges in all those legal procedural shows, who fulfill its "diversity" requirements, get few speaking lines, yet cement the notion that black women have made it all the way to the top—and of the criminal justice system, no less.

At the same time, on any given afternoon, if really forced to, I can turn on BET and see skimpily dressed black women shake their booties to some of the most women-hating lyrics ever recorded. Only an hour and a half later, I can tune into the richest and arguably most influential woman in the entertainment industry, Oprah Winfrey, so famous no one even bothers to use her last name anymore. Talk about being whipsawed between images of utter objectification and stupendous achievement! And enlightened sexism is more complicated—and often more virulent—for African American women because it intersects with the new subtle racism and with misogyny in some sectors of the black community. The age-old charges that black women preside over a matriarchy in which black men have been rendered unwanted or unnecessary pumps up the image of the all-powerful, fearsome female gargoyle on one end of the spectrum; why would this woman ever need feminism, she already runs everything? On the other end of the spectrum, the ethos of enlightened sexism suggests that black women deserve to be objectified and should be rendered powerless because all they really care about are sex and money anyway. In other words, for black women, embedded feminism casts them as Rock-of-Gibraltar superwomen, and enlightened sexism as materialistic jezebels. For both, the power they allegedly have is, of course, a myth.

Now, as (a) a white woman and (b) an *aging* white woman (rather unlikely to be gettin' jiggy wit' 50 Cent) and (c) a white female baby boomer feminist, I know that I am entering treacherous terrain. What right do I have to comment on these images? After all, white feminists in the 1970s really pissed off women of color for ignoring or minimizing their issues and for seeming elitist and exclusionary. As Joan Morgan and other black feminists have made clear, this has not made it easy for African American women to embrace the F-word. And I may know a thing or two (or three) firsthand about sexism, but what the hell do I know, in my bones, in my gut, about racism, let alone about sexism in black communities? Only what I know secondhand. But calling out media images that cast black women as inherently promiscuous, or as typically loud, sassy, and finger-snappin' with attitude, or as lazy, irresponsible welfare mothers should not be left only to our African American sisters. White women have to take a clear-eyed look at them, too, because such images not only hold black women down, they elevate someone like me at their expense.

The media images of black women as brazen, smart-mouthed towers of strength may be a persona I want to transport myself to, pretend to be, laugh at, and laugh with, but I still walk away from the TV or out of the movie theater as a white woman in a white world, where such images have few consequences for me. White women have to appreciate that the big gunny sack of privilege we walk around with—not followed by security guards in clothing stores, typically treated better by doctors, more likely to get that follow-up interview for the job, much more able to get a fixed-rate mortgage—is reinforced by media imagery. Obviously I cannot speak for African American women, but I seek to be their compatriot.[7] The contradictory images of white women and black women, taken separately and together, have at times made more things possible for us all and yet have buttressed enlightened sexism while pitting white women and women of color against each other.

So how did we get to a place where a TV show can have a black woman as a surgeon—albeit a sassy one? Beginning in the early 1990s, despite the ongoing underrepresentation of women of color in all media, there was a rise in the visibility of African Americans in television, in film, and in the music industry. The Reagan administration, with its attacks on "welfare queens," demonizing of African American men as lazy thugs, "crack baby" panics, and its "war on drugs" with its implicit focus on urban blacks provoked a major backlash among a variety of black artists. Black-authored films, TV shows, magazines, and, especially, rap music talked back to these stereotypes and produced an outpouring of popular culture that blacks and whites welcomed.[8] The entertainment industry also discovered that images of "the ghetto" sold.[9] Rap music and videos gave life to the inner city, in a seemingly secret language that most white people didn't know (with words like "diss," "phat," "frontin'," "homie"). And then there were the rhymes, the beat, the break dancing, the graffiti, the baggy pants, the untied sneakers, and the bling. This was not *The Cosby Show* territory, where black folks could become anything they wanted if they just applied themselves and wore the right sweaters.[10]

It was in this milieu that *Yo! MTV Raps* premiered in 1988. This was back in the day when MTV actually aired music videos instead of inane dating games and heinous reality shows. But with the exception of Michael Jackson or the occasional Herbie Hancock or Prince video (ah, "Little Red Corvette"), MTV had been Whiteytown U.S.A., for which it was getting an increasing amount of well-deserved flak, given the growing popularity of rap. So it launched this half-hour show of rap music videos (if my memory serves me correctly, just after school in the late afternoon) and instantly the ratings soared.

Yo! MTV Raps brought hip-hop culture—the music, dancing, slang, clothes, street scenes, style, and its oppositional, defiant stance against the dominant power structure—to a much wider and whiter audience. And while the DJs—Doctor Dre and Ed Lover—and the vast majority of the stars were male, and much of the ghetto-centric, urban ethos was hyper-masculine, women played an integral role in early hip-hop and were not predominantly treated like dirt, as has become de rigueur today.[11] Watching the apolitical trash party videos airing now can make you forget N.W.A.'s song "Express Yourself," which began with images of black oppression under slavery and quickly moved to modern-day police brutality and apartheid in South Africa, or Public Enemy's "Fight the Power." (Go to MTV's *Yo! MTV* Web site to see classic videos that provide an antidote to, say, Lil Wayne's *Lollipop* video, in which a harem of women compete over him.)

When females appeared in these videos, they were dancing fly-girls, as in M. C. Hammer's classic "U Can't Touch This," beautiful escorts and audience members in Digital Underground's "Humpty Dance" (whose lyrics, "Do the humpty hump," are positively kindergarten-friendly compared to what's out there today), or objects of admiring desire in LL Cool J's "Around the Way Girl." There were even men who made fun of the objectification of women (while, of course, then being able to objectify them). Tone Loc's dance single "Wild Thing" parodied Robert Palmer's classic "Addicted to Love" video with its lineup of red-lipped mannequin look-alike females who were obviously mere ornaments. And Sir Mix-a-Lot's "Baby Got Back" video (a number one pop single in 1992) opened with two snobby airheaded white Valley Girls and their "oh my God" reaction to a black woman's butt, which they said made her look like a prostitute, "'kay?" Sir Mix-a-Lot sang the praises of black women's backsides, made fun of the dominant white standard of beauty as promoted in Barbie dolls and *Cosmo,* and urged women to "shake that healthy butt."

At the same time, the video reduced the female dancers to props who were defined entirely by their shaking butts. As the hip-hop scholar S. Craig Watkins notes, "there is a fine line between adoring and annihilating the female body," and that line would gradually get pushed in a more negative direction.[12] Early rap's scathing social criticism of the government, police brutality, racial profiling, and the images of blacks in the media were intermixed with often deeply sexist ways of regarding women, as sexual objects who needed (or wanted) to be dominated.[13] And yet rap was moving toward the gangsta stage, which marked the turn to out-and-out misogyny and sexual violence that gave us, for example, the infamous

Nelly video in which a credit card was swiped through a woman's butt. (In 2004, the women of Spellman College refused to have Nelly come to campus unless he engaged in a dialogue about the sexism of his videos; he refused.)[14]

In addition, a few female rappers broke through. And they were not all forced to wear miniskirts, bikinis, or garter belts. Many black women rappers sought to engage their brothers and listeners in a dialogue about female sexuality and the status of women.[15] They expressed solidarity with black men while also critiquing their sexism.[16] Queen Latifah, MC Lyte, and Salt-N-Pepa, all of whom got airtime on MTV, took on sexual politics, just like their white counterparts in Riot Grrrl. In "Dance for Me," Queen Latifah, in a fabulous army officer's uniform studded with medals (the bottom portion of which consisted of Bermuda shorts) and her Nefertiti-like headpiece-cum-crown, insisted that women could rap as well as men. "A battle, put me in it, I win it," she bragged, and you believed her. More important was her anthem "U.N.I.T.Y.," in which she attacked black men for calling women bitches or hoes. She recounted punching a guy in the eye after being grabbed on the street and then asking, "Who you calling a bitch?" Salt-N-Pepa—wearing, by turns, men's pinstripe suits and fedoras (with cigars), football uniforms, and military camouflage (with guns)—insisted on "Independent" that they were, one minute, "feminine still, yes" and the next "pump a hundred weight bench press." They told men that they didn't need them, and "I make my own money, so don't tell me how to spend it." Yo-Yo, in "Girl Don't Be No Fool," addressed women directly about cheating men and domestic violence: "Guys ain't nothin' but dirt, and they'll flirt with anything dressed in a miniskirt," followed in the next verse by "Homegirl, what's up with the black eye? . . . The man you got is just bad for your health."[17]

These women claimed their voices as legitimate and important; they also asserted their right to be sexually expressive without submitting to dominant white, prissy, middle-class norms about proper sexual decorum for women. The problem was, of course, that this is a trap for all women, with the possible exception of Madonna, who gets away with almost everything. Present yourself as a woman with sexual desires equal to any man's, and as a woman proud of her body, and no matter what your intent you are giving permission to be objectified and, inevitably, cast as a slut.

Hide all this away and you're conforming to double-standard patriarchal hooey about female—but not male—sexual agency being inappropriate and dangerous. This was an even bigger minefield for African American women given the centuries-old stereotypes about their inherent promiscuity. As Salt-N-Pepa found out in some responses to their videos "Shake Your Thang" and "Shoop," "their sexual freedom could be considered dangerously close to self-inflicted exploitation," as the hip-hop historian Tricia Rose noted.[18] Indeed, behind the scenes Salt-N-Pepa were under the near complete control of their writer-producer who bragged, "I wrote records for women from a man's point of view—to be sung by women, 'cause men know what women want."[19] Hip-hop, then, was a complex and complicated brew in the late 1980s and early 1990s—male-dominated but more preoccupied with political critique and white racism than with misogyny, with space for a few female voices who took on sexism, and yet, under and through the beats, an emerging battle of the sexes. But as another, tougher declaration of girl power, it was hard to beat Salt-N-Pepa's "Ain't Nuthin' but a She Thing," in which they noted that women got paid less than a man for "doin' the same damn thing that he can," that men treated women like sex objects, and what made Salt-N-Pepa "mad and crazy" was to be called a bitch and a witch, yet also stupidly cast as the weaker sex, "Underestimate the mind, oh yeah, you're a fool."

As rap music and hip-hop culture in general began to course through the white world, media moguls once again "discovered" the African American audience, as if it had been hidden like the ruins of Troy. The result was an explosion in the number of sitcoms with black folks. In 1986, as part of his never-ending quest to build a media empire the size of Saturn, Rupert Murdoch launched his new TV network Fox (called a "netlet" at the time and predicted as doomed to failure). How would Fox go head-to-head with the three bigger, established networks with all their affiliates and mainstream (if really dumb) hit shows like *Matlock*, *America's Funniest Home Videos*, not to mention blockbusters like *The Cosby Show* and *A Different World*? Hey, wait, *The Cosby Show* and *A Different World*?

The strategy was simple. Fox had already targeted the youth audience with *90210* and *Melrose Place*. But Fox executives knew that African

Americans watched nearly 50 percent more network TV on average than whites, 73.6 hours per week versus 50.2 hours.[20] They also knew that the most desirable audience—young, urban-oriented whites with disposable money—were, with the growing success of hip-hop, looking to black culture for what was cool, innovative, transgressive. And finally, they knew from the success of *The Cosby Show* and *A Different World* that white people would watch shows with black casts, especially if the problem of racism was erased. So, they reasoned, they would sell the new network to advertisers as one that delivered a very specific niche market that the advertisers could target. "Sure, we use black shows to hook the hip white audience," admitted Fox entertainment president Sandy Grushow. "That's one reason we've become the cutting edge network."[21]

By 1993, Fox was airing the largest number of black-produced shows in TV history, and in short order African Americans were a quarter of Fox's audience. Another phenomenon quickly followed. TV viewing became racially segregated. By the mid- and late-1990s the top ten shows in African American households were completely different from the top ten shows in white households; the only point of overlap was *Monday Night Football*.[22] The top three shows in black homes were *Living Single, New York Undercover,* and *Martin.* Yet Fox had also met its goal of getting a crossover audience; 4.1 million black homes tuned into *Living Single,* but so did nearly 4.5 million white homes.[23] To capture just how cynical this strategy was, once Fox had cemented its status as the fourth major network, black-cast sitcoms began to disappear from its lineup: in 1994 alone it canceled four of its six black shows.[24] Once again, black people did the heavy lifting and then were let go.

Exactly how were black women supposed to reconcile the pressures to conform to and succeed in white culture with the pressures, and desire, to keep it real? This question was answered by the Fox hit *Living Single,* conceived by Yvette Lee Bowser, the first African American woman to create a successful prime-time series for network TV. Premiering in 1993, *Living Single* was part of that broader, early to mid-1990s media moment when feminism was the fulcrum of so many shows—*Roseanne, Murphy Brown, Northern Exposure.* It quickly became the most popular prime-time show in African American homes, while drawing a white audience, too.[25] It was filled with black-female-affirming, womanist dialogue, yet aired directly after *Martin*, a show created by the comedian Martin Lawrence and filled with macho posturing.[26] *Living Single* was embedded feminism for black women, while *Martin* became an exemplar of enlightened (or not-so-enlightened) sexism. Separately and together, the two shows staged the war between these two trends in the media and the gender wars between black men and women. While both shows had their fans and their detractors, the consensus among most black critics and fans was that *Living Single* was admirable, warts and all, while *Martin* was a throwback, attacked by Bill Cosby, Spike Lee, and others as bringing the minstrel show back to TV.[27]

In *Living Single* four women—Khadijah (Queen Latifah), Regine (Kim Fields), Maxine (Erika Alexander), and Synclaire (Kim Coles) shared a Brooklyn brownstone and were friends with two men in the building, Overton (John Henton) and Kyle (T. C. Carson). The opening sequence with its rapped theme song showed us right away that these women could dance (sigh) and, through close-up shots of lipstick and fancy shoes, that they were also feminine and upwardly mobile. Khadijah ran *Flavor* magazine, which she had founded, Maxine was a take-no-prisoners attorney, Regine worked as a buyer for a clothing store and shopped 'til she dropped, and Synclaire was Khadijah's naive, slow-on-the-uptake secretary and cousin. Middle-class—even upper-middle-class—success for black women was taken for granted, a battle that had been won.[28]

Two major tensions ran through the show. The first revolved around feminism and men: What was more important, to be accomplished and independent or to be focused on men and finding Mr. Right? (The near impossibility for African American women to find said Mr. Right had kept Terry McMillan's novel *Waiting to Exhale* on the bestseller list for twenty-nine weeks in 1992.) The other main tension, much more implicit than the first, was about assimilation (selling out) versus keeping it real: Could black women be successful in mainstream white society without becoming whitewashed and untrue to who they were? While Yvette Lee Bowser hoped to produce a slice-of-life show about black female friends, Fox executives pressured her to go for a more "male quest," male-oriented set of themes; nonetheless, feminist moments came through.[29]

In the very first episode we learned that Regine—an elitist, materialistic shopaholic who loved all things French and had more wigs than Tina Turner—considered two things about a man, a fine butt and a full wallet. In her bouffant skirt, low-cut top, bows in her hair, and trademark parting line "smooches," Regine confirmed both the counterstereotypical notion that African American women can be as feminine as any white girl, and the stereotypical one that black women won't look at a black man unless he's financially successful (an endless beef, put much more crudely, of course, in all too many rap songs). Maxine, with her beautifully tailored suits and braggadocio about the cases she had won, had clearly made it in the professional world, but in the brownstone she could hand slap Khadijah, roll her eyes, and bring on the sass. We also learned that the boyfriend with whom she was very much in love had left her once she started becoming successful as a lawyer, suggesting a lethal correlation between female achievement and lasting love.

It was slip slidin' in and out of language—code switching—that was the strategy these women used to juggle their different identities. All of the women, with the exception of Synclaire, moved effortlessly between standard white English and black vernacular and slang, verbally proving their ability to be taken seriously in both worlds. This was one of the great pleasures of the show, for white audiences as well as for blacks, because here we gained access, however vicariously, to the truth-telling world of snap. Indeed, it was through language more than anything else that the women made clear they had simultaneously succeeded in whitey town and yet remained absolutely true to black culture. More to the point, it was either through Black Speak, or the physical style of sass, that the women ripped the veneer off of male conceits. Regine could code-switch on a dime (including between English and French), saying things like "You need to embellish" one minute and "The brother ain't called the girl in over a year" the next. *Living Single* insisted that African American women have a rich, lively language all their own that was way cooler and more authentic than anything white girls had. The show celebrated the linguistic vitality of black culture and its exuberance, which endures and gets even richer despite discrimination, injustice, and the relentless, homogenizing lava flow of white culture. These black women cut through the crap of male sexism in a way white girls—except maybe for Roseanne and

Murphy Brown—only dreamed of. Self-doubt? Forget it. And Khadijah and Maxine in particular wouldn't be caught dead fluttering their eyelashes or acting dumb and helpless to get what they want from men. Their language made clear that while they were quite adept at speaking dominant white English, they were not going to adopt white feminine English—sometimes childlike, often equivocating ("you might," "maybe"), overly accommodating, too polite.[30]

With the exception of the dimwit Synclaire, who was quickly romanced by and eventually married Overton, the women were independent sexual agents, interested in their own pleasure and unconcerned about a double standard. They easily eyed men up and down and took them as objects for their visual pleasure: "Damn, he fine," "brother got it goin' on," and "hmm, big feet." In one episode when they were playing Truth or Challenge, Max asked Khadijah this question from a card, "Do you think sex without love is a sin?" Khadijah shot back, "If it is I'll see you in hell," which elicited laughing hoots of approval from the studio audience. Max in particular was unrestrained in her sexual desires and freedom, which compromised her professional status not one whit.[31]

Male bashing happily coexisted in the women's love-hate relationships with men. The acid-tongued and verbally aggressive Max was in a constant war of words with their cocky neighbor Kyle until—yes—we saw that the aggression really masked their attraction. Typical Maxisms about men included: "You'd think after God created dogs she'd know creating men was redundant." "All men are like fine wine. They all start out as grapes and our job is to stomp on them." "Men are nothing but speed bumps on the road to happiness." Regine countered that men were like cheap pantyhose; "at the worst possible moment, they run on you." At one point in the midst of this, the much-less-angry Synclaire asked if they wondered what the world would be like without men. Khadijah answered, "A bunch of fat, happy women and no crime," after which they all high-fived each other, and the studio audience clapped and cheered.

At the very same time that the pursuit of men—for sexual pleasure and emotional sustenance—dominated the show, so did the insistence on female independence and self-respect. This was embedded feminism in action, and not only for black women. From the very first episode Max talked about the importance of women's rights. She and Khadijah told Regine she didn't need a man to get the things she wanted: "You can do anything. You're a woman." In the final season, after Max and Kyle had become involved, he got transferred to London and asked her to go with him. Even though she loved him, Max couldn't do it. As she says to Khadijah, "I'm supposed to follow him like some 1950s housewife, give up everything I've worked for?" And in one of the more famous episodes from the first season, the women tried to crash an all-male poker game Kyle was hosting, and they eventually succeeded. Khadijah beat Kyle's boss, Lawrence, who then turned to one of the other men and said, "I did not come here to get whacked by these bitches." This was, of course, taking on the increasing use of "bitch" in rap, and the studio audience howled in outrage. When confronted by Kyle for disrespecting the women, Lawrence said the word was "just an expression," prompting Kyle to throw him out of his apartment. The episode ended with Queen Latifah performing her feminist anthem "U.N.I.T.Y." Women—especially black women—were in their living rooms yelling "You go! You go!"[32] Talk about feminism being part of a show's DNA.

African American women had a much less charitable take on the lead-in show for *Living Single*, the enormously popular and deeply sexist *Martin*. The comedian Martin Lawrence (the show's creator and star) portrayed a macho-posturing Detroit radio talk show host whose girl-friend (and eventual wife) Gina (Tisha Campbell) put up with his pos-sessiveness and constantly bolstered his fragile ego. Relations between men and women typically consisted of pitched verbal and sometimes physical battles. Gina's best friend, the verbally venomous Pam (Tichina Arnold), hated Martin, and they exchanged insults constantly. Martin had two friends, Cole (Carl Anthony Payne II) and Tommy (Thomas Mikal Ford), but the two other real main characters were played by Mar-tin in drag: his Momma, and his neighbor Sheneneh, Lawrence's vehicle for ridiculing black women, especially poor, uneducated black women. *Martin* relied much more than *Living Single* on broad physical humor and exaggerated gestures that fed into racial stereotypes.

Lawrence tried to have it both ways in the show: to expose black male machismo and sexism as fronts (although, to him, necessary fronts) and, at the same time, to insist that most black women were domineering, aggressive, promiscuous, gold diggers, or all of the above. He clearly had what he admitted was a "love-hate" relationship with women.[33] Typical plots involved Martin bragging on his radio show that Gina, a marketing executive complete with a shiny black briefcase, was totally submissive to him, only to catch hell from her later, or learning that she made more money than he did and being shattered, requiring her to placate him and buck him up. Those defending the show pointed out that it was one of the few to show a loving, monogamous relationship between a young African American couple.[34] But this emphasis on the romance and Martin's pathetic need to always appear manly masked the show's misogyny.[35] It was the hyperracialized images of the women that made it especially controversial.[36]

In show after show the various male characters, including Martin's skeezy, aging, plaid-suit-wearing boss, Stan (Garrett Morris), made it clear that women were, first and foremost, sex objects to be ogled and lusted after. Martin was perennially horny and always asking Gina to "gimme my sugar." The tough and hostile Pam could easily subdue Martin's friend Cole in an armlock; she had little use for men unless they had money. (When asked, "Would you date someone forty pounds overweight?" Pam says, "Yes, if twenty of it was in his wallet.") Even Gina, the successful professional woman, had to restrain herself from getting into a physical fight with another woman, particularly if it was over Martin. Momma Payne—made all the more grotesque because of Lawrence's mustache—was a gyratin' domineering mother who loved to talk trash about others and to "go off" defending her son.[37]

But it was Sheneneh, Lawrence's version of the ghetto "homegirl," who seemed to be his true alter ego when it came to the show's gender politics. Dressed in fluorescent orange or bubble gum pink, midriff-baring halter tops, and loud orange, aqua, yellow, and purple striped shorts, her butt grotesquely overstuffed to look like the Hottentot Venus, covered in gold bling, flinging her hair extensions, and pointing her three-inch-long fingernails, Lawrence's Sheneneh was female belligerence and promiscuity all wrapped up in one girlfriend buffoon. She swiveled and ground her hips and bobbled her neck and head as she talked in her slurred speech. In her first introduction to the audience, Sheneneh accosts Pam and Gina sarcastically as "the little business women," tells Gina to send Martin her way because "I know how to tame that man," and then threatens, "I will bust your ass," which prompts Pam to try to attack her. She was constantly itching for a fistfight when she wasn't itching to get laid. Were African American women unable to get along with each other? Were they physically violent? Were they inherently lascivious? Were they loud, threatening, and domineering? Were they monstrous? Just watch Sheneneh. Sheneneh justified the sexism and the racism—and the powerful intersections between the two—that millions of African American women experienced every day.

That Sheneneh and Big Momma—both offensive drag versions of black women as hard and emasculating—were a Rorschach for Lawrence's actual attitude toward women became clearer in the wake of his various real-life controversies. On February 19, 1994, Lawrence was the guest host of *Saturday Night Live*, and he delivered a truly revolting, female-hating monologue about women's offensive vaginal smells and failure to practice what he considered proper feminine hygiene. NBC's switchboard lit up like the spaceship in *E.T.*, and the hundreds of complaints prompted the monologue to be yanked before the show aired on the West Coast. Lawrence was banned for life from the show.[38] In 1996, Lawrence's wife left him after which he threatened to kill her; she had to get a restraining order and they finally divorced. That same fall Tisha Campbell walked off the set of *Martin*, charging Lawrence with "repeated and escalating sexual harassment, sexual battery, verbal abuse, and related threats to her physical safety."[39]

By 1995, four of the top ten sitcoms, *Roseanne, Grace Under Fire, Ellen*, and *Murphy Brown*, had female leads. But it was male comics who headlined most of the black sitcoms that followed in the wake of *Martin* and *Living Single*. Two exceptions were *Moesha* and *Sister, Sister*, both comedies about teenagers. While *Moesha* wrestled with family struggles, *Sister, Sister*—identical twins separated at birth and reunited at age fourteen—took *The Parent Trap* or *The Patty Duke Show* (in which we were supposed to believe in the concept of "identical cousins") and simply superimposed these white premises on a black cast.[40] The mom (Jackée Harry) was yet another loud, brassy, sassy black woman meant to deliver lines like "They got a mama that can sew like a spider" or to shing-a-ling around the house.

Television's other answer to race was the urban ensemble show: *NYPD*

Blue, ER, Law & Order (the entire franchise), *The Practice, CSI: Miami.*
Here if you mixed in one or two African American women as cops or doctors, you had your get-out-of-stereotyping-jail-free card. Then a show like
NYPD Blue could parade out its endless stream of black hookers, crack-
heads, and negligent mothers. When *ER* premiered in 1994—and I was
there on the sofa every Thursday night pretending that in an age of
managed care, the American medical system would still do right by
its patients—I particularly liked the head nurse, an African American
woman who was the conscience and much needed drill sergeant of the
show. Not only did she not get top billing, in early episodes she was rarely
addressed by her name on the show, so it took a while for us to learn that
this was Nurse Haleh Adams played by Yvette Freeman. There were no
black female doctors on the show until the seventh season (Dr. Cleo Finch,
played by Michael Michele). And while one of the African American
women, physician's assistant Jeanie Boulet (Gloria Reuben), was a prominent and sympathetic character, she had AIDS, and Carla Reese (Lisa
Nicole Carson) became a villain when she tried to take away the son she
had with Dr. Benton (Eriq La Salle) by moving out of state. It was later
revealed that she had lied to Benton; the boy was not in fact his biological
child. So even when it became de rigueur to have at least one token black
woman in the cast, she typically got little screen time and was often deviant or deceptive. Accomplished black women continue to be punished or
are not real women; Angela Bassett, a doctor in the final season of *ER*, was
plagued by infertility and could not have children.

The few dramatic movies geared to and starring African American
women, like *Waiting to Exhale* (1995) and *Soul Food* (1997), featured
beautiful, mostly professionally successful women. But while it was welcome to see black women who were the complete opposite of Sheneneh,
these films still reinforced the tenets of enlightened sexism for black
women: they couldn't hold on to their men; black women and black men
would always be at war; and the most noble black woman was the strong,
self-sacrificing wife and mother who put her family (and her man) before
everything else. Both films threw gasoline on the smoldering gender

wars, and reinforced the supposed Mars–Venus differences between men and women.

Waiting to Exhale was like *The Women's Room* for black women: not one decent brother on the planet. Pretty much every man who came on-screen was a lying, cheating, two-timing cad, an absentee father, or an unemployed, crack-using layabout. Most were totally lousy lays who just jumped on the women, satisfied themselves, and then rolled over. ("Does he think he just did something here? I coulda had a V8," cracks one woman.) As Savannah (Whitney Houston) tells us in a voice-over conveying her inner thoughts, men "lie without a conscience" and "what they're best at is convincing us that we should feel desperate." Bernie (Angela Bassett) had a husband who, after eleven years of marriage, has ditched her for a blond white woman and then seeks to cheat her out of a decent divorce settlement. "It's amazing what can happen when you give a man control over your life," she opines to her friends.

In a brief soliloquy to his girlfriend Robin (Lela Rochon), a drunken Troy (Mykelti Williamson), who has shown up two hours late for a date, articulates the clueless selfishness of black men: "You black bitches are all the same. You complain all the time about don't nobody want your asses don't know how to treat ya. Soon as a brother shows you genuine interest you act simple. And then you wonder why we go out with white women." He then calls her a "raggedy bitch." Later, as the four friends get drunk together, they itemize everything wrong with black men: they're behind bars, too scared to make a commitment, ugly, got bad credit, got little dicks and can't fuck or big ones and still can't fuck, they want to spank you, or be with white women, are too possessive, and just inside-out ugly.

But if this movie was way harsh on black men, *Soul Food* came down on black career women. A family of three adult sisters, their husbands and kids, held together by Big Momma (Irma P. Hall) and her soul food cooking, devolves into squabbling once Big Momma gets sick, lapses into a coma, and then dies. It was Big Momma—the strong, selfless black woman—who, when her husband almost lost their house because of his gambling, cleaned white people's houses "on my hands and knees," took in laundry, and did "what you have to do to stay strong, save the family."

With her gone, the sisters' inability to get along gets worse. The film makes it clear that the truly admirable daughter is Maxine (Vivica Fox), a stay-at-home mother of three and devoted wife to her husband.

The villain is Teri (Vanessa Williams), the attorney who has been made a brittle childless bitch by her success. The script never lets up on her: whenever she walks into a scene, someone is gonna get dissed, typically her husband or her sister Maxine, to wit: "I am the oldest one, I am the responsible one, I'm the one who graduated from law school, you were the one who dropped out when you were nineteen," she snipes. When her husband approaches her affectionately at home and asks her to dance with him, she rebuffs him, and, adding insult to injury, tells him she will not watch his musical performance that night because she is too swamped with work. They eventually divorce. Meanwhile, the third sister, Robin (Nia Long), has gone behind her husband's back to try to get him a job, a move that emasculates him and backfires. This film makes it clear that African American women who are admirable and truly deserving of love are those who put their men first and put up with or support them no matter what. Score another one for enlightened sexism.

Bestriding this entire era and certainly embodying strength, empowerment, and success has been Oprah Winfrey, the quintessential "you go girl." Few in the media have been more dedicated to cheering on women's aspirations than Oprah. From 1986, when her talk show debuted, to the early and mid-1990s when her show swept the ratings, to the book club that produced instant bestsellers, to Oprah's "Big Give," Oprah has been nothing less than an icon and a financial force of nature. And while nearly everyone knows her story of growing up in the South, poor and abused, she seems to have achieved something pretty unusual in the United States: she has almost transcended race. When you say the word "Oprah" to people, I bet the first things they think are "successful female talk show host" or "celebrity"; African American comes after that. A 1996 survey found that 78 percent of Americans had a favorable opinion of her; in 2007, that figure was 74 percent. A 1997 *ABC News / Wall Street Journal* poll found that more Americans admired her than President Clinton or former president Reagan.[41]

Oprah understood white women's envy of the hip, funny, sassy black woman, and made her safe for white viewers. So it is not surprising that while many black women admire and watch her, it is white women who have flocked to her in droves and made her a superstar. On her show, Oprah is our smart, funny, famous girlfriend. The show, of course, has covered all kinds of topics over the years—child abuse, national disasters, makeovers, racism, motherhood, substance abuse, celebrities, cruelty to animals, pop culture, books, and, of course, self-help. Oprah and her audience construct a fantasy, a utopia where white and black women come together as allies and friends. And how many black women, besides Oprah, have launched a magazine named after them, featuring herself on the cover every month, and have it be a hit with white women? Zero.

So while *Time* moaned about the "full Oprahization" of American politics, and others have complained about her book choices, her elevation of the atrocious "Dr. Phil," and her emphasis on individual change versus political action, let's consider what this African American woman has finessed and what pitfalls she still confronts. Oprah's skill has been establishing a powerful solidarity between herself and her studio audience and between herself and the larger, mostly white viewing audience. Like an earlier talk show host, Phil Donahue, she addressed women as if they mattered as citizens, as well as consumers. And, like Donahue, she moved among the studio audience with her microphone, engaging them and soliciting their opinions and experiences. But going one step further, Oprah would hold people's hands while they spoke if they needed moral or emotional support; she addressed both the studio and the home audience directly through the camera; she was obviously empathetic; and she revealed information about her difficult past and struggles with her weight. (Some, particularly black women, saw all this sympathy for white people and emphasis on Oprah's weight as reinforcing the black mammy stereotype.) Unlike A-list movie stars, who rely on some distance and mystery to enhance their aura, TV hosts need to be utterly and recognizably familiar; they must seem sincere, otherwise, they just aren't authentic.[42] When she airs, for example, an exposé on a black wife and mother struggling to rebuild her house after Hurricane Katrina, or another exposé on the sadistic cruelties of puppy farms, you'd have to have a heart of cobalt not to be glued to the screen, and moved.

But Oprah has had another crucial weapon, one that validates her authenticity as a woman with credibility, the real deal: code switching.[43] Oprah is totally in command of both modes of expression and moves effortlessly, and, it seems, intentionally, from standard white English to the use of "ain't," "sistah," "child," "girlfriend," or lines like "an lemme tell ya . . . da force was *definitely* wit' him, honey." Her effortless glide into Black Speak is endearing and almost always gets laughs. It also reminds white viewers that, as a black woman, she has a unique vantage point on white America and a special community membership that they don't. But she's going to let us in. As a daytime talk show host, Oprah speaks for ordinary and even disempowered people, nonelites, and her strategic deployment of Black Speak further emphasizes her brand of populism. Oprah may be a celebrity but she is also "just folks."[44] But it's also this in-group talk—mutually understood slang or language among people with a shared cultural history—that gives these locutions their special "secret code" cachet, until their definitions seep out through the media.

What's so interesting here is that by using Black Speak before a national, predominantly white female audience, and doing so in a direct address to them, Oprah not only marks herself as cool and authentic but also includes the white audience in her hip community.[45] Oprah lets white women into the club, and into a lively and, yes, at times subversive, take on dominant culture. And white women love her for that. For example, in the 1997 show "50 and Fabulous," featuring women in their fifties and early sixties, Oprah introduced Carol, an African American who was fifty-two. Oprah used standard English to verify this fact. But after expressing disbelief at Carol's age, Oprah code switched, saying, "Ya look gooood, girrrl." She then addressed the audience directly. "Fifty looks good. Don't fifty look good, y'all? Fi'ty lookin' goooood . . . um hmmm!" This Black Speak truth, one rarely acknowledged in the likes of *Vogue,* asserts that older women, and older black women, can be and are, in fact, attractive.[46] No wonder the audience cheered and laughed—women want to thumb their noses at the notion that after the age of thirty you're a desiccated has-been, and Black Speak is the ideal outside voice to talk back to the white, sexist, racist, ageist standards of beauty.

Oprah has become the black woman that many white women admire, want to be like, wish they knew. She is, at the very same time, racialized

In their Wonderbras and micro-minis, the Spice Girls proclaimed that they were "freshening up feminism for the nineties," and became the Roman candles of girl power. *(Associated Press/Fiona Hanson)*

Anointed by its fans as "the greatest teen magazine of all time," *Sassy* brought a smart-mouth, defiant sensibility to a new generation, as with this headline: "Do You Need Armpit Hair to Be a Feminist?" The answer was an emphatic "No!" *(Collection of the author)*

WHY LUKE PERRY'S NAME MAKES YOU WANT TO BUY THIS

Sassy

JUNE '92

37 WAYS TO BLOW
a relationship
ACCORDING TO A GUY

REFORMING
teenage
murderers—
SHOULD WE BOTHER?

DO YOU
NEED ARMPIT
HAIR TO BE A
feminist?
THE SASSY DEBATE

U.S.A. $2.00
(CHEAP, HUH?)

Reviled by critics as "stultifying," *Beverly Hills 90210*, with its pompadoured boys and shopping-crazed girls, nonetheless won the hearts of teenage girls, 69 percent of whom said they watched the show in the early 1990s. *(© Roberts Mikel/ Corbis Sygma)*

Building on the success of *90210*, *Melrose Place* followed the multiple, interlocking hookups of twenty-somethings with bodies sculpted like Greek statuary. Its special pleasure was watching how the queen vixen Amanda, played by Heather Locklear, *far left*, would deploy her sexual and corporate powers at the expense of men. *(Associated Press)*

Nicknamed the "Long Island Lolita," teenager Amy Fisher shocked the nation by attempting to kill her thirty-six-year-old lover's wife. Then she was seen on *A Current Affair* saying, "I'm wild. I don't care. I love sex." Was this what girl power meant—girls truly going wild? *(Associated Press/ Mike Albans)*

Janet Reno looked at the masquerade of femininity in American culture and just said no. This made many people—especially late-night comics—deeply anxious, giving rise to an endless stream of Janet Reno jokes. *(Associated Press/Joe Marquette)*

Routinely pummeling stubble-faced, murdering barbarian hordes into submission, Xena (Lucy Lawless) could often make her body go horizontal, the better to kick-box guys into the dirt. You did not—not—mess with Xena. *(Publicity still, collection of the author)*

Sick of seeing girls as always the victims in horror films, Joss Whedon gave us *Buffy the Vampire Slayer* (Sarah Michelle Gellar), in which only a teenage girl could save the world from fang-toothed evil. *(Publicity still, collection of the author)*

A film impossible not to love, *Clueless,* with its triumvirate of Cher (Alicia Silverstone, *center*), Dionne (Stacey Dash, *right*), and their makeover project Tai (Brittany Murphy, *left*), marked the rise of the new girliness in popular culture. *(© Corbis Sygma)*

Although the news media routinely proclaimed feminism to be "dead," this *Time* cover became instantly infamous for suggesting that feminism had devolved into the mini-skirted, stuttering, baby-longing, lovelorn Ally McBeal. *(Reprinted through the courtesy of the Editors of TIME Magazine © 2009 Time Inc.)*

In her feminist-infused routines, Wanda Sykes moves effortlessly between standard white English and black vernacular, and uses her talk-to-the-hand persona to expose the often ridiculous nature of white patriarchy. *(Associated Press/ Paul Drinkwater/NBCU Photo Bank via AP Images)*

Living Single, a hit with black and white audiences, featured African-American women who had made it professionally yet, in their brownstone, could high-five each other and bring on the sass, showing they could move easily between white and black culture. *(© Deborah Feingold/Corbis)*

America's quintessential "you go, girl," and the most successful woman in the entertainment industry, Oprah Winfrey also uses a mix of white English and black vernacular to construct an imaginative space in which women of all hues can come together as allies and friends. (*Associated Press/ Charles Bennet*)

Cosmopolitan has led the way in hyper-inflating the message that a woman's most important assets are her "hotness" and her ability to master every Kama Sutra position. And now, instead of models, celebrities like Jessica Biel, who look even better than they do in real life, grace the covers. (*Associated Press/Marion Curtis, Cosmopolitan*)

The infamous "wardrobe malfunction" at the 2004 Super Bowl halftime show was taken by many as evidence that sex in the media—whose centerpiece was the ever more explicit display of the female body—really had gone too far. *(Associated Press/David Phillip)*

Many women loved escaping to this mythical Manhattan, with no double standard, attractive men everywhere, and abiding female friendships. At the same time, the most important things to the women in *Sex and the City* were men and shopping. *(Publicity still, collection of the author)*

Richard Hatch, *far left*, the winner of the first *Survivor*, poses with fellow finalists Rudy Boesch, Susan Hawk, and Kelly Wigglesworth in happier times. On the final episode, watched by 59 million viewers, Hawk attacked Wigglesworth as "two-faced" and "manipulative" and voted her off the island, showing, once again, that women will always stab each other in the back. *(Associated Press/Kevork Djansezian)*

Reality TV shows like MTV's *The Real World*, with its stereotypes of hot girls getting into catfights over guys, became the ground zero of enlightened sexism. Here is the cast from the heinous *The Real World: Sydney*, in which the men assessed their female roommates as follows: "I'm a boob guy; I like big ones." *(© Steven Marcus/Reuters/Corbis)*

In *Mean Girls*, "the plastics" policed their own appearances as relentlessly as they tormented and sabotaged the lives of others, suggesting there might be a connection between having to be lean and tending to be mean. (© *Michael Gibson/Paramount Pictures/Bureau L.A. Collection/Corbis*)

It wasn't enough to torture the women of America with their TV ads. Now Victoria's Secret aired entire TV specials, in which the only ideal body type was a size zero ectomorph with Pamela Anderson's breasts attached. *(© Scott McDermott/ Corbis)*

With schemes that would make Machiavelli drool with envy, *Gossip Girl* follows the web- and text-based mutually assured destruction enacted by various Queen Bees, including Serena (Blake Lively, *left*) and Blair (Leighton Meester). *(Associated Press/Charles Sykes)*

One of the central features of celebrity culture has become the relentless surveillance of women's bodies for who is too fat, too thin, too flabby, and who has anything resembling "cellulite." *(Courtesy of American Media, collection of the author)*

As if constantly patrolling women's bodies, faces, hairdos, and clothing isn't enough, the celebrity press has introduced the "bump patrol," a creepy combination of stalking and CIA-style surveillance that seeks to pry inside a woman's womb. *(Courtesy of American Media, collection of the author)*

Male pundits like Tim Russert were shocked that a "self-avowed feminist" like Hillary Clinton would show "some emotion" during the New Hampshire primary, as if all feminists have had their tear ducts surgically removed. *(Associated Press/ Elise Amendola)*

Seeking to wink her way into the vice presidency, Sarah Palin embodied her own version of pit bull feminism, in which she sought to take advantage of the benefits created by the women's movement so she could undo them once she got into office. *(Associated Press/J. Scott Applewhite)*

Law & Order's tough-talking Lt. Anita Van Buren (S. Epatha Merkerson) is respected and taken seriously in a male-dominated profession. She offers the fantasy of a woman who gives orders and tells it like it is without any efforts to please or placate the rhino-skinned male detectives she works with. *(Publicity still, collection of the author)*

Between multiple surgeries and musical beds, *Grey's Anatomy* presents a utopian, multiracial world in which women get to advance to the top of their field, saves lives, compete with men, talk smack to their male bosses, and still have great sex. *(Publicity still, collection of the author)*

Ripping the veneer off the myth of domestic, suburban bliss, *Desperate Housewives* especially trashes the standards of perfection surrounding motherhood and exposes the constraints of gender roles that men and women are forced into. *(Publicity still, collection of the author)*

through her Black Speak (cool, an in-group member of black culture) and yet de-raced (a very rich, successful Everywoman).[47] As an African American woman who has succeeded so spectacularly as a talk show host and as a publisher of a magazine, Oprah seeks to personify empowerment for all women. This cause has indeed become a passionate crusade for Oprah: "Behave Your Way to Success," which she offered through "Change Your Life TV." She has added a considerable dose of spirituality to her mix of behavioral advice so while we can learn in O magazine "How to Lose Weight After 40" (answer: you can't), we also get "a practical guide to the spiritual side of life."[48] Personal "healing" and self-actualization have become, in Oprah's world, the true path to power.

Her effort to fill the spiritual void in many people's lives has not come without criticism, with some ridiculing her as "Deepak Oprah."[49] But the main critique of the Oprah empire has been its relentless emphasis on individualism: self-improvement, self-help, private solutions to public problems. In the age of George W. Bush, when no amount of public activism was going to change his devotion to dismantling every institution he could, from the FDA (Food and Drug Administration) to the EPA (Environmental Protection Agency) to affirmative action and antipoverty programs, Oprah's own giveaways and the volunteer and charitable efforts she encouraged in others made sense. For example, in February 2003 Oprah made an African American woman named Fannie, who had raised her dead sister's three kids as if they were her own, "Princess for a Day," buying her a much-needed new car and providing maid service for a year. In April 2008, when Oprah learned that Fannie's home in New Orleans, which had been devastated by Hurricane Katrina, still had not been reconstructed, she arranged for a private builder to expedite the work while Fannie and her family stayed in a Hilton. Since we all know how catastrophically the Bush administration had bungled the entire Katrina disaster, at least Oprah was reminding people that New Orleans was *still* a disaster and urged people "not to forget." Indeed, some researchers have found that watching shows like *Oprah*, which often focuses on family and child welfare issues, increases people's support for government programs like national day care, greater funding for education, and universal health care.[50] But exactly what were people supposed to do? And what about all the other poor black folks, Fannie's neighbors, whose homes were still piles of rubble? And did making Fannie "Princess for a Day" turn her into an object of white women's pity, and let the rest of us off the hook from rallying for anything more systemic?

Leaving aside whatever shrewd commercial calculations went into it, there is little doubt that Oprah is genuinely committed to improving women's lives. But advancing personal empowerment is hardly the same thing as advancing a feminist political agenda.[51] "Change Your Life Television" involved a de-emphasis on political issues and the showcasing of Oprah's individual generosity and people's "inner revolutions." The exhortation to "do something" and to achieve your own dreams requires consumer goods—fancy leather-bound journals for chronicling your dreams, the right chair or chenille throw for the most satisfying reading, the right food, clothes, or cosmetics to energize yourself.[52] The persistent structural inequalities that keep millions of women, and particularly African American girls and women, trapped in crappy jobs, deteriorating neighborhoods, and unhealthy environments typically can't be overcome simply by pulling up your bootstraps or finding your spiritual center. And Oprah's own rags-to-riches story, always cast as the result of enormous personal drive and talent, further dramatizes that with individual will, anyone can make it, which we know is not necessarily true.[53]

Oprah personifies the massive contradictions—and illusions—that run through how women are portrayed in the media. On the one hand she embodies embedded feminism as the richest woman in the entertainment industry, who renders such success for women a given and seeks to use her power to provide role models for other women. On the other hand, she is an entertainer, and what she produces—her show, her magazine—must sell products or they will fail. Thus, the empowerment fantasies on offer are personal, not collective, they are about "me," not about making things better for all girls and women. In fact, if I come to feel, like, really empowered, having written in my journal while drinking herb tea after having done my yoga, wouldn't I be so at peace, so blissed out, that I'd be completely happy with exactly the way things are?[54] All of this erases the need for continued feminist politics. The Oprah dynasty affirms—indeed, demands—that women turn within and improve themselves instead of turning outward and storming the barricades. Women's

advancement is a solitary, narcissistic process, not a mass, cooperative one.

So within the various places where we see media images of African
American women, the contradictions, the mixed messages are everywhere. The gulf between Oprah's insistence that women, especially black
women, can achieve anything, and Nelly's reduction of black women to
eager, rutting pornographic strippers in "Tip Drill" is as big as the
Andromeda Galaxy and just as tough to get across. Meanwhile, with too
few exceptions, accomplished black women are invisible or tokens in TV
dramas and film, and working-class and poor women of color of all
races and ethnicities—who really could use more kick-butt advocates
in Washington, D.C.—are simply absent.

But let's turn back to Dr. Bailey on *Grey's Anatomy*, and the pleasures
and perils of sass. By the show's fourth season, she is the mother of a
toddler, and her husband, Tucker (Cress Williams), stays home to take
care of the child while she works her incredibly long and demanding
hours. Tucker is getting resentful. When we see them at their home in
the morning, he is shown folding laundry, driving home how emasculated he has become. But they agree to have lunch that day so they can
talk. Not only does an emergency surgery come up, it also is an operation Bailey has to perform on a white supremacist who has a swastika
tattooed on his belly, and who won't let Bailey operate unless a white
man is also present to make sure, as Bailey puts it, "that I don't kill his
crazy white behind." Complications ensue, and she is later and later for
her lunch date until finally her exasperated husband leaves. How's that
for a choice: save the life of a neo-Nazi (showing that black women can
do this and rise above racism) versus saving your marriage (showing a
black man that he really matters).

Things get worse in the next episode when Tucker has to rush their son
to the hospital because the boy managed to get into Bailey's office, where
a bookshelf fell on him, breaking various ribs and rupturing internal
organs. It was, Tucker suggests, all "those medical books" that injured
him, and he also implies that Bailey left the baby gate to the office open;
worse, Tucker charges, the child went in there because "he went lookin' for

his mama and wound up in the hospital." This was right out of 1940s and 1950s melodramas when working mothers were always punished with dead, injured, or ungrateful children who had been neglected because of mom's job. At the end of the episode the child is fine, but Tucker has moved out.

On the one hand, it was great to have Bailey further humanized, especially as a deeply devoted mother. On the other hand, why did it take something as massive as the tragedy of her child nearly dying to "feminize" her? Why is Bailey the only woman on the show who doesn't get to be sexy and sought after? And why did her husband have to come off as castrated by his strong, accomplished wife? Why the need to punish her and strip her of love? If you're strong and "sassy," must you automatically be by yourself, the lone matriarch yet again? And while white women like me will always be crazy about (and fantasize about being) women like Wanda Sykes, we also have to appreciate what "sassy" withholds. As Sykes herself told *Ms.*, "Just don't call me 'sassy.' That bothers me when they call me that. It's like there is no substance or nothing to say. I am out there saying something, you know what I mean?"[55] The truth-speaking, talk-to-the-hand persona may feel wonderfully liberating to many of us, but it is also an archetype that trivializes black women and all that they can be. Worse, we also see how the sassy woman—maybe too outspoken, maybe too big for her britches—evokes the insistence that she be put in her place.

And, indeed, the overweight, jive-talkin', verbally aggressive black matriarch is commonly someone to laugh at, not to laugh with. Her power is way scary, ridiculous, and played for laughs—by men. In Martin Lawrence's *Big Momma's House* movies (we've had #1 in 2000, and #2 in 2006, with #3 on the way), he is an FBI agent who goes undercover as the elephantine, boogalooing, smack-talkin' "Big Momma" who kicks white guys in the nuts, whacks them upside the head, and succumbs to numerous pratfalls that make fun of her obesity, her clumsiness, and her asexuality. Big Momma competes with Tyler Perry's Madea in *Madea's Class Reunion* (2003), *Diary of an Angry Black Woman* (2005), *Madea's Family Reunion* (2006), and *Madea Goes to Jail* (2009), the last of which instantly grossed over $75 million.[56] She, too, is brawny (one character calls her "Jemima the Hutt"), hurls warnings and insults like switchblades, and has "an anger management problem," as evidenced by her tendency to pull out a gun and shoot it when she's pissed off. She is not a fantasy for me, like Sykes and Bailey. She's a buffoon, a joke, and a warning about black women—especially older black women—having power.

So while the success of Wanda Sykes, Queen Latifah, and Oprah Winfrey may let us pretend that we don't need to take on the burdens of feminist political struggle because, whoa, we can just make patriarchy like talk to the hand, Big Momma and Madea are bracing reminders of how little power, in actuality, black women still have. Hell, they're more likely to be represented by black men than by their own damn selves! This is the chimera of power and the squelching of power, dancing together, twins, still, after all these years, in the darkness.

6

SEX "R" US

"Can you unbutton the top button of those jeans and push them down?" instructs the unseen horny male pervert behind the camera. The nervous young woman in the TV ad is poised to oblige. In a companion ad, a young girl appears to be auditioning for a triple-X-rated film; the off-camera degenerate tells her not to be nervous as she slowly unbuttons her dress. In yet another, the leering voice urges a young man with a blond pompadour to tear off his shirt, saying, "You got a real nice look. How old are you? Are you strong? You think you could rip that shirt off of you? That's a real nice body. You work out? I can tell."[1] Speaking for much of the nation, one reporter observed that these commercials looked like "runaway kids coaxed from bus stations by exploitative adults."[2]

When right-wing conservative religious groups and liberal feminists find themselves spooning in ideological bed together, chances are that it is about one thing: sex. And that was the case when Calvin Klein—who in 1980 gave us fifteen-year-old Brooke Shields purring, "Nothing comes between me and my Calvins"—released a series of print and TV ads in August 1995 uniformly denounced as bordering on kiddie porn. The soft-core ads in magazines like *YM* and *Mademoiselle* featured slim, white, mostly blond pubescent models in various stages of undress, their hands in their jean pockets or hooked over the waistband to enable them to pull the jeans down even lower. They looked directly and provocatively into the camera. The TV ads described above and showcased on MTV made people especially crazed because they looked like D-level stag films from the 1960s. (Inquiring minds can see the ads on YouTube.)

Outrage roiled from the conservative American Family Association and the Catholic League to women heading rape crisis centers, as critics ventured that maybe this pedophilia marketing strategy was a bit too debased, even for American advertising. Klein quickly yanked the campaign and within two weeks the Justice Department had launched an investigation into whether his use of underage models violated child pornography laws. Undaunted, Klein still slapped giant photos of young men—but this time in their early twenties—wearing nothing but bulging briefs and hair gel on the billboards of Times Square. In 1999, to promote Calvin underwear for children (what happened to underpants by Carter with dinosaurs on them?), he launched another campaign featuring high-definition black-and-white photos of boys who appeared to be around four, and girls who appeared to be between four and seven, jumping on a sofa in nothing but their Calvins. This time the ads were pulled within twenty-four hours.

Despite the controversy surrounding the Klein campaigns, they were a harbinger of two trends that gained considerable steam in the late-1990s: the rampant return to the often degrading sexual objectification of women, and the increasing sexualization of children, especially girls. Books with titles like *Striptease Culture, Pornified, So Sexy So Soon,* and *The Lolita Effect* have documented the mainstreaming of pornography and its lopsided negative effects on females.[3] Here's what our increasingly pornified media have been telling girls and women: dress like a streetwalker but just say no—or dress like Carrie Bradshaw (what *were* some of those outfits?!) and just say yes. Old-fashioned American prudery has always been an important component of keeping women in their place. So has pornography. A culture that is prudish *and* pornographic—how's that for a contradiction to navigate?[4]

The pornification continued to expand and to move down the age chain. The Bratz dolls, launched in 2001, with their Sunset Strip hooker outfits, make Barbie look like a priss (although a very stacked priss); the selling of thongs that read "eye candy" to seven-year-olds; the transformation of Britney Spears from teen pop star to midriff-baring, breast-implanted hootchie mama; the promotion of pole dancing as a great new exercise regimen for women; "Little Diva" makeover parties for girls as young as five—well, even those of us who truly believe that sex is and should be a healthy, normal, pleasurable part of life started getting very uneasy.

As a result, a new female icon began to take center stage: the sexpert. Think *Cosmo*, Carrie Bradshaw, Monica Lewinsky. The sexpert knows a lot about sex, is comfortable with sex, initiates and enjoys sex on an equal footing with men, and talks a lot about sex with her girlfriends. The fantasy was that because of feminism and girl power, there was a new "sex positive" environment for women, and the double standard had been completely eliminated. The reality, of course, was different: this liberation came at a price. In exchange for this freedom—indeed, because of this freedom—young women were supposed to dress like call girls and had to start learning how to do this at an ever younger age. The sexpert persona came, in part, from the desires of young women for sexual freedom and equality, to enjoy sex without condemnation, and to have their sexuality seen as healthy and normal. But this *is* America, where there is little that can't be repackaged and sold back to us for a profit.

Here's the twist that emerged. Some young women wanted sexual equity with men: that's a claim for equal power. They didn't want to be mere sex objects, they wanted to be active sexual agents. But while true and total sexual equality between men and women is still too threatening, it has nonetheless proved lucrative to flatter women that they have it. So the media began to highlight this message: it's through sex and sexual display that women really have the power to get what they want. And because the true path to power comes from being an object of desire, girls and women should now actively choose—even celebrate and embrace—being sex objects. That's the mark of a truly confident, can-do girl: one whose objectification isn't imposed from without, but comes from within.[5] You have to admit, this is a very slick contortion.

The best way to gain this kind of power is to cater to what men want. And you're not acquiescing to men or to patriarchal sexual requirements:

by submitting, you're in the driver's seat! Thus, in the hands of, say, *Cosmo*, the sexpert appreciates the ultimate requirement to please *him* (even at her expense or discomfort if necessary), to reassure *him* about *his* performance, and to constantly monitor and refine her ability to look sexy and to do what *he* wants and needs. This persona of the sexpert is almost always white, young, heterosexual, slim, busty, beautiful, and middle- or upper-middle-class (i.e., the media's target demographic).[6] She is ideal for the age of enlightened sexism because she is a hybrid of empowerment *and* objectification. In this way, women's hopes for sexual equity have become wrapped up in glossy images that sold jeans, underwear, magazines, music videos, and TV shows and allowed Victoria's Secret to conquer the malls of America. And as the image and prevalence of the sexpert colonized more media outlets and hailed ever and ever younger girls, her image polarized women and men, especially along generational lines.

Take me—I was in my twenties and single in the 1970s, during the era that the movie *Boogie Nights* infamously brought to life. And I did believe, then and now, that sexual equality goes hand in hand, as it were, with political and economic equality. So I didn't want my daughter, when she came of age, to be confronting the double standard or to be told that she had to figure out how to look sexy and then "just say no." That said, I didn't feel it was necessary for her to be invited by the radio to sing along, at age fourteen, to Eamon's classy 2004 hit record "Fuck It, I Don't Want You Back," with the immortal lyrics "Fuck what I said, it don't mean shit now" and "Fuck you, you hoe." Ditto for Shaggy's "Wasn't Me," which urged her to "Picture this, we were both butt-naked banging on the bathroom floor." Or there was 50 Cent bragging metaphorically, "I got the magic stick," which evoked Lil' Kim's somewhat less allegorical response, "I got the magic clit." The Beatles' "Why Don't We Do It in the Road" suddenly seemed like an Osmond Brothers song.

Now, if you don't think that something really sick is going on in our country about girls—I mean really little girls—learning that their main asset is strutting their stuff, then you haven't watched TLC's abominable *Toddlers and Tiaras*, the behind-the-scenes reality TV show about beauty pageants for girls just out of (or maybe still in) diapers. With their spray-on tans, "flippers" (fake teeth inserted into the mouth to hide baby teeth gaps), fake eyelashes, and bare midriffs, these babies learn how to swivel their hips and push out their chests as they sashay before judges, including balding older white guys, as if they were Gypsy Rose Lee. Gross. How did we get here?

The prudery of the media, and television in particular, first began to melt under the heat of the sexual revolution, producing more risqué fare like *Dallas* and *Dynasty* in the late 1970s and 1980s, but it was in the 1990s that a much higher infusion of sex began to course through the media as advertisers zeroed in on the rising numbers of teenagers in the population. It was a simple commercial calculation: in their effort to imprint brand loyalty on this distinct, edgy, rebellious generation, the advertisers figured, not incorrectly, that sex sells, especially to adolescents. They were also tapping into the "girl power" moment and using it to sell as well. So for some of us, the issue wasn't that young women wanted to be sexual agents in their own right. It was that an increasing number of corporations were seeking to profit from this desire to their own ends.

The news media, and especially the bottom-feeder tabloids, expressed outrage over the trend and yet, not surprisingly, used it to sell their own magazines and TV shows. Just a year and a half after Klein's peepshow ads wheedled young girls to "give me a smile" or slavered, "I like the way those jeans fit," the country woke up to a lurid post-Christmas crime. Six-year-old JonBenet Ramsey—1996's American Royale Miss and 1995's Little Miss Colorado, was found dead, having been sexually assaulted and strangled. Her parents had reportedly put her to bed after a day of opening presents and awoke on December 26, 1996, to find her missing and a ransom note demanding $118,000. Hours later they found her body in the basement. In short order the parents came under suspicion but were not charged; the crime has never been solved.

The television and cable networks, magazines, and tabloids went on a JonBenet bender. And what riveted the country was the endless video loop of this tiny girl in various very, very grown-up outfits at her various pageants—a gold-star-appliquéd, white satin Vegas showgirl leotard with a feathered train showcasing her legs, a black-and-white striped satin cocktail dress with a huge, Amazonian feathered headpiece and her hands assertively on her hips—singing and dancing in a very alluring way. In one clip we saw her modeling a sailor suit to music, during which she stripped off a jacket to reveal a backless dress.[7] She was fully sexualized, her blond hair done up like one of Dolly Parton's wigs, her face heavily and meticulously made up with bright red lipstick, her butt shaking back and forth in her satin pink cowgirl outfit. We saw her posing provocatively for the judges in her black or silver pumps, one knee bent in front of the other as she held up the flouncy trim of her skirt. These same images, as still photos, were plastered all over the tabloids. Here was an aping of adult female sexuality as staged in floorshows that seemed, at once, a parody and a tragedy.

The case exposed the thriving subculture of beauty pageants for little girls and raised questions about the judgment and motives of parents who encouraged their daughters to parade their little bodies around as a competitive activity. *Newsweek* cited executives from modeling agencies who asserted flat-out, "You do not put lipstick on your 6-year-old," and quoted child psychologists who denounced the emphasis on looking good and pleasing others as unhealthy for girls. The contestants, the magazine observed, were "child-women in boas and high heels" and the pageant world was "seemingly oblivious to advances in feminism that have brought women into Little League, military academies and the Supreme Court" and instead emphasized "the timeless art of catching men's eyes."[8] What might have seemed like a "fairy tale" life for a little girl, being pampered and envied for her beauty, now seemed perverse, however fleetingly. Because whatever outrage there was, it didn't leave lasting footprints; on the contrary, even more thongs and midriff-baring halter tops seemed to flood the size 3-to-6X shelves of Kmart.

Abercrombie & Fitch, not to be outdone by Calvin Klein, and in fact relying on his photographers, launched its *A&F Quarterly* in 1997, a catalog in the form of a glossy magazine that promoted a lifestyle of Caucasian group sex, going down on your date at the movies, and mastering alcohol drink recipes like "Brain Hemorrhage." Denunciations ensued, especially since the "magalog" was pitched as much to the under-eighteen set as it was to their older brothers and sisters. A partial list of those who lined up against the *Quarterly* included Mothers Against Drunk Driving, the attorney general of Michigan, the lieutenant governor of Illinois, the National Organization for Women, and the Concerned Christians of America. Right-wingers saw all this sex undermining "family values," and feminists saw it as objectifying women and exploiting girls, at a time when Americans were confronting the AIDS epidemic and the spread of sexually transmitted diseases, and when the United States also had the highest teen pregnancy rate of any industrialized nation.

Many women, and especially young women, in the age of girl power, were tired of having their sexuality seen as something dangerous or shameful, something they had to deny or censor. Feminists who expressed concerns about new pornification of women's bodies were dismissed as hating sex, but their real concern was that reducing women to their sexuality undermines their march toward full equality. Were women supposed to revert back to the 1950s and try their best to look and sound like Jayne Mansfield while men controlled the reins of power? Or were they to take their cues from Madonna's music videos and embrace a sex-positive stance?

As Carrie Bradshaw might have asked herself as she typed into her laptop (if she had indeed asked slightly more broad-scale questions), was this new heightened sexuality in the media good for women, or bad? Confounding the controversy further was how far down the age chain all this was moving: Did we really want five-year-old girls trying to be sexy? Who were they being sexy for? If the answer was (a) Uncle Bob; (b) the twelve-year-old boys around the corner; or (c) their priest, you could see why people—especially parents—were having conniption fits. And yet the conniption fits didn't matter. Not one bit.

"99 SEX FACTS YOU'VE NEVER HEARD BEFORE!" (Right. That's if you missed the last issue.) "Secrets of Male Arousal: A Surprising Trigger to His Deepest Sexual Cravings." "Be a SEX GENIUS!" "Little Mouth Moves That Make Sex Hotter." "Orgasms Unlimited." "Touch Him *There!*" By now you know where we are: the red hot and/or shocking pink pages of *Cosmopolitan*, the magazine for the "Fun, Fearless Female." Ever since Helen Gurley Brown transformed it in 1965 from a quasi-cultural and literary magazine into one where, as the *Harvard Lampoon*'s 1972 parody put it, you could learn how to decorate your uterine walls, *Cosmo* has been the pioneer in addressing young women as confident and obliging sexperts. In the 1970s, college women were more likely to read *Glamour* or *Mademoiselle*, as both magazines, and *Glamour* in particular, intermixed features like "How to Get a Better Butt Fast" and "The Art of the Pedicure" with articles about how to advance in your career and change a tire, and updates on congressional legislation of interest to women. (Yes, really.) Many also felt that being a "Cosmo Girl"—one whose main goals were to be hyperfeminine and to please men—was a bit too stereotypical and downmarket.

But with the rise of enlightened sexism, things began to shift. In 1997 a new editor, Bonnie Fuller, took over from Brown and replaced the "Cosmo Girl" moniker with the new "Fun, Fearless Female" label. Fuller slashed or dumped coverage of travel, food, and pets and ramped up coverage of beauty and fashion and put a Bunsen burner under the sexual content. She replaced the anonymous cover girls in plunging necklines with celebrities in plunging necklines. Within a year ad revenue was up more than 20 percent, newsstand sales were up 16.5 percent, and monthly circulation had surged to 2.7 million.[9] After only eighteen months at *Cosmo*, Fuller would move to *Glamour* and *Cosmo*-fy it, virtually eliminating the feminist sympathies that *Glamour*'s longtime editor Ruth Whitney had, for decades, sandwiched between bra ads and exercise regimens. Fuller's successor at *Cosmo*, Kate White, has made even Fuller seem like a prude.

A tour of *Cosmo* covers from 1992, "The Year of the Woman," to the present, shows how much more explicit the sex has become, even in this journalistic red light precinct. Here are some sample wimpy PG-rated cover lines from 1992: "How to Make Him Like You as Much as You Like Him"; "How to Get Over a Bad Love Affair"; "How to Survive Being Dumped"; "10 Ways to Recover Your Energy When You're Oh So Tired."[10] These read like a Girl Scout manual by today's standards. Other articles even covered political and workplace issues: "Cosmo Girls Describe the Shock of Date Rape"; "The Lady is a Pol . . . Politics' Top Women Reveal How to *Win*"; "Ten Tips for Getting Along with Coworkers"; and two you would never, ever see in today's *Cosmo*, "Volunteerism—What You Gain by Giving" and, get this, "Who's Afraid of Verdi and Puccini? Not You!," a primer about the joys of opera.[11]

Five years later, when Fuller took over and further tarted it up, we began to see a shift (and an obsession with underlining): "More Foreplay Please! Men Dish Details on What They'd Love to Do to You"; "Make Him Beg for It! How to Fire Up His Desire in Bed"; "What Makes a Woman Bedable? Men Let You in on the Surprising Things That Make Them Lust After You" (where you could "find out if you have the secret sex appeal that makes men melt"). Still, in 1997, there were none of the sex manual illustrations one has come to expect today. And the contradictions between pleasing men and being politically and economically empowered riddled the magazine. "So Mad You Feel Like Writing Congress? Here's How" and "How to Kick Butt When You're the New Kid. Master the Maze of Your New Office's Politics" sidled right next to "Big Butt Be Gone—The Fastest Way That Works" and "His Point of View: Why Men Really Do Prefer Nice Girls." In "How Different Are Men from Women?" we were told "Not at all,"[12] which is not quite the publication's point of view today.

By 2002, the jam-packed covers screamed "Blow His Mind! Lock the Doors, Dim the Lights, and Try This Naughty 'Number' Tonight"; "Turn-On Tricks; How to Make Him Ache for You All Day Long"; "His Pleasure: Here Are Four, Yes, Four, Levels of Male Bliss. Here's How to Take Your Guy Through the Roof"; "#*&@! And Other Stuff He Wishes You'd Say in Bed"; "Sex Survey; 7000+ Guys Spill: The Special Kiss They Crave; The Spot They Wish You'd Find; The Move You Should Lose Pronto"; and "40 Sex Secrets of Women Who Are Great in the Sack."[13] Within ten years, and with the turn of the millennium, Cosmo had gone from "Zonked? Restoring Your Will to Get Out and Meet Men Again" to "Dirty Sexy Sex" and "67 New Sex Tricks Including the Tongue Swirl That Will Push Him Over the Edge." Older sections or articles on work or politics were replaced with the sections "Man Manual," "Love and Lust," and "You, You, You." Narcissism is, like, way cooler than politics.

Cosmo, like most women's magazines, has the insistent "Hey you! Yeah you, girl" direct mode of address, and the flattering initial salutation is to a confident "girl in the know" who wants to do "whatever you damn well please."[14] She takes men as sex objects (the monthly "Guy Without His

Shirt" eye candy). She is the sexpert par excellence, whose main capital in the marketplace of relationships is her shapely, well made up, and femininely dressed body, her sexual knowledge, and her sexual skills.[15] She must juggle all this, however, with not being remotely threatening to men. As "How to Be a Superhottie" advised, "Although a cool-chick vibe will reel in a man, it's your softer side that'll hook him."[16] There are two voices in *Cosmo*, the savvy female one who knows all about how to please him, and the voices of allegedly "real guys" who also provide the inside skinny on "his point of view" and tell you how to behave.

So what do these voices say are the sexpert's main duties? What is she like and what *should* she be like? Certainly there are the monthly Kama Sutra articles with titles like "Your Orgasm Guaranteed" in which women are actually urged to "Be Selfish" and not to be so obsessed about the guy's pleasure. But three pages later will be "His Secret Sex Trigger" and two pages after that "Don't Forget to Do This in Bed," both primers on what "he wants."[17] Readers learn how to "Blow His Mind!," about "The Lingerie Looks He Loves," "The Sex He Craves," how to "Touch Him There!," "His Secret Pleasure Zone," and "What Makes Sex Exciting for Him."

Advice here? One is struck by how much sex must always be a calculated pose, a performance, while looking utterly spontaneous. The advice is also often wildly contradictory. In one issue we're told, "Ambush him when he gets home" and yet, from one of the "real guys" we hear, "I hate when girls try way too hard to be sexy." "Giggle—sexily" offers one column, while in "Guys Speak Out" we learn, "Excessive giggling on dates tends to annoy me." (The weirdest sex advice was to look over your shoulder at your guy "during doggie-style," which I believe might require the neck turning radius of Linda Blair in *The Exorcist*.) My totally favorite part of the sex tip articles aren't the illustrations of the positions (we had posters of those in 1969), but the advice by so-and-so "Ph.D." who has typically written a book titled something like *How to Dress Like a Whore and Screw Like an Angel*. (Note to self: next book project!) *Cosmo* is filled with these Ph.D.s—I'm clearly moving in the wrong academic circles as I've never met anyone who has written *Naughty Tricks and Sexy Tips* (Pam Spurr— great name!—Ph.D.) or *Touch Me There!* (Yvonne K. Fulbright, Ph.D.).

A range of other less "fearless" instructions repeatedly jump off the pages of *Cosmo*, however. Women are relentlessly posited to be really annoying nags. In "4 Reasons He's Not Talking," the first bullet point asks, "Is it something you did?" and then immediately answers, "Maybe." What might that be? "You undermined him" in front of others by "bust[ing] his balls" in public and "singeing his manhood." Or, you just talk too much, "harping" and "yammering" about "dumb stuff" the guy is "not interested in talking about."[18] *Cosmo* teaches you "how to rein in your bitch reflex with your guy" and warns about veering into "nag territory." Pissed about something he did? "Before you lay into him about what he did wrong, point out something he's done right."[19] Advice from guys themselves? "Ask me to do something for you and you'll remind me that I'm a man. On the other hand, tell me how to do something and you'll remind me of my mother."[20] Another guy's pet peeve? "She nags me to eat healthy."[21] Tiptoe, girls, tiptoe.

While men are still the boss and must be pleased and placated, their egos are as fragile as snowflakes. In the July 2007 issue, for example, "men like to feel needed and valued, and women who have endured hardships bring out their protective natures." About a dozen pages later, in case you've forgotten already, "Guy Spy" reminds you that "men crave feeling needed." You must also "acknowledge his physical assets" so "he'll feel like a stud."[22] In this world men are as uncomplicated as a butcher block. "Beer. Naked babes. A big-screen TV. One of the great things about guys is that they're pretty uncomplicated creatures." Yet two paragraphs later we learn that when it comes to relationships with women, men are so unfathomable that only *Cosmo* can "help you comprehend the male mind."[23]

Conforming to the Barbie aesthetic of femininity and walking the razor-thin line between sexy and slutty is also essential. "50 Things Guys Wish You Knew" embodies the complete tutorial. Lesson #34: "Close-cropped hair. Cut upper-arm muscles. Stubble on your legs. Some women can get away with these attributes, but most of the time they remind me of a guy's body. So if I see them on a girl, I'm completely turned off." Lesson #37: "I'm totally in favor of you wearing skimpy clothes when we're out with my pals. Reveal enough to make them want you but not so much that they assume they can easily have you." (Ugh—quasi-pimping here?) Lesson #46: "Just because I occasionally look at other women in your presence doesn't mean I don't love you or don't find you hot. It just means there's someone wearing an outfit more revealing than yours is."[24] In an especially creepy installment of "*Cosmo* for Your Guy," men were instructed to "throw her on the bed, and pin down her arms as you get on top of her." Date rape, anyone?

So wait, what if you have the most successful magazine for young single women and it's filled with scantily clad women (and men) and advice about sex? Isn't that what *men* like? It turns out that *Cosmo* editors had learned that there were men (boyfriends, husbands) sneaking peaks at the magazine and that a new genre of publication, the "lad magazine," was doing very well in Great Britain. *Maxim*, originally launched in Britain in 1995, came across the Atlantic in April 1997, boasting it was "The Best Thing to Happen to Men Since Women." *Maxim* quickly became the mother ship of enlightened sexism. (The inaugural issue celebrated the "guy lifestyle" of beer, babes, and sports and proclaimed, "Leave that toilet seat up proudly!")[25] Its covers and inner pages showcase barely clad starlets and celebrities in *Playboy* poses (legs spread, cleavage leaning into the camera) with abject, slavering commentary like "she set our hearts racing" or she "keeps looking for ways to make us forget about her swimsuit-model body—and keeps failing." In 1999 it began issuing its annual "Hot 100," "The Ultimate List of the World's Most Beautiful Women." By 2002, *Maxim*'s circulation had soared to over 2.5 million, and by 2006 it was beating out *Glamour*, *Seventeen*, and *Redbook* (but not *Cosmo*).

So here's the thing about *Maxim*. It shamelessly objectifies women and reduces them to their body parts (their breasts in particular) and, as a result, has been the subject of a host of protests and criticisms. ("Finding the Inner Swine," quipped *Newsweek* and added, "you think the feminist movement never happened.")[26] *Maxim* got away with not seeming pornographic because there were *some* clothes on the women (since its inception it has had a "no nipple rule").[27] And talk about using irony as a shield! As its first woman-as-inoculation editor put it, "It's not about pictures of girls. . . . It's about the stance."[28] The irreverent, frat boy, "harmless fun" tone insists that men are slaves to their gonads and live to ogle women in string bikinis not because they're sexist but because they can't help themselves since women—well, young, slim, busty, mostly white, gorgeous women—have all the power anyway. This is *Jackass* country: men are not invincible like James Bond and they know there's a new gender regime out there.[29] Thus *Maxim* and other lad magazines deflect charges of sexism: they know sexism is stupid and retro, so why would they be sexist? Only some clueless old maid who only looks at the covers and doesn't get the jokes would think that.[30]

Maxim's "stance" is that it worships beautiful women and that its readers are often inferior to them: less cool, lazier, not as smart, dorkier, and very possibly not as good in bed. "Sexy, Funny, Smarter Than Us" proclaims one headline about its cover girl. In an April 2000 feature, "Fun with Women," one tip suggested taking your date skeet shooting but warned, "Because this game is about hand-eye coordination—not strength—it's quite possible your girlfriend will whip your ass." At the same time, women are stereotyped as "enjoying things that will bore you to tears—antiquing, winetasting, anything vaguely involving Gwyneth Paltrow," and, unlike *Cosmo*, the magazine features articles about "guy" topics like new techie devices, cars, sports, and travel.[31] Older women are repellent: a tip advising men to take a date to an art auction concludes, "You can always use the bidder's paddle to fan away the perfume of the old biddies next to you"; a feature on the fun of drive-in movies shows an image of Bette Midler on the screen with the caption, "A leading cause of car sickness."[32]

Maxim is *Mad* magazine with babes; as such, it is often very funny. Its 2000 countdown of the "30 Worst Albums of All Time" featured Vanilla Ice's *Hard to Swallow* with the quip, "Rarely do you come across an album quite so aptly titled." Yanni and John Tesh's *The Endless Dream* evoked, "We at *Maxim* don't throw the phrase 'worse than Hitler' around lightly. . . . But really, the twin pestilences of Yanni and Tesh infecting the same album?"[33] *Maxim* also parodies the very things that make it successful, like its subtitle for its new products feature "Stuff"—"Fill Your Inner Emptiness with Material Goods."[34]

But it is this "it's all a joke" veneer that gives enlightened sexism such a protected perch. In a piece dumping on Philadelphia as a "glorified [bathroom] break" between New York and Washington, the editors quip, "The only things that make Philly worthwhile—cheesesteaks and wasted Penn girls."[35] (Again, date rape anyone?) A 2008 article about having sex with coworkers was illustrated with a model wearing a black bustier, garter belt, and stockings—is this how men are to imagine their female colleagues?—and claimed, without accompanying data, that "wary male bosses are rarely the aggressors anymore . . . more women are now taking the lead." Indeed, "Female bosses aren't afraid to move on underlings, either. 'I screwed one of my interns,' confesses Margo, a 31-year-old head recruiter. 'I loved that he was intimidated by me because it meant I had control in bed.'"[36] Here sexual harassment is turned upside down and its continued disproportionate impact on women negated.

For its part, *Maxim* itself has been heavily staffed with women over the years (some imported from *Cosmo*), who claim that with the sex and relationship advice, "*Maxim* makes better boyfriends. It makes better husbands."[37] Perhaps. But in its aggressive reclamation of an allegedly immutable beer- and libido-driven masculinity, and its view that women fall into two categories, "hotties" and worthless, *Maxim* resuscitates the mantras feminists skewered nearly forty years ago: that women's only value comes from their sex appeal, that women are rarely fully fledged people but things to be used by men for their sexual pleasure, and that there is only one narrow standard for sexiness, the size zero D-cup starlet. Not all the self-denigrating jokes about fetid jockstraps, making "that sound" with your hand under your armpit, or snarky articles about "the world's suckiest sportscasters" changes that.

Television, too, witnessed a revolution in the depiction of sexually suggestive and even explicit material, which helped pave the way for the sexpert. In 1975, in response to concerns about too much crime, violence, and sex in prime-time television, the networks agreed to a "family viewing hour" from 8:00 to 9:00, which would be restricted to programming acceptable to all family members, including smaller children. It didn't last long. The Hollywood creative community felt the "family viewing hour" violated its First Amendment rights and sued. In some cases ratings suffered when shows were moved to a later time slot, and the courts ruled in 1976 that the FCC (Federal Communications Commission) had not followed the proper procedures in implementing the policy. Nonetheless, the networks continued in the late 1970s and much of the 1980s to embrace the idea in practice and aired shows like *The*

Cosby Show, Who's the Boss?, and *Highway to Heaven* between 8:00 and 9:00. On most shows sex was portrayed through innuendo.[38]

Then came the competition, first from Fox, then from the other net-lets, as well as from all those movies on cable, and from the home video and DVD market. If the networks wanted to hook viewers—especially young viewers—into the lead-in 8:00 prime-time slot, and *Beverly Hills 90210* or *Melrose Place* or *Martin* were roping them in at Fox, well, they had a business to run. In September 1995, for example, one of my favorite shows, *Cybill*—with the sardonic Maryann (the fantabulous Christine Baranski), who drank as much as Boris Yeltsin, spent her time shopping and ogling the buns of young men, and lived to wreak vengeance on her rich ex-husband Dr. Dick—moved from its 9:30 time slot to 8:00, and I had to stop tuning in. Nor could I watch *Friends*, easily one of the best sitcoms ever, in its early years, or *Mad About You* after July 1993 when it moved from 9:30 to 8:00. Now, I am not a prude. (I sound like Richard Nixon: "I am not a crook!") But I had to stop watching all this because I didn't think my daughter, then six, was quite ready for references to hookers, masturbation, and intercourse and I wasn't quite ready to explain to a first grader what those meant. (Hello, Nick at Nite.) I was uneasy about the onslaught of all the R-rated fare, and also about the greater negative implications for girls.

I wasn't alone in my uneasiness. As *The Hollywood Reporter* announced in 1995, "with programmers chasing the 18–49 demographic, parents and kids are at a loss as to what to watch."[39] There was, as researchers have put it, "an explosion of televised sexual content" on broadcast and cable TV, and thus television began to overexaggerate the centrality of sex to everyday life.[40] (Indeed, heavy viewers of soap operas tend to overestimate how often real-life people have sex.)[41] The sexual content of prime-time shows—both scenes and references—increased from 43 percent in 1976 to 75 percent in 1996.[42] By 2005, 77 percent of prime-time shows contained sexual content. (I don't know how things are in your house, but 77 percent of the "content" in my home concerns things like who fed the dog and whether the electric bill got paid.) A lot of this is merely talk about sex, but when eight-year-olds understand that a sitcom reference to whipped cream means a guy intends to squirt it all over his wife and then lick it off, we can understand parental concern.[43]

In the 1999–2000 season, almost half of the characters who became sexually involved with each other had either just met (this would be *Melrose Place* territory) or had no romantic relationship.[44] So it's not just talk; the number of sex scenes per hour nearly doubled between 1998 and 2005. And it's been shows like *Dawson's Creek—90210* set in a Massachusetts swamp in which parents humped on the living room coffee table and a high schooler was seen kissing a female teacher twice his age, all in just the first episode—that further cemented the marriage between teen audiences and sexual fare. According to the Kaiser Family Foundation, among the twenty most-watched shows by teens in 2005, 70 percent included some kind of sexual content and 45 percent included sexual behavior. The number of sex scenes per hour in top teen shows was 6.7, even higher than overall prime time, which showed 5.9 sex scenes an hour. While many young people couldn't wait to tune in, their parents were looking for the V-Chip—which was worthless since only their kids knew how to program the damn thing. Some didn't think their kids should be having sex before their braces came off.

But it's the way girls and women get depicted when sex becomes so foregrounded that is of concern, and not without reason: there's evidence that watching such shows encourages gendered stereotypes about sex.[45] Whether it's through the jokes, insults, and innuendo of sitcoms or the semi-random bed-hopping and terminally dysfunctional relationships of nighttime soaps, TV serves up a menu of scripts that play a central role (especially in the fantasyland of "abstinence only" sex education) in shaping young people's understandings about sex. It's a gradual and cumulative process, and since young people still—despite Facebook and their cell phones—spend more time with TV than any other mass medium, what TV conveys about girls, women, and sex matters.[46]

So what have been the dominant scenarios? In the early 1990s, the template got laid down. Boys and men in the TV shows most popular with adolescents were sex-driven, "always ready and willing for sex anytime, anywhere." This meant that boys and men—they could be in third grade or they could be geezers—constantly made sexual comments assessing women's bodies, which was seen as totally fine, even funny. For example, in an episode of *Blossom*, an adolescent boy said of a teacher, "My algebra tutor is like a major babe." Then there were those Diet Pepsi ads in which, first, six-year-old boys playing soccer stopped dead in their tracks to ogle Cindy Crawford and comment on Pepsi's "new can." A few years later the male appreciating her hotness was a newborn in a maternity ward; never too zygotelike, never too ancient, to take the liberty of commenting on a woman's body. One of the guys on *90210*, anticipating meeting some young women, predicted, "These are going to be the most awesome girls we've ever seen. Girls with legs all the way to their necks." (Sounds like something unfortunate from a Salvador Dalí painting.) Sex was recreational, and often a competition, with the guys doing the scoring, the girls and women as prizes.[47] Another study found that in dramas like *Dawson's Creek* and *Party of Five* aimed at young people, even though girls were sexually active, just like the guys, things were more likely to end badly for the girls if they took the sexual initiative—humiliation, disappointment, rejection, and guilt.[48] But then—at this high-water mark of girl power—a premium cable show sought to twist these scripts like a pair of tighty whiteys.

Now how's this for a publicist's dream? You're about to launch an edgy new show with the unambiguous title *Sex and the City*. It's based on the love lives of four successful, beautiful, white, upper-middle-class heterosexual single women in New York who have active and often very uninhibited sex lives. The early episodes focus, in part, on blow jobs and threesomes: this is not *The Mary Tyler Moore Show*. In late January 1998, just five months before the show's debut, one of the most sensational sex scandals ever breaks: the president of the United States has been having an Oval Office sexcapade with a twenty-four-year-old intern, Monica Lewinsky. Bill Clinton denied having had "sexual relations with that woman" because reportedly they never had intercourse; primarily, she serviced him through oral sex. He reciprocated the favor with a cigar (even *Sex and the City* didn't go there). We learned that, sexually liberated young woman that she was, she made the initial moves on him by flashing him her thong; this was no passive victim, but a "fun, fearless female" right out of the pages of *Cosmo*.

We should not underestimate the impact of the Clinton–Lewinsky scandal, which brought oral sex to the nightly news and produced possibly the only best-selling special prosecutor's report the press had to publish with this advisory: "WARNING: The following report contains sexually explicit language." All throughout the winter, spring, and summer of 1998, references to multiple blow jobs (while he was negotiating deals on the phone, no less!), dirty phone sex, and the infamous semen-stained blue dress were everywhere: certainly on the "family hour" nightly news, on the front pages and covers of newspapers and magazines, blaring from the radio, on *Nightline* with Ted Koppel, on Sunday morning's *Face the Nation*, on talk shows and late night comedy shows. There were national debates about whether oral sex was "really" sex. (Clinton claimed the Bible, of all sources, said it wasn't! Fifteen-year-old boys around the nation have thanked him ever since.) Parents accustomed to watching *The Today Show* or *Good Morning America*, or listening to *Morning Edition* while eating breakfast and packing lunches, had to explain to third graders what the hoopla was all about.

Bob Schieffer, the courtly CBS reporter, noted that all of a sudden he was hearing female coworkers "using euphemisms that up to now were only whispered about in the ladies' room or out behind the barn somewhere." He added that they were openly using slang terms for sex acts that he had never heard before at work. The *New York Times* added that the news and all the subsequent Clinton jokes had suddenly made it acceptable to participate in "frank sex talk" at work.[49] As our fascinated neighbors to the north put it in the *Toronto Star*, "No detail is too sordid, no adjective too racy, and no whisper of gossip is too juicy to repeat about the allegations of a sexual affair between President Bill Clinton and former White House intern Monica Lewinsky. It seems the entire nation ... is talking about sex, hearing about sex, reading and/or writing about sex, and one imagines from all this, thinking constantly about sex."[50] (If Clinton's stiff penis could now be part of everyday discourse, why not Bob Dole's limp one? Just a year later, in 1999, Dole began hawking Viagra in TV ads.) By the time the premiere of *Sex and the City* aired on June 6, 1998, you could say that the way had been, well, paved. Was there an outcry when, in the first episode, we saw that Carrie (Sarah Jessica Parker) had just received oral sex from an old flame? Puleeze—how 1997.

What made *Sex and the City* so revolutionary was that it was a sex-positive show from a female perspective. And unlike *Melrose Place*, the women here who jumped from bed to bed were classy, not trashy. You simply would not apply the word "slut" to any of the main characters, including Samantha. Indeed, sex was an integral, taken-for-granted part of the upscale single woman's life, and not something instrumental she used to get back at former lovers, other women, or as part of a career advancement plan. This made millions of women—at least those that could afford HBO—sigh "thank you."

The show was narrated by Carrie's voice-over and captioned for us by the typings on her laptop as she worked on her weekly newspaper column. She met almost constantly with her three BFFs: Samantha, the libertine (Kim Cattrall); Charlotte (Kristin Davis), the "prude" who was, nonetheless, sexually active and labeled by Carrie a "Park Avenue Pollyanna"; and Miranda (Cynthia Nixon), the cynical, independent lawyer who enjoyed sex for its own sake and, as Carrie told us, had decided that "all men were assholes." Here we slipped into a girl-friendly world of shopping, parties, yoga classes, and leisurely dining out filled with very frank talk about sex, men, and relationships. While Carrie was meant to provide our main point of identification—she had the best boyfriends, was the friend all the others went to and trusted the most, and the stories were from her point of view—we could also try on Miranda, Samantha, and Charlotte for size, or occupy some imagined space between them. And we inhabited a female fantasy version of Manhattan—beautifully lit, no crime, no dangers to women of being out on a dark street at 3:00 A.M. trying to hail a cab, no STDs, no poverty, no people from Jersey in tacky warm-up suits (hey, I'm from Jersey; I know from Jersey)—where the women could afford to buy whatever they wanted and live in nice apartments, constantly ate out, and drank as many cosmopolitans as they could hold and never gained weight. Plus, despite their griping about the men in their lives (or lack thereof), they met cute ones by the battalions every week—at cemeteries, in elevators, at gyms, gallery openings, bars—who weren't gay or married. And the sex was almost always "amazing." My kind of town!

The first episode set up certain premises that were, at the same time, filled with truth and with gender stereotypes. Carrie tells us about the thousands of great single women in New York who travel, pay taxes, spend $400 on Manolo Blahniks, yet are alone. "Why are there so many great unmarried women and no great unmarried men?" Carrie asks. This was also Mars–Venus territory: women wanted love and marriage while attractive men would rather have their balls waxed than enter a monogamous relationship. In early episodes Carrie and "person on the street" types speak directly to the camera, and we meet "toxic bachelors" who say that women should forget about marriage, while other men observe that women in New York may complain about being single but they also refuse to give a chance to guys who are too fat, too short, too poor, or too nice.

But just when we think that all we'll get is the single-women-are-all-desperate-for-a-man bilge, or that men and women are so fundamentally different that commonalities are impossible, we then meet the women, who are debating whether women should give up on love and have sex just like men. The very last word you'd use to describe Samantha is desperate. "This is the first time in the history of Manhattan that women have had as much money and power as men," she asserts, so women can have the same luxury "of treating men like sex objects." Which they do, often. Samantha has zero interest in getting married, let alone having children. When Carrie goes out and has sex with an old flame, she thinks, "I just had sex like a man. . . . I felt powerful, potent, like I owned the city." In another episode, Samantha gives voice to the opinion that giving oral sex to men was empowering to women: "You may be on your knees but you've got them by the balls." In "The Fuck Buddy" (season two), Charlotte is shocked to learn that all three of the other women have a guy they can call solely for sex with no other attachments or commitments. Throughout the series, the women are active, assertive sexual agents and while they all meet men who disappoint them or break their hearts, they are not censured or punished for having sex "just like men."

Directly contradicting the frequent Mars–Venus assertions are sensitive, caring men who fall in love, want to get involved and commit, only to be rejected by the women, which actually happens in real life. Miranda dumps Skipper because he is too nice (as did every woman he met); Charlotte has to leave her husband, Trey, because he can't get it up; and Carrie can't commit to her cute, nice boyfriend Aidan (John Corbett) because he doesn't go out to the clubs or provide the sharp edges for Carrie to bounce off of, and file herself against, that Mr. Big (Chris Noth) did. Even the elusive, can't-commit Big finally comes around, realizing (although it takes him six years) that Carrie is "The One."

The women's conversations are also informed by feminist sensibilities. They denounce living in a culture that "promotes impossible standards of beauty" where even the gorgeous Charlotte hates her thighs. (And, as an added bonus, Samantha proclaims that she loves the way she looks.) They attend a baby shower that makes the isolation and intensive mothering of stay-at-home suburban motherhood look pretty lethal: one mother confesses to the camera that she now has an Internet lover while another admits, "Sometimes I climb into the kids' tree house, light up a joint, and listen to Peter Frampton." (I hear you, sister.) In the second season, at their regular Saturday breakfast, the conversation revolves around Carrie's ex, Big, the fact that Charlotte's current boyfriend is constantly grabbing his balls, and the puny, cornichon-sized penis of Samantha's current boyfriend. Miranda loses it. "How does it happen that four such smart women have nothing to talk about but boyfriends?" she demands. "It's like seventh grade with bank accounts. What about us? What we think, we feel, we know? Christ! Does it always have to be about them?"

We see the subtle sexism Miranda experiences at the hands of her mortgage officer when she buys her own apartment; he asks if the down payment is coming from her father, even though she is a successful attorney. The mortgage paperwork itself emphasizes the oddness of her being a single woman. After an ensuing panic attack about possibly dying alone, Miranda calls Carrie, who assures her she'll always have her friends.

There is, indeed, a constant emphasis on their sisterhood, the priority that female friendship takes over everything else, and a cardinal sin is putting current boyfriends before your female friends. (As Big puts it to Samantha, Miranda, and Charlotte in the next-to-the-last episode, "You're the loves of her life; a guy is lucky to come in fourth.") It is also a big mistake to lose yourself in a relationship, to have the man's goals and ambitions overthrow your own. Toward the end of the series Miranda is beside herself that Carrie would quit her job and follow Alexander Petrovsky (Mikhail Baryshnikov) to Paris, giving up her life to "live his life." Miranda can't believe Carrie would abandon her column, insisting,

"That's who you are." Carrie counters, "That's not who I am, it's what I do." Carrie is wrong, and Miranda is proved right.

But even something as silky as *Sex and the City* had its snags. In the Mars–Venus department men, especially Big, were inscrutable, and the women spent countless hours of mental energy trying to decode their motivations, asking of so many male behaviors, "What do you think it means?" Thus, the "common sense" of the show was that women obsess about men and relationships to the exclusion of almost anything else in their lives, except shoes. Indeed, when you spend the amount of time they do dissecting men and their behaviors, how can there be any cognitive resources left for anything else? Male bashing, while good for laughs, also furthered the notion of the Great Divide. In the first season Miranda proclaims that men will soon be obsolete as women no longer need them to have children or sex, given the new high-tech vibrators like the infamous "rabbit." Samantha opines that "men aren't that complicated, they're kind of like plants," and admits that she has "given up on the idea that you could talk to men."

Unlike real women, this foursome did not talk about their work and related office politics, books, movies, current affairs, national politics, or their families. When Carrie begins dating a New York City politician, she admits to him that she has never voted—ever. Even 9/11, a searing event for New Yorkers, did not make it into Carrie's world. This is because, in part, if you're a producer thinking about syndication, you don't want the show dated by references to Clinton, Bush, or terrorism, and you don't want to offend viewers' political or aesthetic sensibilities. But this is another example of how commercial exigencies—the need for a show to be evergreen—promotes an image of women (even these women) as much more unidimensional and superficial than they are in everyday life. Nonetheless, that millions of women loved escaping into this timeless world of shopping and female bonding was confirmed during the opening weekend of the film version of the show in May 2008. Defying expectations and deservedly mediocre reviews, *Sex and the City* knocked *Indiana Jones and the Kingdom of the Crystal Skull* out of its top slot; now there's some girl muscle.

Sex and the City paved the way for two other major hits, *Desperate Housewives*, which premiered in 2004, and *Grey's Anatomy*, which made its debut the following year. *Desperate Housewives*, a picket-fenced fusion of drama, mystery, comedy, and soap opera, was more about the women's relationships than their sex lives, but Gabrielle (Eva Longoria) could now say in the premiere of a broadcast network show, "An erect penis doesn't have a conscience," with Lynette (Felicity Huffman) responding, "Even the limp ones aren't ethical." Gabrielle was having an affair (which involved steamy bubble baths and naughty lingerie) with her teenage gardener, who was still in high school. Outrage? Middle America couldn't get enough. *Grey's Anatomy*, purportedly about the competitive, high-stress lives of surgical interns, was also about who was sleeping with whom, and especially about who was sleeping with her superior at work. That crown-jeweled demographic, women aged eighteen to forty-nine, loved the blend of workplace drama, female accomplishment, and sex. By now it all just went together. Or did it?

You would have thought the Virgin Mary had been defiled on national television. At America's most sacred event, the Super Bowl—well, unless you were not on the planet on February 1, 2004, you know where this is going—the country was introduced to a new euphemism, the "wardrobe malfunction." First P. Diddy and Nelly strutted around the halftime stage grabbing their crotches, and Kid Rock graced the stage as well, wearing an American flag with holes cut in it for sleeves and crooning about having "a bottle of scotch and watching lots of crotch."[51] Then Justin Timberlake and Janet Jackson humped and grinded their way through a medley of their own tunes, supported by pump-that-pelvis, rutting backup dancers in garter belts and red panties. (The *Washington Post* characterized Timberlake as "following Jackson around the stage like an old hound after a bitch in heat.")[52] When the duo got to the family-friendly line "I'm gonna have you naked by the end of this song," Timberlake pulled off Jackson's black leather breastplate to reveal one very naked boob. Well, except for the sun-shaped nipple shield.

The country went ape shit. As the highest-rated Super Bowl yet, an estimated 90 million people were watching, but the key number was that as many as one in five kids between the ages of two and eleven had been exposed to the flash and trash exhibition.[53] CBS's switchboard nearly blew up from the call volume.[54] The Parents' Television Council immediately condemned the show for indecency and the FCC reportedly got more than a half million complaints from viewers who didn't think their potato-chip-munching kids, who had tuned in to watch fully armored beefalos pummel each other, should have to see Janet Jackson's breast. The FCC launched an immediate investigation and it eventually fined CBS $550,000 for violating indecency rules. On the floor of the Senate, Zell Miller of Georgia fulminated (which is what Zell Miller does), "Does any responsible adult ever listen to the words of this rap crap?" and likened the event to running over a skunk: "The stink stays around for a long time . . . the scent of this event will long linger in the nostrils of America."[55] PepsiCo, one of the game's long-standing and biggest advertisers, threatened to pull out of future Super Bowls unless the company received assurances that such an incident wouldn't happen again. (Why? Because people were talking much more about the "wardrobe malfunction" than about the big-ticket Pepsi ads.) MTV, which had produced the halftime show, was effectively banned from ever doing it again.

The obvious hypocrisy of the outrage was not lost on some. As then presidential candidate Howard Dean put it, "Considering what's on television these days, I think the FCC is being pretty silly about investigating this."[56] The same society in which it had become commonplace to deploy underclad women's bodies, especially their breasts, to sell almost everything (okay, maybe not dental floss or air-conditioning units) was now upset about a split-second boob reveal? But that was precisely the point: while some saw the incident as nothing more than a somewhat crass and really tacky publicity stunt by Janet Jackson (who had an album coming out) and no more shocking than, say, Madonna and Britney Spears locking tongues onstage during the MTV awards (also viewed by millions of young people), others saw the whole halftime show as evidence that sex in the media—whose centerpiece was the ever more explicit display of the female body—really had gone too far. "This flash of breast," noted USA Today in its front-page story, "on national television during a beloved annual sporting event seen by millions of families, suddenly became a culminating moment in a long-simmering culture clash."

But the real hypocrisy was that it was the violation of the "beloved" sporting event, not the overexposure of an African American woman, that had people howling in outrage. After all, wasn't Janet Jackson just doing what we had come to expect of black women in rap music videos: shaking their booties and putting as much of their bodies on display as possible? You want a sexpert, who dances around a swimming pool in her bikini, lives only to please men, and never speaks? Just turn on BET or VH1 when they're showcasing rap or R&B videos.

Hip-hop historians and journalists disagree over what the turning point was, and they emphasize that sex and violence were always part of pop and rock music (let's not forget the white strippers and pole dancers of Mötley Crüe's "Girls Girls Girls" or the watermelon-breasted woman in a simulated gang rape in Sam Kinison's utterly vile "Wild Thing"). It's just that by the early to mid-1990s, sex and violence had come together, particularly in gangsta rap videos, in a combustible and increasingly incessant diatribe against black women. This was not enlightened sexism—this was pure misogyny. Was it N.W.A.'s 1991 song "She Swallowed It," which, in addition to the lyrics you can easily imagine, had lines like "The bitch will let you rape her" and "they even take de broomstick at the butt"? Was it 2 Live Crew's infamous CD *As Nasty as They Wanna Be*, in which black women were cunts, bitches, and hoes who had "dicks rammed down [their] throats" and "semen splattered across [their] faces?"[57] Was it comparable (or worse) lyrics by the Geto Boys, Ice Cube, or Snoop Dogg? And in so many of these songs, when black women weren't the deserving recipients of sexual violence they were hypermaterialist gold diggers who only used men for money, or "skeezers," "hootchies," and "chickenheads" who would do you and your entire posse if you wanted.

Many who adored rap, and understood all too well how the mainstream criticisms of rappers fed into white racist attacks on black men, found themselves in a newly complicated battleground. Black critics like Nelson George and S. Craig Watkins denounced "the woman-hating inclinations in corporate hip hop" in which women were "pictured in one degrading pose after another."[58] And as in white culture, the battle lines over the mainstreaming of pornography often fell out along generational lines, with older people outraged by these depictions and younger people—although hardly all—simply taking them for granted. Still, as Watkins notes, many young African American women were asking, "We love hip hop, but does hip hop love us?"[59]

As the conventions around rap videos ossified, the bevy of women meant to decorate the set, now referred to derisively as "video hoes," had to be light-skinned, curvaceous, and gorgeous, and utterly adulate the male rappers.[60] How ossified is the rap video formula? I, a fiftysomething white woman, could produce one. Watch this. Cue the music. Opening scene: out struts our male rapper and maybe he is joined by another male rapper in a guest appearance. They enter the obligatory limousine the length of a bowling alley and discover that it is fully stocked with a harem of latte-hued (never espresso) gorgeous young women whose sole and animating desire is to pleasure the men. The women—clad in microminis, leopard print (black women as fierce, feline animals), and cleavage-exploding dress tops cut down to their navels—are driven, sometimes two or three at a time, to sidle up to, kiss, fondle, kneel before, and/or dance provocatively in front of the very self-satisfied bling-covered men (do they really need more than one woman to get it up?). These women—whom we later see dancing and gyrating during the now obligatory poolside scene—must be silent, mute, voiceless, only to be looked at. The men, by contrast, are powerful, macho, rare, and unattainable, and the multiple women must use their bodies and sexuality to compete for them or, if need be, to share them. Preferably, there is also a scene of a woman lying prostrate on a bed as the camera pans her body, chops it up into its most important parts, and shows her squirming with delight as alone, eyes closed, welcoming our voyeuristic gaze, she fantasizes about her man. (I propose that this latter scene accompany typically transcendent lyrics like "She's grinding on my dick," from "Falsetto," by The Dream.) Final scene, end of song. There's your video. Straight out of the male chauvinist pigsty.

Nonetheless, there were women who sought to use the persona of the sexpert to their own advantage, to assert the legitimacy of their own sexual agency, and to talk back. Various women rappers sought to reclaim the word "bitch" and reconfigure its definition as "an aggressive woman who challenges male authority."[61] The female gangstress—street tough, defiant, intimidating—was another icon who used whatever means she had to (prostitution, drug dealing, stealing) to survive in the postindustrial inner city.[62] Da Brat, with her man-sized clothes and head full of fabulous braids, produced soul-infused songs whose softer musicality was counterposed by her tough-talking bragging about "not too many hoes can hang with me" and, in "That's What I'm Looking For," making various gorgeous men with ripped abs serve as sexual objects for her.

Seeing what the industry and the audience rewarded, other women, most notably Lil' Kim and Foxy Brown, embraced black leather bustiers and sequined pasties as the way to make a fortune. If black women's bodies sold music, why not profit off your own body instead of letting some guy do so? In one of her more talked-about photos, Lil' Kim appeared on the cover of *Interview* magazine in 1999 wearing nothing but a Louis Vuitton leather hat and Vuitton insignia stamped all over her body. You say we're obsessed with high-end consumer goods and sex? Well, here you go, in your face. In "Queen Bitch" (her boast about herself), Lil' Kim offered a soft-porn slideshow of herself in various states of undress and, in one shot, wearing a black T-shirt whose white letters read, "Got Dick?" bragged about being rich and getting sexually serviced by men while "I watch cartoons." For obvious reasons, Lil' Kim became hugely controversial among African American women. As the hip-hop scholar Angie Beatty reports, many female fans "celebrate[d] the chutzpah of these artists who have become the unapologetic bitches that they themselves either are or wish they could be." Of course these battles to resist sexist constructions of themselves were not without peril. Efforts to reclaim words like "bitch" have made virtually no dent in its ongoing pejorative use. Beatty's study of female rappers showed that the more control they had over the writing and production of their albums, the less likely they were to use self-denigrating language; the more control male writers and producers had, the more likely you were to hear "bitch," "hoe," and women talking smack about one another.[63]

In addition to affirming that black female power stemmed from how hot you were, gangstresses celebrated female violence, criminality, and female-on-female hatred, rivalry, and even physical attacks. Well, so what, it's only party music, right? But it turns out that the heavy viewing of these videos may be risky to African American girls' sexual health.[64]

Recent studies have found that African American girls who were heavy viewers of gangsta rap videos were more likely to have hit a teacher, more than twice as likely to have been arrested, nearly twice as likely to have had multiple sex partners, and more likely to have acquired a sexually transmitted disease than girls who were light viewers of such videos. Of course no one can claim a direct causal relationship here, but nonetheless these videos do tell young women, repeatedly, which behaviors to model, and which ones will get you the admiration of men and the fear or respect of other women.[65] Other studies have shown that after white males and females watch black women performing sexually titillating songs in music videos, they offer distinctly negative assessments of black women.[66] And what happens after adolescent African American boys watch your typical rap video? They express a preference for the more white, European standards of beauty repeatedly on display there.[67]

Both inside and outside of rap, other women sought to defy the imprisoning commercial edicts imposed on them. Lauryn Hill, Eryka Badu, Missy Elliot, TLC, and Me'Shell Ndegeocello created music and videos in which they were strong and independent, and, in songs like TLC's huge hit "Unpretty," urged women to reclaim the self-esteem that men and fashion magazines sought to take from them. In the video, a young woman's boyfriend makes clear from a computer simulation that he'd like her to get a boob job. She goes in for the surgery, but backs out after seeing another terrified young woman having her implants removed. She runs screaming from the place and starts taking up self-defense instead. Missy Elliot sought to take a leaf out of Madonna's playbook—combine representations of strength, toughness, and agency with a sexualized image. But when she performs the fabulous "Work It," in which she is claiming her sexual desire and availability very much in the affirmative without, in the video, stripping down to a push-up bra and thong, how is this read? As reinforcing the stereotype of the hypersexual black woman, or as achieving control over her own sexuality?[68] Or both? At the same time? Damned if she do and damned if she don't.

The December 2007 story was so big it made the front page of the *New York Times*. Jamie Lynn Spears, Britney's sixteen-year-old kid sister and the star of Nickelodeon's squeaky-clean *Zoey 101*, was pregnant by her nineteen-year-old boyfriend. And everyone was shocked, shocked, shocked. There was plenty of derision for Spears's mother, who was surprised because Jamie Lynn was "never late for curfew," as if sex only happens after 11:00 P.M. Jamie Lynn herself said, "I was in complete and total shock," apparently not appreciating one of the more significant outcomes of having sex. Then, six months later, another squeaky clean teen star, fifteen-year-old Miley Cyrus, of the massive hit *Hannah Montana*, created a comparable ruckus by posing barebacked with a Lolita-style come hither look (tousled hair and all) for *Vanity Fair*. (Actually, the more fully clothed photo with her father Billy Ray Cyrus in which they looked like lovers was much more disturbing.) The first line of the article? That Cyrus's favorite show was *Sex and the City*. Here are two famous young women who have embodied what it's like to pilot through the crosscurrents of prudery and pornography.

So what's a feminist to do? Young women today have never experienced a media environment that didn't overexaggerate the centrality of sex and "hotness" to everyday life. This is the way of the world for them. Many older women—their mothers, aunts, grandmothers—who grew up in different times (even though, take our word for it, there was plenty of sex), have watched this blitz on young women with concern. Shocking as it may seem to the likes of Rush Limbaugh, it's not that we don't think they should enjoy sex. (God, just putting the words "Limbaugh" and "sex" in the same sentence produces dry heaves.) Many of us welcome sex-positive media fare that throws a vodka martini in the face of the double standard and celebrates women's right to enjoy sex without censure.

But if *Sex and the City* has been such a phenomenon, why is there, on my campus and many others, the "walk of shame" that only applies to girls walking back to their dorm rooms or apartments in the early morning hours after spending the night with a guy? And when the objectification of women's bodies is sold as "empowerment" à la *Girls Gone Wild*, I am awed at how our notions of sexual liberation have been turned inside out. Girls and women are three times as likely as men to be sexually objectified to sell products in ads. The media construction of the sexpert might be fine in *Sex and the City* but more complicated in *Cosmo*, where on one page sexual pleasure is a woman's right but in so many of the others her main duties are to make sure, first and foremost, that *he* has his "mind blown" and is never made angry, resentful, uneasy, insecure, or threatened by a woman. And I'm sorry, it's sexist for girls to be expected to provide blow jobs for guys and get nothing in return.

It's this insistence on the part of enlightened sexism—that what continues to disproportionately benefit boys, men, and corporate America is really liberating to girls and women, and is just "laddish," harmless fun—that merits ridicule from us all. So does the selling of the sexpert image to ever younger and younger girls: rather than being merely pretty or cute, now they're supposed to be "hot" and project sexuality, even if they're seven years old, or, as on *Toddlers and Tiaras*, three.[69]

Stocking the prime-time airwaves with sexual activities and allusions also has particular consequences for girls. Girls Inc., the child advocacy organization, reported in 2006 that many girls find the imposition of the sexpert persona very stressful. As one tenth grader put it, "You are expected to be very sexy and attractive but at the same time are condemned for the sexuality that you portray." Many of these girls hate that "in my school, boys think they have a right to discuss girls' bodies in public."[70] This is a lose-lose situation. If you don't dress like a high-class hooker you're a dork; if you do, you're slutty. And as Jane Brown and her research team at the University of North Carolina have found, kids with the highest levels of sex in their media diet during the ages twelve to fourteen were 2.2 times more likely to have had sexual intercourse when aged fourteen to sixteen than those who had the lowest levels of sex in their media diets. The media serve as a "sexual super peer for girls, especially those who hit puberty early." Exposure to sexual content in the media, she found, accelerates white adolescents' sexual activity and increases their risk of engaging in early sexual intercourse. Black teens, by contrast, were more influenced by their parents' expectations and friends' sexual behavior than they were by the media.[71]

This might not be such a big deal, depending on the age of the teens, if the United States weren't completely bonkers about sex education and if these same TV shows contained references to safer sex or to sexual risks or responsibilities. But they don't: among all the shows with sexual content, only 14 percent make any reference to risks or responsibilities, and for the top shows among teens with sexual content, only 10 percent do.[72] The Guttmacher Institute reported that in 2002, "one-third of teens had not received any formal instruction about contraception," and the figure was even lower for black teens. For girls, there has actually been a decline in how many have received such instruction since 1995. Then, only 8 to 9 percent of teens got abstinence-only instruction (without any mention of contraception); by 2002, thanks to the Bush–religious right approach to sex education, the figure was up to 21 percent for girls and 24 percent for boys.[73] Study after study has shown that abstinence-only sex-ed programs are failures. So, as the amount of sexual content in the media has increased, exposure to thorough and reliable sex education has decreased.

Some consequences here? When teens have sex at a younger age, they are less likely to use contraception. Thirty-four percent of young women become pregnant at least once before they reach age twenty, and the teenage pregnancy rate in the United States remains anywhere from three to ten times that of other industrialized countries, even though their teens have sex at the same ages and rates that ours do. Early initiation into sex is also a risk factor for sexually transmitted diseases, which has been especially lethal for African American women. Indeed, in the summer of 2009 the Centers for Disease Control reported that teenage pregnancies and cases of syphilis rose sharply during the Bush administration after years of decline and that it was in southern states, with the greatest emphasis on abstinence, where the increases were greatest.[74]

Life for girls and young women in the pornosphere also can be really confusing. In 2007 the American Psychological Association issued a report that concluded that the rampant sexualization of girls was undermining their self-esteem and jeopardizing their physical and psychological health because they were learning at ever younger ages that their value came primarily from their sexual appeal and behavior. Cosmo, Maxim, and so much else in the media are adamant that girls' sexual desirability to men is much more important than girls' own desires, health, or achievements.[75] It's not surprising then that the sexualization of girls has been linked to depression, anxiety, and eating disorders. But at the same time, another experiment showed that when applying for a managerial position, the women who appeared more sexy got rated as less competent and less intelligent than the more conservatively dressed applicants.[76] There's that fine line again. And there are many studies showing that boys and men who live on a regular diet of all this stuff typically have more sexist attitudes and are more accepting of sexual harassment, interpersonal violence, and the myth that women invite rape.[77]

This was driven home to me not long ago when I went to pick up my daughter at her college dorm. As I waited for her to come out, a young man walked past wearing a T-shirt that read:

THINGS TO DO:

YOUR SISTER

YOUR MOM

No doubt this douche bag bought it from the Web site for Roadkill T-shirts, which advertises a woman wearing one with a firecracker on it that reads "Bang Me," and another showing a stick figure of a man giving a woman oral sex that reads "50,000 Battered Women and I Still Eat Mine Plain." Any guy wearing the "Things to Do" T-shirt on a college campus anytime between the founding of Harvard and 1998 would have been expelled, beaten up by other guys, or had two tampons shoved up his nose and his mouth taped shut by a gang of women until he agreed to transfer. Not today. (It is a testament to how well my daughter has trained me not to deliberately embarrass her that I did not vault out of the car and take him out myself.)

At least we got *Little Miss Sunshine*, a film nominated for best picture of 2006. Here a totally dysfunctional family jump-starts its VW bus across Arizona and California so that the daughter Olive (Abigail Breslin) can compete in the Little Miss Sunshine beauty pageant. As the contest unfolds we see all the JonBenet types with their huge hair, cover girl makeup, and pole-dancer outfits, and we know that poor, slightly chubby Olive doesn't have a prayer. But then she comes out for the talent portion, doing a striptease number taught to her by her recently deceased grandfather, and dancing to none other than Rick James's "Super Freak." As we hear James sing, "She's a very kinky girl, the kind you don't take home to mother," Olive rips off her various tuxedo parts, twirls them in the air, and hurls them into the audience. What is so perfect about the moment is that Olive is, indeed, unlike all the other contestants, a completely unsexualized preteen girl; she doesn't even get it that her performance has anything to do with sex. The stark contrast between her erotic dancer performance and her un-made-up, round, innocent kid face and body dramatizes how sick the entire pageant is and how really bizarre it is to have little girls participating in such a spectacle. It's even richer that Olive's performance, which explicitly mimics stripping, scandalizes the judges and observers while they remain utterly comfortable with the more pedophilic, soft-porn (and thus more insidious) stagings of the other girls.

Little Miss Sunshine was one of those brief moments when the culture looked at the cultivation of the sexpert, starting with grammar school girls, and "just said no." But it was a blip, one of the few speed bumps in the harlotization of American girls. In fact, Howard Lee, an executive at the TLC cable channel, said—presumably with a straight face—that *Toddlers and Tiaras* was inspired by *Little Miss Sunshine*. TLC, by the way, stands for The Learning Channel. The WE channel is following suit with *Little Miss Perfect*, presumably because the sexualization of girls is meant to be seen as harmless, funny, or both. Isn't this one of the creepiest triumphs of enlightened sexism?

So the question of whether the sexualization of our culture is good or bad for females may not quite be the right one. More important is *how* girls and women have been sexualized, how that's different from the way men have been, and what the consequences might be. Because while an increased frankness about sex in the media might indeed seem to be a liberal, even progressive advance from the days when *The Catcher in the Rye* and *Lady Chatterley's Lover* were censored, the content of this media, the way girls and women appear in them, may often be as sexist as it ever was.[78] The new hedonism and all the sex-positive talk to, about, and among women in the media, which seemed so fresh, new, and controversial, was the shiny cellophane that helped mask a Mars–Venus discourse about men and women being fundamentally different—and thus maybe not equal. It also deflected our scrutiny away from the underlying message: women were nothing without Mr. Right and so they had to do anything they could to land him. This is sexual liberation?

7

REALITY BITES

In the spring and summer of 2000, when not much was happening except what would turn out to be the most consequential presidential campaign in modern history, America became transfixed by a new show: *Survivor.* Eight men and eight women volunteered to be marooned on a tropical island filled with palm trees, venomous snakes, vipers the size of baby dinosaurs, rats, pulsating phalanxes of ants, and a series of contests, dares, and obstacle courses right out of an Outward Bound run by al-Qaeda. Every three days at a "tribal council"—on a set that appeared to be the place where all those Tiki dolls from the 1960s went to die—someone was voted off the island. The last one left would be "the survivor" and win a million bucks. When the show premiered in May, it reeled in 15.5 million viewers. By the time of the season finale on August 23, when Richard Hatch, a.k.a. "that naked fat guy," won, 51.7 million viewers tuned in, more than had watched the Academy Awards and 12.3 million more than the most-watched episode of the top scripted show in the country, *ER.*[1] Even better, the show brought in viewers to CBS beyond the Polident demographic it had become known for: it lowered the median age of the network's prime-time viewer from fifty-three to forty-eight.[2] (A delicious aside: as of this writing Richard Hatch is serving four years and three months in federal prison in West Virginia for tax evasion. The judge said Hatch "lied repeatedly" on the witness stand. Yum.)[3]

The bumper crop era of "reality TV" had begun, and in short order we got *Big Brother* (summer 2001), *The Amazing Race* (spring 2002), *The Bachelor* (March 2002), *The Osbournes* (spring 2002), *The Mole* (summer 2002), *Joe Millionaire* (January 2003), *America's Next Top Model* (May 2003), *Newlyweds: Nick and Jessica* (August 2003), *The Apprentice* (January 2004), *The Swan* (April 2004), *Laguna Beach* (September 2004), *My Super Sweet Sixteen* (January 2005), *The Hills* (May 2006), and the increasingly notorious *Jon & Kate Plus Eight* (January 2007), to name only a fraction of the offerings. You will notice that the onslaught began in earnest after 9/11, when you might have thought the media would give us just a tad more information about the rest of the world. But what we got instead was voyeurism, exhibitionism, sadism, and the mass sedation of brain cells. And of course there were debates and revelations about how "real" the shows really were.

But except for Fox's universally reviled February 2000 show *Who Wants to Marry a Multi-Millionaire* ("slave market," and "the great whore-dom," the press moaned), in which fifty women paraded around in bathing suits strutting their wares for a rich man they couldn't even see and hadn't met—all in the hopes of being chosen to marry him instantly on camera (even though, it turned out, he had restraining orders in his personal history)—there's been precious little comment about how women have been portrayed in reality TV.

Yet a close look at reality TV reveals it to be the ground zero of enlightened sexism. Now I'm not suggesting a conspiracy or anything (I don't think), but if you wanted to create a new genre of TV shows based squarely on the assumption that women now have full equality with men—so equal they can go head to head with men in a larvae-eating competition or in locking horns with them for a top corporate position—and then demonstrate how, in the end, women rarely have the right stuff, it would be reality TV. In the phony and contrived egalitarianism of many reality TV shows, there is an unstated yet emphatic insistence that women have the same capabilities and power as men—the gains of feminism are very much taken into account. And then some of the central principles of feminism—most crucially, the importance of female solidarity to achieve gender equity for all women—are dramatically, insistently, and publicly trashed to make it abundantly clear that not only is sisterhood not powerful, it is also utterly impossible. In other words it is *precisely* these shows, where female freedom, independence, and equality are completely acknowledged, that seem especially devoted to the repudiation of feminism.[4] So let's see how under the guise of "the real" we get some of the most retrograde images of girls and women to grace the small screens of America.

Indeed, the notion of female "portrayals" reveals the problem: if reality TV is truly real, then women aren't being scripted or forced into roles or stereotypes, right? They are just "themselves," and this is how women really are—especially when given independence and physical and mental challenges—when the cameras just happen to be turned on them: bitchy, self-loathing, catty, conniving, slutty, narcissistic, dumb. Reality TV is another post–network era hybrid, and depending on the genre, blends the elements of game shows, beauty pageants, adventure series, sporting events, and soap operas. Nonetheless, most reality TV shows, despite fake, hokey boardrooms or torch-lit tribal councils with pseudo-Neolithic campfires, rely heavily on the conventions of the news and of documentaries. Thus, we get handheld camera work, infrared shots at night, cutaways of the current location, on-camera interviews, interview material used as narration and as voice-overs of the action, and sound bites and assessments from expert sources (like The Donald or plastic surgeons). The participants themselves tell the story, like the eyewitnesses we have come to trust in breaking news, to give firsthand accounts about real events. They talk directly to us, the audience, telling us how they feel and how they see things.

So even though what's fun about watching reality TV is questioning how real it is (or isn't), the way these shows are shot screams, "This is really real."[5] The news/documentary visual style is meant to stoke our confidence that the representations of many of the women are true, natural, genuine. The introduction to the granddaddy reality show of them all, *The Real World*, begins, "This is the true story of seven people . . ." Never mind that the show's editors have to cut down seventy hours of videotape each week to create one half-hour episode, leaving sixty-nine and a half hours in the circular file.[6] We are urged to forget about the incredibly selective and deliberate casting, the calculated, often out-of-sequence editing, everything on the cutting room floor, the rest of these women's lives, the women who never made it on or would rather eat earthworm feces than ever, ever audition for such shows (even the ones that require them to eat earthworm feces).

Another reason, perhaps, that women of all ages haven't united to torch the sets of *The Swan*, *The Bachelor*, or *The Real World*—or sent the creators of *My Super Sweet Sixteen* to a secret detainee camp staffed by mattress salesmen and disgruntled postal workers—is that we aren't supposed to take these shows completely seriously. In fact, we're not even supposed to admit we watch most of them lest people conclude that we are half-witted chumps who can't tell good TV from bad. (In the online forums and chat rooms about reality TV, many admit to being hooked, and then feel they must emphasize that they tune in primarily to laugh at the shows. The few shows that are talent competitions, like *American Idol* or *Project Runway*, are exceptions.) If reality TV is mostly sensationalist trash, just "mindless entertainment" and often self-consciously kitschy to boot, it's easy to conclude that its consequences are minimal.[7] Indeed, many of these shows wear their tastelessness and sexism like a badge of honor (think *Are You Hot?* where Lorenzo Lamas deployed a laser pointer to highlight women's physical flaws). If they blare "we are obviously *the* most vulgar products of the media industry," then we can't possibly be unwitting dupes of mass culture because we have already been invited to watch them with condescension. Such shows insinuate that they know that we know that they know that their depictions of women are retrograde or exaggerated or unrepresentative of 97.3 percent of American females. They urge us to assume a distinctly ironic stance while watching, to nestle in a bath of superiority, judgment, and disdain that insulates us from being implicated in the tawdriness or sexism of the show. So it is in reality shows, in particular, that ironic sexism comes into full flower.

The contest shows, like *Survivor* and *The Apprentice*, rest on the "level playing field" conceit. Here, in the outback of Australia or the concrete jungle of Manhattan, smarts and cunning are as important as physical strength, so women have just as much of a chance of winning as men.

Moreover, while men won in the first seasons of both these shows, a woman won the second *Survivor* and the third *Apprentice*. There certainly have been moments on reality TV when women have been shown to be resourceful, shrewd, and strong. And there's little evidence that girls and women just buy into these shows hook, line, and sinker— indeed, women loved making fun of what a dope Joe Millionaire was and the Web is filled with howls of derision over *Laguna Beach* and *The Swan*. So what's the problem?

Having been chained in a chair for weeks and weeks watching a sampling of this fare (the equivalent of donating your brain to science), I now offer my field notes on how the female of the species comes off in reality TV.[8] And because most of us see these shows as very carefully constructed to produce the desired conflict, drama, and tension, it is not possible to view these portrayals as somehow accidental or innocent, let alone documents of how women "really are." Indeed, as the *New York Times* reported in the summer of 2009, the producers of *The Bachelor* deliberately stoked the drama among the women through a combined cocktail of sleep deprivation and "bottomless glasses of wine." When things got too boring, "they sent out a production assistant with a tray of shots." As one contestant put it, "If you combine no sleep with alcohol and no food, emotions are going to run high and people are going to be acting crazy." Added another, "The producers know that alcohol ignites emotions and you get better responses for TV." Add this to crafty editing, and watch the faux fireworks go off.[9]

As reality TV has evolved in the early twenty-first century and become formulaic, one of its biggest formulas has been to rely on stereotypes, like "the slut" and "the bitch," and to insist that women be defined by their relationships with and assessments by men. As a woman who worked as a "resident psychologist" on one of these shows reported, she was "struck by how embedded in the show's narrative were the common stereotypes of gender" and how it was in the editing room that "the nonconscious ideology of sexism" took control of the footage.[10] It is in reality TV where the spritzy new girliness of chick flicks and women's magazines in the late 1990s began to curdle into something more reactionary.

But first—given that so much of reality TV is widely acknowledged to be schlock and that even the initially interesting shows, like *Survivor,* start composting after the first season or so, why do so many people watch it? The networks and cable channels love reality TV because it's so much cheaper to produce than scripted shows, as it requires minimal writing and no high-priced A-list celebrity talent. And they make sure that reality TV is flattering to us: we are either hailed as obviously superior to the dysfunctional or superficial participants in the show (*Wife Swap, My Super Sweet Sixteen,* every parent on *SuperNanny*) or as highly competent judges with just as much expertise as anyone to assess which participants are worthy of admiration and which ones should be asked to get off the screen (*America's Next Top Model, American Idol, Dancing with the Stars*). What woman couldn't feel superior to the beautiful, rich, and famous Jessica Simpson on *Newlyweds* when we saw that she had no idea how to do the laundry, cook the simplest meal, read a price tag, or survive a camping trip? Indeed, that these people have stooped to go on reality shows and we haven't suggests that we aren't desperate, needy media whores willing to give up our privacy in exchange for fleeting fame. At the same time, the fact that ordinary people are now on TV suggests that anyone can become famous or is worthy of celebrity status—even us in our ratty bathrobes on the couch. And many reality TV shows highlight vengeance and humiliation; some seem to be trying to reach into our chests and pull out our often thwarted desire to get even, with a coworker, a former friend, a former lover.[11]

As viewers, we relish the unpredictability of these shows, meaning we are as authoritative as the next guy in forecasting what may happen the next week, who will get fired, who will be asked to leave, who will hook up. On *CSI* or *Law & Order,* we have a pretty good idea of how things will resolve, and Horatio and Jack McCoy will certainly not be voted off the island. And who are we, mere mortals, to judge these two icy, commanding men who know their jobs so well? But reality TV is a carnival barker, calling us in as active participants to serve as judges and juries of "ordinary" people, to bring to bear our own social, moral, and gender norms on predicting what should, should not, and will happen next, on who should get his and who should get hers. On *American Idol* we choose the voice and singer we like best, agree or disagree with Simon (Paula likes everyone), and wait to see if we are part of or at odds with the media plebiscite that eventually determines the winner.

People also enjoy not knowing quite how much of the show is real and how much isn't—that, too, provides a source of speculation and debate. We can be our off guard, relaxed, trusting leisure selves and our on guard, skeptical working selves at the same time. We are at once consumers and yet productive: interrogating the editing, the sets, and the other signs of manipulation and reinforcing very particular norms. I mean, how phony is Trump's boardroom (which was built specially for the show)? The cameras and reverential music unveil it as if we're entering Chartres, with the close-ups of the gold door handles, the pew of black and golden chairs with sunbeams strategically lighting them, and The Donald, the sun god, as if from heaven itself. But then we cut to the Donald-wannabes chatting in the suite, or getting lost in New York, and the documentary form kicks in. These shows contradict themselves, willfully blending what is constructed (the tribal council, the Bachelor's handing out the rose) with what seems spontaneous, and then dare us to figure it out.[12]

By having people talk directly to us about themselves and others on camera, reality shows actively spark quasi-intimate relationships, in which we feel we know these people we've never met, identify with some, and even hate others.[13] We were supposed to throw Doritos at the TV whenever we saw the dreaded Omarosa on *The Apprentice*, yell at the witless parents on the nanny shows, and, of course, cheer for our favorite American Idol. Various online chats, in which people express outrage over who the most recent Bachelor has chosen or sent home, or talk smack about members of the latest version of *The Real World*, demonstrate how effective many of these shows are in engaging our emotions and loyalties.

What all this adds up to is that we get to judge, and we are encouraged to enforce a set of powerful, and sexist, gender codes when we put the women in our crosshairs. Even as we dismiss particular situations or conflicts as exaggerated, even staged, we still use these situations to infer some "truths" about women's proper roles and behaviors. By surrounding people with cameras 24/7, these shows do insist that life is a performance, a constant, incessant, always scrutinized presentation of self. So what do they tell us about how women *should* perform in our relationships, our friendships, our work, and how we actually *do* perform? What are the tenets of this code?

Before proceeding, allow me to offer a small smorgasbord of quotations made to or about women culled from my weeks of indentured viewing.

"I'm a boob guy; I like big ones."
"[This is] a henhouse of mixed female emotion."
(The Real World: Sydney)

"She's an emotional lady."
"A scheming, conniving bitch."
(The Apprentice)

"You're two-faced and manipulative."
(Survivor: Borneo)

"I make trouble all the time . . . I have fought over a guy with a roommate before." "She's hot . . . her breasts are always on my mind."
"You're a tramp and a whore!"
(The Real World: Las Vegas)

"Can you imagine LC and Kristin fighting over you?"
"We're doing what girls do when things aren't going their way. Shop!"
(Laguna Beach)

"I don't like my legs, my boobs, I don't like to show my body at all."
"Bring out her femininity. It's gonna take a lot of work."
"She's very emotional."
(The Swan)

"She's not exactly a size two."
"The car looks better than she does."
(America's Next Top Model)

"Her face is a crime scene."
(Extreme Makeover)

There's plenty more where these came from, but you get the idea. Male privilege is simply the unstated, taken-for-granted foundation of most of this genre. There are no equivalent, constantly repeated mantras about men being too emotional, or unable to get along with each other, or slurs on their sexuality (calling a man a "player" is not the same as calling a woman a "slut" or a "whore"), or obsessive emphasis on, say, the size of their penises (unless the guy is black, of course), or on their appearance in general.

Now, to the gents reading this, it's hardly news that *The Real World* and other reality shows reinforce various stereotypes of men, especially the one about most men being so sex-crazed, irresponsible, and dumb that they follow wherever their wood leads them, the consequences be damned. All they have to do is see the aforementioned "big ones" and all reason, judgment, and discretion vanish. The first *Survivor* gave us the lazy, card-playing black man who had fathered children out of wedlock; in *SuperNanny* and *Wife Swap* the dads are often as clueless as cement when it comes to raising kids. But the pigeonholes the women in these shows are typically cast into are more plentiful, narrow, and recurring, and while they often build on stereotypes from the past, they also articulate new ones for the present. And there is a generational divide: the reality shows on MTV geared to young people usually have the most inane images of women.

There's also often a devolution in these shows—as they progress from season to season, the girls and women become more buff, more busty, more catty, more caricatured. One reason the women have become more starletlike is that the exposure that has come to so many on reality TV has prompted legions of aspiring actors to look to these shows as their path to stardom. And the producers believe that catfights produce boffo ratings. *The Real World* is a case in point. When it premiered in 1992 and was set in New York City, the premise was to take seven people in their late teens and early twenties, each of whom had a job or an ambition, and place them together in an apartment with the cameras rolling constantly and see what happened. (Those raised on *The Real World: Las Vegas* or *Hawaii*, not to mention *San Diego*—a nonstop binge-drinking barf fest—or the truly heinous *Sydney*, are strongly urged to watch the first season to see how low things have gotten.) In 1992 the housemates debated what constituted racism, went to a political rally and a pro-choice demonstration, and one of them, Julie, spent the night on the street with a homeless person to better understand her situation. There was virtually no drinking and no sex among the housemates, no comments about the women's breasts, and no fighting among the women over any of the guys. In fact, Julie, a white girl from Alabama, and Heather, an African American rapper, became close friends during the show.

Fast-forward to *The Real World: Las Vegas* or pretty much any season after 1998. Here's the by now petrified formula. Take seven buff twenty-somethings (so they're the legal drinking age), say three males and four females. They can be white, black, or mixed race, but they must conform to specific requirements. The guys should be ripped, the girls potential *Playboy* material: all females should have cleavage and at least one must be a 36D. (Various of *The Real World* women have gone on to pose in *Playboy*.) The guys should be drawn from one of the following categories: player (essential), racist, homophobe, southern hick, insensitive lout, good boy waiting for the right girl, bad boy, gay guy. The girls must fulfill the following roles: self-proclaimed party girl and proud of it, self-centered bitch (preferably blond), emotional wreck, slut, bimbo (also preferably blond), nice girl, innocent girl who becomes a party girl, alpha slut who steals guys from other girls. As the girls are introduced to the audience they should say things like "I get really courageous when I drink . . . I want that guy and by the end of the night, I will have him" or "I'm not used to girls getting more attention than me . . . if other girls do get more attention I'll be sneaky." Place them in an apartment that resembles a Saudi palace for five months with cameras everywhere (except, in a lone nod to tastefulness, the loo) and watch to see if "people stop being polite and start getting real."

Except what you're really supposed to watch for is which girl will become the slut, which girls will fight with each other, which girl is the bitch, which guy is the player, and which guy is the biggest asshole. They aren't allowed to have TV (who wants to watch other people watching TV?) or listen to music (interferes with the audio). Only very rarely do books, newspapers, or magazines appear in the home, and these tend to have titles like *Las Vegas for Dummies* or *What Women Really Want . . . And How They Can Get It*, which we assume is not about running for Congress. Political rallies and homeless people are verboten; clubs and bars must be frequented every night. We never hear one word about these women's aspirations—not that we hear about the men's, either. As Daniel Carlson on the Web site Pajiba.com put it, "There was a group of people whose sole purpose was to screw on camera . . . as if the dumbest and hottest kids at your high school had been dropped into a giant terrarium with a sixer of PBR and five hits of X and told to just have a good time."

Well, back to the task at hand. Despite all the ways in which reality TV repeatedly gets down on one knee (just like the Bachelor himself) and beseeches us to watch with an arched eyebrow and bemused grin (or grimace), and however much we oblige, the genre still does serious cultural work and offers, as one writer put it, "the worst clichés of gender indoctrination you can imagine."[14] So here's my top ten list of enlightened sexism in action, under the pretense of simply depicting "reality."

1. Women Are to Be Judged First and Foremost by Their Appearance.

I know, I know—like what else is new, right? But reality TV has made this reduction of women to their faces, figures, clothes, and specific body parts actually worse than it was back in the 1950s. The Miss America pageant may have lost its berth on network TV, but who needs it when you have *The Swan, The Bachelor, America's Next Top Model, The Millionaire Matchmaker,* and *Are You Hot?* Reinforcing this is the message that men act— they do things—while women must simply appear. In *The Apprentice,* obviously, the men and the women all had to compete by taking action. But back in the suite, it was the men we saw working out in the gym while the women gossiped, fought, or put on more lipstick. On *The Real World:*

Las Vegas, same thing—the guys worked out in the gym, but we never saw the women doing this—we saw them grooming themselves and applying makeup. On *Laguna Beach* where, it's true, nobody did much of anything except go to the beach or drive their Beemers, the guys at least played golf or organized charity events, which the girls found, like, so boring. They, by contrast, got their nails done. If the beauty-industrial complex needed additional propaganda for its insistence that, without its arsenal of products you are never, ever good enough, reality TV shows totally fit the bill.

All of the young women on *The Real World* must be, in the argot of the show, "hot." The first thing we hear the guys say about the girls never has anything to do with their personalities, character, or their intellect (as if!)—it's about their hotness. It's not just that they must put on bikinis whose tops can barely contain their large American bosoms and jump into a Jacuzzi with all the guys the first night in the apartment so we can see how hot they are. The female roommates must express anxiety that the other girls are hotter than they and the males must tell the camera how hot (occasionally the words "pretty," "gorgeous," and "sexy" are used) all the girls are. Sometimes a guy will tell the camera the girls are so hot he can't wait to be seen with them in public, or that he's attracted to one of the girls he met twenty minutes ago. In the notoriously bottom-feeding Sydney installment, the blond Trisha boasts that all of her friends are just like her, hot. Later we see Cohutta (yes, his real name) on the phone with his grandfather, who (yuck) asks if the girls are hot and Cohutta assures him they are and that, in fact, a hot one is lying on the floor right in front of him.

MTV's other hit reality shows, *Laguna Beach* and *The Hills*, set in the breeding ground of prototypical female hotness, southern California, all emphasize the importance of blond hair and boobs. Projections about the future include daydreams like "If you and Stephen had babies they'd be so good looking" and pronouncements about female body image are "too skinny is definitely unattractive, but there's a fine line between skinny and unattractively skinny."

When *The Apprentice* premiered, several of the male contestants weren't remotely close to the men you'd see in a Ralph Lauren ad (and, indeed, looked more like the guys you'd see at work, sometimes worse), but all of the women were slim and conventionally attractive. As *Survivor* evolved, the guys became more muscled, the women younger and more beautiful (with a typical "outcast" exception with tattoos and piercings or a woman who was just too old, who were quickly dispatched at the tribal council).

In *The Bachelor*, the first of the romantic competition reality shows, it was simply a given that all the women would be between twenty-one and thirty-five, slim, conventionally beautiful, and look really good in a bikini and hot tub. Ditto for *Joe Millionaire*. But it was the makeover shows that not only emphasized the primacy of female beauty to female self-worth, but also upped the ante on putting women's faces and bodies under constant and scathing surveillance.

America's Next Top Model—a favorite of many of my female students—takes fourteen aspiring models, and the show's star and guru, Tyra Banks, sets them up with photo shoots, "go sees" with top designers, television commercials, and fashion shows. Each week someone is eliminated ("I only have one photo in my hands," intones the self-important Tyra solemnly) until one is declared the next top model and gets a contract with the Ford modeling agency. (Just as *The Bachelor* doesn't actually marry the woman he chooses, these winners do not actually become real supermodels.) The women are not necessarily drop-dead gorgeous without their makeup and hair styled, and some are anxious, filled with doubt, insecure (just like us!), others are confident and feisty (just like us!). The show urges us to identify with various of the contestants, to judge them, and to root for them. By the end of the season you're emotionally exhausted: the show is structured so we are meant to believe that the two finalists have really taken Tyra's deeply felt and totally excellent advice (more on that in a minute) and you often like them both and don't want either one to lose. Because the emotional drama and struggles of the women to succeed suck you in, it can sometimes be easy to forget (and to forgive) that the show, after all, pits women against each other based on their looks, their ability to pose for a camera, and their personality traits.

The women are scrutinized by everyone: themselves, the other contestants, the fashion designers, the photographers, Tyra, and, of course, you. It is drilled into them (and thus, us) that first impressions are crucial. In one episode a designer faults the size of a contestant's hips and humiliates her by measuring them with a tape measure (her thighs, too) in front of everyone. At the end of each episode the judges—a photographer, a fashion editor/stylist, maybe a male model, a guest judge and, in the early seasons, the totally bitchy former model Janice Dickinson—rate how the women walk, pose, look in clothes, follow directions, and the like. The judging enacts every woman's dread of having her appearance ripped apart behind her back. Sample comments are: "Norelle's walk belongs in a circus"; "Eva's too short"; "she'll never be America's next top model"; she "has too much flesh"; "Eva's hands look like baseball mitts."

What is especially shrewd and insidious about *America's Next Top Model* is that, at times, it incorporates critiques of the modeling and beauty industry, so it can seem enlightened while perpetuating obsessions about thinness, never being pretty enough, and the notion that only celebrity will validate you. In "Cycle 3," which aired in 2004, the contestant Toccara hopes to break through as the first "plus size" top model. But the designers have no clothes that fit her and the various people she encounters make her feel ashamed of her plus size. Tyra acknowledges in the judging that Toccara indeed confronted size discrimination; nonetheless, Toccara is eliminated from the competition. (Other seasons had aspiring "plus size" models, too, also ejected before the final round.) Tyra repeatedly acknowledges that models (models!) face incessant criticism all the time, and "If you want to be a top model you have to suck it up." She gives contestants hypocritical advice about the need to avoid or conquer eating disorders when we know how most models are able to fit into a size zero. And, in a show whose premise is to pit women against each other, Tyra counsels the contestants that you have to think about sisterhood because you will be around women all the time, and need to trust them. (Sure.)

The myth that these shows propagate is that if you're beautiful, you have it knocked—all else will follow. But at the same time they show us that we can never be beautiful enough; some other woman, even more beautiful, will be chosen by the bachelor, or pursued by the hunky guy in *Laguna Beach*. Needless to say, such shows provide an excellent selling environment for the multibillion-dollar diet and beauty industry that needs us always, always, to envy the future selves we will become if we just use Oil of Olay or Dexatrim.

2. Women Need to Compete Over Men.

Vying, often desperately, and against formidable competition, for the attention of one and only one man was the premise of *The Bachelor, Joe Millionaire, Millionaire Matchmaker,* and others with this seraglio format. *The Bachelor,* which debuted in 2002, features a carefully selected lunk of a guy—usually named Alex or Aaron or Andrew—who is presented with a harem of twenty-five also carefully vetted young women, all slim, all conventionally pretty, most of them white and blond. (By the fall of 2006 the Bachelor was an Italian "prince," the way, say, that the composer of "Purple Rain" is a prince.) After a serial sampling of this array of female pulchritude in typical everyday locales like hot tubs and stretch limos, the Bachelor rejects them one by one until he has chosen the one he likes the very best. Then they are supposed to get married. (They don't.)

It was not unlike a 4-H competition of prize heifers, except the women did weigh less, got to go to fancy resorts, and had not been dragged there against their will with a rope. To us baggy-faced types who once railed against the sexism of the Miss America pageant (in what now seems like the Cretaceous era), we could not believe what we were seeing on *The Bachelor,* or, even worse, that the show had become such a success. It prompted concern about the survival of its competition over on NBC, the Emmy Award–winning drama *The West Wing,* which actually featured interesting, strong women characters.

But even in the non-bordello formats, girls and women routinely compete and even fight with each other over men: this happened on *Laguna Beach, The Real World,* and, most repulsively, for the attention and approval of the Donald on *The Apprentice.* As *The Real World* has devolved, there have been dueling flirtations among the women for the same guy, with the alpha sluts in particular trying to seduce someone else's crush or date right in front of her face. Therefore it makes sense that:

3. Women Can't Get Along with One Another and Will Stab Each Other in the Back.

If you were one of the nearly 59 million viewers who tuned into the last thirty minutes of the first *Survivor,* you will probably not soon forget the tough-talking, double-negative-spewing truck driver Susan Hawk vindictively ripping into Kelly Wigglesworth, one of the two finalists. Initially Sue and Kelly had become friends, had allegedly bonded as women, were partners in an early alliance against some of the others, and at one point vowed that they would work together against all the men so that a woman would win. But Kelly starts working both sides of "the tribes," which Sue sees as traitorous, and Kelly eventually votes Sue off the island instead of the despicable Richard. Just prior to the final vote, Sue sucks on her wrath like a toffee, telling Kelly and the national viewing audience that Kelly is two-faced and manipulative. Sticking the shiv farther in, Sue tells Kelly she hopes that it will be her vote that gives the prize to Rich (which it is), and, further, that if she were to see Kelly dying of thirst she wouldn't give her any water, she would just let the vultures have her. Mee—fucking—oww. Although the widely hated Richard Hatch (if "the fat naked guy" wins, predicted David Letterman, "there's going to be rioting in the streets, there's going to be looting")[15] is much more manipulative than Kelly, Sue turns on her former female ally, costing her the prize. So here are two women who have tried sisterhood—explicitly affirming the feminist principle of female solidarity—only to show how absurd and unattainable this principle is in reality. By the sixth season of *Survivor*, we would get a "battle of the sexes" with all-male and all-female tribes. While the guys bond affably as they build their hut, the talons flip out like switchblades from the women's fingers and the backbiting and spite render them dysfunctional.[16]

As the genre evolved, the impossibility—indeed, the preposterousness—of sisterhood, the inability of women to work together harmoniously, the fragility of female friendships, and the inevitability of female catfights became staples of reality TV. It was hardly surprising that there is typically "tension" in the "ladies' villa" on *The Bachelor*, "kind of like a little catfight . . . 'he's mine,' 'no, he's mine,'" as one of the bachelorettes put it; "it's been really stressful and cliquey." But this was true even when women were supposed to be cooperating *against* men.

On the first season of *The Apprentice*, the Donald initially divides the teams up by gender. Now, it's true, the all-female team wins the first four competitions, leading the Donald to quip, "I'm starting to think I may never hire a man again." (Right.) But despite this, the takeaway message from the first season is that all-female teams are dysfunctional. The men may have had one clinker in the group—an overly amped-up Trump brownnoser named Sam—and may have criticized each other's approaches or ethics, but we never see them clawing each other's eyes out like the women.

Each team's first job is to select a name for its "corporation," which, as the breakout female villain Omarosa tells the camera, should have been easy, "but when you've got eight women," she laughs, "it became a three-hour ordeal." When the women tackle their first task—to sell lemonade in Manhattan—Kristi tells us there is too much talk and "a lot of attitude" as we see the women all speaking at once, failing to listen to one another, and disagreeing. The cameras then cut to the men and their project leader Troy, who is "keeping everyone positive." As soon as the women return to the suite, they start fighting with one another, which the men do not. The very next episode begins with the women fighting again, this time over how to choose the next project manager. After their reward for having won this challenge (the design of an ad campaign), which involves their being flown by private jet to a swanky restaurant in Boston, the fighting resumes in the limo as they return to the plane, with Ereka calling Omarosa a bitch and Omarosa countering that Ereka is "a baby" and "emotionally unstable." One of the women says she has never seen women yell at each other in a professional setting the way she sees women do so here; but maybe that's because in the "real world," we're meant to assume that they're tempered by their male counterparts?

After four men are fired, Trump has to reconstitute the teams so they are equal in number, and two of the women express huge relief at being on a mixed-gender team, which eliminates the tension they say is inherent to all-female teams. As the contestants are whittled down, the various women's hatred of one another explodes in the boardroom; by contrast, when two of the men, Troy and Kwame, are pitted against each other and Troy gets fired, the two men vow their friendship and hug.

MTV specializes in catfights in shows like *The Real World*, *Laguna Beach*, and, of course, *The Hills* with the infamous breakup between former BFFs Heidi and Lauren. *The Real World: Sydney* features an instantly infamous series of battles between Trisha and Parisa ("Why don't you learn to like someone who wants to fuck you?" with the retort, "Why don't you go back to your boyfriend that I hope dumps your ass because you're a slut?"), culminating in Trisha pushing Parisa, which prompts Parisa to threaten, "I will slam your head into the wall if you touch me again." (Chat rooms quickly emerged with people voting whether they were on Team Parisa or Team Trisha.) "I can't stand that girl . . . she tried to insult me," sniffs one woman about another on *The Real Housewives of New Jersey*. On *America's Next Top Model*, Tyra warns her wards that even best friends talk about each other behind their backs. The contestants tell the camera they can't stand living with other women because it quickly becomes "like junior high school." This is because, unlike their calm, reasonable, rational male counterparts . . .

4. Women Are Overly Emotional and Obsessed with Relationships.

"The female creature is inherently psychotic," sums up the noted psychological authority Isaac, one of the roommates on *The Real World: Sydney*. Here the women are so erratic, so volatile, and so thin-skinned that they fight over making grilled cheese sandwiches. The Donald also singles out female emotion as a big problem in *The Apprentice*. When one of the contestants, Heidi, learns that her mother has been diagnosed with cancer and is to be rushed into surgery, she cries, prompting one of the men to tell the camera, "She's an emotional lady," as if a man might not have an identical response to such awful news. Another of the women, Ereka, is dismissed as not Trump corporation material because she is "an emotional girl," "couldn't control her emotions," while the out-of-control male hysteric Sam, who was fired early on, did not earn the same label. Whether a woman is "too emotional" to withstand fourteen surgical procedures on *The Swan* (after which you look and feel like you've gone fourteen rounds with Muhammad Ali in his prime) is a frequent "concern" expressed by the condescending male plastic surgeons. And being "too emotional" on *America's Next Top Model*—even if you're supposed to pose for a photograph with a tarantula on your face (yes!)—sends you packing.

Women cry all over the place on these shows, and men rarely do. Men are rational, women hysterical. Freud would have loved it. Because of these wild emotions, females are utterly occupied with relationships: boy drama, who's nice, who's not, who's a bitch, who's talking about whom behind their backs, parent-child relationships. The notion that females might be citizens who care about anything beyond the confines of their bedrooms, kitchens, or stretch limos is unthinkable, ridiculous.

Anyone who has seen, in real life, a man at work punch a hole in the wall, storm out of a meeting in a huff, throw a tantrum, scream at coworkers, fall desperately in love with a colleague, or get utterly despondent over a bad turn of events (and I have seen all these things) knows that being "emotional" is hardly confined to the female of the species.

5. Women Should Be Sexy, but Not Overly Sexual.

Here it is, the impossible line to walk. Sexual display and sex appeal are everywhere on reality TV with the bikinis, miniskirts, and cleavage-baring tops on *Survivor*, *The Real World*, *The Bachelor*, *The Swan*, *My Super Sweet Sixteen*, and so forth. Women are supposed to be very "hot," but not a tease or a slut. The mixed messages career all over the screen. Women on *The Bachelor* who sit on the guy's lap without an invite, or just start making out with him, are often belittled as "too aggressive" by the other "bachelorettes," but sometimes such ploys work. On the first season of *The Apprentice*, the women's team beats the men's team in the first four challenges and are shown as using their sex appeal to do so. We see them kissing male customers and allegedly passing out their phone numbers to sell lemonade; choosing a sexually suggestive, phallic design to promote a private jet company; and, in a special low, casting themselves, in midriff-baring tops and black spike boots, as the "Planet Hollywood Shooter Girls" (after Hooter's, another establishment that would have been firebombed by pissed-off women in 1974). In each case, their sexuality helps them win. Yet the Donald, of all people—squire only to busty supermodels—has to warn them that they are "coming close to crossing the line" and that using their sexuality was "unnecessary." So, what's a girl to believe, her victories or the Donald? And where, exactly, is that line?

6. The Worst Thing a Woman Can Be Is a Bitch: Strong Women Are Bitches and Rich Women Are Bitches.

The bitch—assertive, snotty, self-important and self-absorbed, confrontational, outspoken, hypercritical, a threat to men and a danger to other women, and, typically, rich—has become one of the required stock characters in reality TV. Girls and women are supposed to be nice—considerate, cooperative, nurturing, supportive, even-keeled, soft-spoken, kind. They should never be self-centered, angry, unsmiling, judgmental, unpleasant, emotionally withholding, lazy, insecure, or cocky. They must be able to take criticism from experts and then change, right away. They should never appear to be strategizing to win. Deceit works for men but not for women. Women who are powerful or competent, but don't smile enough, or are not as socially accommodating as they should be, are cast as bitches. Women who try to outwit or outplay—you know, try to win the game— without being nice enough are "manipulative" or "two-faced." The first two women to win *Survivor* were the "nice girl" who took care of others and liked to cook.[17]

Whoever violates these edicts is a bitch. Certain women—Sue from the first *Survivor*, who could spearfish better than the guys and complained that some of them did not have "enough balls," Omarosa from *The Apprentice*, the venom-tongued Janice-the-judge from *America's Next Top Model*—became iconic bitches par excellence. But bitchiness is everywhere, and the word "bitch" is thrown around freely. In the opening episode of *The Real World: Sydney*, when we meet Trisha, her first thought is whether there will be "a bitchy girl" she won't get along with. (There is.) And it is inevitable that well-to-do women and girls are bitches because they're self-centered and have been spoiled rotten. All of the *Real Housewives* series, from Orange County, from New Jersey, whatever, pivot on women who have way too much time on their hands and who make Matterhorns out of molehills as they talk trash about each other to their confidante, the camera.

7. African American Women Are Lazy, Threatening, Have a Chip on Their Shoulder, Are Not Marriage Material, or All of the Above (Except for Tyra Banks).

The Apprentice's first African American woman, Omarosa, who was cast as and eagerly played the bitch, was voted the most reviled reality contestant of all time in a *TV Guide* survey in the summer of 2005. As she said to one of the white women, "You're very intimidated by black women, right?" Ramona, on the first *Survivor,* who was ill at the beginning of their marooning, was also portrayed as lazy and not pulling her weight; she was the third woman voted off the island. On the second season of *Survivor,* another African American woman, Alicia, was also branded as the bitch who had to be voted off because her strength was a threat to others.[18] *The Bachelor* pretends it's enlightened by including African American women and other women of color in the initial harem, but usually they get eliminated between the second and fourth weeks.[19] A judge on *America's Next Top Model* once criticized a contestant because her "look" was "too Afro-centric." Frank, on *The Real World: Las Vegas,* tells his mixed-race roommate, "That's your role, you're the black bitch." There are no such stereotypes on *Laguna Beach* or *The Hills,* as African American women may not be permitted in these precincts—except, perhaps, to clean the rich girls' bathrooms.

8. Women (Especially Blondes) Are Shallow, Materialistic, and Live to Shop.

On *Laguna Beach,* like, when the blondes talk, like, every other word is like "like," and their central activities are like planning parties, going to concerts, sunbathing, and like pointing out which other blonde is like totally spoiled. Bravo's *Millionaire Matchmaker* is based on the premise that most women would prefer a rich guy to, say, a sane one or a nice one. And do we even need to go to the gated community of *The Real Housewives of Orange County,* not to mention New York or New Jersey? Here in the land of exploding clothes closets and kitchen islands the size of Olympic swimming pools, women's lives revolve around parties, dance lessons, and incredibly banal social dramas about who allegedly insulted whom. Of course, reality TV would be deemed deeply boring by its producers (and antithetical to advertising and product placement) if we saw women talking about books, religion, the health care crisis, politics, poverty, justice, law, spirituality, or the lack of decent day care. (It's left to the fictional shows like *Law & Order* or *Boston Legal* to provide an environment for women to engage in such topics.) But how many busty, dumb, superficial, materialistic blondes can one TV genre take? It was the bitchy "hot" blonde Trisha on *The Real World: Sydney* who shoved the brunette Parisa over who got to use the telephone (and thus got kicked off the show). And then there were the ultimate tributes to blond dumbness, *Newlyweds*, *The Anna Nicole Show*, and *The Simple Life*. It's possible that the representation of Jessica Simpson as dumber than a box turtle was exaggerated for *Newlyweds* (as when she famously asked her husband whether she was eating tuna or chicken because it was "Chicken of the Sea"), but did we have to be shown over and over that she couldn't cook, hated to do laundry because "then you have to fold it" and "that sucks," failed to look at price tags or the charge slip while shopping and then was shocked by the bill, and said to her husband "I made an uh-oh" after spilling water on the floor? Who would think that attractive blondes might be able to pass the MCATs after this?

9. Housework and Child Rearing Are a Woman's Domain.

Now we get to the reality shows that don't showcase women in bikinis, hot tubs, and nightclubs, the domestic intervention shows like *Wife Swap*, *Trading Spouses*, *SuperNanny*, and *Nanny 911*. In the carefully staged *Wife Swap*, the wives of two totally opposite households—say, rural, fundamentalist, pig farmers in Iowa and atheist Manhattan socialite stockbrokers—trade families for two weeks, and we see the kids and the husbands through the eyes of the transplanted wives. The kids are either totally spoiled and undisciplined or forced to shovel pig manure at 5:00 A.M., make their own clothes, and walk ten miles to school. The husbands are either oblivious to their kids' needs—forcing them to be homeschooled, or, more accurately, car schooled, because he likes driving around the country in his old VW van—or they are abusive louts. At the end we see the desperate wives reunited with their equally crazed families, and the wives say what needs to be fixed or changed in the other's household. Here the women are the authorities, and caveman husbands who have been utterly untouched by feminism and never help around the house or participate in child rearing come in for a world of hurt. The message is that these guys should "help," because it's too much to ask that they be fifty-fifty partners with their wives.

However, the wives have not just been pitted against other husbands and kids, they've been pitted against each other and must issue judgments—the mothers are too permissive or too strict, they spend too much time hovering over their kids or not nearly enough time with them. Message board forums on Web sites like RealityTVWorld.com show how much viewers love to be shocked by the extremes of both families and to judge them all as "idiots" compared to themselves. But the unstated assumption underpinning everything is that however much husbands need to "help," the domestic sphere is rightly and necessarily the province of women. In the nanny rescue shows, in which children routinely bite or assault their mothers, or (in one of my favorites) will only pee outside in their mother's flower garden, the parents are both guilty of really dumb child rearing practices. But again, it is much worse being a bad, clueless mother than a clueless father.

10. Lesbians? What Lesbians?

Not much to say here because not much to cite. While Richard Hatch won the first *Survivor*, and other openly gay men have appeared in various reality shows (including, most notably, *Queer Eye for the Straight Guy*, but also subsequent versions of *Survivor* and *The Real World*), lesbians have remained virtually invisible.[20] Is that because lesbians raise the dreaded specter of feminism, of women happily loving and indeed getting along with other women?

So, Back to the Future.

If all of the above sounds like the basic tenets of the feminine mystique circa 1958, then there you have it, but all packaged up in the cellophane of irony. Take that, you humorless feminists: the producers' intention is not *really* to take women back to the Stone Age, it's actually to exaggerate and then mock what patriarchy stands for so we all have a good chuckle. We know full well that you know that it's ridiculous to think anyone would really find marital bliss on *The Bachelor* or that most young people are as preoccupied with vodka shooters and threesomes as those on *The Real World*.

Having said that, if women do get into catfights all the time, can't get along, are preoccupied with boy drama, and are narcissists obsessed with their appearance, isn't some sexism, well, justified? Reality TV doesn't only resurrect various sexist stereotypes, it also resurrects approval of them. And studies have shown that when young men are exposed to such stereotypes, they are more inclined to treat women as sex objects or approach them in similarly sexist ways.[21] Many young women are so inured to the onslaught of bimbos and alpha sluts that, as one *Real World* viewer put it, "It's been like beat into your head so many times. You're kind of like numb to it. You don't even notice it anymore."[22] But here's what researchers have noticed. When women are exposed to the sorts of stereotypes that abound on reality TV, they are less likely, when asked to perform a task after viewing comparable drivel, to want to assume leadership roles and more likely to choose a subservient position.[23]

At the same time, women's attraction to shows like *The Bachelor, Super-Nanny, The Hills,* or *Wife Swap* tells us something about women's experiences in the age of enlightened sexism. We know that we are judged, constantly, based on our looks, "niceness," and domestic skills, especially child rearing. Female viewers see an array of personas on reality TV, identifying with some and rejecting others, as we calibrate what kind of woman can and deserves to succeed. *The Bachelor* has, in its various seasons, offered highly normative female "types" into which most women allegedly fall, and ropes viewers into damning certain behaviors while applauding others. In season two, for example, Helene, the one the bachelor Aaron finally chose, was enormously popular with young women—chat rooms confirmed this—because she was cast as "the smart one." She also had a confident sense of humor and was not overly adulatory of The Man the way some of the other contestants were. Young women did not like contestants who were too wimpy, too needy, too airheaded, too manipulative, too untrustworthy, or too backstabbing. Thus, shows like *The Bachelor* urge girls to place themselves on a postfeminist scale of femininity to determine how far they have to go to please men without losing all shreds of their own identity and dignity. In the process young women calibrate, for better and for worse, what kind of female traits are most likely to ensure success in a male-dominated world.

But reality TV also insists that there's no such thing as patriarchy anymore. Any woman can become the Survivor or the Apprentice. Verbally abusive husbands who refuse to wash the dishes on *Wife Swap* are throwbacks to an unenlightened yesteryear; the straight men on *Queer Eye* must learn to shop for clothes, cook, clean their apartments, and get their backs waxed if they're ever going to get a decent woman. And the Bachelor, poor dear, must agonize incessantly on camera about how really, really hard and painful it is to hurt twenty-four of the women laid at his feet. It is essential that he perform the role of the sensitive New Age guy so he doesn't seem like the john that he is.

Finally, reality TV promotes a turn within, a gazing at our navels, a fixation with our bodies and relationships, and the ideology of individualism. And I'd like to suggest that while such a turn is not good for any of us (especially given the massive erosion of international news on the networks and CNN), it's especially bad for women. No one expects reality TV to compete with the BBC World Service. But it's on television dramas like *Law & Order* and *ER* where one has been asked to contemplate issues like restrictions on civil liberties during wartime, or the lack of health insurance, or debates about Muslim women wearing head scarves. Reality TV, by contrast, is fundamentally dedicated to ignoring and denying the real.

By exhorting us to insert ourselves into the interpersonal relations of preselected, mostly white, mostly young people whose major concerns are staged as highly narcissistic and vapid, reality TV reinforces the outdated mantra that we females should not worry our pretty little heads about anything beyond the kitchen or the bedroom. And we should especially turn our backs on feminism because the "level playing fields" on reality TV show it to be no longer necessary. More important, who needs it? When the producers deliberately put females in situations that require solidarity, what happens? Brawls, rivalries, conflicts, feuds, tiffs, contention. On reality TV, female alliances are impossible; these are the ties that will hurt you, and will break your heart. So who can women really trust, really bond with, really get true support from, and ultimately throw in their lot with? Yep, only one other choice: men.

8

LEAN AND MEAN

I have a hypothesis. In the early twenty-first century the size zero—which, by my calculation, means you take up no space—was the dress size that young women were supposed to aspire to fit into, while still filling up a size 38D bra. During this same period, there was supposedly an epidemic of "queen bees" and "mean girls" trolling the halls of America's high schools (or the Internet) looking for weaker girls whose exposed throats they could sink their fangs into. Food deprivation tends to make one irritable. So does trying to squeeze into size zero short shorts. But enlightened sexism tells us that these beauty standards are actually empowering because they turn men into helpless, salivating dung beetles, and are allegedly promulgated by women for women anyway, so why take your low blood sugar out on the guys? Ergo, female self-starvation and the prospect of having water balloons surgically implanted into your chest led to female-on-female bullying. What do you think?

Okay, so the causal chain is a bit stretched. But we need to explain this odd constellation of thinness tyranny, the new mammary mania with its mainstreaming of breast augmentation and other cosmetic surgery, and the alleged mean girl phenomenon. Why did about 247,000 women get breast implants in 2004, when only 32,000 did in 1992?[1] What accounts for the emergence of the new cultural star, the hot mean privileged girl bitch? Only five or so years earlier, in the wake of Mary Pipher's 1994 bestseller *Reviving Ophelia*, there was widespread concern about teenage girls having zero self-esteem and learning to silence themselves rather than give voice to their opinions and ambitions. Now (because of girl power?), teenage girls had suddenly morphed into strutting, supremely confident, Machiavellian cyber-bullies? How much was the whole "mean girl" hysteria simply a media panic, and how much of it actually captured, however hyperbolically, an inchoate, unspoken frustration—even fury—among girls and young women, about the bargain they were supposed to make, that in exchange for having independence (sort of), they had to look better than Jennifer Aniston in a bikini, no matter what?

These were the new, revised, incredibly contradictory images of girl power at the turn of the twenty-first century: real power came from having a slim, young, hot body but to get it you might have to be anything but powerful—prostrate on a gurney—which was, in a nice twist, sold as a new technology of power for women. And girls now had so much power—too much, in fact—that it had turned them into beasts of prey. So let's think about the relationship between "lean" and "mean," and why the former might lead to the latter.

There have been two stores that my daughter has either had to drag me into or that I have finally refused to enter: Abercrombie & Fitch (about which I have already unburdened myself) and Victoria's Secret. I really hate Victoria's Secret a lot, being instantly accosted by the ever-hovering black-suited officious young women, being dwarfed by larger-than-life black-and-white photos of breasts the size of Mount McKinley bursting out of Ipex bras. But the main reason I really hate Victoria's Secret is that through their ubiquitous ads, stores in every mall in America, and their regular TV "specials," they have repeatedly asked the question "What Is Sexy?" and then told us there is one and only one answer: Giselle Bundchen, in 2007 the highest-paid supermodel in the world. Well, okay, there *have* been other supermodels in their ads with a "body by Victoria"— Claudia Schiffer, Heidi Klum—but the body type is always identical: Barbie. This is enlightened sexism's ideal female form. The fantasy on offer is that genuine girl power really comes from a Dream Angels push-up bra. And the message is clear: your body is your central, crucial resource in establishing your net worth as a female, and if it isn't like Giselle's, well, aren't you kind of worthless? Or at least really deficient? Do you get to have all that "freedom" and "control," the ads keep promising, if you don't at least try really hard to look like Giselle? Welcome to the most important female sport: the Hotness Olympics.

Anyone thinking that the tyranny of the breast hadn't returned—but done with a wink, and all in good fun—missed "The Breast Christmas Ever" from Clear Channel, the radio station behemoth that banned hundreds of songs after 9/11, including "Hit Me with Your Best Shot" and anything by Rage Against the Machine (we all know those jihadists really pump themselves up to Pat Benatar). They also banned the Dixie Chicks from their stations because they found their criticism of George W. Bush tasteless. No such censorship for "The Breast Christmas Ever." Starting in 2004, in markets around the country like St. Louis, Sacramento, and Detroit, girls and women, including high school girls, could enter a contest on the radio station by submitting an essay about why their breasts were deficient and needed to be bigger, and if they won, they got free breast augmentation surgery as a Christmas present.[2] Now we are supposed to relax about the equation between a woman's breasts and her worth—why, we're even supposed to celebrate it and regard it with an ironic stance—hey, isn't it kind of funny to obsess about women's breasts because really women now have it all, can do it all, can be anything they want so this whole breast obsession is just really a lighthearted, silly, stupid joke, right? This is clearly the thinking that prompted Abercrombie & Fitch to produce girls' T-shirts that read, "Who Needs Brains When You Have These?"

The actual irony here is that a de-emphasis on breasts and the celebration of a more androgynous form actually accompanied both women's drive for legal equality in the 1920s and the drive for social equality in the mid- to late 1960s and early 1970s. Mammary mania, by contrast, has accompanied trends like the rise of "the feminine mystique" when all women were supposedly capable of was making marshmallow Jell-O molds. During the women's movement we had hoped that the media's ridiculous obsession with women's breasts would attenuate, if not stop altogether. And, in fact, in the 1960s, what with the fashion icons Jackie Kennedy and Audrey Hepburn, and the models Jean Shrimpton and

Twiggy, the mammary mania of the 1950s gave way to a slimmer silhou-
ette. Being flat-chested was fine, even stylish. (A most welcome change
for certain of us.) While few of us could be, or wanted to be, as thin as
Twiggy, we didn't expect that we could be that slim and also have Jayne
Mansfield's boobs.

How things have changed. Today, young women are not supposed to
desire either the bodies of Marilyn Monroe (too zaftig) or Audrey Hepburn (too flat-chested), but an impossible melding of the two, in which the
ideal body type is, well, the body of a lanky twelve-year-old boy with
Pamela Anderson's breasts attached. As the imaginary camera pans up
our bodies, we are supposed to be perfect ectomorphs until the camera
gets to our breasts—then it is time to photoshop in the cup-runneth-over
hooters. It goes without saying that such a body type is one rarely found in
nature. And it hasn't just been Wonderbras and Victoria's Secret that have
insisted on the renewed importance of cleavage to a woman's self-worth
and desirability. So have the covers of *Cosmo*, *Maxim*, the *Sports Illustrated* "swimsuit issue," *Girls Gone Wild*, and other breast-flashing fare,
the girls exploding out of their bikini tops on *Laguna Beach*, and the
fact that there's a restaurant chain called Hooters. Even the boss on
House, Dr. Cuddy, and the female forensic researchers on *CSI* flash cleavage typically reserved for "gentlemen's clubs."

In this environment, it is no surprise to find that young women
today are more dissatisfied with their bodies than previous generations;
one study of women of different ages noted a "body obsessiveness verg-
ing on the pathological" among some women born in the 1970s and
1980s.[3] We all know about the dramatic rise in anorexia and bulimia in
recent decades. Indeed, the pressure to be very thin and dress the right
way has gotten worse since 2000. In a 2006 survey, girls said they felt "we
have to be skinny to be successful"; one seventh grader noted, "There is
too much pressure from the media to be ultra thin and to have big boobs
and blonde hair . . . you have to look like a supermodel to fit in." More
than half of the girls in grades three through five (!) said they worry
about their appearance.[4] The percentage of girls who think they're overweight has reportedly tripled just since 1995.[5] And according to another
study, the number one wish of girls between the ages of eleven and seventeen is to lose weight.[6] And what body part are young women most

dissatisfied with? Breast size. What to do if they're not just right? Hello Dr. 90210.

But something more intense and coercive started happening in the late 1990s and beyond through Victoria's Secret and its ilk: the marketing of emphatic femininity. And this seems a response to the threat of all that scary unleashing of girl power. Now that girls and women were taking up more space collectively in the workplace, in schools, on our media screens, we were urged to take up less space individually: hence the size zero.[7] Between the return of stiletto heels (talk about revenge!), miniskirts, and plunging halter tops, the pandemic of TV makeover shows, brazen promotion of cosmetic surgery for girls of all ages, and the unremitting "Best and Worst Beach Bodies" in all the celebrity rags, multiple sectors of the media have become the Robocops of the beauty-industrial complex, insisting on our confinement in Barbie-land.

So what they police, in addition to our thinness, the horror of cellulite, and the abomination of wrinkles, is whether we are emphatically feminine. That's the bargain, the price we're supposed to pay for having freedom and independence: we must reassure everyone that we're still girls, not at all threatening, not remotely lured in by anything resembling feminism. Because feminism cannot be allowed once again to rear its monstrous, Medusa-like head.[8] And if the media have drummed into us over the years that feminism equals combat boots, unshaven legs, and no makeup, then plunging necklines, fuck-me pumps, and plenty of mascara advertise that we are going nowhere near that form of discredited rebellion. So we must scrutinize ourselves microscopically, not just for the usual flaws—flat hair, love handles, pores, as we always have—but for signs of insufficient adherence to this forceful, pointed code of femininity. Even in the wake of 9/11, which should have directed the media spotlight elsewhere, and nearly forty years after the women's movement, TV makeover shows have instructed us to fix our attention, almost cannibalistically, on other women's bodies, too: which parts should be cut up, thrown out, replaced, enhanced, reduced. Nobody gets to escape without consequences. And what does this mean for girls and women? In addition to inhabiting a weird sort of third-person perspective on our faces and bodies—watching ourselves being watched by others—experiments have shown that this amount of self-scrutiny can be so mentally and emotionally demanding that it can sap the energy and confidence needed to focus on other things.[9]

And what makes it worse now are all these technologies of the body we're supposed to take advantage of and indeed express gratitude for. The Marquis de Sade would slaver over these. Face peels (acid on the face), dermabrasion (a Black & Decker applied to the face), dermaplaning (ditto, but with woodworking equipment?), lasers, liposuction (vacuum cleaner applied to offending area), and, of course, scalpels, it's right out of *The Bride of Frankenstein*. While all these procedures supposedly "enable" us to look like we're twenty-eight forever, they actually require that we do so.[10] And then there's computer enhancement that makes even models and actresses, who already look really great, look even more perfect so they can torture the rest of us even more.

The British feminist scholar Angela McRobbie speculates that underneath the enforced femininity now expected of girls and women, because we're all so freaking "empowered," is what she calls "illegible rage." Study after study has shown that being expected to be as thin as Kate Moss can prompt a certain subsection of the female population to try to live on a Tic Tac and a Diet Coke a day or to eat like normal people and then go throw it up. More commonly, but just as wasteful of female time, energy, and self-esteem, is the constant obsessing about one's diet and weight. And feminism, by the way, provides zero inoculation against this. We all know this: we know that trying to look like all those semi-emaciated models in the fashion magazines makes girls and women sick; the pathologies produced are taken for granted, it's like a little anorexia, whatever. In fact, we bond over this, share our woes over this aspect of being female, our entrapment by these standards of physical perfection.[11] At least this is an acceptable form of female solidarity. Better to have a little bit of an eating disorder, or a really weird relationship to food, and a hatred of your own body, than defy the whole thinness-beauty regime and be thought of as unattractive (bad), unfeminine (really bad), or a feminist (like totally odious).

All this effort to try to look remotely like someone in *Glamour*, matched by the inevitable failure to do so, creates a certain dyspepsia among the female population: hence McRobbie's "illegible rage." Back in the day, feminists had fun mocking the media images of women and took special delight in giving out awards to the most stupid, sexist ads of the year. (Do you know how much fun it was to walk through the subway in New York City and see ads with stickers plastered on them that read "This Ad Insults Women"?) But now, because we "have it all," and feminism is dead and unnecessary, mounting a similar critique would be uncool, even ungrateful. I mean, aren't the very same ads and magazines featuring all those starved, underfed models also overflowing with the constant appeals that we all have "freedom," "independence," "control," and "power"?[12] So by selling us the "faux feminism" of freedom through skin creams and control through pantyhose, they urge us to substitute consumer feminism for the real deal.[13] It's still feminism, right?

But McRobbie thinks there's something else going on here as women, and young women in particular, lament the gap between image and reality and the impossibility of bridging it. Whether they know it or not, they are missing feminism. There is an anger, however repressed, about how unforgiving this new boilerplate femininity is and an instinct, however thwarted, to fight back. There is a desire for female solidarity based on having to figure out how to live, still, in a male-dominated world, rather than on having to lose five pounds.

Girls and women, with plenty of help from Lancôme, Diet Pepsi, and the bathing suit industry, have learned to turn this sense of loss and this anger in on themselves, of course. But with the rise, and hyperinflation, of the mean girl dramas, the media have done something else: provided fresh new scripts for where girls should really direct their frustration and rage—against one another. In other words, the media—some more consciously than others—have acknowledged girls' exasperation, and the mandate imposed on them to compete in the Hotness Olympics. But since the late 1990s this has been converted into the Queen Bee Olympics and the titillating spectacle of girl-on-girl aggression. In other words, they have taken this "illegible rage," redirected it, and made it visible as the sadistic, white, blond, buxom female posse hunting down the crybaby flunkies of the hotness code. If the size zero, coupled with breasts the size of watermelons, are sold as markers of female liberation and empowerment, and on top of that we see that the actual enforcers of this are the mean girls, then the real source of this—the advancement of enlightened sexism—gets off the hook and remains in the shadows.

Well, before we get to meanness, let's look at leanness. Being slim, even skinny, has of course been an ideal for decades, but in addition to the new hooters, the women's magazines have added something else. Even as a "body by Victoria" became the new norm, women have also been urged to love their bodies as they are. *Glamour*, for example, has repeatedly inter-leaved its ceaseless diet, exercise, and fashion features with articles like: "The New Meaning of Thin," which argued that the thinness ideal was "not psychologically healthy"; "Silence the Dieter in Your Head," which encouraged young women to "boycott the $35- to $50-billion-a-year diet industry" and "make dieting a feminist issue"; "10 Signs You're (Finally!) at Peace with the Mirror"; "Body Confidence Special: The Ultimate Love-Your-Body Guide," which included "Relief! How to Shut Up the Body Police"; and "How to Love Your Body As Is." Talk about bait and switch! You're supposed to love your body as it is but only if it looks like one of their models demonstrating the exercise routine that ensures you'll lose forty pounds by Friday.

The women's magazines often give voice, especially in their letters to the editor pages, to complaints by readers that the models seem a tad cadaverous. But then they would of course totally ignore the complaints (talk to the hand, girls), or dismiss them as wrongheaded. To choose just one example, in *Vogue*'s April 2002 "first ever Shape Issue" (you're kidding, yes?), the magazine "celebrates the female form in all its glorious variety." These varieties included tall, short, curvy, pregnant, and thin. Except that they are all size two (or maybe zero) with large breasts. Even the pregnant model, who, it turns out, is nineteen and "would rather flaunt my belly than hide it," is also a size two. The letter from the magazine's editor acknowledges that "we receive countless letters attacking the models for the way they look. 'Too skinny' is the usual complaint." But then she huffs about a "simple truth": "To be slim and fit is healthier than to be seriously overweight and 'out of shape.'" Well, that settles that. Our choices as women are anorexic versus blimp. Actually, the choice is even narrower—Kate Moss with implants.

It is *Vogue*'s job and that of the countless other women's magazines to remind women that their most important task is to police the boundaries of their bodies. One study found that 78 percent of the covers of frequently read women's magazines made some reference to bodily appearance and over 60 percent explicitly mentioned diet, exercise, or cosmetic surgery in their headlines.[14] This regulation, we are reminded, requires considerable time, mental energy, and attention. Crucial to *Vogue*'s strategy is to acknowledge women's legitimate charges that the magazine promotes an unattainable and, in fact, unhealthy body image and then to assert that such charges are false and wrong, and that the true progressive position for women (because it's healthy—don't you love it?) is to embrace hyperthinness as a body ideal. Enlightened sexism in action: reconfigure antifeminism as feminism.

Well, we've had these fashion magazines around a long time, but in the early twenty-first century there debuted another very instructive weapon in the arsenal of emphatic femininity: the makeover shows, which made cosmetic surgery seem only slightly more unusual (and painful) than going to the dentist. Drawing from the timeworn before-and-after makeover genre of the women's magazines, these shows took what might have been a four-page magazine spread and turned it into an hour of bodily scrutiny and dissection. *Extreme Makeover* premiered in 2002, and initially paired a man and a woman, each of whom hated how he or she looked and hoped for the usual menu of procedures. After only four episodes, the show began pairing women more frequently; it never paired two men in the same show. First we were introduced to the totally selfless, utterly altruistic plastic surgeons, dermatologists, and cosmetic dentists, whose only calling was to enact "miracles" and change these people's lives. Then the candidates themselves offered unsparing self-criticisms of their looks. The men typically needed missing teeth replaced or capped (one guy lost his teeth riding a bull in a rodeo), maybe a nose job, liposuction on beer bellies, and an exercise routine. The women invariably got all this, and more, plus breast augmentation.

One would have to be pretty heartless not to root for many of the people who came on because they were such underdogs, felt so awful about themselves, and often wanted to do this for their partners. And it was in these makeover shows that we saw the central role of class, where the professional, educated, successful people schooled those beneath them about the crucial role proper appearance plays in acceptable upward mobility. And another equation was made completely clear: cosmetic surgery was as much, if not more, about emotional empowerment, boosting your self-esteem, becoming a new and better person, and having your entire life changed, irrevocably, for the better. There were no risks, no regrets (even when the women's smiles had that postsurgery Kabuki stretch to them), and no mention made of the need for subsequent, serial surgeries. If your exterior changed, then, ipso facto, your interior did, too, and always immediately and for the better.

In *The Swan* ("the most unique competition ever!"), Fox's 2004 offering of psychic mustard gas to the female population, "ordinary women" who hated their faces and bodies, and often had stories about being made fun of because of their looks, applied to "turn their lives over to a team of cosmetic and plastic surgeons" and go through "a brutal three-month makeover," the Parris Island of beautification. This was *Queen for a Day* with scalpels. The show was reviled by critics—"hurtful . . . repellent . . . obscene," wrote Robert Bianco in *USA Today*—and on TV.com various of the episodes get community ratings of "terrible" and "abysmal." But its lead-in show was Fox's ratings blockbuster *American Idol*, and *The Swan* retained 76 percent of *Idol*'s audience, nearly 15 million viewers.[15]

And, as dreadful as it was, the show should not be dismissed as irrelevant simply because it was banal, ridiculous, and crude. For its vulgarity came from the fact that, unlike all the glamorous "after" images in *Vogue* or *Cosmo*, it made all too explicit the narrow physical standards to which women are expected to conform, the sad degree to which women internalize these standards, the lengths needed to get there, and the impossibility for most of us to meet the bar without, well, taking a box cutter to our faces and bodies. The show had the poor taste to expose, however inadvertently, how much work it was to put on the masquerade of femininity, in contrast to the suggestions in *Glamour* that all it took was a new eye shadow, different skin cream, or a new pair of shoes. *The Swan* was offensive because it took all the hidden work women are supposed to do to be considered attractive and revealed it to be incredibly time-consuming, painful, lonely, expensive, and, in the end, stupid.

So, this show merits our attention because it dramatized in detail what it means that women are, first and foremost, to be looked at. Each week, two different women, after having gone to Los Angeles to subject themselves to the knife, the gym, a shrink, Jenny Craig, and the overall "coaching" of the collagen-engorged Nely Galan, were unveiled in a chateaulike studio. The one who had undergone the most heroic transformation—that is, was a completely unrecognizable version of her former self, was chosen to move ahead for the final Swan pageant. The other one got sent home looking like a Mae West female impersonator.

At the beginning of each episode, a team of experts—mostly Los Angeles plastic and cosmetic surgeons—viewed an initial videotape of the pathetic "average woman," who was hardly hideous and instead looked pretty much like women from everyday life. Here the women pointed out their various offending body parts—noses too big, stretch marks from pregnancy, imperfect smiles, and always boobs that are too saggy, too small, or both. Often crying into the camera, the women repeatedly insisted that happiness, success, and love are impossible without conventional beauty. It was de rigueur that husbands or boyfriends be interviewed who said they loved the women and thought they were pretty much just fine the way they were, but that the relationship, and especially their sex lives, were suffering because the woman had no self-esteem. Thus, the "brutal three-month makeover" in this show was never about conforming to patriarchal standards of beauty, but about empowering women to be all they could be. Don't worry, it gets worse.

After the self-flagellating video, each of the experts itemized what he (or the lone female dentist) planned to do to the woman to make her "beauty pageant material": "You do breast augmentation"; "she needs to be feminized"; "nose job"; "we'll change her strong masculine teeth" and give her a "feminine smile"; and so forth. Then, in imagery not unlike that used by the Pentagon to monitor bombing attacks, the woman's body—clad only in gray Hanes underpants and a saggy old sports bra— appeared on the screen next to a rotating model of the female body with grid marks on it, just to give things a nice *Battlestar Galactica* touch. A bulls-eye was superimposed over the offending body part with an X marking the target of the proposed surgical strike. Then, after all the imperfect parts had been visually put in the crosshairs, our evening gown–clad and bling-laden hostess Amanda Byram itemized yet again all the serial procedures—multiple liposuctions, da Vinci veneers, breast augmentation, brow lifts, fat transfers to the lips, tummy tucks—that each imperfect body would undergo. Of the show's sixteen contestants, only three did not undergo breast augmentation.

The final kicker of every episode occurred when each woman came out, transformed, to the applause of the various surgeons and coaches and to Byram's gushing praise. During their three-month ordeal the women were allegedly kept away from mirrors—everyone else could see, scrutinize, and assess them, but they couldn't see themselves. Talk about being the blindered object of the gaze! So they had to walk up to a huge mirror hidden behind a curtain, and when they were ready, the curtain lifted and they saw their new selves. Of course there was much scream-ing and crying and exclamations of "I look beautiful." But the truly creepy part was when the women regarded their reflection and said, "Is that me?" or "I don't even recognize myself." This was supposed to be empowering, transforming: that as a woman, you were so subject to Rodeo Drive standards of beauty that it was better to no longer see your true self in the mirror than to fail to conform, to measure up.

Not to be outdone, the following winter MTV aired the truly abysmal *I Want a Famous Face*, in which young women who wanted to look like Britney Spears, Pamela Anderson, or Jennifer Lopez got breast implants, cheek implants, eyebrow lifts, liposuction, and lip implants. (There were the occasional guys who wanted to look like Brad Pitt or Elvis, but the makeover candidates were overwhelmingly female.) But even the nonscal-pel shows enforced the makeover, most notably *American Idol* (where it's true, the guys were redone, too, although rarely told to lose weight) and we also got *What Not to Wear, Fashion Police*, and *Style Court*.

By 2004 even the American Society of Plastic Surgeons (ASPS) was getting a bit nervous about people's "unrealistic, unhealthy expecta-tions about what plastic surgery can do" and issued a warning that "patients should be wary of surgeons who claim they can make a person look like someone else."[16] "No, we can't make you look like Brad Pitt or Angelina Jolie," insisted one doctor, adding, "No, we can't do five different proce-dures in one session," and "No, cosmetic surgery will not make your life a dream."[17] These doctors had a reason to worry: a 2007 study by the ASPS asserted that four out of five cosmetic surgery patients reported that they had been "directly influenced to have a procedure by the plastic surgery reality television shows they watch." The association warned again about "unrealistic expectations," apparently to little avail, especially for younger women.[18] A 2003 survey by *Self* magazine found that 56 percent of women in their thirties and 51 percent of women in their twenties would consider cosmetic surgery, compared to only 27 percent in their fifties.[19]

In 2006, Americans spent just under $12.2 billion (yes, with a *b*) on cosmetic procedures; from 1997 to 2006, there was a 446 percent increase in the number of said procedures.[20] (Here's a bright spot to the financial collapse of 2008; total expenditures had dropped by $2 billion that year.)[21] Don't think those Ipex ads were working? Between 1998 and 1999 alone, there was a 51 percent increase in breast implant surgery, which represented nearly a 500 percent increase since 1992. By 2006, breast augmentation had become the number one cosmetic surgical procedure for women (nearly four hundred thousand surgeries that year), and while more men were having cosmetic procedures, women still accounted for 92 percent of them.[22]

Had people forgotten that in 1992 David Kessler, the commissioner of the Food and Drug Administration, had banned silicone-gel implants on the grounds that they weren't safe? Although there hadn't been many studies about the effects of implants, some of the surgeries had complications: in many women the tissue around the implants scarred and hardened, and in about 5 percent of women the implants ruptured, releasing the silicone gel into women's bodies and causing the breast to collapse. The biggest fear was that the silicone would lead to a variety of autoimmune diseases. Litigation followed and news coverage of plastic surgery soared; in the 1970s, *ABC News* aired two stories about plastic surgery; in the 1990s, it aired sixty. The jump was similar on the other two networks.[23] In 1994, the major manufacturers of breast implants set aside $4.25 billion in anticipation of a major class action settlement.[24]

You would think that these findings would put a damper on breast augmentation. But not when you have the juggernaut of enforced hyperfemininity. Out came new implants filled with saline (sterile salt water), which are believed to be safer than silicone because if they blow up or leak, they will only release salt water—not silicone gel—into the body. It goes without saying that some women with breast implants, particularly those who had them for reconstruction after breast cancer surgery, or had been trying to fill up a 32AAA, reported that they had experienced significant improvement in their quality of life. But this is hardly a group large enough to keep all those Dr. 90210s out there in new Beemers.

Here's what we didn't hear much about from all of those self-satisfied, patronizing, wallet-fattening doctors on *The Swan*. Implants still have risks. Saline breast implants can rupture, change shape, and, er, "shift position." (Does one then point up and the other down?) They can also cause infection, pain, and loss of feeling in the nipple or tissue of the breast. Because the implant is a foreign object, the body will typically form scar tissue around it. The tightening and squeezing of this scar tissue is called "capsular contracture," and may produce hardening of the breast tissue, rippling of the skin, and changes in breast shape. It also may cause pain, sometimes severe, which can require surgery to remove the scar tissue or replace the implant itself. In other words, implants may require additional breast implant surgeries. And implants can interfere with breast-feeding and the detection of breast cancer. Breast implants have a limited life: they can last sixty years, or just six weeks. And then, in 2006, the FDA under the Bush administration reapproved the use of silicone implants.[25] Sure you wouldn't want to take the $3,500 and go to the Bahamas instead? Despite all this, from 2002 to 2003, according to the American Society for Aesthetic Plastic Surgery, the number of girls eighteen and younger who got breast implants nearly tripled, from 3,872 to 11,326.

Maybe it's because I grew up idolizing the likes of Audrey Hepburn, or that the women who emerged as major stars when I was in my twenties—Diane Keaton, Sally Field, Meryl Streep, Glenda Jackson, Faye Dunaway, Barbra Streisand, Sissy Spacek, Mary Tyler Moore, Mia Farrow—were hardly known for their breast size; their breasts were utterly irrelevant. Maybe it's because there simply weren't TV shows and magazine articles all over the place about breast augmentation, and that my friends who were well-endowed often found their large American breasts to be an equally large pain in the ass. But getting implants just wasn't something many women even considered in the 1970s. So the explosive rise in this surgical procedure (especially when we hear women say they want to go from a B to a C or a C to a D)—as one ad promised, "You Won't Just Turn Heads, You'll Break Necks"—shows that the media have hardly been ineffective in selling this bill of goods to women.

But here is the big Catch-22. Now we were all supposed to be stacked, and if you weren't, well, you weren't hot. But if you got implants, weren't you just a gullible tool of the beauty industry whose boobs would feel like rocks and point to the ceiling even if you were standing on your head? Films and TV shows have been filled with fake boob jokes and the celebrity rags delight in trying to expose who's had work done and who hasn't, especially on their boobs. And some old stereotypes, dating back at least to the 1950s, still held sway: Women with large breasts are dumb. Women with large breasts and blond hair are really dumb. Women with large breasts are sexier than women with small breasts. Women with small breasts are smarter than women with big breasts. Women with small breasts and smooth, dark hair are classy. Women with large breasts are promiscuous. Women with small breasts are frigid. Enlightened sexism has worked very hard to restore the principle that women are to be judged by the size, uplift, and cleavage of their breasts. And whatever their size and shape, they're never just quite right.

Is all of this making a lot of girls and women sick, deformed, furious, or all of the above? Highly entertaining Web sites like "The 15 Worst Celebrity Plastic Surgery Disasters You Will Ever See," "Worst Celebrity Boob Jobs," or "Bitten & Bound: The Not So Pretty Side of Hollywood" invert the whole before-and-after makeover conventions, because the "after" photos are terrifying. Bulgy lips distended by collagen, asymmetrical cannonball boobs, cheeks that look like they're stuffed with golf balls, frozen faces that can no longer move, all accompanied by snarky, derisive commentary like, "Your artificial fat lip looks fat and ugly. . . . You can probably get punched in the mouth for free if you try hard enough." And while the women of America have been worked over so well by the beauty-industrial complex that there are hardly any of us who don't think—no matter what we weigh—that we could still stand to lose another five pounds, there was also a backlash against hyperthinness. A series of highly publicized deaths in the fall of 2006, most notably that of the Brazilian fashion model Ana Carolina Reston, whose tomato and fruit diet got her down to eighty pounds (at five feet eight inches) before she died, created a scandal (however temporary) in the fashion industry. That fall Madrid's Fashion Week had banned underweight models from the catwalk and then Milan followed suit, forbidding models with a body mass index of less than 18.5. But efforts to impose a similar ban in New York failed—not surprising given that Americans spend more money on dieting products than on education.[26] In January 2007 the Council of Fashion Designers of America issued vague, voluntary guidelines about protecting models and urging those with eating disorders to get help, but it did not specify what constituted being too thin.[27] That would impose unreasonable constraints on the industry and we in A-mer-ka don't do that.

And is doing anything to stay thin all that bad? Not if you take the highly publicized Kate Moss scandal as a morality tale. After London's *Daily Mirror* published a picture of her in September 2005 allegedly using cocaine (which is helpful in making food seem unnecessary), various companies like Burberry, Chanel, and H&M said they would no longer use the superwaif in their ads.[28] But within two months, Burberry welcomed Moss back to "our family," she was promoting mascara, and she had signed on to model for an Italian designer. Five months after that, Calvin Klein signed her to a $1 million deal.[29] Is it worth snorting coke to stay at ninety-five pounds? Sure sounds like it. At the same time on billboards and in magazines around the country we saw Dove's "Campaign for Real Beauty," launched in September 2004, which featured real women, not actresses or models, in bras and underpants and not stick thin, to counter the Kate Moss standard of beauty.[30] Within a year, Dove's sales rose 12.5 percent, and rose another 10 percent in 2006.[31] (Of course Unilever, the company that owns Dove, also owns Slim-Fast, so go figure.)

In the midst of all this we learned about the "real" problem—an obesity epidemic in America. By 2007, 25 percent—one quarter of U.S. adults!—were said to be obese.[32] This is hardly surprising given the food porn seducing us—the ketchup dripping ever so voluptuously down the curves of the burger, the caramel stretched, stretched, stretched just to the snapping point, the beer cascading into the sweating glass—and these ads just after the Jenny Craig ads! Talk about a sick relationship with food. As the feminist activist and author Jean Kilbourne has pointed out in her video *Slim Hopes*, advertisers tell us that the way for women to stop feeling bad after a crappy day or heinous breakup is to eat a half gallon of ice cream (in secret, of course). So, there was a thinness ideal few could meet, and many weren't bothering, yet undoubtedly felt bad about it. And the contradictions are huge, the mixed messages irresolvable. So: Be a size zero! No, wait, that's unhealthy! Love your body! No wait, it's not good enough the way it is! Love your body, part 2! No, wait, we're all obese! But there's one group for whom the messages are decidedly not mixed: the dreaded older woman.

Things are not so good for me, the Vintage Female, when I look in the mirror, especially after reading *Vogue*. Oh my God, do I need work. The eye bags the size of wontons are enough to make any plastic surgeon weep. I will never be envied with this face, just pitied. I may not be the target market for a boob job, but Botox, laser peels, face-lifts—anything to eradicate evidence of aging hectors women of my age at every turn. And here's my problem, as I understand it from reading various issues of *Vogue* over the years. My face is like a piece of real estate, I'm the landlord, and I have a really serious deferred maintenance problem. "Think of your face as a house," advised dermatologist Patricia Wexler. "Collagen is your spackle. Fat is your foundation. And SoftForm is your framework." SoftForm is a "rubbery tube" from "the famed Collagen Corporation" that gets inserted into "puppet lines" between one's mouth and chin or into "thin, flat lips." "Women and men are bound to queue up for SoftForm," *Vogue* predicted, and helpfully offered the firm's toll-free number.[33]

Well, what if you are uneasy about inserting these little pipe cleaners in your face, since complications may include "infection . . . a common, but treatable risk," "migration," and "extrusion" (eeeww)?[34] Well, you could still have fat or collagen injected into your face, but "fat and collagen are gradually absorbed by the body, so patients wind up back at their dermatologists every couple of months for routine maintenance."[35] (Where does the fat and collagen go? To your ass, would be my guess.) Fillers include bovine collagen (yes, from cows), Cosmoplast (holy bris milah, it's foreskin collagen!), and Cymetra (holy Frankenstein, cadaver collagen). The same issue of *Vogue* reported that a plastic surgeon had recently been "gunned down by a disgruntled facelift patient." Wonder what the level of "extrusion" was there.[36]

But I've already screwed up big time. Because it now turns out that it's no longer okay to wait until you're sixty or so and look like Andy Rooney to have any work done. You have to start in your thirties, even your twenties. "There isn't much you can do for a 60-year-old," sniped Paul Jarrod Frank, another dermatologist. "But you can do a lot of preventative work on a younger woman." *Vogue* reported with a straight face that, with advice like this, "Suddenly, his practice has diversified."[37] I bet. "Until the age of 21, the way you look depends on your parents and God," the magazine advised. "After that, it's all up to you—provided you have the cash or can qualify for credit."[38] Hello Citibank. Collagen injections—at least $400 a pop—are "great for someone in her 30s just starting out in the process of maintaining and correcting. When it wears off, all you need is a quick shot and you're set for another couple of months."[39]

Vogue's stable of plastic surgeon sources also began to recommend that women start the surgical process early, as "the best and longest-lasting results are achieved on younger patients due to the elasticity of their skin."[40] Because aging "creeps up on you . . . decade by decade . . . cosmetic procedures are necessary even in the 20s." In fact, the magazine asserted, cosmetic surgery "is now a . . . relatively hassle-free method for upkeep, even age prevention" and "a necessity for anyone with a decent income." Returning, repeatedly, to the building trades metaphor, *Vogue* emphasized that dermatologists study the "skin's architecture," that collagen is one of its "building blocks," and that women must be committed to regular maintenance, because now cosmetic procedures are like "hair coloring or dental work."[41] The machines being invented—the "Lyra laser," the "VersaPulse laser"—sound like something from Darth Vader's arsenal. And then there's Artecoll, "a collagen infused with Plexiglas particles," if you want a little acrylic in your face's overall structural design.

Of course, there's always Botox to freeze those pesky facial muscles. In 2005, Allergan, the maker of Botox (and the world's largest producer of breast implants), launched a major ad campaign aimed at women between thirty-five and forty-nine, in which the three best reasons for getting the shots were "Me, myself and I." (There were nearly 2.8 million

Botox injections performed in 2007.)[42] But Botox can be "jostled" and move to a muscle where it wasn't intended and give you "droopy eyelid." After a Botox injection you shouldn't shower, bend over (no shoe shopping, girls), nap, or look down until the next day, warns Dr. Pat Wexler, lest such unwanted migrations occur. No using a hair dryer either, in case it melts the Botox beneath the skin. Or a neighboring muscle can overcompensate for the frozen one and produce what's known in the dermatology business as "'the Mr. Spock' . . . a freakishly arched brow."[43]

Then there's the nuclear option, the surgical face-lift. In recounting hers, one woman wrote that the day after surgery "I am a mass of mutilation stacked upright in bed" and, two weeks later, "My body has oozed more than I knew it had to spare." After recounting other grisly details, she advised "keeping bags of frozen vegetables on hand" to throw on your face to "diminish swelling." But in the end it was all worth it: "The surgery translated into an attitude boost that all the money on earth couldn't buy."[44] I don't know, a stiff gin and tonic sounds like a pretty good alternative to me. But the gin and tonic won't substitute for this—a friend of the woman's, in her mid-forties, "concedes that I might look a tiny bit younger than she. (I am older.) This incident alone has made the surgery worthwhile."[45]

All of this is forcing women to develop their own face-lift politics. On the one hand, in a culture where, like it or not, women are still judged first and foremost by their appearances, and where looking too old might even cost you your job, "Why grow old gracefully," as Nicole Richie put it, "when you have the technology to prevent it?"[46] On the other hand, why subject ourselves to shoving Elsie the cow's or dead people's collagen into our faces, let alone undergoing bruising surgery, just to enrich the plastic surgeons of America and to reinforce the sexist double standard in which aging men are distinguished and older women are not? (Then there's the feminist-wimp response that fuses the previous objection with a deeply fervent desire to never have needles, laser beams, or scalpels touch one's body unless one's life is at stake.)

Even actresses, for whom youthful beauty is typically equivalent to employability, are divided on the issue. Kate Winslet has claimed that she would never have surgery or Botox, and Diane Keaton has declared herself opposed as well, whereas Jennifer Aniston has said, "Sure, I'd have a face lift. . . . Anything that makes you feel better, go for it." Since I don't know anyone who's had Botox (at least, not to my knowledge), I find Cameron Diaz's observation to be a deterrent: "It looks like their faces are dead in that one place."[47] Then there were the studies, beginning in 2007, which found that the suicide rate among women who had received breast implants was twice the suicide rate of the general population.[48] So there's an alarming relationship between being deeply unhappy, being unhappy with your body, and having liquid-filled plastic bags surgically inserted into your body that kind of contradicts the whole "boost your self-esteem" line about the real reasons to have cosmetic surgery.

To challenge the concern that the cosmetic procedure frenzy is just another way to oppress women, and to extract any unsightly swelling in their checkbooks, words like "choice" and "empowered" seek to equate having work done with being truly liberated. Virginia Madsen, the star of Sideways and a spokesperson for Botox, likened getting "injectables" to a healthy lifestyle choice like working out and eating properly.[49] Allergan markets its breast implants as sources of "power, freedom, individuality and self-confidence."[50] Cosmetic surgery is thus presented as a feminist way for women to exert control over their bodies and thus their destinies. In this way, succumbing to patriarchal standards of female beauty is the latest expression of women's liberation; pretty nice twist, you have to admit. To decide not to go under the knife, under these circumstances, is not a "choice" but an admission that you don't care enough about yourself and don't have enough self-esteem to tackle the requisite deferred maintenance. Never mind that health insurance doesn't cover any of this either; take out a loan or slap it on your credit card.

Many older women are deeply torn by these face-lift politics: many see cosmetic surgery as simultaneously oppressive and liberating.[51] As I look down and wonder what happened to my knees, or watch my neck collapse—hello, scarves and turtlenecks!—I, like millions of baby boom women, would like to look as young as I feel, to compete in a youth-oriented culture, to still be able to wear skirts that aren't floor length, and not to have one of my dearest friends call me whenever she sees me on TV to ask when I am finally going to have my eyes done. But I'm also inclined to offer an obscene gesture to ageist, sexist dismissals of older women, and am disinclined to be a bigger dupe of the beauty industry than I already am (my Sephora bills are strictly between me and my daughter). And I really, really do not want to have knives and needles stuck in my face the results of which might make me look like I was trapped in one of those astronaut-training G-force centrifuges for a month. Because conquering aging is, of course, one of the biggest fantasies of all.

So, now that we've reviewed leanness—which I hope has left you some-what irate—let's move on to meanness, and the connection between the two. In 2002, Rosalind Wiseman's *Queen Bees and Wannabes* and Rachel Simmons's *Odd Girl Out: The Hidden Culture of Aggression in Girls* both became bestsellers. Wiseman, who had already begun doing workshops at schools around the country to handle girl-on-girl "relational aggression," was also profiled in a cover story in the *New York Times Magazine* and featured on Oprah. Tina Fey optioned Wiseman's book and turned it into the 2004 hit movie *Mean Girls* with Rachel McAdams and Lindsay Lohan as the main backstabbing, evil bitches. As we've previously noted, during these years, catfighting, duplicitous females became a media fave: on *The Real World, The Hills, The Apprentice, America's Next Top Model.* By 2007 we had the gold standard of teen female meanness and betrayal in *Gossip Girl,* especially in the first season.

This was something of a rapid turnaround from the allegedly meek, self-doubting girls whose plight had kept Mary Pipher's *Reviving Ophelia* on the bestseller list from 1994 to 1997. Pretty soon there were stories about widespread cyber-bullying or net-bullying, with gangs of girls reportedly using text messages, MySpace, instant messaging, and plain old e-mail to torment and humiliate their prey. And in 2007, the press went crazy over a story about a thirteen-year-old girl named Megan Meier who hanged herself after a woman—posing as a boy online—told her that the world would be a better place without her.

It's not that Wiseman and Simmons weren't on to something. We all know that vindictive mean girls do exist. We also know they are nothing new. (For those of you not around in 1956 who want to see the original blond-pigtailed preteen from Hades, catch Patty McCormack in *The Bad Seed.* No wimpy cyber-rumors for her, she killed a classmate and set a janitor on fire. Only a bolt of lightning could stop that evil spawn.) So I am not belittling the cruelties that girls can and do inflict on each other. And we have heard true-life tragic stories of malicious girl bullying. Communications technologies that permit the instant sharing of private information can also provide the bully anonymity to make all this faster and easier. But this new media archetype, that of the teen girl—especially if she was rich—as a little Leona Helmsley in training, seemed a bit out of proportion to what was really going on. Did the teen and preteen girls of the country go from being Cinderella to Cruella De Vil in five short years?

Both *Queen Bees and Wannabes* and *Odd Girl Out* used pretty broad brushstrokes ("every girl has a role in cliques," Wiseman asserted) and plenty of eye-clawing anecdotes to suggest that the mean girl phenomenon had reached epidemic proportions.[52] They offered no scientific studies documenting a new explosion of this behavior. Never mind, this was a hot story. Consulting firms popped up around the country to target the scourge. A 2007 study of the Pew Internet and American Life Project, however, reported that only 7 percent of its teen girl respondents had had an embarrassing picture of them posted online and only 16 percent had had rumors spread about them online.[53] As the lead researcher told MSNBC, "the results were unexpectedly tame, given all the media attention focused on the problem of cyber-bullying." Overall, studies show that about 20 percent of kids in school experience bullying—meaning 80 percent don't.

But here's the interesting part. While girls rarely bully boys, "girls are frequently victimized by boys at school." Indeed, much of the bullying that girls actually endure is really sexual harassment by boys—crude jokes, sexual propositions, lewd gestures, inappropriate touching or grabbing, and degrading comments about girls' appearance, body parts, and sexuality.[54] And despite the shocking headlines about girls who kill themselves as the result of mean girl manipulations, studies show that it's sexual harassment in particular that has greater negative outcomes for girls, who internalize the attacks and may become depressed, withdrawn, and anxious.[55] But hell, that was old news: we already knew that from the Clarence Thomas–Anita Hill hearings. And how can you make a funny chick-flick comedy out of that?

When the film *Mean Girls* premiered in May 2004, it became a number one box office hit and brought in $25 million its first weekend, more than anyone expected. Seventy-five percent of the audience was female.[56] Written by the incomparable Tina Fey, the script faithfully represents Wiseman's overstatements in *Queen Bees* about how epidemic girl meanness was—in the climactic scene about girl bullying, every single girl in a school-wide assembly claims to have been a victim. (There are no questions about or any scenes showing boys bullying or sexually harassing girls.) But through its humor the film also captures some important truths about the possible roots of girl-on-girl malice. Here we meet "the Plastics," whose Queen Bee, the rich, blond, gorgeous Regina (Rachel McAdams) is so adulated that she is carried to gym class on the shoulders of two hunky male athletes. Cady (Lindsay Lohan), home-schooled, in Africa no less, until her junior year, is adopted by the Plastics and learns their ways. Karl Rove had nothing on Regina, who wrecks girls' lives by spreading rumors that they are lesbians or calling their mothers and, pretending to be someone from Planned Parenthood, says their daughter's test results are in.

But the Plastics have strict, self-imposed rules they have to live by, too: no jeans except on Friday, ponytails just once a week, no tank tops two days in a row. We later learn that Regina has had a nose job. In Regina's bedroom, she and her two slim, pretty friends stand in front of the mirror and itemize what they hate about their own bodies: their hips, their calves, their pores, their hairlines. In public, however, they use their sexuality as a weapon, to steal boys from other girls and to make other girls envy them. (In an especially telling and disturbing moment, we see Regina's little sister, maybe eight or so, watching *Girls Gone Wild* and then lifting her little shirt in front of the TV screen.) The Plastics are, then, a caricature of female solidarity: when girls bond, this is the kind of trivial crap they actually focus on.

Mean Girls and *Queen Bees and Wannabes* show how the tyranny of narrow, unforgiving standards of femininity and hotness compel girls to police themselves and punish those who fail to live up to these standards, or refuse to take them on. So the mean girl icon simultaneously acknowledges that girls have every right to feel oppressed by the "body by Victoria" ideal, but then directs their anger away from broader social forces (like patriarchy) and onto each other. Being a hottie takes time, work, and money; girls who are too tomboyish or athletic or political or intellectual don't have their leg caught in the trap and are getting away with something the conformist girls aren't, so they deserve to be ostracized. Girls have learned to be "enforcers of their own oppression," calling each other sluts and whores, imposing even more ridiculous rules on themselves than the beauty-industrial complex does and mocking girls whose clothes, hair, figures, or social status aren't just right.[57] And despite the popularity of all the warrior women in thongs on TV and in the movies, it remains utterly unacceptable for real girls to be physically aggressive or even to express anger. Thus, as Cady tells us in *Mean Girls*, "All the fighting had to be sneaky."

The icon of the mean girl—entitled, pampered, conceited, vindictive, overly sexualized, too big for her britches—justifies simmering sexist resentments that with Title IX, girl-only science classes, federal girl power programs, girls are now getting too big a piece of the pie.[58] It is therefore crucial to uphold enlightened sexism by making the story about girls attacking other girls, and not about boys or right-wingers going after them. If, after all this corrective social policy aimed at sports and academic achievement, the best girls can do is to spread false rumors about each other and impose "pink Tuesdays" on themselves, then why bother? If we try to redress sexism only to have the girls turn out to be even more empty-headed than any card-carrying male chauvinist pig might have claimed, well, weren't the sexists right all along? Didn't girls need to be put back in their place?

The mean girl takes us right back to Amy Fisher territory, reminding us that teen girl sexuality is threatening if it isn't properly controlled and contained. And because these mean girls are so willing to use sex as a weapon, and to flaunt their hotness with miniskirts, Playboy Bunny Halloween costumes, and provocative strutting across the lunchroom or at any A-list party, aren't they asking for it?

The image of the mean girl also became a great lightning rod for simmering class resentments about the increasing maldistribution of wealth in the country. Why be really pissed at the Bush tax cuts? Tax codes are hard to follow and that would be "class warfare" anyway. Why rail at CEOs who make anywhere from two hundred to four hundred times what the rest of us make while their companies fire people and plunder their pensions? We don't know these guys and what could we do anyway? But take an image of a really rich, size zero princess (a blonde for L.A., throw in a brunette for the Upper East Side of Manhattan), whose parents indulge her every whim and to whom money is no object, who is vindictive, petty, and superficial, who doesn't deserve and shouldn't have the wealth that she does, and who channels all her energy into ruining the life of some other equally wealthy, shallow girl. Now there's an icon of class animus we can really sink our teeth into. I already feel my blood boiling. But we can also make fun of this panic about the overweening power of rich teens. Which leads us to the totally delicious *Gossip Girl*.

Created by Josh Schwartz and Stephanie Savage, the same people who brought us *The O.C.*, and simply transplanted the exact same show to the Upper East Side of Manhattan (some of the actors even look alike), *Gossip Girl* follows the sexcapades, palace plots and intrigue, and the warring Queen Bees' attempts at Web- and text-based mutually assured destruction, often assisted by their Caligula-like fellow student Chuck Bass (the perfectly slimy and gorgeous Ed Westwick). The original Queen Bee, Serena van der Woodsen (Blake Lively), whose last name evokes old New York Dutch roots, has gone away to a boarding school for a year only to be dethroned by her former BFF, the truly scabrous Blair Waldorf (Leighton Meester), whose reign is then challenged by the upstart blonde, Jenny Humphrey (Taylor Momsen). All of this takes place at an impossibly hoity-toity prep school that looks like the Houses of Parliament. Typical dialogue: Blair tells Serena she doesn't have a chance of getting into her top college because "Brown doesn't offer degrees to sluts." In between trying to annihilate one another's reputations, social standing, and personal relationships, the principals engage in sex on bar stools, drink martinis in posh New York bars (even though they're all juniors in high school), smoke pot, and, most important of all, text message and go online to read and dish dirt. Indeed, the biggest stars of the show, beside the twenty-something actors we're supposed to believe are sixteen, are the girls' over-the-top outfits and their cell phones. (Hello, successful product placement by Verizon.)

Unlike other comparable soaps aimed at the eighteen-to-thirty-four demographic, *Gossip Girl* did not become a runaway hit on television its first season: each episode drew only about 2.5 million viewers. But it generated enormous buzz and was a big hit online: for a while fans could watch it on CW's Web site for free, and it was among the top shows downloaded from iTunes.[59] In August 2008 it won six Teen Choice Awards, including those for best TV show and best "breakout show." By the fall of 2008, the CW enjoyed a 41 percent increase in viewers on Monday night, and a 143 percent increase in female viewers aged eighteen to thirty-four.[60] Once you give yourself over to it, *Gossip Girl* is the televisual version of heroin. I mean, even Wallace Shawn is in it!

What makes this show smarter than it deserves to be, and perfect for its time? Aside from the clothes and the ever-comforting message that the rich are just as miserable—no, maybe even more miserable—than we are, *Gossip Girl* buys into and repudiates various elements of enlightened sexism. And its mocking tone and fantastically implausible plot lines, which draw from the conventions of online celebrity journalism, allow us to view the whole enterprise ironically while still getting sucked in. We get this right away from the arch female voice-over of the anonymous "Gossip Girl" blogger who dishes the dirt ("This just in . . ."), delivered flawlessly by the actress Kristen Bell (*Veronica Mars, Forgetting Sarah Marshall*). Her voice dripping with sarcasm, and seeming to look down on the mere mortals from her perch on Mount Olympus (or the royal palace of Monaco), a typical Gossip Girl report goes, "Gossip Girl here. Your one and only source into the scandalous lives of Manhattan's upper elite . . . It takes two to tangle and girls like these don't go down without a fight." Or another: "Spotted on the steps of the Met, an S and B power struggle . . . Did S think she could waltz home and things would be just like they were? . . . Did B think S would go down without a fight? Or can these two hotties work it out? There's nothing Gossip Girl likes more than a good catfight . . . and this could be a classic." Later in the season, the cunning and duplicitous Georgina appears, who is even more treacherous than Blair (Gossip Girl calls her "the spawn of Satan"), and seeks to blackmail Serena *and* steal her boyfriend from her.

So, we get the stereotype of girls as shallow and vindictive social climbers, obsessed with conspicuous consumption, who can't get along and are destined to get into serial catfights, especially over boys. These are girly girls, frequently squealing when in groups and awash in bright pastels, huge, shocking pink patent-leather handbags, reeling under headbands adorned with Minnie Mouse–sized bows. And these are real bitches here, impressively calculating for sixteen-year-olds, who choose feel-good moments—an intimate family dinner, or a large, public announcement of a charitable donation—to out a closeted homosexual teen or expose a female rival's alleged drug addiction. They have a way of cocking their heads with complete confidence and widening their eyes just so when they've said something especially devastating. They steal someone's cell phone and then send damaging gossip from it; or they steal a man's cell phone in a bar and figure out how to call his girlfriend, and say they were just making out with him. Use your computer to access information or help with your homework? As freakin' if! It's a miracle the girls don't fall down the stairs at school, so glued are their faces to the smutty text on their cell phones.

But that's also the show's point—it's all so exaggerated (made more so by Gossip Girl mocking, "You all know you love me, XOXO") that we have to view the whole enterprise with an in-the-know smirk: these *are* caricatures, and most girls, even really rich ones, are not such superficial, sexually predatory black widows. Gossip Girl herself delights in the girl fights, but by announcing them snidely, and inflatedly, "Game on, Ladies" or "Hey Upper East Siders. We hear that World War III just broke out and it's wearing knee socks . . . this one's to the death," she also conveys how overblown the notion of girl-on-girl violence has become. And the heart of the show—and these soaps *do* have to have heart, after all—is the same as it was nearly twenty years before on *90210*: what really matters is friendship, family, and honest, loving relationships. When Blair, at the end of the first season, very publicly busts the scheming Georgina (the hint is that she'll be off to reform school), it's because she and Serena have patched things up and become BFFs again—which is what most of us wanted.

It is here that we see the triumph of enlightened sexism and of the rebellion against it, and the role irony plays in both. What with the new size zero, mammary mania, and the mass promotion of cosmetic surgery to females of all ages, the drumbeat message is the same as it ever was—appearance for women is everything, and you don't measure up—only even more ballyhooed, blaring, demanding. And the new empowered girl, given everything through "girl power," had turned into a monster, because what girls' power really did, according to these fables, was magnify their essential traits—pettiness, cattiness, emotional vapidity, materialism, and a desperate need for a guy. The hot, mean girl bitch was yet another warning about female power run amok and about what happens when girls stop being the most important thing they're supposed to be after "hot"—nice. What *Gossip Girl* shows is that irony works not only in offering sexist, retrograde images of women with a wink; it also works in making fun of such fare. And we need this arch, empowered irony as we confront another newly engorged carbuncle of enlightened sexism, celebrity culture.

9

RED CARPET MANIA

There we all are, waiting in the checkout line to buy dinner. (For my version of the South Beach diet, that would be a can of tuna and the 2.5-liter jug of sauvignon blanc.) We cannot escape. Everywhere, hot pink or canary yellow headlines bellow, "She's Due May 2!" "The Truth About That Night!" "Deadly Eating Disorders!" "Oprah Betrays Gayle!" "First Photos of Her Bump!" "Why Tom Won't Marry Katie!" "Britney Committed! Inside Her Ordeal!" "EXTRA! 66 Celeb Babies!" "Rihanna's Tragedy!" The photos, exclamation points, finger-pointing arrows, quivering question marks demand that we look at them, wonder about them, identify with them, envy them, hate them: the celebrities of America. We, the females of America, are to measure our own worth against them, and to fashion ourselves through them. We must walk through the gauntlet of magazine racks, a highly compressed and unavoidable photo gallery, their faces and bodies dominating every publication. Some of them are glowing and gorgeous; others, having been caught by a photographer with their faces contorted in some kind of shriek, look crazed or deranged. Most humiliating of all, various women, especially in the *Enquirer's* and the *Star's* "Worst Beach Bodies," have been caught—yes—sporting cellulite.

Fame is heavenly; fame is a curse. But fame is the flame, and we are the fluttering, envious, resentful, curious moths.

Celebrity culture has moved from the margins of the mass media into its auricles and ventricles. And the relentless manufacture of celebrity culture has all the earmarks of a business plan, and one directed especially at girls and young women. Women—which ones are to be admired and which ones loathed—are the drivers of celebrity journalism; they are also its main market. Sure, Tom Cruise may be a crazed Scientologist who locks his wife up like Rapunzel, and Mel Gibson may down one too many tequilas while reading, yet again, *The Protocols of the Elders of Zion* while sticking voodoo pins into a rabbi doll. But it is the women—Jen, Angelina, Lindsay, Julia, Tyra, Nicole, J.Lo, Britney, and all the girls of *The Hills* and *Gossip Girl*—who propel the magazines off the racks.

And, ah, the numerous fantasies they offer. So many rich, successful women. Girls and women get to shop 'til they drop; are bombarded by free gifts and other swag; date or marry impossibly handsome men; are adulated for being distinct, gifted human beings; have friends who are also famous (and, thus, allegedly fun or interesting); get the best seats at restaurants; go to over-the-top, Taittinger-drenched parties; have the cutest babies and, two days after the kids are born, weigh less than they did when they got pregnant; have husbands who are full partners in raising the kids; and win countless awards and recognition for their work. At the same time, these dazzling knockouts get dumped, betrayed, and cheated on, just like us. Even they have slumps in their careers, make deeply unfortunate fashion choices, gain too much weight, drink too much, or get hooked on drugs. They have what we wish we had, will never have, and yet even they—the most beautiful, admired, deferred-to women in the world—are also subject to the vicissitudes of living in a man's world. They escape; yet even they can't escape. While celebrity journalism puts these women in the spotlight, and gives them a voice and a platform we don't have, it also constantly polices them and their femininity. So one fantasy is that there is a place where women can, indeed, "have it all." But the contradictory (and reassuring) fantasy is that these gorgeous, wealthy luminaries can't "have it all," either. And if they can't, neither can we.

On this particular evening in the supermarket, slack-jawed shop-
pers were confronted by multiple photos on assorted magazines of the
same five white people: Brad Pitt and Angelina Jolie ("Brangelina"),
Tom Cruise and Katie Holmes ("TomKat"), and the Liza Minnelli melt-
down of the millennial generation, Britney Spears. Between January
and early September 2005, Jolie, Pitt, and/or Jennifer Aniston were on
the cover of *In Touch* thirty-three times. By late 2007 and early 2008 it
was all Britney, all the time. As *Rolling Stone* reported, paparazzi agencies estimated that Spears constituted 20 percent of their coverage in
2007.[1] While celebrity gossip has for years relied on sensationalism, it
now draws increasingly from the conventions of the news, with daily
breaking stories, scoops, and latest developments—the construction of
a continuum—that one simply should not miss.

On the one hand, as I stood there eager to get my hands on a cork-
screw, a portion of me did wonder what Brad Pitt sees in Angelina Jolie
that he ceased to see in Jennifer Aniston. Or why Tom Cruise—who, after
all, dumped one of the great beauties and gifted actresses of our time,
Nicole Kidman—would jump up and down on Oprah's sofa like a cricket
on Ritalin chirping his undying love for a former star of *Dawson's Creek*.
Cruise's outburst immediately became as embarrassing as when Sean
Penn declared on *The Tonight Show* during his love affair with Madonna
something to the effect that she was more important than "any whale."

On the other hand, of course, I do not care at all about Lindsay Lohan,
let alone Nicole Richie, and half of the people in *US Weekly* I haven't even
heard of. But I—Vintage Female and, even worse, college professor—am
not the target market. My daughter is the market, my female students are
the market, girls in middle and high school are the market, and women
in their late twenties and early thirties are the market. (This doesn't mean
there isn't celebrity journalism for men. Sports coverage has moved
squarely in this direction, too, with lots more about male athletes' personal lives, homes, and cars. But *US Weekly* and its competitors are primarily female territory.) Indeed, among the college students I teach, at one
of the top universities in the country, I am astounded by how much they
know about the lives, dating histories, food preferences, pet ownership
records, and employment timelines of celebrities. Stand back for a minute
and just think how bizarre it is to live in a culture where we have such

completely asymmetrical relationships with utterly distant, unknown people: we know plenty about them, identify with them, sympathize with them, want to emulate them, and they have zero idea who any of us is.[2]

Little in the media divides women across generational lines more than celebrity culture: the mothers I know would rather line gerbil boxes with *Life & Style* than have their daughters read it. Okay, I might want to learn, in the checkout line, that Mr.-authority-on-all-relationships "Dr. Phil" and his wife may be splitting (after screaming matches and throwing things, woo-hoo!), or that the adorable Reese Witherspoon may have found new love with the adorable Jake Gyllenhaal. But all the "red carpet" mania, the rabid, crazed paparazzi attention to misbehaving girls, the "Worst Beach Bodies"—I think it's nuts. It rots girls' and women's brains and is the perfect example of how the media try to get us to focus on the mental equivalent of Twinkies instead of on, say, knowing who our senators are, where India is, or why the Children's Defense Fund matters.

So why do young women care about who's wearing which outfit (and wearing it better), who's "hot" now, who's dating whom, and babies, babies, babies? (The hypernatalism in particular has become thermonuclear.) They attend to it because it's entertaining and escapist, of course. And despite how evanescent, banal, and femininity-obsessed it is, think about the alternative daydream that celebrity culture offers. Women and girls are absolutely central to this parallel universe—they matter symbolically and economically. They are the center of attention. Corporate profits rest on them. Unlike schoolteachers, day care workers, or secretaries, these women are not paid less than they're worth, but *more* than they're worth, often much more. And unlike in the business or political worlds, families and children are of utmost importance. Women in this realm work long hours, have careers, and are still able to have families because they have the support to do so. There are no hungry or deprived children—hell, we don't even see them screaming "no!," throwing tantrums, or throwing up. Decent, admired men here are the polar opposite of Dick Cheney—they're guys like Ben Affleck photographed taking their children to the park or out for ice cream, centrally committed (according to these candid snapshots) to their families and the domestic sphere. It's always sunny. You can always go to the beach. You have a personal trainer. There's no war, no people without health care. I wouldn't mind such a world (except for the fact that I'd have to lose thirty pounds and get a face-lift to fit in).

But wrapped in this shiny cellophane are persistent, unforgiving primers on what constitutes successful femininity, and what does not. Julia Roberts, successful. Britney Spears, not so much. And there is plenty for girls and women to deplore about the gender norms that these magazines ram down our throats. Celebrity journalism drives home the message that the gender tightrope for women is gossamer-thin and precarious. And celebrity journalism claims to tell women—the visible famous ones and the invisible rest of us—how to walk it. That celebrity magazines and Web sites have proliferated like North Korea's nuclear arsenal has only increased the fusillade.

Where, in the olden days, one would find *Glamour* and *Vogue*, and, believe it or not, even *Newsweek* or *Time* (yes!) near the checkout conveyor belts, now there are primarily the warring celebrity and gossip magazines that pay for those upfront racks: the old warhorse *People*, embattled now by *US Weekly*, *In Touch*, *Inside TV*, the newly celebritized *TV Guide*, the upstart British import *OK!* (which often pays celebrities to be in its pages and thus sucks up to them shamelessly), and the *Star*, the *Enquirer*, and the *Globe*. These formerly black-and-white tabloids, loved for their features on UFO visitations and interspecies offspring, have long since moved to exposés on the weight fluctuations and rehab recidivism rates of the rich and famous. They've gone glossy as well, which has helped them get advertisers other than palm readers and those promising that their "miracle" sauna suit will help you lose forty pounds in two days. Indeed, celebrity magazines, not counting *People*, raked in $150 million in advertising in 2003; by 2006, that had soared to $560 million.[3] There are now so many of these rags that *Advertising Age* has a word for the genre: "celeb-azines."[4] Although I can't be sure about this, I imagine that most of us in the checkout line feel like a Strasbourg goose, funnel down the gullet, being force-fed this unrelenting stream of calculated commercial swill. But it wouldn't be there if it didn't sell.

And sell it does. Or did. In the first half of 2005 alone, *US Weekly*'s paid circulation increased 24 percent over the previous year, to 1.7 million, the *Star*'s increased 21 percent to 1.4 million, while *People* led the pack at 3.7 million.[5] (The Jen–Brangelina dirt was the bonanza that year.) By 2005, entertainment or celebrity news consumed more space in magazines than any other topic.[6] Between 2006 and 2007, *OK!*'s circulation jumped 54 percent, and *US Weekly* and *In Touch* rose another 5 to 10 percent.[7] Many fans didn't buy just one of these mags, they bought two or three at a pop. By 2006, these weeklies had a combined circulation of over eight and a half million.[8] Snarky celebrity Web sites like PerezHilton.com, TMZ.com, Gawker.com, X17online.com, and Pink is the New Blog, which have sprung up like toadstools since 2005, offer junior high school headlines like "Brit Can't Go Wee-Wee Without Watchers?" and are appointment surfing for millions, especially women aged sixteen to thirty-four.[9] But here's another silver lining of the Great Recession: 2009 headlines like "Celebrity Magazines Post a Downturn in Sales." After the heated growth of 2003–07, some of these rags posted double-digit declines in the second half of 2008, the circulation of *In Touch* crashing 29 percent, *Life & Style Weekly* 30.7 percent, the *Star* 10 percent, and the *Enquirer* 11.2 percent (not nearly enough).[10]

Nonetheless, gossip, celebrity obsession, and celebrity worship have become the herpes of the mass media, highly contagious, blistering previously celebrity-free media zones like the news. When Britney Spears shaved her head in February 2007 it was a lead story for two days on CNN, "the most trusted name in news." Celebrity culture is a media phenomenon and a determined, profitable media production, and as media outlets have multiplied, celebrities, real and manufactured, have spread out like millipedes. We have celebrity chefs, celebrity CEOs, reality TV stars who become celebrities, and on and on. The rest of us are famine victims, starved of this level of achievement and accolades.[11]

The central beat of celebrity journalism is about feelings: love, hate, heartbreak, despair, resentment, joy. The rhetoric is that of the family and intimate relationships. It is a world governed first and foremost by emotional ties.[12] Celebrity journalism extends our sense of family, as celebrities are brought into our domestic realm and we into theirs. This is a fantasy rarely laid out, say, by politicians in Washington, a fantasy of belonging to a like-minded and moral community that values love, loyalty, and nurturing behavior and disdains betrayal.[13]

We also get hooked because we can inhabit a variety of sensibilities in quick succession as we flip through *People*—from trusting, credulous fan of someone like Jennifer Aniston (who is enormously popular with my students) to smug, skeptical cynic sneering at Nicole Richie.[14] (I know, you only read *People* at the dentist's.) And we can also try some of the celebrity personas on for size; some we might identify with because we may feel we have something in common: we may look a little like them (though probably not as good) or feel we share the same personality traits or inner struggles. Any similarity, however iffy, validates that we, too, might matter. When we temporarily merge with the celebrity, we can test out new possibilities for our imagined, potential self. We take on her identity and temporarily lose our own.[15] So there's the pleasure of imagining being transformed into someone better, more glamorous, more assured. It is this oscillation between similarity and difference—entering an imagined world where our fantasies about beauty, wealth, love, and fame can be fulfilled, yet also being reminded that we already have similar qualities (or even better ones) as the stars—that makes diving into the pages of *People* or *US Weekly* so satisfying.[16]

It's also easy to get hooked because the mode of address to the reader is intimate and direct: the magazine is your best friend with the latest insider info, talking to *you*. You get to be part of Jennifer Aniston's inner circle, too. Unlike the *New York Times*, which would never have headlines like "What Was Eliot Spitzer Thinking? His Secrets Inside!" celebazine titles seek to engage you, to turn you from a passive recipient of information to an active adjudicator of the moral issues involved. With so many magazines, entertainment news shows, and Web sites following so many of the same celebrities on a daily basis, calling them by their first names or nicknames, addressing them in such a personal fashion, and even making fun of them, the strategy is to cultivate the notion that we have an ongoing relationship with these stars, that we are in on their lives and thus should engage with them pretty much the same way we do with people we know. The participatory ethos of the magazines and especially the Web sites, where you can comment instantly about celebrity behavior, allows you to become part of the story. (Comments to photo of Kelly Ripa in a bikini on PerezHilton.com: "Jesus, eat something," "The belly button is frightening," and "Eeeewww! She looks like she has the body of an 80-year-old man.") You, too, can join the Greek chorus online, defending or denouncing the stars.[17] If we feel more involved with them, surely we'll come back for more, yes? Ka-ching.

The scandals, betrayals, bad behavior, and admirable or appalling maternal skills (Britney driving with her baby in her lap) invite us to participate in a particular moral universe where we can be full-fledged authorities and get to judge the rich and famous.[18] And with each question, betrayal, triumph, or crisis, a judgment *is* required; it is a given that you are an authority on such matters and will bring your own social knowledge and moral compass to bear on the topic at hand. You, in your ratty bathrobe with your uncombed hair, are hailed as having every right to evaluate these rich and famous people and to speculate about their futures. Yes, we get to envy them, but we also get to condemn them. What are these women doing right, and what are they doing wrong? What's causing problems for so-and-so? Are babies in so-and-so's future? Is X tearing couple Y apart? Will so-and-so get married? Rumor has it that X is pregnant, and X "has made no secret of her desire for kids." And our magazine friend will tell us secrets that give us privileged insider info: we'll get the scoop on "Katie's Secret Plan to ESCAPE WITH SURI!" or Christina Aguilera's admission, "What I've Kept Secret."

So why did this matter in the age of George W. Bush? Why did celebrity gossip dilate so much in the wake of 9/11? One might not initially see a connection between the style of the Bush administration and the rise of celebrity culture, but the impact of those attacks and the Bush administration's response to them, as well as the media's, provided a perfect hothouse in which celebrity culture could bloom. This is hardly to suggest that most people, especially the young, avidly followed national affairs in the 1990s and then stopped dead cold at the turn of the century. After all, celebrity journalism was on the rise in the 1990s (think O.J., Monica, JonBenet), as was sensationalism, and the news in the summer of 2001—when President Bush received a memo titled "Bin Laden Determined to Attack Inside the United States"—was dominated by shark attacks and endless speculation about the murdered congressional intern Chandra Levy.[19] Immediately after 9/11, celebrity journalism plummeted, and you would think that more media attention might have been paid to the broader world. But instead, with major help from the media, we pulled a big collective quilt over our heads and got back to the doings of the Osbournes and Anna Nicole; a year after 9/11, celebrity journalism had returned to its previous levels and then began to soar even more.

Bush, Dick Cheney, and Donald Rumsfeld told us that the way to respond to 9/11 was to go shopping. And they made it clear that they were going to do what they wanted, public and world opinion be damned. They were going to invade Iraq; they were going to deny the existence of global warming; they were going to give tax cuts to those who live in starter castles; they were going to veto health care for poor kids; they were going to try to eliminate Title IX and further undermine women's reproductive rights; they just did not give a rat's ass. We—especially girls and women—were utterly irrelevant. Unlike die-hard evangelicals and corporate moguls, we had no role in judging or influencing or even denouncing what the government did. Plus everything was staged, fake, and relentlessly macho, from the now infamous "Mission Accomplished" Bush-dresses-up-as-Top-Gun moment to the way Bush was photographed in front of Mount Rushmore so his profile seemed part of the rock face. So why follow politics or national or international affairs? It was a bunch of spin anyway, over which we had no say. We were *supposed* to be fatalistic.

But we were still part of a nation, and stories about which we can have strong opinions are part of the glue that binds us together in this imagined place called "America." Celebrity gossip became even more mass-produced, it sold (so it proliferated even more), it was a lot less scary and confusing than stories about al-Qaeda. We could talk about it with anyone without getting into a political fight, and we could use it to affirm our own opinions about right and wrong. At times our opinions even affected the success or failures of the stars—to wit, Tom Cruise's falling currency after his Scientology blather and bashing Brooke Shields about her postpartum depression treatments. The Bush style, with all the brush clearing and "bring 'em on" rhetoric, was insistently hypermasculine; no room for "girlie men," let alone actual girls, here. By contrast, celebrity journalism's entire raison d'etre is that the opinions, tastes, and judgments of females are centrally important. They matter. A lot.

In short order we got *Celebrity Fit Club 3*, *Celebrity Showdown 2*, *40 Greatest Celebrity Feuds*, *Celebrity Mole*, Celebrities.com, E! online, Gawker (and then Stalker!) Celebrities Eating Dot Com, TMZ (online and on TV), *Celebrity Apprentice*, *Dancing with the Stars*. What's next—a new reality series, *Celebrity Proctologist*? *Baby People*? ("Adorable Emma Holmes-Cruise plays it cool in her Missoni for minis while making mud pies.") Why is there such an enormous appetite for celebrity gossip? Especially since to be a fan—a real, devoted, know-every-detail-of-her-life fan—has often been cast as kind of pathetic, like you don't have a real life of your own, or you're an easily influenced tool of the Hollywood publicity factory.[20] "Fan," after all, comes from the word "fanatic" and has suggested an obsessed individual, the kind who thinks Elvis is still alive or goes on YouTube wailing, "Leave Britney alone." How did we come to this pass? It wasn't always like this—really.

Now, ever since the rise of tinseltown there have been fan magazines and celebrity journalism; even Edward R. Murrow, the personified gold standard of journalistic integrity, started the TV show *Person to Person* in 1953, in which he interviewed the likes of Zsa Zsa Gabor and Marlon Brando in their homes. Boomers grew up with *Photoplay* and other fan magazines whose bread and butter for years was Elizabeth Taylor. (Liz Steals Eddie from Debbie! Liz Near Death! Liz Dumps Eddie for Burton! Liz Gains 400 Pounds!) But what we have today is of a different order of magnitude. One important turning point occurred between 1974, when *People* magazine began publication, and 1976, when Barbara Walters— just beginning her humiliating and no doubt infuriating brief stint as co-anchor of the *ABC Evening News* with the notorious male chauvinist Neanderthal, Harry Reasoner—also started her "Specials," the celebrity interview shows in which she excelled, and famously got to ask people what kind of trees they felt they were.

By March 1981, when Ronald Reagan, the first movie actor to become president, was shot by John Hinckley Jr., who was trying to impress another celebrity, Jodie Foster, and a new, syndicated TV show *Entertainment Tonight* premiered, Americans began to get a sense that celebrity culture was assuming a much more commanding role in their culture. The Reagan administration celebrated elitism and wealth and legitimated greed, which further helped to inflate celebrity culture. The year 1984 brought us *Lifestyles of the Rich and Famous* and its host, the braying, unctuous Robin Leach, who wished his viewers "champagne wishes and caviar dreams" as he showed us the preposterously swanky homes and resorts of the super rich. By the late 1980s, when Dan Rather included accounts of problems in the Robin Givens–Mike Tyson marriage on the *CBS Evening News*, we knew we had come a long way from Walter Cronkite.

The radiation of the tentacles of celebrity culture has been driven further by the media consolidation of the 1980s and beyond, as the conglomerates have bought up publishing houses, news outlets, movie theaters, amusement parks, record companies, television stations, cable systems, and the like and insisted on "synergy" and maximum profits from them all. And twenty-four-hour cable television, with all its competing, insatiable programs, needs to be constantly fed; celebrities are the fodder. Unholy alliances within these media behemoths mean that all kinds of cross-promotions can be launched that seem utterly natural or spontaneous when they are anything but. Thus the winner of CBS's *Survivor* is immediately booked on CBS's *Late Night with David Letterman*, those "fired" by the Donald on NBC's *The Apprentice* end up on *The Today Show*, and so forth. A story in Time Warner's *People* can also serve as a story or interview on Time Warner's CNN. Each media mastodon has multiple ways—and a pressing need—to promote its own celebrities, adding to the glut. Of paramount importance are ratings, sales, buzz, profits. Celebrities, whether adored or reviled, triumphant or mired in the tar pits of scandal, deliver these.

By 1992, with the premiere of MTV's *The Real World*, everyday people began to be stars of their own lives. Talk shows like *Sally Jesse Raphael*, *Montel*, and, most notoriously, *The Jerry Springer Show*, invited people with no prospect of ever being on the inside of the TV screen to get a flickering taste of fame in exchange for exposing their personal problems (real, exaggerated, or invented) on national television. After the enormous success of *Survivor* in 2000, television witnessed the metastasizing of reality TV in which contestants could find themselves featured in *People* magazine and appearing on *The Today Show*. Now previous "everyday people" Heidi Montag and Spencer Pratt, the SoCal Barbie and Ken types from the reality show *The Hills*, became the celebrity unit known as "Speidi." (Until they split. But then got married.)

As celebrity culture has proliferated as an industry, then, it has also become a routine part of people's daily lives. While it's still sort of embarrassing for some of us to load up on the likes of *US Weekly* at the end of our grocery order, glossies like *InStyle*, the swanked-up *Star*, the TV shows with celebrity moles, or dancers, or apprentices, the spreading of celebrity culture everywhere has normalized both knowing about celebrities, and wanting to know about them. It was no longer mortifying to be aware of, say, the details of the Anna Nicole Smith saga in 2007—it was part of everyday discourse. The story swamped CNN and it took work *not* to know the latest. Celebrity journalism shrewdly positions readers not as dupes or cynics, but as having "inquiring minds," for whom it is entertaining and challenging to try to fill in the blanks, to figure out what might be "real" and what is PR hokum or paparazzi truths.

Despite the enormous outcry against predatory photographers after Princess Diana's death in 1997, the ranks of the paparazzi have swelled since then. Some credit this change in part to the former *Cosmopolitan* editor Bonnie Fuller, who in 2002 took over as the editor of *US Weekly* and transformed it from a sleepy also-ran to *People* into a powerhouse. It was Fuller who pioneered the magazine's sections "Stars—They're Just Like Us!" and "Hot Pics!" in which we see them walking their dogs or going to the supermarket.[21] As others sought to imitate her success, the celebrity rags proliferated. Fuller herself later moved to American Media where she brought the same paparazzi-driven sensibilities to the *Star* and the *Enquirer*. So beginning in 2002 there was an even bigger and more competitive market for all those candid shots—some of which could rake in six-figure prices—and this market swelled further with the rise of the online celebrity sites.

Paparazzi firms became very big business, and everyone from former pizza delivery guys and valet parking attendants wanted a piece of the action, becoming photographers overnight. On any given evening in 2007, between thirty and forty-five paparazzi stalked Britney Spears; X17, the largest agency in Hollywood, figures it raked in $3 million on

Britney-related photos alone.[22] So there is a self-fulfilling industrial cycle that kept Britney in our faces 24/7. And the most important thing being produced here is a newly shame-free, avid audience—us.

Another reason for the success of celebrity journalism has been a significant increase in the number of teenagers in the country since the millennium. Teens and young adults tend to be major fans and followers of celebrity news as they try on and forge their own identities.[23] We all have to develop a story about who we are, what we care about and stand for, what we hope to do with our lives, and what we do *not* want to be like. The vast arsenal of celebrity profiles, successes, and disasters provides raw material, resources we can try on, weave in, and reject as we construct our self-identity.[24] And this has been especially true for young women who have been told that in this age they have to be supergirls. How to be sexy but not overtly sexual? How to have a career and a family? How to have success and male approval? In an age of collapsed courtship rules and "hooking up," how to find a guy and have a long-term relationship? These are the questions about combining femininity and success that week in and week out, the celeb-azines dramatize. And who else to provide the right answers than female stars who seem to have cracked the code?

So what are some of the rules in celebrity culture's manual for women and girls? Successful femininity rests on a combination of luck and true grit. Stories about getting discovered, being "destined" for success, and "making it" tap into the hope that we are not merely part of some nameless herd or mass, but that each of us will eventually be recognized as special and distinct. For those of us stuck fuming in line at the Division of Motor Vehicles, or placed on endless hold and never able to talk to an actual human on the telephone, or trapped in Dilbert's world of undifferentiated cubicles at work, or stuck in arbitrary rule-bound asylums of high school, the daydream of vaulting over these barriers makes celebrity culture a place we'd like to be. Who dares to cut in line in front of a celebrity? To interrupt a celebrity? To make her get a hall pass? It does seem, in fact, that the more bureaucratized everyday life becomes, the more we desire the deference, the acknowledgment of our individual qualities, the special treatment that being a celebrity provides. So being, somehow, a girl with an aura is crucial.

But nothing is more important for females in this world than self-regulation. Realizing your destiny requires major and serious self-monitoring—of your figure, face, hair, outfits, behavior, sexuality, and maternal practices. Being a good judge of character, in potential boy-friends or husbands, and in friends, is also essential to your success and happiness. If you choose wrong, you could end up with someone like Jude Law, who is screwing your nanny on the side, or, worse, Tom Cruise, who takes total control of your life. You must also be a perfect consumer, knowing exactly which outfit to wear at all times, which restaurant to patronize, which baby clothes to buy, which car to drive. You also need to manage your career well. Ideal women here are independent—they have their own professions, money, and sources of success—and yet are com-pletely reliant on the love and approval of men. And they get that approval because their economic independence is tempered by their hyperfeminin-ity. And finally, you must adopt the correct middle-class values of deco-rum. Paris Hilton? Too rich and too spoiled to appreciate the importance of hard work and achievement. Britney Spears? Too uncontrolled to grasp that shaving your head or marrying beneath your new station marks you as unable to transcend your trailer trash origins. Reese Witherspoon? Just right.

To be just right, female celebrities must devote their time, energy, and attention to their appearance above all else. They are supposed to be a toned size zero, maybe a size two, but nothing lower and nothing higher. As we all know, being overweight is cause for withering derision, and here the magazines assume the stance of a totally disgusted boot camp drill sergeant. Typical were the *Star*'s captions over a shot of the actress Vivica Fox in a bathing suit drinking bottled water: "Let's hope that's *diet* water. . . . Curb Your Tummy!" Kate Moss (!) was told to "tone up her midsection," and Jennifer Love Hewitt was busted for her "love handles." The *National Enquirer* sniped that "Rosanna Arquette has a beach ball for a belly," that "Queen Latifah doesn't deprive herself—and it shows!" and her "roly-poly bulges" inspire a comment that "Martha Stewart's well-rounded cooking skills might have helped make her a little too well-rounded!" Poor Reese Witherspoon, at the beach with her kids, was pictured with a yellow circle drawn around her stomach and the shocking pink caption "Just a pouch!" The *Star* asked, "What's up with Reese Witherspoon's belly?" and then answered its own question. "She's Not Pregnant. . . . IT'S BLOAT! . . . Since she is not pregnant, maybe it's just a sign that it's time to hit the gym!"

Being too thin is also bad, but a cause for dismay and panic instead of ridicule. "Shocking trend: Stars flaunt their stick figures," blared *In Touch* in December 2005. Yellow circles drawn over the offending parts identified "twig shoulders," "bony back," and protruding "ribs." "Stars used to show off their cleavage," complained the magazine "Now they show off collarbones."[25] "SKINNY S.O.S.!" brayed the cover of the *Star* in July 2006; "Star's Scary New Affliction—Foodophobia and It's Contagious!" "BARE BONES!" the magazine screamed one month later as white arrows pointed out that Nicole Richie's "collarbones are more concave," "her stomach skin hangs looser," and "there's less meat on her arms" than just three months earlier.[26] *In Touch* used white arrows to point to Lindsay Lohan's "rail thin arms" and "protruding elbow and wrist bones" as it advised the actress in 2009 that she "needs to gain 25 pounds" or risk "infertility, osteoporosis, heart problems and even death."[27] Now, to be fair, these magazines have also started trashing men's bodies, jeering at those with "man boobs" or who are "man blobs" or "beached males." While these beach body spreads insist that superficial appearances are crucial for everyone, and suggest that their scrutiny is completely egalitarian, the fact remains that women's bodies are most frequently and prominently at the center of the bull's-eye.

So what else do the women of La-La Land do, according to these publications? They shop, change their outfits all the time, date, party, have $2 million weddings, pine desperately for babies, have babies, get divorced, and, through all this, compete ferociously with each other. Indeed, what is especially striking (as with reality TV) is the constant pitting of women against each other, the endless conflict—"LC Wrecks Heidi's Wedding"— which is the price they pay for being in the magazines' female-dominated world. And it's not just the "feuds" or "showdowns" (i.e., catfights) between a current wife and an ex-wife or two former BFFs. The competition is over every detail of their appearances and behaviors and there is very little room for error. They are made to compete against each other, and we are meant to compete with them.

Every celebrity magazine now has the de rigueur visual lineup, based primarily on red carpet photos, of women wearing the same or similar outfits and then judging who looked the best, typically based on the minutest details. *In Touch* features "Who Wore It Better?" in which two celebs are juxtaposed against each other in the same dress or outfit; one gets a circle with a check mark titled "she did." The loser has worn shoes that are "too heavy (and just don't match)" or her bust is "bursting out of the dress."[28] *Life & Style* has "Who Got It Right?" in which we learn, for example, which celebrity wears polka dots better. In "Red Carpet Ready?" celebrities are actually made to compete against *themselves*. The same woman—Hilary Duff, Katherine Heigl—is seen in two different outfits at different events and in one she is labeled "ready" and the other "not ready." The "not ready" might result from a dress that makes the star's "upper body look very large" or "flattens her bustline."[29] In "Hot or Not?" in the same issue of *In Touch*, Perez Hilton compares women's current and previous hairdos; either the woman's current self loses to her past self, or vice versa.[30] No aspect of a woman's appearance is too puny or insignificant to criticize: *In Touch* also presents celebrity "tanning blunders" (visible tan lines, uneven tan). The *Enquirer* has its weekly "fashion hits & misses" in which some women are exhorted to "Trash Your Stylist," the fashion blunders are so egregious. The *Star* has "The Worst of the Week! The Stars' Fashion Violations" and "Star Style & Error."

But whatever their blunders, we still don't look like them. To close the gap, articles provide tutorials on how to get their "look." Consumerism is a religion here and everything, from what you wear to where you eat lunch, requires careful determined and incessant shopping. Consumption is presented as the primary path to true self-actualization and product placement is ubiquitous.[31] The *Star* offers "Updos You Can Do!"; *OK!* tells us how to "Match Her Makeup" and "Simple Tips and Tricks" to transform office wear into a "party-worthy" outfit. Not a buff size two? Try Pilates, organic sprout lunches, thrice-weekly workouts with your personal trainer, as Heather Locklear does. There's tons of "hot" stuff we must have—this week, a hot red handbag, next week, hot boots, hot shawls, hot jewelry, hot nonfiction books about the Iraq War. (Okay, I made that last one up). *OK!* takes us inside celebrities' homes (and these photos of stars "relaxing" as they sit in a frozen pose in their living rooms look less lifelike than Madame Tussaud's), and at the end of the tour we learn how we can get "the look" of so-and-so's house simply by buying a similar lamp, vase, or carpet. And think this is devoid of public policy concerns? *Life & Style* in 2009 took us inside an "ecofriendly makeover" presided over by one of the *Real Housewives of New York City* in which we learned where we could get picture frames made from "naturally shed buffalo horns" and a chair made from "plant material." (Might that be wood?)[32]

Pregnancies and births (as well as engagements and weddings) provide great opportunities for product placement and advice on how you can get the crib or stroller that J.Lo got. So it's not just that motherhood is destiny, it's also hip and fun because there's so much to buy that will make you just like them! You accessorize your baby and your baby accessorizes you. Stories about the latest baby slings, baby designer clothes, and baby showers pitch products like "one-of-a-kind, hand-painted sneakers" for infants ($195) or a "Platinum and Diamond Bezel-set Baby Bracelet" ($1,320). Such wretched financial excess is rendered thrilling here; huge income disparities are glamorous and just make sense. Shopping is life. (No maternity leave or day care where you work? Surely the bracelet will remind your baby that she really is special.)

In this world successful women can't get along with each other; they "clash," "butt heads," and "fight," particularly over scarce resources: attention and decent men. The real or alleged feuds between celebrity women ask you to take sides, and usually the woman who lost her man to someone else is cast as more sympathetic than the one who stole him away. These are high school sensibilities at their finest. Here female agency is exemplified not in landing a big role or producing a hit film or record; it's in scheming to humiliate her rival. In the never-ending Jen–Brangelina saga of 2005 and beyond, Aniston was typically the victim, Jolie the vixen. To pick just one random issue of *In Touch*, for whom the story was the equivalent of Watergate, Angelina was "flaunting her new family." Was she "doing it deliberately . . . to send Jen a message?" Well, an insider revealed, Jolie was "capable of anything!"

Now here's the plot Jolie allegedly hatched. Aniston had a film, *The Break-Up*, coming out on May 29, 2006. So nine months to the day before this, Jolie, somehow knowing the exact release date of the film, and able to conceive on a dime, deliberately got pregnant so that she would have her and Brad Pitt's baby two days before the premiere of *The Break-Up*. This was a "deliberate attempt to sabotage her big movie opening—taking the spotlight off Jen."[33] Talk about family planning with a vengeance! Women fight over everything; the pettier, the better. "Julia Roberts & Sheryl Crow duke it out over babysitter," revealed the *Enquirer* in July 2007. According to this story, Crow had hired Roberts's former nanny, who specializes in infants, but when Roberts found out, she offered the nanny "big bucks" to come back. Sheryl was "livid over Julia's dirty tricks." As relationship authority Paris Hilton "told" *OK!* in September 2006, "You can't trust women friends . . . there is too much jealousy and cattiness." Male relationships, when they are featured, are not cast in this catty light—they betray women, not each other. But for women, sisterhood is not powerful; it is impossible.

The two biggest hopes blared repeatedly are finding a loving relationship (ideally, with a "soul mate") and then having children. Because they're celebrities, success is already a given. So the most common and interchangeable stories are about relationships starting, blossoming ("The Romance Gets Hotter!), and deteriorating. The near compulsory heterosexuality screams at you from every page, as no woman is truly complete without a guy. Women *must* be in a romantic relationship, and these are always "blissful" and "perfect" until the nasty breakup. "Until I was married, I never had a strong man I could rely on, who would take care of me," asserts Christina Aguilera, according to *US Weekly*.[34]

Losing your man is a tragedy, but remaining childless is a thermonuclear disaster. It's as if the makers of Pampers, Gerber's, and Legos owned these magazines. Babies are always "a bundle of joy," only produce "baby bliss," bring "new meaning to life," and make the man love the mother "even more now than he did before." Babies always bring couples "closer together." Clearly, no projectile vomiting, sleep deprivation, thwarted adult conversations, or fights over whose turn it is to go to the playground in those households. If you have twins, you get "Twin

Bliss!" "Twins are double the work but twice the fun," confides *In Touch*; here Charlie Sheen, former party animal and client of Hollywood hooker Heidi Fleiss, announces, "The Twins Made Me a Better Man."[35]

Two-inch headlines like "BABY NEWS" and "HOLLYWOOD'S BABY BOOM" are constantly recycled. Let's just take another issue of *In Touch*, this one from July 2006. Jennifer Aniston reportedly "made no secret of her desire to have a baby of her own . . . rumors continue to swirl that she's already pregnant."[36] (False.) Aniston has been mercilessly badgered for years about having children. The cover of the *Star* blared in huge, marigold-colored headlines in the spring of 2009 "MOM AT LAST" and announced that Aniston—on the advice of Brad Pitt, no less—was adopting a baby boy and was planning a $250,000 nursery with hand-painted murals, a $1,200 changing table, and a baby monitoring system presumably designed and installed by NASA.[37] In "Is Their Age Difference TEARING THEM APART?" we read that Cameron Diaz wanted to settle down but younger boyfriend Justin Timberlake did not. Why? A "confidante" reported, "Cameron's biological clock has begun to tick."[38] Four pages later, we read that Christina Aguilera "is already planning her next project: starting a family!" And you?

This brings us to the hypernatalism of celebrity journalism and its most invasive new beat, the "bump patrol." Ever since a nude and fully pregnant Demi Moore graced the cover of *Vanity Fair* in 1991, display of one's belly has become less embarrassing and even glamorous; for many, it seems required. When I was pregnant you would never, ever wear a bikini (well, unless you were Princess Diana); now you're supposed to flaunt your protuberance. The *Star* has featured its "Bump Brigade" and "How to Dress a Bump (and Not!)" that showcase stylish maternity wear that is "HOT!" and, of course, a host of pregnancy fashion don'ts (most worn by Britney Spears).[39]

Well fine, it's nice not to have to feel like Moby Dick and to have maternity clothes that aren't like army tents. But pregnancy has now become compulsory for female stars: they must have a baby to fulfill what is allegedly every woman's innate dream to become a mother. If they don't have children yet, we are assured they desperately want to in the future. If they have one, when is the next one coming? If they have two, what about three? Julia Roberts was constantly hounded about having kids until her twins arrived. George Clooney, by contrast, is not hounded about when he will reproduce. Jennifer Aniston's breakup with Brad Pitt was blamed on her alleged refusal to have children, as was her breakup with Vince Vaughn. We are back to the 1950s—you are not a real woman if you don't have kids. Just imagine a female celebrity saying, "Kids? I don't think so. They would interfere with my career plans. And they're a pain in the ass." OMFG!

Thus, for the celebrity rags a new scoop developed: being the first to detect what has come to be called a woman's "bump." Telephoto lenses now zoom in on the midsections of scores of female celebrities accompanied by speculation about whether she's pregnant or simply ate too much for lunch. (To wit: the *Enquirer* bragged that it was "weeks ahead of other media in reporting that Jennifer [Lopez] and hubby Marc Anthony were expecting.")[40] Am I the only one that finds the "bump patrol" to be a truly creepy cross between stalking and government surveillance? Borders are patrolled, prisons are patrolled; women's wombs? In the *Star*'s "1st Look at Her Bump!" a fluorescent yellow circle over Nicole Kidman's abdomen was accompanied by "Her baby bump exposed!" Now they feel they have the right and duty to get inside a woman's uterus. The circles and arrows drawn on and around the alleged "bump" visually emphasize that a woman is, in the end, governed by and reduced to her reproductive organs. What's worse, they exclaim that what goes on in there is not her private business, but everyone's public business. In other words, when it comes to pregnancy, there is no right to privacy. See where this leads?

The one thing worse than not procreating at regular intervals is being a bad mother. Again Britney has led the way here in just saying no to car seats and to scheduled custody hearings. But we also see photos of babies wearing sun hats, with a caption praising the good mother for protecting him from the sun. In "Nicole Richie BACK ON BOOZE," the real scandal is that "she is risking her newborn baby's health" because she was seen "drinking white wine at a Los Angeles hotel." In my experience "drinking white wine" makes motherhood possible, but not in the hypersurveillance world of Hollywood motherhood.

At the same time that we envy celebrities their privileges, we also resent them for having what we don't. So the other side of envying these women their alleged fantasy lives is schadenfreude—taking malicious delight in the misfortune of others—which has also become an essential ancillary pleasure of celebrity culture. Ordinary girls and women feel all too keenly the constant scrutiny we're put under and the impossibility of measuring up, so being able to feel superior to millionaire blond actresses has its therapeutic moments. Most of us have to go to nine-to-five jobs; we have to watch what we spend; we don't get to marry and divorce beautiful new people every three years; we are not supposed to be "difficult" or "high maintenance." Celebrities don't have to play by any of these rules. They don't have to rein in their various appetites (except, for women, hunger, sex, and drinking). They get to escape from these confines—at least, up to a point. Because while we envy this, we also don't want to let them get away with it: we need to see some of them humiliated and put in their place.[41] So when Kathie Lee Gifford, who for years had smugly trumpeted her perfect marriage, perfect family, and perfect Christian values, got exposed in 1996 as an absentee sweatshop operator, it was scrumptious. It got even better when her husband, Frank—who she bragged on her TV show was a "sex machine"—got caught in a hotel room with a stewardess.

A crucial factor in the spread and new legitimacy of celebrity journalism has been the shield of irony in covering celebrities, especially online, or on TV shows like *TMZ*. The sarcasm, the witty and often juvenile wordplay, the special sections on "drunks," "train wrecks," and "fights," the overall knowingness and ridicule convey that it's okay to follow celebrities, even obsessively, because we see through them, are above them, and mostly laugh at or pity them. This cultivated ironic stance confirms our cultural superiority, our detachment from celebrity spin, our distance from such "low culture."[42] The Web sites have made it their particular mission, as David Samuels put it in the *Atlantic Monthly*, to "shred the toilet-paper thin reputations built by studio publicists and New York magazine editors."[43] Headlines like TMZ.com's "Britney Chaos, Take 7,241," "Britney and Heidi Sing Duet, World Nears End," and "Winehouse Trashed, Planet Saved" are typical of the snotty, derisive, and, yes, highly entertaining tone that then allows us to indulge in celebrity tracking. Photo captions like "Canada's national newspaper, the *Globe & Mail*, has written this great article basically summing up why Avril Lavigne is such a douche. We're getting it framed," are typical of

PerezHilton.com, who pioneered in scrawling irreverent Magic Marker comments over photos of celebrities. TMZ.com, featuring a random video of topless women out to dinner, quipped, "We have no clue who they are, but after celebrating a birthday inside the Hollywood sushi house, these classy ladies made out, shook their booties and one popped out of her limo's emergency hatch to show off her jiggly bits. You're welcome, you are now dumber."

Some of the biggest scandals involve women who drink too much, party too much, and fail to regulate their sexuality. Britney Spears, who clearly went through a phase in which she was intent on shoving the norms of proper feminine decorum in the face of the paparazzi, famously revealed that she was wearing no underwear when stepping out of a car. This created a furor. And it is the snotty Web sites in particular like TMZ .com and PerezHilton.com that cultivate a mocking, even contemptuous stance toward celebrities. They also get to have it both ways—they feature stills and videos of "slutty" and "trampy" aspiring and actual female celebrities behaving badly and then condemn them for it.

A sense that a woman's fame or reputation is undeserved stokes strong resentments about justice and fairness. People loved to revile self-promoting celebrity party girl Paris Hilton (a small sampling of online comments: "Paris is trash," "rich, spoiled bitch," "drunk, ugly ho," "cocaine addled drunken slut") and exulted in her 2007 prison sentence. Online chats with titles like "Am I the only person that doesn't hate Lindsay Lohan?" or "Why is everyone hatin' on my girl Angelina?" include your basic, garden-variety antagonism ("I hate this skank" about Lohan). In an Angelina chat, "Overheard" referred to Jolie as "a huge publicity whore" who gets her fans to think she's "Mother Teresa when she is anything but." These can be seen as a way of displacing people's completely legitimate resentments over the social inequalities and injustices of American society in which someone like Hilton, through the accident of inheritance, can party all night while millions of other women aren't sure if their paychecks will last through the end of the month.[44]

Given that the Web pages must be refreshed constantly throughout the day, the paparazzi who supply these sites go after men and women. But there is a particularly creepy dynamic in having the overwhelmingly male photographers disproportionately stalking young women like

Spears, Hilton, and Lohan. And what they praise is women who are, in their terms, willing to "give it up"—meaning the ones who cooperate with them to produce a good photograph. They hate "surly male stars" who ignore, elude, or insult them, but it does not undermine a male actor's reputation or masculinity if he lashes out at the photographers. The women are judged by a different standard—they must be "nice," "sweet," as it could very much hurt a woman's feminine image if she was seen as angry or aggressive. In this way, despite whatever mental illness or instabilities Spears may have been suffering from, she certainly emerged for a while as a conscientious objector to this straitjacketed femininity.

With the Manifest Destiny of celebrity culture, the dominant norms about success and happiness for girls and women simply take economic achievement and stability as a given. Precious little attention is ever devoted to how the singer or actress herself might have studied, trained, chosen songs or parts, strategized with her managers, sought to become more involved in production, or really did anything with her brain to get to where she is. Few lessons there for the rest of us. But there are ample lessons about physical self-scrutiny and behavioral self-regulation because it is always and only the most attractive, most perfectly slim (but not too thin), "nicest," most caring and nurturing and best-dressed who will get preferential treatment and the love and approval of others.

The celeb-azines are strict, exacting manuals on how to comply with these demanding norms of beauty and feminine decorum. Women are supposed to be admired for how they appear, not what they can do professionally. In an uncertain geopolitical environment, which girls and women have been told they can't possibly understand or influence, at least in celebrity land they can try to maintain and control their bodies and themselves. Then, so the fantasy goes, they can control their lives.

So here's the deal with the devil that celebrity culture asks us to make. We enter an illusory female-centric world where women matter symbolically and economically, where good men love their wives and children, and where men who keep their wives under their thumbs (especially through whack-job religions) are bad. We become part of an imagined community in which our judgments about all things emotional and relational matter and where female expertise in such fields is a given. We have the pleasure of gaining allegedly insider, forbidden knowledge and the cognitive pleasure (yes) of solving the jigsaw puzzle of celebrity gossip by ascertaining what's true and what isn't, who's naughty and who's nice.[45] We enter the glittery, sunny precincts of L.A., indulge in fantasies of envy and revenge, express our outrage over stupid or immoral behavior, and feel superior to those entering rehab, caught making dumb racist jokes, or stuck with a really lame boyfriend. We can feel, at once, aspirational for our future selves and pretty lucky with what we have. But enlightened sexism exacts a price, and it's not small.

The bratty tone and ironic distance that celebrity journalism, and especially the Web sites adopt can give us the Teflon we want: I'm just looking because I'm so much more together and normal than Britney or Lindsay and get to pity how far she's fallen. But in the midst of all this, celebrity culture tells girls and women in no uncertain terms that they cannot beat the system, ever. The women we see may be rich and successful, and some of them may enjoy considerable autonomy, if not outright control, over their careers. They may be businesswomen, may oversee their own production companies, may make major financial decisions. So they can be empowered and empowering role models. But that's not what we learn about them. Rather, their faces, bodies, hair, outfits, behaviors, relationships, and mothering skills are what they are ultimately judged by, and are under relentless, withering, microscopic scrutiny. If they don't conform to—and bolster—the standard conventions of successful femininity, they will pay. And when they are policed, we are all policed.

So while celebrity culture transports us into a fantasy world of female privilege where it seems, at first blush, that these women have it made with their luxury houses, hunky, beefcake boyfriends and husbands, designer gowns, endless parties and Oscar, Golden Globe, or Emmy statuettes, and stress-free child rearing, the reality is somewhat different. Behind the scenes, beyond the pages of *In Touch*, the *Star*, and *People*, Hollywood is still very much run by men; only 9 percent of major film directors are female, for example. Of the top 250 domestic grossing films in 2008, women comprised only 16 percent of all directors, executive producers, producers, writers, cinematographers, and editors. Twenty-two percent—nearly a quarter—of the films released in 2008 employed not a single female director, executive producer, producer, screenwriter, cinematographer, or editor. There were no films—zero—made in 2008 that failed to employ a man in at least one of these roles.[46] If this doesn't sound like a system we used to call patriarchy, then I don't know what does. (Oh, yes I do—Congress!)

And what does this industry tell us? Luring us in with women we envy, admire, and may even want to emulate, women we like to think have some power, this industry and its celebrity rags lay down the law. The women who deserve to be at the top are young, beautiful, poreless, slim, wrinkle-free, toned, busty, typically white, wealthy, stylish, nice, heterosexual, and maternal. They are nothing without a man, and really nothing without children. Just like in 1957.

10

WOMEN ON TOP . . . SORT OF

Okay—here's a quiz about women and the news media. Recently there was a woman who commanded the national stage, attempting to take on a role no woman had before. She was, of course, attractive—she had to be—and had a set of skills that made her seem right for the job. Indeed, there was a sector of the population, especially other women, devoted to her. But some Americans—particularly male pundits—remained deeply uncomfortable with ambitious women. Women aren't supposed to be ambitious, there's just something so, well, unfeminine about it all. And they shouldn't have power, that's kind of scary. And it's just, still, a little preposterous that a woman could hold such a commanding position. Pretty soon there were rumblings that behind the scenes, this woman was difficult, a bitch, a diva. She couldn't really do the job. People didn't like her. She was ruthless, not a team player. So she deserved not to succeed. Indeed, there would be smug satisfaction when she stumbled or failed. Was this woman (a) Hillary Clinton, (b) Katie Couric, (c) Martha Stewart, or (d) Sarah Palin? Uh-oh—it was all of them.

Now, I don't think the following disquisition on foreign policy—"As Putin rears his head and comes into the air space of the United States of America, where do they go? It's Alaska. It's just right over the border"—is a grammatical or intellectually reassuring utterance by a candidate for vice president of the United States. Nor was the candidate's inability to name a single newspaper or current affairs magazine that she read on a regular basis. But what's striking here is the way that the other three women on our list—a very accomplished lawyer and U.S. senator; the first sole female anchor of a network news program (and the journalist to expose Palin for the ignoramus that she is); and a hugely successful media mogul—were dismissed or maligned along exactly the same lines that Sarah Palin was. Divas. Bitches. Incompetent. Didn't deserve to succeed. Too girly or not girly enough. Shouldn't be on top. And these women were subject to much cattier commentary than their male counterparts, including plenty, and I mean plenty of meows from men.

Now, if full equality for women has been achieved, as the sibilant whispers of enlightened sexism like to pretend, then Hillary Clinton's candidacy would not have sent the male pundits of America into such a tizzy. After a while they seemed like all those torch-bearing villagers in *Frankenstein*, desperate to destroy the monster. And it wasn't just that she was a woman; after all, Palin was a woman, and she did not arouse nearly the heebie-jeebies from the guys that Clinton did (which is saying something). This is because in addition to being female, Hillary Clinton was known to be a f . . . fem . . . femin . . . feminist. Cue Edvard Munch's *The Scream*. Clinton in fact personified what, under the tenets of enlightened sexism, can never, ever happen again: the reemergence, the ascension of feminism. It was this determination, however unconscious and repressed, to exorcise forever any possibility of a revived feminist agenda that prompted the guys, in their cold sweats, to circle the wagons. And I say this as someone who was not a Hillary supporter, primarily because she backed the war in Iraq from the beginning and for too long and, ironically, because I felt she had drifted away from feminism by trying to be as tough and bellicose as the guys when it came to foreign affairs.[1]

Let's review what happened to Hillary. Yes, her policy positions got major coverage and millions of men, as well as women, voted for her.[2] At the same time, journalists and pundits became obsessed with her laugh (a cackle?), commented on her cleavage, speculated about the deep symbolism of her blue pantsuits (comfort?), and cast her as a bitch and "she-devil" who nonetheless got where she was only because, as MSNBC's Chris Matthews insisted, people felt sorry for her because her husband cheated on her. Matthews also likened Clinton to Nurse Ratched and Eva Peron and said that she and her "loyal lieutenants . . . are ready to scratch the eyes out of the opposition."[3] (When Nancy Pelosi was about to become the first female Speaker of the House of Representatives, Matthews asked a guest if Pelosi was "going to castrate Steny Hoyer," the House majority leader.)[4] Joe Scarborough called Clinton "very shrill" and asked about her "house-keeping skills."[5] (And yours, Joe?) There were endless comparisons to the lethal bunny murderer in *Fatal Attraction* for which at least one guy, Steve Cohen (a Democratic officeholder from Tennessee), apologized.[6] Note how all of these comments are not substantive criticisms, but are trivial-izing and seek to reduce her to her physical features or to liken her to famous female villains.

This smart, attractive blonde reportedly made men—or, at least, Tucker Carlson—"involuntarily" cross their legs out of castration anxiety.[7] In commenting about Clinton's strategy in an upcoming debate, Matthews asked, "Well, everybody's wondering where she's going to swing. Will it be above the belt or below the belt?"[8] Mike Barnicle, yucking it up with the guys on *Morning Joe*, compared Hillary Clinton to "everyone's first wife standing outside a probate court." (Not clear where Barnicle got the joke, given that he was forced to resign from the *Boston Globe* amid plagia-rism charges in 1998.) Clinton was taken very seriously yet cut down to size and even demonized because she was a woman—especially an older woman, an accomplished woman, and a feminist. Tim Russert found it ironic, and was befuddled, that a "self-avowed feminist" would show "some emotion" during the New Hampshire primary, as if all feminists have had their tear ducts removed, all the better to master their karate moves. Male commentators in particular dismissed the moment that Clinton teared up as nothing more than a crass ploy to try to get votes.[9] You cannot, it seems, permit the notion to circulate that feminists might actually have human characteristics.

Such coverage did not cost Hillary Clinton the nomination; other fac-tors were at work. But Tucker Carlson, Freudian analyst that he is, put his finger on it, as it were; the guys got really anxious about protecting their cojones whenever they imagined a female president. In this ter-rain, women are held up simultaneously to often deeply contradictory standards—could Clinton, a girl, really be commander in chief? Or was she too tough and unladylike for the job?

So why didn't Sarah Palin face the same treatment? It's true, by the time she was catapulted, like an *American Idol* contestant, to the dead center of the national stage, there had been so much coverage of Hillary's sexist treatment that some of the guys were chastened. And the Republicans are known for being much more aggressive in defending their own than the weenie, spineless Democrats. But Palin also was not a feminist; she hated everything feminists stood for—except being allowed to run for national office. And the combination of her Neanderthal views (surprising the world's paleontologists, for example, with her claim that dinosaurs and humans coexisted just six thousand years ago) and her astounding political illiteracy almost made her off-limits, she was so clueless. So it wasn't until after the election that Palin got the old sexist one-two punch from the guys. Former aides to her running mate, John McCain, began leaking like crazy that she really was as dumb as a peach pit and thought Africa was a country, not a continent, that she was a diva and had tantrums, that she was difficult and uncooperative, and that it was she, not her handlers, who insisted on a $150,000 wardrobe makeover. How much of this was true was unclear, but it was all easy to believe because she was a woman, and an ambitious one at that.

Indeed, it was precisely because Palin was not a feminist, but was seeking to take advantage of the opportunities that feminism had made possible for her, that it was women who would have to take her down. When John McCain chose her as his running mate, his calculation, such as it was, seemed simple. It was clear that millions of Democratic women were deeply disappointed that Hillary Clinton had not won the nomination, and many felt that sexism had played a role. So McCain, ignoring that most of these women were, still, Democrats, figured he'd choose a female running mate and steal all those Clinton votes away from Barack Obama. And he figured he'd get a twofer, because Palin was really conservative—a no-abortion-even-in-the-case-of-rape-or-incest conservative, an antienvironment, pro-gun, aerial-shooting-of-wildlife conservative—which would help him with the wing of his party who didn't like how all "mavericky" he sometimes got about issues like campaign finance reform.

So here was McCain's first insult to women: that anyone with a uterus, no matter how inexperienced, would be an acceptable sop to female voters. As if women are really that dumb, and that easily bought off. Equally galling was this avowed antifeminist (and her antifeminist political party) suddenly using feminism as a shield and a cudgel. Sarah Palin, in her peep-toe shoes, tried to walk the line between pit bull, "hockey mom," and hottie. So she offered us her own version of "pit bull feminism": you have the appearance of feminism—alleged superwoman, top executive, and mother of five—with a repudiation of everything feminism stands for and has fought for. The hypocrisy of pit bull feminism was breathtaking. Suddenly, right-wing pundits and politicians— previously the most outspoken fault finders of working mothers and castigators of unwed teenage mothers—denounced as sexist anyone who questioned whether the mother of an infant could handle the job of vice president, and insisted that the pregnancy of Palin's daughter Bristol was a private matter. Just for the sake of comparison, the social critic Charles Murray, longtime darling of the right and vehement critic of teenage pregnancy, proclaimed, "I want to make the behavior of having a child when you aren't prepared to care for it extremely punishing again."[10] And Bill O'Reilly, part of the posse saying people couldn't go near Bristol Palin's pregnancy as an issue, had recently referred to the parents of Jamie Lynn Spears as "pinheads" for not preventing their sixteen-year-old daughter from getting pregnant. At the same time that the Republicans were embracing their newfound inner feminism, the convention delegates proudly sported huge campaign buttons that read "Hottest VP" and "Hot Chick."

So here was a woman who was anti-choice, anti–sex education (that worked out well), anti–day care, using the gains of the women's movement to run for office, and to silence those who might have a few questions about her qualifications. Pit bull feminism was about exploiting forty years of activism, lawsuits, legislative changes, and consciousness-raising—all of which Palin benefited from—in the hope of undoing them all if she managed to get into office. Her record in personnel matters— trying to fire her town's local librarian, trying to get her brother-in-law fired—and her smug, mocking stance in her acceptance speech at the Republican convention, suggested a vindictiveness off-putting to millions of women who have sought, and not without success, to bring more empathy and humanity to workplaces around the country. Palin also proved herself on the campaign trail to be one mean customer time and again, accusing Obama (stupidly) of "palling around with terrorists" and of working with "a former domestic terrorist," which evoked cries from the audience of "terrorist" and "kill him." Reportedly the McCain folks had to tell her to cool it, especially as death threats to Obama increased in the wake of these rallies. Helluva gal.

For thinking women who know how much harder women often have to work just to be seen as competent as their male colleagues, this spectacle of an uninformed, inexperienced, vindictive woman who sought to get over by winking at the camera during interviews and debates was the opposite of everything they had fought for; it turned feminism inside out. This is why it took Katie Couric—no doubt seriously underestimated by Palin's handlers—and Tina Fey, two shrewd, smart women in male-dominated fields, to expose Palin as a fraud. Charles Gibson of *ABC News* just clumbered around in his interview with Palin, but Couric and Fey went right at the issue that mattered: competence. Because Palin made a mockery of all they had accomplished. And in a terrific flourish, it was CNN's Campbell Brown who denounced the McCain campaign for refusing to let Palin out on her own to talk to the press, charging that they were keeping her on a "chauvinistic chain" and treating her like "a delicate flower that will wilt at any moment."[11]

It was the news media and its coverage of prominent, successful women that provided a Rorschach of lingering, jittery anxieties about women and power. Here, in the news, there remained a deep, unyielding contradiction between and discomfort with "female" and "power." Forty years after the women's movement, "female" is still equated with being nice, supportive, nurturing, accommodating, and domestic—not compatible with anything that might involve leadership. "Power" is equated with domination, superiority, being tough, even ruthless. These two categories simply are not supposed to go together. If some woman seeks to meld these polar opposites, our cultural magnets start spinning out of control, screaming "incongruous" and, even louder, "inappropriate." Let's take another notorious example, Martha Stewart.

Now, I admit right off—I have never been a fan, and my house shows it. That I would be presumed to have the interest, let alone the time, to clean my potting shed (or to have a potting shed!), raise chickens that lay celadon-colored eggs, or stencil the driveway has always struck me as preposterous. And there has been a tyranny about the Martha Stewarti-zation of America with standards of decorating, housekeeping, and entertaining unattainable without a SWAT team of chefs, maids, and Pottery Barn sales associates. Plus, didn't we think that behind the peace-ful Zen of the old Martha Stewart calendar (Tuesday: mulch, read books; Wednesday: plant petunias, hire new pool boy) was a ruthless control freak who probably got all this done by terrorizing her staff? So was I gratified, as I read about her legal troubles, surrounded as I was by dust balls the size of tumbleweeds, coffee splotches on the counter, and the dying ficus in the corner? Uncle.

Nonetheless, Stewart was a hugely successful businesswoman and I, inveterate slob, am not her target market. And she was so successful because millions of women loved her advice, her aesthetic, and her vali-dation of work in the domestic sphere as valuable, even an art. But when Stewart was accused in 2002 and then convicted in 2004 of lying about an insider trading deal, out came the long knives (the Global Santoku Chef's knife, perhaps?). The coverage of the Enron scandal, which began in 2001 and featured massive fraud by Kenneth Lay, Jeffrey Skilling, Andrew Fastow, and others that bilked thousands of Enron employees and investors out of their life savings, simply didn't have that mix of ani-mus and ridicule that animated the orgy of anti-Stewart schadenfreude. Yes, it's true, they weren't celebrities. But they also weren't women.

The source of the taunting jokes about the "Domestic Diva," the "Doyen of Decorating," and the "Style Princess" ("To Do: Slipcover Oven, Embroil Self in Scandal")[12] was the extreme discomfort of having the concept and realm of "the domestic" put together with the concept and the realm of "powerful CEO." The woman who tutored other women in how to make their homes elegant, diaphanous havens in a heartless world should, according to our gender scripts, be as kind, noble, and gentle as the fairy godmother in "Cinderella." Instead, "the diva of domesticity turned tough tycoon."[13] She was "driven," and the trial emphasized "her long perceived flaws—that she's mean, arrogant, a control freak."[14] Reports emphasized that she had screamed at her broker's assistant and hung up on him.[15] A Shakespeare scholar told USA Today that as with King Lear,

"Hubris is her fatal flaw."[16] There was the obligatory courtroom reporting about her hair and her outfits as she stood trial, but much of the emphasis was on her temperament and the gap between her tranquil, home-loving public image and her alleged ruthlessness in private.

Now, I have no reason to doubt that Stewart may be a prima donna with an entitlement problem and a temper. But why do we find these traits more delicious than comparable accounts of male leaders? The State Department official John Bolton reportedly once chased a female foreign-aid worker down a hall in a Moscow hotel while screaming like a crazy person, among other weird behaviors, but he still became George W. Bush's ambassador to the United Nations. (Okay, it's true, Bush had to slip him in as a recess appointment when Congress was away. But imagine if Bolton had been a woman and done this!) What do people think the character flaws of Enron's Jeffrey Skilling might have been? Arrogance, perhaps, lousy management skills? Or Kenneth Lay, deceptive liar and just as big an entitlement problem with his yachts, multiple homes in Aspen, and $200,000-plus birthday parties? Yes, there was outrage over the Enron guys. But the backbiting of the Clinton and Stewart coverage reinforced the notion that these women were uppity, went where they didn't belong, and should get back in their place, fast.

Even America's *Today Show* sweetheart Katie Couric did not fare much better once she announced that she would become the first sole female anchor of a nightly network news show, filling "the seat," as was repeatedly emphasized, of the former news god Walter Cronkite. Months before she stepped into the anchor role, failure was predicted, and not without a touch of relish. "Women have had little success as evening news anchors," opined Stephen Winzenburg in *USA Today* in the wake of the announcement, "and Couric appears to lack the necessary skills to be the one to change that trend." The real trend, of course, was to substitute speculation for actual reporting. Winzenburg continued, "The anchor is the quarterback of the evening news team," and given which gender quarterbacks usually are, that eliminates 51 percent of the population from the top news job.[17] "The perky princess of morning TV is heading to the night shift" was the let's-treat-her-like-Chatty-Cathy lead line in the *Daily News*, which chose to quote a male tourist who said, "She's known for her legs. . . . I'd probably still watch her on CBS because she's hot."[18] Its subheadline was "Men Left in Dust as She Flees NBC," in reference to how her new salary symbolically castrated the other male anchors. "Some question whether Couric has the chops to make the transition from morning TV," reported the *Philadelphia Inquirer*. "The fear of the naysayers," noted the news media analyst Andrew Tyndall, "is that Katie spent so much time doing cooking segments and having her colon looked at, no one will take her seriously."[19] (Never mind that both Tom Brokaw and Charles Gibson went to the anchor's slot after stints on their networks' morning shows.)

The scrutiny and prognostications were endless, and mostly filled with predictions of disaster. The Associated Press and *TV Guide* conducted one of those instant polls asking people whether they'd rather see Couric remain at *Today* or move to the CBS anchor post, and 49 percent voted for the morning show versus only 29 percent for the anchor slot. The *St. Petersburg Times* said, "Some critics said Couric's hiring was a desperation move by CBS."[20] And in a gallant gesture to his new colleague, Andy Rooney— who would never, ever be allowed to remain on *60 Minutes* looking like that if he were a woman—told the press, "I don't think people at *CBS News* are enthusiastic about having her here. She doesn't fit the image that we have of ourselves, as a hard-news operation, a Walter Cronkite kind of news operation."[21] (Oh, like those hard-hitting Andy Rooney essays on the merits of semicolons?) As Sally Quinn pointed out in the *Washington Post*, when Tom Brokaw and Charles Gibson became anchors, there was not the same angst about their morning-show roots, alleged lack of "gravitas," or, obviously, their outfits.[22] And when male hysterics like CNN's Lou Dobbs go berserk over immigration or China as the revived yellow peril, no one suggests he's a tad too overwrought because of that Y chromosome.

When Couric debuted on the *CBS Evening News* on September 5, 2006, she smashed the ratings records, bringing in 13.6 million viewers, CBS's largest audience in eight years. Much of this came, of course, from the hype and the curiosity factor. There was great attention paid to her black shirt and skirt topped by a white blazer—"made her look chubby," sniffed the *Washington Post*; "tasteful," countered the *St. Petersburg Times*.[23] When she interviewed the *New York Times* columnist Thomas Friedman, she did sit in a chair across from him, as is customary, which allowed her to "show her legendary legs."[24] Unfortunately she, and CBS, seemed to be as confused about how her gender and her roots in morning

TV might inform the newscast, so there was an odd mix of hard news, a "Free Speech" segment featuring people like Morgan Spurlock and Rush Limbaugh whom nobody wanted to hear from, and the airing of the first baby picture of TomKat's baby Suri, which people really hated. Viewership fell off quickly, possibly in part because of these early stumbles in the format of the show, and within weeks Couric's broadcast was back in third place. So it is indeed ironic that two years later it would be Katie Couric (we are forever in your debt) who helped save Western civilization through her history-making interviews with Sarah Palin.

But you want to talk scary, like really, really scary? How about a black woman with power, married to a black man with power? Holy Afro! For much of the 2008 campaign the media had no idea what to make of the elegant, Princeton- and Harvard-educated Michelle Obama (except, of course, her clothes). But the stereotype of the "angry black woman" was so pervasive and so available that Fox News, *National Review*, and the Internet rumor mill had no trouble trying to pin it on her. She said she was proud of her country and all of a sudden she was "angry"? Arrgh. Then, of course, there was the infamous *New Yorker* cover with Michelle Obama as a gun-toting, fist-bumping terrorist, intended as a joke but maybe not so funny. When her husband won the nomination, her approval rating was reportedly around 43 percent, kind of in the ratings tank for a future First Lady. Even after Barack Obama's inauguration, Juan Williams—juiced on the fumes of *The O'Reilly Factor*—referred to Michelle's "militant anger" and described her as "Stokely Carmichael [a 1960s radical black activist] . . . in a dress." These guys had seen one too many *Big Momma* or *Madea* movies, in which the main black female character had only one impulse: to execute verbal and physical jujitsu on anyone, especially male, who dared trip her hair trigger. Sassy—even the slightest hint of sassy—must, in real life, be policed, contained.

Michelle Obama had been a vice president at the University of Chicago Hospitals making a six-figure salary, served on six boards, and, indeed, had been her future husband's adviser at the Chicago law firm where he started out.[25] But her predecessor as First Lady, the reassuringly (to some) bland Laura Bush, had rebranded the position, after Hillary Clinton, as one best filled by a stay-at-home mom who organizes her cleaning products via the Dewey decimal system.

So—sigh—the makeover began. Michelle Obama has had to pay dearly for the perception that she might be a talk-to-the-hand woman. She went on *The View*, she read to schoolchildren, she planted the famous White House garden, she tended to her kids, she shopped at J. Crew: she became the "mom in chief." When she accompanied her husband on his first European trip in April 2009, the press referred to her visit as a "conquest," and spilled a great deal of ink and engorged a great deal of air time over her outfits and whether she and the French First Lady, Carla Bruni Sarkozy, really had a fashion smackdown and, if so, who won.[26] By May 2009, her favorability ratings had soared to 76 percent, higher even than her husband's.[27]

But as evidence that too many people in this country still have way too much time on their hands, a new controversy emerged about Michelle Obama favoring sleeveless dresses. Her first official photograph (gorgeous, by the way) featured her in a black sleeveless dress that some huffed was too informal and "out of season," since it was still winter.[28] In a *New York Times* blog entry titled "Michelle Obama Goes Sleeveless, Again," about her appearance at her husband's first speech to Congress, we learned even more about what was so troubling here: her arms are "long and muscular"; they are "super sculpted," the result of "years of effort," her "arms pop out, rippled and gleaming." Typical online responses to this were "Why is this in the political blog? Doesn't this belong in a style blog? All the issues this speech tackled and you're talking about Michelle Obama's arms?" and "Why is this even posted as 'news'! I admire her for her strength and individuality, not what she wears (or doesn't). It seems like you want so badly to pigeonhole her. . . . Good Luck!!!"[29] Thank you, sane people of America.

Spring 2010. Nine o'clock at night, maybe ten. You click on the remote. And here you enter a different realm than the one offered in the news. On one channel is an entire group of female surgeons who divide their time between saving lives and having affairs; on another, a fiftysomething blonde is one of the most shrewd, conniving, and successful litigators in the United States. On the other channels, police investigators, chiefs of police, high-level hospital administrators, FBI agents, whiz-bang computer specialists, attorneys and law partners, business executives, and even a female president. All these women, concentrated in high-profile, male-dominated lines of work—law enforcement, medicine, the White House. Hey, do women have it made, or what?

But it's not just what they do or whom they preside over. It's what they get to say. These were ultraconfident Ironsides who seemed to have studied the art of the put-down at the feet of Don Rickles. Imagine that you are in your place of employment, and a man you supervise proposes doing something that violates workplace procedures. Might you say, "This idea of yours is a no-go . . . however, if we find ourselves reduced to pursuing alternatives of a dubious legal nature, or, should the sun explode, I promise to reconsider your suggestion"? Or, if another man you supervised initiated a sexually suggestive conversation would you say, "Since I'm your boss, I can't return your sexual banter, but I will say for the record that if I were looking for [someone], he would be taller. He would be better looking. He would be more evolved than a junior in high school." Welcome to the withering, direct, bitch-slap smackdown of female bosses on TV. Talk about taking your authority seriously. And, also, taking no prisoners.

By 2007, when it was clear that a woman was going to make the first really viable run for the presidency, Americans had already gotten used to seeing, on dramatic television shows, in a few movies, in the news, a growing number of women in positions of power. Whether it was Lieutenant Anita Van Buren on *Law & Order*, President MacKenzie Allen in *Commander in Chief*, President Allison Taylor on *24*, Deputy Police Chief Brenda Leigh Johnson on *The Closer*, White House Press Secretary C. J. Craig on *The West Wing*, the benighted boss of Dr. House, Lisa Cuddy, or the numerous other high-level professionals on so many dramatic TV shows, the image and idea of women on top, at least in entertainment programming, had become utterly natural. Newsmakers and government officials like Madeleine Albright, Sandra Day O'Connor, Condoleezza Rice, and Nancy Pelosi further cemented this new common sense. And it was this embedded feminism—of course women could play with the big boys, even be their bosses—that enlightened sexism crashed up against and sought to erode.

Now, in real life, things are not quite so egalitarian as they may seem in the fantasy realms of our nation's small screens. With the media's eagerness to present "aspirational" shows and characters—meaning viewers will fantasize about moving up and so will be in a good frame of mind to think about buying Estée Lauder "Teint longue tenue" or a Cadillac—most "real women" and what they do in "real life" are erased in favor of fantasies of power, achievement, and control. Nancy Pelosi aside, only 17 percent of Congress was female in 2009. Women are still only 14 percent of all police officers, and only 1 percent of police chiefs are female.[30] How many female CEOs are there at *Fortune* magazine's top 500 companies? Fifteen.[31] Law schools may be graduating more women than ever—almost the same number as men—but in 2005 only 17 percent of the partners at major American law firms were women.[32] Women account for half of all medical students, but in 2007 only 20 percent of new surgeons were women.[33] What this means is that, in addition to overrepresenting female achievement by showcasing doctors and lawyers instead of secretaries and day care workers, TV also overstates women's conquest of the professions.

Something else is happening, too. For many people, their main exposure to female bosses or other women with power comes from the media, and from TV in particular. So what have these media images told us about women in authority? What lessons might viewers have taken away from these multiple and often contradictory representations of female bosses? What did these women have to do to be taken seriously?

Well, being stony helps. So does being thick-skinned, and mastering the art of the cutting remark. It started with *Hill Street Blues* in 1981. There had been precious few dramatic TV shows featuring professional women in positions of power, and here we got the cold-as-ice, tough-as-titanium, gorgeous public defender Joyce Davenport (Veronica Hamel) who never smiled in public, was anything but deferential to men, and spoke with the various police officers in the precinct as if her words were themselves blunt instruments. Shortly we learned that, behind the scenes, she was romantically involved with the precinct's captain, Frank Furillo (Daniel J. Travanti), and that she cultivated a public "don't-mess-with-me" persona so her authority would not be challenged because of her romantic alliance with the boss of all the cops she had to deal with. Davenport, the lacquer-hard lawyer, stood in contrast to Furillo's ex-wife Fay (Barbara Bosson), a high-pitched, flighty, often emotionally overwrought mother who was always badgering Furillo for more alimony. The template here was that women in positions like Davenport had to be verbally as tough as—or tougher than—men, emotionally forbidding on the job, and never show any inclination to compromise.

The Davenport character eschewed any hint of feminine personality traits on the job, a mode followed by Lieutenant Anita Van Buren (S. Epatha Merkerson) on *Law & Order*. Only here, Van Buren was herself the boss of a series of street-hardened, rhino-skinned male detectives like Lennie Briscoe (Jerry Orbach), Mike Logan (Chris Noth), Rey Curtis (Benjamin Bratt), Ed Green (Jesse L. Martin), and Joe Fontana (Dennis Farina). You didn't mess with these detectives, but you *really* didn't mess with Van Buren. The dream here was that being a woman did not matter at all to her doing her job. She talked tough, took her authority completely seriously, and didn't take any crap from anyone. With a fabulous voice that somehow mixed honey and gravel, she gave direct orders like "Arrange some lineups," "Set it up," and "Find out what you can" without ever offering girly verbal qualifications like "Could you . . ." or "You might . . ." or "Would you mind . . ." that women have been so socialized to do.[34] She would challenge her detectives, demanding, "Tell me again why you don't wanna slap the chains on [a suspect] tonight?" When her detectives told her that the witnesses in a case had all been placed together in the same conference room, she raised her eyebrows and asked, scathingly, "Where they can compare notes?" (Oops, Briscoe.) Sarcasm was a weapon she used not infrequently, and to great effect.

Suspects fared even worse. When one guy brought to interrogation asserts innocently, "I don't know why I'm here," Van Buren purses her lips and responds, "How about hiring guys to play bumper cars on the West Side Highway. Ring a bell?" She then pulls a chair out from the table in the interrogation room and commands, "Have a seat," which he does not hesitate to do. In another episode a doctor challenges her authority and demands to see his patient, a suspect in a murder case. Big mistake. "Until you have more stars on your collar than I do, Doctor," she tells him witheringly, "you can't demand a *damn thing*." (Can I please say, the next time a D student demands an A because his great-uncle knows the president of the university, "Until you earn a Ph.D., you can't demand a damn thing"?)

Now while it's true that I don't really know any female police lieutenants, the women I do know in positions of authority don't talk like this—hell, even the men I know in positions of authority don't talk like this—although, it's true, I'm in academics, not in criminal justice, even though sometimes there are striking similarities. Van Buren and others like her offered a wonderful fantasy, not of how to look, but how to talk: straight, direct, with zero hint of trying to please or placate man, with zero fears of not being liked if she were strong, tough, even aggressive, and with no one ever calling her a bitch. One of the great appeals of the show was that the men and women worked as partners, as equals, sometimes with the men on top, other times with the women there, and with none of the sexual-romantic entanglements so common to so many ensemble workplace shows. Van Buren was one of the guys—just as tough, just as no nonsense, just as inclined to think the worst of people—with few of the soft, accommodating edges most women have had to learn to cultivate on the job. And it was very much the show's understanding that this was the ideal. In season eleven (whew!) of the show, we got an equally big treat—Dianne Wiest as interim district attorney Nora Lewin, the "steel fist in a velvet glove," as show creator Dick Wolf called her. These women wore their power as comfortably as a silk chemise.

On the other hand, we also got less enviable types like Dr. Kerry Weaver (Laura Innes), the chief of emergency medicine on *ER*. Dr. Weaver was initially and consistently cast as the female boss from hell: a martinet who loved bureaucratic rules way more than people, who made snap decisions that were frequently wrong, who chewed her staff out in public, and who seemed to have antifreeze flowing through her veins. As a result, her staff resented her, defied her, and sought to undermine her authority. She was an unreasonable bitch, and thus deserved the impudence she got. She offered a weekly primer on how *not* to be a woman with power, and a suggestion about what happens to women when they get it, and like it too much.

In a characteristic episode, which begins with a warning that, once again, Weaver is "on the warpath," she opens the back of a parked ambulance to find Dr. Malucci (Erik Palladino) having sex with an EMT. She instantly tells him he's fired and slams the door. (Moments before, Weaver had unilaterally taken a patient away from one doctor and given the case to another, so we were squarely in "snap decision" territory.) Malucci, however, refuses to accept his termination; he asks, "What do you want from me, a formal apology?" which of course would have been a good start. She erases his name from the board matching doctors to cases; he writes it back in. Malucci then goes to Dr. Greene (Anthony Edwards), below Weaver in rank, and says, "She thinks she fired me." Greene then seeks to persuade Weaver to relent, obviously not drawing from *How to Win Friends and Influence People*: "You can't get rid of him just because you two don't get along. Hell, if that were the case, you'd have to fire all of us."

After Greene delivers this condescending bit of advice to his superior, Malucci simply puts himself back on the job and begins to see patients without Weaver's knowledge. Once she finds him out, she insists he is still fired. His response? To yell the following: "You're a sad, coldhearted bitch, you know that? You may not like me, but nobody here likes you. You know why this stupid ER's so damn important to you, lady? . . .'Cause it's the only thing that you've got in your life. Nazi dyke." In real life, if it turned out that doctors were screwing female EMTs on the job and the bosses did nothing, we're talking a Peabody-award-winning exposé on *60 Minutes*. But within the context of the show these antifeminist and homophobic insults seem on target and thus perfectly justified.

Weaver's problem, according to the show, was that she took her authority way too seriously for a woman and loved power for its own sake. Unlike Lieutenant Van Buren, Weaver had no sense of humor and no ability to use cynical jocularity to smooth the skids of her demands. She also insisted that her decisions and her diagnoses were always right and refused to ever admit she was wrong: rigid, rigid, rigid. Finally, she had the empathy of a cinder block. She knew little about and exhibited no interest in aspects of her staff's personal lives that might be affecting their work. In an especially Weaver-punishing episode, she sends a very reluctant staff member out in a drenching thunderstorm to buy a present for a birthday party her son is going to attend, and the staffer gets struck by lightning. (How's that for a script dramatizing the consequences of female power gone too far?) Even the at-home, non-doctor types on their sofas can see the fallout of her tyranny, but not the callous, oblivious Weaver. She even yells at him, "What the hell happened to King Funshine?" until she finally realizes what's happened. Without a whisper of an apology, Weaver at least orders the staffer to be hooked up to a cardiac monitor.

Weaver was *ER*'s poster girl for bad female bosses, and the traits to be avoided at all costs. And we repeatedly saw the price a woman would pay if she was perceived as autocratic, overly demanding, and insensitive: everyone would hate her and defy her authority. The show was especially cruel to this woman (and, starting from the beginning, and over the years, she was hardly the only one), made all the worse by the fact that she eventually came out as a lesbian. While her relationships with her partners and her son seemed intended to humanize her, Kerry Weaver remained the abrasive, power-hungry, career ladder–climbing bitch who was much more keen to impress grant-funding agencies and insurance companies than to have the admiration or respect of her staff.

On the other end of the spectrum, what if you were too empathetic? This was often the Achilles' heel of Detective Olivia Benson (the irresistible Mariska Hargitay) on *Law & Order: Special Victims Unit*. Partnered with Detective Elliot Stabler (Christopher Meloni), the two investigated often grisly sex crimes, and this required considerable toughness from Benson. But unlike her male counterpart, she repeatedly relied on her "gut," her instincts, based in part on the depth with which she connected with the children and young women who were disproportionately the victims on *SVU*. In cases when they had no hard evidence that abuse was occurring or a crime had been committed, Benson still snooped around, trusting her feelings and thus getting slapped with desk duty or nearly violating the law. Benson was also one tough-talking gumshoe—"This is *my* case. *I'm* the lead detective on this one"—and she responded to attorneys' arguments with an emphatic "Bull!" She also had no compunction about shooting bad guys, and in one episode when a stalker stabs her in her own apartment, she clobbers the perp into submission with a book. (My kind of defense!)

Nonetheless, the unstated premise of the show was that women are inherently more empathetic than men and that they do—and should do—the bulk of the emotional work of their organization. And because it's a given that girls and women are more likely to be the victims of sexual assault than boys and men, Benson had a special tie to the victims in her cases. She was the one they wanted to talk to, she was the one who knelt by their side and stroked their hair after an attack. Her intuition, her "I've got a feeling" moments—her emotional intelligence—played a central role in some cases being pursued or certain victims being believed. In a debate among the detectives about whether a transgender person might be guilty of a crime, Benson asserts, "*I talked to her . . . I don't think she's a violent person,*" and that's supposed to settle it; when a little girl calls her to say she is being abused, the other cops think it's a hoax, but not Benson, and in the end her hunch proves correct. For those of us who have seen "women's intuition" ridiculed as faulty, irrational, or fictitious, yet also mystified as evidence that females have an emotional radar system more awesome than the Strategic Air Command, the fantasy that emotional sensitivity can be combined with the ability to slam a sexual pervert to the asphalt ASAP is not without its appeal.

Which brings us to *The Closer*. Here we had Deputy Police Chief Brenda Leigh Johnson (Kyra Sedgwick), a police detective who had moved from Atlanta to Los Angeles, bringing her big southern hair and accent, to crack high-profile murder cases. A CIA-trained interrogator, Chief Johnson was brought into the LAPD by her former boss (and lover), Assistant Police Chief Will Pope (J. K. Simmons), and put in charge of a new "Priority Murder Squad," much to the instant resentment of all the men she was either now in charge of or had to work with. In the first episode, she strides into a murder scene, and after inspecting the decomposing corpse more closely and instantly finding more clues than any of the men had, quickly ascertains that the cops on the scene hadn't obtained a search warrant and hadn't followed procedures. One steps forward and offers, "No need to be a bitch about it," to which she responds, "Excuse me, Lieutenant, if I liked being called a bitch to my face, I'd still be married." (You go, girl!) Justifying his choice of Detective Johnson to one of the hoof-stomping bulls in the unit, Pope explains, "She's not Miss Congeniality . . . but she's a closer." This hardly mollifies the men in the unit, who submit an en masse request for transfers.

The hook here was the bringing together of the kind of tough, gritty police work Lieutenant Van Buren had to do with the personal style—the talk, the hair, the print dresses, the "y'alls"—of, say, the head of Savannah's Junior League. Could this kind of stereotypical femininity be inhabited by someone who had to break murderers in the interrogation room and bust the chops of her coworkers? One fantasy of *The Closer* is that the two really can go together; the other was that you needed the big hair and "y'alls" to make up for the toughness. Each show, especially in the first season, was as much about women needing constantly to assert, reassert, and claim their authority as it was about the murder case at hand. Instantly, the premise of the show was that this southern belle had to be a ballbuster, and had to confront explicit sexism, resentment of, and disrespect for her authority, gruesome murder scenes and even more gruesome autopsies, and hostile suspects and their attorneys. She did so by pretending the resentment wasn't there, exerting her authority over all the guys by giving them a host of orders, some demeaning yet eventually quite fruitful, and by—yes—being ten times better than all the rest of them.

Self-doubt? No, ma'am. Chief Johnson was typically eighteen steps ahead of everyone else when figuring out a crime and her interrogation techniques always delivered the goods even when, at first, the guys watching her on their video screens were certain she had blown it. The constant lesson here was that knowledge is power—the more you research, compile, and analyze, the more you know and follow the rules (which often her male subordinates wanted to ignore), the better able you're going to be to trump the big boys.

This was not the sort of Queens-talkin' interrogation smackdowns preferred by Andy Sipowicz (Dennis Franz) on *NYPD Blue*. No, Chief Brenda Leigh Johnson came in all feminine wiles, real polite like, expressing her sympathies, smiling, drawling, seeming all nurturing and naive. As she got people to trust her, she would then back them into a corner with all the information she had about them and the case and, in the end, they would confess, much to the awe of the sexist old grumps under her, like Detective Andy Flynn (Anthony John Denison), Detective Lieutenant Provenza (G. W. Bailey), or Captain Taylor (Robert Gossett). Her southern manners—lots of "pleases" and "thank yous" often delivered with a smile—were a constant weapon, used disingenuously to lull suspects into complacency and sarcastically to defuse the irritation of her male coworkers who didn't want to follow her orders. She wasn't intimidated by anyone—not her boss, not the FBI, not the criminal slimebags she busted. In her management style of these guys, Chief Johnson seemed to be drawing less from *In Search of Excellence* or *The Managerial*

Woman than from *How to Raise Teenagers Without Killing Them* or, perhaps, *The Dog Whisperer*. My hunch is a lot of female viewers who supervise employees have found this instructive.

In the first season Detectives Flynn and Provenza and Captain Taylor often went behind Chief Johnson's back to try to undermine her authority. It didn't work, but it did show what this woman was up against, working in not just a male-dominated workplace, but one over-populated by Neanderthals. The show made absolutely clear that rank sexism, as embodied especially in the white-haired Detective Lieutenant Provenza, who referred to suspects as bitches or "lesbos," was not only out of touch and offensive, it interfered with your job by making you a stupider man. When any of these guys interrupted her as she was briefing the unit about a case and proposed something quasi-legal, or suggested that she didn't know what she was doing, she thanked them for their input, ignored their suggestion, and forged ahead.

To soften the character, Chief Johnson had an uncontrollable sweet tooth, had a boyfriend in the FBI, and was deeply empathetic with female crime victims. She was the classic steel magnolia, embodying how femininity and command-and-control executive authority were not mutually exclusive. In a scene that seemed designed to make this clear, Chief Johnson is in her office, where she is temporarily housing kittens her cat had just produced. She is having a showdown with the rival head of Robbery and Homicide who usurped her authority earlier in the episode only to extract a false confession from the wrong suspect. He was forced to apologize. While picking up and petting the kitties (how soft can you get?), she says, "I don't want an apology from you. I want an acknowledgment of my rank. I want an understanding that you are beneath me (she paused for emphasis) in the chain of command. And I want you to be officially warned that if you make any attempt to undermine my investigations, Chief Pope will recommend an inquiry by internal affairs, which is, I believe, the established procedure when investigating an insubordinate officer." (I am woman, I will not purr.)

That women could, and needed to, combine pearls with brass knuckles was reaffirmed on *Boston Legal*. Crane, Poole & Schmidt was the testosterone-infused law firm dominated by the wildly narcissistic and mentally faltering Denny Crane (William Shatner) and his best friend, the unmarried lothario Alan Shore (James Spader). Halfway through the first season, in strides Shirley Schmidt (Candice Bergen) to help take control of a firm that, at times, also seems on helium. In her first scene, Shirley barges into the men's room while Alan is taking a pee. "Who the hell are you?" she demands. After their exchange, in which he tries to flirt with her and she insults him on multiple fronts, she comments on the small size of his penis and leaves the room. Shirley made it clear she owned the place, would give as good as she got, and would take absolutely no crap from anyone. Nonetheless, a running joke was that Denny in particular still found her "hot" (they had had an affair long in the past) and had an inflatable Shirley doll to fulfill his fantasies. Because Bergen was nearly fifty-nine at the time, and because of the deliberate eccentricity of the show, one was never sure whether *Boston Legal* was affirming that older women could still be thought attractive, or ridiculing such a notion. But what did matter was that Shirley Schmidt was sexualized from the beginning, some of her clout stemming from her sexual power over the men in the firm.

Shirley did not resort to the "please" and "thank you" rhetoric of *The Closer*; she was direct, often blunt. When firing a female attorney she says, simply, "You're fired," and when the woman protests she shoots back, "What are you going to do, sweetheart, sue me?" When passing another female attorney in decidedly nonprofessional clothes, she asks her name and then says, "Very nice outfit, Sally," and then adds sarcastically, "Can you spell? Wear something more appropriate. Pretend you're a lawyer." In a subsequent episode she has to chastise Alan for sexual harassment, warning, "That kind of behavior isn't tolerated at Crane, Poole & Schmidt." First Alan asks what exactly did constitute sexual harassment and then asks if it also applies to senior partners. "Go subscribe to *National Geographic*," she instructs him. "Make a list of all the places you'll never get to visit. Add to that list Schmidt." When lawyers in the firm screw up a case she says, directly, "I'm not happy with either one of you." Between her often aggressive, insulting (and witty) comebacks and more straightforward, unadorned issuing of orders, Shirley inhabited her authority as effortlessly as she did her suits and scarves.

By the time we got to a TV version of a female president, the short-lived *Commander in Chief*, the fusing of toughness with femininity was complete. MacKenzie Allen (Geena Davis) was the vice president, and the dying president had asked her to step down so someone "more appropriate" could take over, more specifically, the Republican Speaker of the House, Nathan Templeton (Donald Sutherland). Allen refused and became the first female president of the United States. *Commander in Chief* led the ratings in its time slot on Tuesday nights in the fall of 2005 until *American Idol* began airing opposite the show in January 2006. ABC replaced the show's producer, put the show on hiatus, and then moved it to the Thursday 10 P.M. death slot, where its ratings plummeted. But while it was on, millions got to fantasize about what it would be like to have a woman run the country.

President Allen combined a crisp executive style (commands to assistants like "Make the call happen," "Let's get this done," "He needs to hear this from me directly," "I want to know ten minutes ago") with instinct ("I feel it in my gut") in which, for example, she went off script during an address and called for a popular uprising in a small, coca-producing country somewhere in Latin America. She constantly had to parry the efforts of Speaker Templeton to screw her over one way or another, in between dealing with terrorists, incipient wars, and the like. *Commander in Chief* made it quite clear that a woman could do this, almost to a fault: President Allen's solutions to varying crises combined getting as much information and input from her advisers with her own gut reactions, and her solutions were almost always just right. Even for a male president, this would be a completely unrealistic illusion.

One thing was clear—the accomplished women in these shows could not look like Janet Reno. When you eyeball some of the cleavage that Dr. Cuddy in *House* or most of the female forensic scientists in the variously located *CSIs* had to sport as they leaned across their desks (or cadavers), we see how essential feminine display has been in these depictions as a kind of inoculation against (or undermining of) the feminism embedded in their roles. In this media terrain, women are held up simultaneously to feminist and feminine standards, and must fulfill both, but with a bias (still) toward the feminine.

So we got both: utopian visions of women in power for whom their gender was a nonissue—or was eventually rendered a nonissue—and omens about women in power being emotionally stunted and unnatural—

the bitch—or too tied to their feelings and instincts. The ideal seemed to be the steel magnolia, with contradictory messages about whether to be heavier on the magnolia or the steel. But even the ones regarded as sexy or feminine—Shirley Schmidt, Brenda Leigh Johnson—were verbally combative, masters of the put-down. They made even the more user-friendly female bosses pretty intimidating.

Is this how most women managers or women in power are in real life? Various studies suggest that rather than verbally busting their coworkers' balls or acting like Dr. Weaver–style autocrats, the majority of female supervisors are "team builders," more open and accessible than men, more tolerant of and able to deal with different styles and personalities, more likely to solicit advice. They are, again in contrast to the tough-talking broads on TV, actually more likely to praise coworkers and to mentor and motivate them. It is male managers who are more likely to punish coworkers, despite everything we've learned from *The Devil Wears Prada*.[35] This doesn't mean, necessarily, that women are better managers than men, but many of them are different because of how women have been socialized, and thus they are quite at odds with the leathery, acid-tongued law enforcement and other types so dominant in the media. But if you thought that females in power had brass balls, and might be more intimidating or unsympathetic or acerbic than men in power, it's not hard to see how one would have these stereotypes reinforced. At the same time, all these confident, linguistically brawny women personified the assumption that, whether they deserved it or not, women have smashed the glass ceiling. Who in their right mind would think there would ever be a need for a revitalized feminist politics with hard-bitten, flinty, successful women like these at the top?

Figure this one out. We women of America are supposed to stare endlessly and longingly at the beautiful actresses and models of the world, admiring and envying their faces, bodies, and clothes. But we are not supposed to desire them.[36] Because even with the new gay visibility and lesbian chic, love between women is still more verboten on the screens of America (except for porn for straight men) than is love between men. I mean, by now, between *Queer Eye for the Straight Guy*, *Will & Grace*, *Six Feet Under*,

Brothers & Sisters, and even, OMG, *The Sopranos*, we've had gay men or gay male couples everywhere. But lesbians? Not so much. Yes, there was *The L Word*, sequestered on Showtime, the cast of which was so beautiful that it prompted the eminent queer theory scholar Eve Sedgwick to write, "I would like to order up some characters with body hair, ungleaming teeth, subcutaneous fat, or shorter-than-chin-length haircuts. Oh, and maybe with some politics."[37] And there were the occasional lesbian flirtations on *Roseanne*, *Sex and the City*, *Ally McBeal*, and *Friends*, but not the explorations of ongoing, long-term relationships that we've seen with gay guys on network programming.

And with Katy Perry's song "I Kissed a Girl"—she was drunk, "don't know your name, it doesn't matter, you're my experimental game"—and Madonna's attention-grabbing lip-locks with Britney Spears and Christina Aguilera on the 2003 MTV awards, women kissing women (or more) also came out, as it were, as a "fashionable 'add on'" to otherwise conventional sexuality.[38] Other famous media scenes, as when Ally and Ling kissed on *Ally McBeal*, only cemented the women's realization that they were adamantly heterosexual.[39] The Jennifer Aniston–Winona Ryder kiss on *Friends* ran during sweeps week to increase ratings.[40] What happened to Ellen DeGeneres once she came out in 1997? There was much hoopla, but her show got canceled and then her girlfriend Anne Heche ended the relationship and married a man. After that, there were very few lesbians as regular, let alone lead characters, on TV or in films.

DeGeneres—possibly one of the most gifted physical comedians since Lucille Ball—finally ended up with her own talk show, where her sexuality remains in the background, much as it does for MSNBC talk show host Rachel Maddow. It is as hosts of talk shows—and let's not forget Rosie O'Donnell, who waited until her talk show ended to come out—that lesbians seem to be most acceptable to TV programmers. Embedded feminism has not yet gotten to the point where we can see a female version of the couple Scotty and Kevin in *Brothers & Sisters*, and in the realms of enlightened sexism, lesbianism must be divested of any political, feminist implications and only be manifested in its most guy-friendly forms—meaning really hot babes who kiss each other in front of men.[41] So here we are again, in on-the-one-hand, on-the-other-hand territory. If out lesbians can have their own talk shows, including political talk shows, and no one cares—and people, including men, are fans—then isn't that prima facie evidence that feminism has truly broken all barriers for women? On the other hand, if ongoing, semirealistic lesbians or lesbian couples must either be lipstick lesbians or really few and far between on the screens of America, isn't that evidence of the continuing, lumbering conquest of enlightened sexism?

Indeed, why are lesbians so scary? Well, aside from the fact that they don't need men romantically or sexually, they often have feminist politics and look at the fashion magazine standard of female beauty and just say no. Unlike the guys in *Queer Eye*, who are shopping swamis who know every emporium from Crate & Barrel to the Sharper Image to Aveda, lesbians who figure they really can get by without Maybelline, forty-two shades of MAC lipstick, or a lifetime membership at Bally Total Fitness are a huge threat to our dominant religion, consumerism. Don't need men and don't need shopping? Time for the Exorcist.

Okay, class, let's review. On dramatic TV, despite the preponderance of male cops, mind readers, lawyers, mentalists (?), doctors, private investigators, and the like, the extent to which we see women in top positions exaggerates women's conquest of male-dominated professions and implies that women have done much better in career-land than they remotely have. These escapist images also erase the plight of millions of real-life women whose annual income is about the same as the price of a new Ford truck. Now I love Dr. Bailey and her counterparts and am, indeed, grateful for the embedded feminism that has brought these women, instead of more ditzy, superrich "real housewives," into my living room. But when paired with the ongoing, infuriating news coverage of real women in positions of power, with the bimbettes in hot tubs on MTV, and with the crossing out of what real women put up with every day, what we get is "women's issues" or "feminist politics" erased from the national blackboard.

Meanwhile, as the nightly news—all of it, including cable—cuts back on investigative and international reporting, focuses increasingly on health and lifestyle stories about the benefits of walking or the possibilities of curing male-pattern baldness, or on who wore it better, Michelle or Carla, coverage of ordinary Americans, and especially women, continues to decline. Even with the Great Recession, and its increased attention to foreclosures and job losses, what's happening to women remains virtually ignored. According to a 2008 study by Senator Ted Kennedy's office, the unemployment rate for women began to increase: their real median wages dropped by 3 percent in 2007 alone, and they were 32 percent more likely to hold subprime mortgages. Indeed, women, and especially women of color, were much more likely to have been targeted by predatory lending practices. The unemployment rate for single mothers was higher than the national average, and by March 2009 it was 10.8 percent.[42]

At the same time, as the Great Recession worsened in late 2008 and 2009, three out of every four jobs lost—often in fields like construction and manufacturing—were sustained by men, meaning that many families were, for the first time, relying on a woman's paycheck, which is typically lower—sometimes much lower. In the average family where both spouses work, the wife brings in only 35.6 percent of the family's income.[43] Women are more likely to be in part-time jobs, too, meaning no health insurance or unemployment benefits.[44] This is a big change in American life, where increasingly women are the main breadwinners in their families, yet continue to earn less than men.

And guess what else a lot of these women are doing? Being mothers and, maybe on top of that, tending to aging parents. So this leads us to one more important and spirited battle between embedded feminism and enlightened sexism, the battle over motherhood. If, as we are to believe, full equality has been achieved, then why were women being told they ought to be "opting out" of work, the better to be stay-at-home moms? And why does motherhood cost women so much in lost income and job advancement, as documented by Ann Crittenden in her book *The Price of Motherhood*, in a way that fatherhood never costs men?

In one corner was the "new momism," a highly romanticized and utterly demanding set of standards about perfect mothering that are impossible to achieve.[45] The new momism requires that you devote your entire physical, emotional, and psychological being, and the GDP of Japan, to raising the perfect child, the one who learns Mozart in the womb, speaks French by the age of five, so that by his sophomore year in high school, he is rescuing remote tropical villages from the ravages of leprosy. How is a mother to do this? An instantly infamous article in the

New York Times Magazine from October 2003 had the answer: "opt out" of work. The cover headline asked, "Q: Why Don't More Women Get to the Top? A: They Choose Not To." The subtitle read, "Abandoning the Climb and Heading Home." Illustrating the article was a photograph of an angelic white Madonna in her Ann Taylor outfit with what appeared to be the Hope Diamond on one finger, several selections from Tiffany's bracelet department on her wrist, and a toddler in her lap, to represent all these American mothers who were "heading home." Reportedly this story engorged the *Times*'s inbox with an unprecedented amount of hate mail from really pissed-off mothers.

Ever since the debut of "the mommy track," the women of America had been subjected to these stories about mothers seeing the light and chucking it all for Junior's sake. The format was almost always the same. Five women who went to Yale and, say, the Harvard Business School, married to men whose salaries equaled the operating budget of Walmart, decided to have kids and then quit their jobs and—poof!—there was a national "movement" of mothers not only rejecting the workplace, but feminism as well. This article, written by Lisa Belkin, herself a former *Times* reporter who decided to quit and write freelance instead, followed the template perfectly. Only here the privileged white women we met from the "Opt-Out Revolution" were Princeton alums (as is Belkin) or from other elite universities who then went to work in law firms or newsrooms.

This final drumbeat of enlightened sexism was a slap at mothers who do work for a living, because they need to, want to, or both. It was also, of course, yet another assault on feminism as misguided, irrelevant, out-of-date, or all of the above. As one of the mothers told Belkin, "I don't want to take on the mantle of all womanhood and fight a fight for some sister who isn't really my sister because I don't even know her." (And because she might not be as privileged as I am.) The biggest problem with this and similar stories was the emphasis on "choice"; supposedly sensible, devoted mothers who truly cared about their kids chose to "opt out." But despite the headlines, what we learned inside the article was that the first two women we met, one an attorney, the other a television reporter, were confronted with speed-up at work—fifty-five- to seventy-five-hour weeks—at the same time they were having children. Both asked for shorter and more flexible hours and were turned down. Their "choice" was to maintain their punishing schedules or to quit. I am sorry, but this is not a choice. As one of these women admitted, "I wish it had been possible to be the kind of parent I want to be and continue with my legal career."

Then there was the old selective use of statistics problem. There was no empirical evidence at all that mothers were "opting out."[46] The article emphasized findings from a recent survey in which 26 percent of women in senior management said they did not want a promotion. So that meant nearly three-quarters *did*. And how does that compare to men, many of whom don't want high-stress jobs either? We then learned that *Fortune* reported that in a survey of 108 women in high-powered jobs, "at least 20" have chosen to leave. Maybe I'm dumb at math, but doesn't that mean that four-fifths have not made this "choice"? Katha Pollitt and others trashed Belkin's other statistical sleights of hand in the piece, which overstated how many mothers were actually "opting out" of the workforce. In fact, the most interesting thing about the article was its buried lead. The real story here was not about mothers "choosing" not to work. It was about the ongoing inhumanity of many workplaces whose workaholic cultures are hostile to men and women alike. Americans work anywhere from six to nine weeks a year longer than most Europeans; many "high-powered" jobs like corporate attorney are lethally boring and stressful to both genders.

Finally there was the biology-is-destiny problem. Whenever you need to keep women in their place, it's always good to cite examples from the animal kingdom. (Baboons were used here.) There were the usual disclaimers about the misuse of biology, but nonetheless we mothers (but not fathers?) are allegedly driven to protect our kids and "seeking clout in a male world does not correlate with child well-being." So apparently earning a decent salary did not correlate with being able to take care of your kids.

Not to be outdone, *Time* ran an equally infuriating cover story in March 2004, with the huge blue headline "THE CASE FOR STAYING HOME: Why more young MOMS are opting out of the rat race." The cover illustration was an angelic little blond boy dressed in white (what the *&%??) clinging to his mom's equally white pants leg, looking up at her wistfully. Mom herself was cut off at the waist; no need to see her face. Inside, of course, amid the stats about women dropping out was, again, the real story: workplaces so demanding, day care so expensive or nonexistent that working mothers and fathers were going nuts.

Marc Cherry, the creator of *Desperate Housewives*, must have been mainlining these articles or, more accurately, the bile they raised. Because when his show premiered the following fall, and ripped the veneer off of the myth of domestic female bliss in the suburbs, people, and especially women, could not get enough. We had Bree (Marcia Cross), the Martha Stewart clone, whose domestic perfection made her entire family feel like they were in a Turkish prison; Susan (Teri Hatcher), the hapless mother whose kid was more sensible than she was; Gabby (Eva Longoria), totally uninterested in having children because they would interfere with her affair with her high school student gardener; and best of all, Lynette (Felicity Huffman), the high-powered corporate executive forced to quit because of her four kids, and who couldn't handle raising them without popping some of their ADD medication herself.

In an episode mothers talked about for months, which aired the Sunday of Thanksgiving weekend in 2004, Lynette is trying to survive a typical day at home, with her sons smashing pots and pans on the furniture and turning the stereo up to DEFCON 1 levels. Her response? She starts screaming at them, smashes a bowl on the kitchen floor, and throws a jar of peanut butter through the kitchen window. She finally snaps and runs out of her house, unloading her kids on Susan, saying, "I can't do this, it's just too much," and drives off. Susan and Bree get a sitter for the kids and find Lynette sitting on the ground, weeping in a soccer field. As Lynette confesses her reliance on speed she says, "I love my kids so much. I'm so sorry they have me for a mother." Bree assures her she's a great mother, but Lynette says, "No, I'm not," and adds, "I'm so tired of feeling like a failure." When Bree insists that Lynette just needs some help with her kids, Lynette speaks for every mother harassed by the new momism when she says, "Other moms don't need help. Other moms make it look so easy." Susan and Bree then tell her how hard they found it to be mothers of little kids. Lynette cries, "Why didn't you ever tell me this?" Bree admits, "Nobody likes to admit that they can't handle the pressure." "We should tell each other this stuff," Lynette sobs. Mothers across the country cried from their sofas, "Yes! Yes! Yes!"

A backlash was brewing against the new momism; we got books like the long-overdue *The Three-Martini Playdate*, *Sippy Cups Are Not for Chardonnay*, *Confessions of a Slacker Mom*, and *Even June Cleaver Would Forget the Juice Box*, to name just a few of the outpouring of books—not to mention the hilariously confessional Web sites—talking back to the expectations placed on mothers who also must live with the worst public policies of any industrialized nation to support mothers and families. Motherhood, how horribly it is supported, how much it punishes the female parent, how much it guilt-trips women who are, like, really good mothers compared to, say, my grandmother (who routinely yelled at my father, "I'll paint the walls with your blood")—this is the ultimate unfinished business of the women's movement. Young women today are making crucial decisions about which careers to pursue based on which ones they think they can have and also have children.

So are women truly on top? No. And until policy makers wake up, male pundits get their boxers untwisted over remotely competent women, *The Bachelor* goes on permanent hiatus, Hooters goes out of business, the news media shows us how unequal things still are for millions of girls and women, and every Fortune 500 company in the country has day care and paid maternity leave instead of $360 billion in bonuses for five white guys, they won't be. But most women don't want to be on top. They just want to be side-by-side: with their sisters, their friends, their daughters, and yes, believe it or not, with their men.

THE F-WORD

SCENARIO I

Spring. It is sometime in the future. Saturday morning. The feminist mom—now a grandmother—still looks like she just got shot out of a wind turbine and has a cheap Metamucil hangover. She is about to babysit.

Her daughter—smart, accomplished, hardworking—is struggling to figure out how she can possibly juggle the demands of her job, which she loves, and the demands of her new baby, whom she adores. Her place of employment allows only six weeks of unpaid maternity leave, does not offer flex time or part-time work arrangements, and does not have a day care center. Day care for her is an uneven patchwork of live-in nannies (which she can't afford and doesn't want), unlicensed and wildly variable in-home day care arrangements, and a state-of-the-art child center staffed by women with master's degrees in child development who make $28,000 a year, where the waiting list to get in is seven years and the monthly cost is the equivalent of four car payments. The daughter, who typically worked at least fifty hours a week prior to the baby's arrival, has been told that she can't cut back to forty hours—it's either keep up the fifty plus, or quit. She doesn't want to quit, can't afford to quit—she and her husband need the salary and the health care benefits—but she wants more time with her two-month-old baby and hasn't found any decent, affordable, available day care. On this morning, the feminist mom will take care of her grandchild so her daughter and her husband can go out and have a conversation about what to do. Her daughter, weaned on "girl power" and all the "can do" consumerist feminism of the early twenty-first century, has come to label the bill of goods sold to her in the media as "ersatz feminism."

Prior to arriving for her babysitting gig, grandma has gone to buy a few things for her new granddaughter. And she thought things had been bad when her own daughter was little! Then there were the hot-pink-colored, Barbie-stuffed aisles for girls and the battleship-gray-colored, armament-stuffed aisles for boys at Toys "R" Us. Now there is Jessica Simpson's line of "Diapers for Her" with "Daddy's Little Hottie" printed all over them, next to her latest exclusive product, potty training thongs. "Baby's Little Make-up Kit" is prominently displayed next to the pole-dancing game for girls, recommended ages: three and up. Kmart is showcasing its kindergarten training bras.

Not much has improved in the media or political environment. Despite Don Imus getting temporarily fired for referring to a guest's five-year-old daughter as "hootchie mama jailbait," the hottest trend in music videos is first-grade girls in bikinis bumping and grinding around swimming pools. The upcoming television season features a sitcom called *Boobs*, a new reality TV show called *Celebrity Gynecologist*, and a documentary on Spike TV hosted by former Harvard president Larry Summers titled *Why Women Are Dumber Than Men*. *Maxim Jr.* targets seven-year-old boys.

As was the case in 2009, the United States still ranks sixty-ninth in the world in terms of number of women in national legislatures (only 17 percent of the seats in the United States House of Representatives are held by women, whereas in Rwanda it's 56 percent).[1] America continues to rank twenty-ninth in infant mortality rates, seventeen places *lower* than it did in 1960, and now behind Cuba, the Czech Republic, and Hungary, and tied with Slovakia and Poland.[2] While 163 other countries on the planet offer paid maternity leave, and 45 provide paid paternity leave, the United States does not. Unpaid leave, if you can even get that, is the best we do.[3]

As in 2005, men with just a high school degree earn more on average than a woman with an associate's degree.[4] Indeed, it is still the case that the majority of poor people in the United States are women, and the gap in poverty rates between men and women is wider in America than anywhere else in the Western world.[5] Women are still segregated into low-paying jobs, just as they were in 2007, when (unlike what we saw in the media) nearly half—43 percent—were confined to just twenty occupational categories where the median income is just over $27,000 a year. At the same time, just as in 2009, women are still expected to bear the major costs, in time and money, of caring for children and aging parents: nearly 70 percent of unpaid caregivers of older adults are female.[6]

But all these issues and facts are invisible to the country's news media: as in 2006, of the thirty-five hosts or cohosts of prime-time cable news shows, twenty-nine are white men. On the Sunday morning talk shows, men outnumber women by four to one. And still, only 28 percent of the broadcast evening newscasts are reported by women, just as in 2006.[7]

The feminist grandma, still an academic nerd, has been reading about the consequences of all this. Girls, bombarded by the unabated demand to be really sexy while also being told that they can—and must—just say no and excel at academics and sports, are reporting enormous stress at having to be all things to all people at all times.[8] Girls continue to go to college in record numbers, but they learn automatically to rule out certain careers, because they know that it will be impossible to combine them with having a family—but not so for their male counterparts. And most women continue to be tracked into low-paying "pink collar" jobs that don't pay enough to support them, let alone a family. The dumb blond, narcissistic "real housewives," catfighting, wedding-obsessed, baby-obsessed stereotypes in the media mask and justify this inequality, as does the relentless blitzkrieg against women with power by the pit bulls of talk radio and cable TV news.

In fact, researchers have documented the persistence of "ambivalent sexism," a seemingly paradoxical amalgam of hostility and chivalry toward women. Some men resent that women have come too far—hostile sexism—while others put them up on a pedestal—benevolent sexism. But many men hold both negative and positive attitudes toward women that sustain enlightened sexism: they feel protective toward certain kinds of women (mothers or girlfriends who are nurturing or submissive) and hostile toward those who fail to conform to such feminine scripts and want to have the same opportunities and responsibilities as men. As the researchers note, benevolent sexism might seem harmless, even noble, "but its effects can be devastating" precisely because it's so insidious. For example, as one older male supervisor put it to the feminist mom's daughter, he did not advise her to quit her job because she didn't have the ability to do it anymore now that she had a baby. Instead, he said, "Now you should stay home because women are so much better at child care; there's nothing I admire more than a truly devoted mother and babies need their mother's care full-time, don't you agree?"[9] See—social order maintained, women back in the home, men holding more economic and political freedom, choice, and power.

When the daughter and her husband return home, the grandmother is presented with two choices. The husband has the opportunity to work nights while her daughter will work days. Between the two of them, they can cover day care, although they will never see each other except around noon on Sundays. Or the grandmother, recently and blissfully retired, and with other plans, can do full-time day care. She goes home and ditches the Metamucil for some Tanqueray.

SCENARIO II

Spring. It is sometime in the future. Saturday morning. The feminist mom—now a grandmother—still looks like she just got shot out of a wind turbine and has a sauvignon blanc hangover, having ditched chardonnay long ago. She is not about to babysit. Instead, she and her daughter are taking the baby to the park, because her daughter has six months' paid maternity leave. After this leave, her daughter will bring the baby to her organization's federally funded and licensed on-site day care center, which only costs, on a monthly basis, the equivalent of one car payment, as there's a payment scale based on what you can afford. The new centers, established around the country and widely available, have been funded, in part, by eliminating the tax loophole that allows hedge fund managers to pay only a maximum 15 percent rate instead of the 35 percent imposed on top income earners—which has raised nearly $15 billion in five years—

and by raising the taxes paid by the very rich.[10] In addition, given that in 2007 the United States accounted for 45 percent of the entire globe's military spending, and these expenditures had increased by 202 percent between 1998 and 2007, this seemed like another area where some more family-friendly reallocations might occur.[11] Welfare "as we know it," the mean-spirited and vindictive Temporary Assistance for Needy Families, which Barbara Ehrenreich reported is nicknamed "Torture and Abuse of Needy Families" by its recipients, has been reformed to actually help poor mothers and their kids.[12]

How has this happened? Baby boom women, watching their daughters struggle, remember the power, energy, and success of the 1970s women's movement and, now, with more time on their hands, start organizing. They unite with their daughters' generation, a not insignificant number of people given that they were that burgeoning cohort of teenagers and twentysomethings in the first decade of the twenty-first century. But now they are grown up and pissed off at discovering that they are not close to "having it all." Their Facebook and MySpace pages, once devoted to parties, fun photos, and gossip, now include comments about pay inequities, sexual harassment, the lack of decent day care, and how stupid it is that Hooters has served as the basis for a new sitcom. Blogs, twitters, YouTube all pulsate with the discontent. They've taken their motto from the 1976 movie *Network*: "We're mad as hell and we're not going to take it anymore."

The movement becomes known as the F-Girl initiative. The "F" of course stands for feminist, but emphasizes that it has been turned into a dirty word. Saying "I'm an F-Girl" is emphatic, is assertive, and spans generations. F-Girl simultaneously reclaims the word "feminism," but also rebrands it as cool, hip, and mouthy, because, as Jessica Valenti, the founder of the Web site Feministing.com put it, "The smartest, coolest women I know are feminists."[13] F-Girl videos go viral on YouTube, Oprah features F-Girl activists, and the Spice Girls do another reunion tour, a part of whose proceeds go to support lobbying efforts on behalf of America's women. Various F-Girl blogs emerge, and women of all ages start doing the unthinkable—finding time to meet with each other to compare experiences and press for change, locally, nationally, or both.

Immediately, *F-Girl* magazine—modeled on the old *Sassy*—is launched, along with a Web site, blogs, twitters, and, last but not least, a political action committee. The magazine is an instant hit, just the way *Ms.* was in 1971. It makes fun of the media, bogus makeup and cosmetic surgery claims, and dumb fashion trends, it provides juicy political gossip about who's proactive on women's issues and who's a jerk, and it brings the plight of poor women out of the shadows. One of its favorite features is its "Before and After" makeover send-up. For example:

Before: You sit alone reading *Cosmo* or *Glamour* or *Vogue* and, on the one hand, you're cheered up because you tell yourself you will buy that new $90 skin cream that will finally make you look like Giselle Bundchen, but on the other hand, you realize you will never be as thin as the five-foot-nine-inch, 110-pound models. You get depressed and eat a quart of Ben & Jerry's Cherry Garcia.

After: You host a margarita party for your friends; each one must bring a recent fashion magazine. You tear out the most offensive ads and articles, with the skinniest models and most backassward advice and, felt-tip pens in hand, decorate them with sassy, righteous comebacks. (The magazine covers themselves are often excellent material here.) Then (this is why the margaritas are so important), take them to public restrooms in restaurants, bars, academic buildings, women's dorms, and tape them up on the inside of the stall doors. Repeat once a month.

F-Girl also loves trashing celebrity journalism and its incessant hectoring of women to have babies, babies, and more babies while also maintaining that size zero figure. So they take all the features of *US Weekly* or the *Star* and reverse the roles. Thus we get "Who Wore It Better, Brad Pitt or George Clooney," which gives us nice eye candy and makes fun of how women are pitted against each other, a twofer. But they also add comparisons like "Who Made It Worse, the Producers of *Bride Wars* or *Real Housewives of Atlanta*?" with the appropriate eviscerating commentary. Taking special aim at the heinous, invasive violation of the "bump patrol," they start "Scrotum Patrol," with a canary yellow circle around Tom Cruise's crotch and the caption "*F-Girl* exclusive, Tom's sperm poised to produce baby brother for little Suri."

Another popular feature is "Who Deserves It More?" Pictures of American mothers are juxtaposed with pictures of French and Danish mothers, captioned with accounts of our crappy family policies versus theirs and the tagline, "Are we any less deserving or hardworking than French or Danish women?" But "Who Deserves It More?" also features poor, unemployed, or recently laid-off women and compares them to, say, Bernie Madoff's wife, to drive home how the increased concentration of wealth in the hands of fewer and fewer people since the 1980s has especially screwed women. And "Who Deserves It More?" goes international, asking why the girls and women of southern Sudan don't deserve an education (96.5 percent cannot read or write) or why the pope doesn't think the women of Africa deserve to have condoms to fight AIDS.

F-Girl chapters have sprung up all over college campuses, where more privileged young women raise money for scholarships for poorer girls, as education is the best guarantee of getting women out of poverty. They also identify pharmacies that refuse to fill prescriptions for birth control pills and stand at their doors posing as insurance salesmen, so no one will want to enter. The First Lady has ensured that certificates be issued for free annual mammograms and pap smears for cervical cancer for women who cannot afford them, following Japan's lead in the summer of 2009. Building on *Ms.* magazine's "No Comment" feature showcasing offensive ads, the "Stop the Insults" campaign has established its own YouTube-style Web site showcasing the most retrograde images of women in film, TV, magazines, and on the Internet with detailed information on which advertisers supported them and, thus, which products you should never let darken your door again. Massive picketing and demonstrations at the network and cable channels have brought in more women with feminist sensibilities as commentators and reporters. And now that there's nationally funded day care, more women can and do run for political office. The "100% solution" is the new mantra demanding pay equity so that women, on average, earn the same as men, and gain access to higher-paying jobs.

After their time in the park, the feminist mom and her daughter take the baby home; Dad will watch her now—as it is utterly expected that partners share child care fifty-fifty—and they will go get pedicures and a drink.

I don't know about you, but I really do prefer Scenario II. It may seem, right now, like the impossible dream, especially given the current federal deficit, looming problems like global warming, health care, and terror-ism, and Congress's seeming inability to do anything decent that matters to most Americans, let alone women. But who would have thought, in 1963, when the Kennedy Commission's Report on the Status of Women documented the widespread discrimination that women faced, that only ten years later the unthinkable—women going to law and medical schools, women getting credit cards in their own names, women with small chil-dren working outside the home in increasing numbers, abortion legalized, women reporters hired by networks, the double standard trashed—would all have occurred? Yet still, the Kennedy Commission, get this, recom-mended paid maternity leaves (yes, paid) and affordable day care, which we still don't have and which we need and deserve.

What happened in the late 1960s and early 1970s was a rejection of the prevailing common sense about girls and women—a misogynist and confining conception of their roles, their capabilities, their destinies. The consciousness-raising group, one of the most important inventions of the women's movement, enabled women to see which myths and ste-reotypes held them down. Once they punctured those and saw through them, they then got political. And these women, whether they were high-profile activists or newly divorced mothers of small children enter-ing the workforce for the first time, changed the damn world. And very few of us—with the exception of troglodytes like Glenn Beck—want to go back to what existed before.

It's time, once again, to shake up our current common sense that has, yes, folded certain feminist sensibilities into itself, but exiled others to ideological Siberia. And the media, while certainly including and even at times promoting feminist aspirations, have also played a central role in the construction of a more constricted worldview. The media have exhorted us to concentrate our psychic energy on celebrities, logos, diet-ing, and face-lifts and to flee from political involvement. They have paraded battalions of rich, spoiled, privileged, famous, or entitled women before us—whom we are to regard with a mix of envy and ironic condescension—and rendered the majority of women in the United States, and the inequality they still face, invisible. More to the point, poor women, lower-middle-class women, working-class women, most women of color, overweight women, women over sixty-five, are all portrayed as irrelevant losers with whom "we"—the presumed middle-class and upper-middle-class audience—should feel we have nothing in common. Because the kind of people who predominate on radio and TV talk shows are white men, what they focus on (Hillary's laugh) and what they ignore (anything resembling "women's issues") generate a kind of fatalism about what might be possible. At the same time, feminist activists, leaders, and writers rarely get on TV, and they are the ones who have all kinds of visions and ideas about the way forward. And finally, way too many in the media have reproduced and displayed the right-wing effigy of feminists as grumpy, man-hating, deliberately unattractive, humorless whiners.

The time is long overdue for us to reclaim the F-word and ridicule this stereotype, because it is this caricature of the feminist as ugly, aggrieved, anti-sex, anti-men, and anti-fun that keeps women in their place and strives to ensure that nothing resembling a women's movement will ever regain the momentum of the late 1960s and early 1970s. All my friends, including nearly all my men friends, are feminists, and here's what they're really like. My women friends, to varying degrees, like nice clothes, know what mascara is and even use it, have a terrific sense of humor, are (to my eyes) beautiful, and love kids, their own and others'. And get this—we actually like men, often a lot—some of us even married them! And still like them. In fact, some of our best friends really are men. And why are my men friends feminists? They are husbands who respect and value their wives and have seen what they've had to put up with over the years; ditto for their sisters. And they are fathers of daughters: few things can make a man a feminist faster than having a daughter and being told she might not be as good as a boy and can't have the same opportunities as he can. Plus, unlike the Mars–Venus line that men and women are fundamentally different, *The Shriver Report* documented that men and women want the same things out of life and the same things from a romantic partner. Most men now also agree with women that government and businesses need to provide equal pay, more flexible work schedules, and better child care.[14]

We can have, and deserve to have, everything that was laid out in Scenario II, and more. It is not impossible, unaffordable, or unnecessary, as enlightened sexism continuously insists. It will take time, energy, and patience, but it can also be gratifying and energizing getting there. We need to make fun of and ridicule the media images that seek to keep us down, divide us against each other by age, class, and race, and insist that we spend so much psychic energy on our faces, clothes, and bodies that nothing is left for ideas, social change, or politics. At the same time, we also need to praise those media images and individuals who advance women's interests. Young girls—our daughters, our nieces, our friends' kids—need to learn how to talk back to the media at ever younger ages, and boys need to see how they are stereotyped, too. We can do more to boycott products and activities that seek to turn little girls into hooker look-alikes, and attack once again a double standard in which sexually active girls are sluts but guys are studs. There is so much that the women's movement accomplished and changed for the better, but there is serious work to do. In particular, motherhood, pay equity, female poverty, violence against women, and the acceptability, even celebration, of sexism: this is the unfinished business of the women's movement.

Talking back to the media may seem inconsequential or fruitless—and indeed, it only has a limited effect in bringing about change—but look at some of the great stuff we get to see now that we never saw in, say, 1985. But that's not the point—it's not necessarily about them, it's about us, and changing what we can imagine. It's a first step, and a not unimportant one. More of us can get involved in issues we care about, learn about political organizing, donate to organizations dedicated to improving the lot of women and children, even run for office. After all, who would have believed we could elect an African American man president of the United States?

At the end of *Where the Girls Are*, back in 1994 when my daughter was four, I wrote that while I expected her and her generation to have the same struggles with media images that the baby boomers did, I also suspected that they would wise up to it sooner, "that they will be less patient and less willing to compromise." This was my hope. "For she will see with her eyes and feel with her spirit that despite all this, women are not helpless victims, they are fighters. And she will want to be a fighter too." It's possible I was overly optimistic. But really, haven't we had enough? Isn't it time, Buffy-style, to take a giant stake and drive it right through the beastly heart of enlightened sexism? Because I think that, in our heart of hearts, we do miss feminism: its zeal, its audacity, its righteous justice. So let's have some fun, and get to work.

NOTES

INTRODUCTION: FANTASIES OF POWER

1. Christina Hoff Sommers, *The War Against Boys: How Misguided Feminism Is Harming Our Young Men* (New York: Simon & Schuster, 2000).

2. American Association of University Women, "Behind the Pay Gap," 2007, www.aauw.org/about/newsroom//presskits/paygap.cfm.

3. For an excellent rant against and analysis of this new sexist fare see Ariel Levy, *Female Chauvinist Pigs: Women and the Rise of Raunch Culture* (New York: Free Press, 2006).

4. See the superb essay by Yvonne Tasker and Diane Negra, "Feminist Politics and Postfeminist Culture," in their coedited collection, *Interrogating Postfeminism* (Durham, N.C.: Duke University Press, 2007), 2.

5. Rosalind Gill does a superb job of summarizing postfeminism in the media in *Gender and the Media* (Cambridge, U.K.: Polity Press, 2007), 40.

6. I am adapting this term from Sut Jhally and Justin Lewis's term "enlightened racism" from their book *Enlightened Racism: The Cosby Show, Audiences, and the Myth of the American Dream* (Boulder, Westview Press, Colo.: 1992).

7. This entire discussion of enlightened sexism is indebted to Angela McRobbie's pathbreaking work on postfeminism. See, for example, "Notes on Postfeminism and Popular Culture: Bridget Jones and the New Gender Regime," in *All About the Girl*, ed. Anita Harris (New York: Routledge, 2004); see also Gill, *Gender and the Media*.

8. The most astute scholar of postfeminist media is Angela McRobbie, and this book draws from her crucially important book *The Aftermath of Feminism* (London: Sage, 2009).

9. McRobbie, *The Aftermath of Feminism*, 11.

10. For the definitive discussion of backlash in the 1980s see Susan Faludi's *Backlash: The Undeclared War Against American Women* (New York: Crown, 1991).

11. For a recent take on the stereotyping of feminists by a young feminist, see Jessica Valenti, *Full Frontal Feminism* (Emeryville, Calif.: Seal Press, 2007).

12. This need to "take feminism into account" so it can be rejected is central to McRobbie's argument.

13. Gill, *Gender and the Media*, 90.

14. Cited in Marcyliena Morgan, "Hip-Hop Women Shredding the Veil: Race and Class in Popular Feminist Identity," *South Atlantic Quarterly* 104 (Summer 2005): 436.

15. Gill, *Gender and the Media*, 109.

16. Susan Faludi, *The Terror Dream: Fear and Fantasy in Post-9/11 America* (New York: Metropolitan Books, 2007), 21–45.

17. Ibid., all cited on 21.

18. McRobbie, "Notes on Postfeminism," 4.

19. Gill, *Gender and the Media*, 40.

20. Ibid., 267.

21. Gill emphasizes this point as well in ibid., 39, 266–67.

22. Ibid., 40.

23. Thanks to Robin Means Coleman for the girl-on-girl violence point.

24. Gill, *Gender and the Media*, 111, 81.

25. "Consumer Entertainment Spending Hits Post-WWII High, Pointing to Saturation," Kagan Insights, www.marketingcharts.com/television/new-tech-driving-interest-in-entertainment-media-1942. November 10, 2005.

26. This notion of fun house mirrors comes from Todd Gitlin, *The Whole World Is Watching* (Berkeley: University of California Press, 1980).

27. Stuart Hall, "Encoding/Decoding," in *Culture, Media, Language*, ed. Stuart Hall (New York: Routledge, 1980). And I want to thank my daughter, Ella, for pointing out that these days a negotiated reading of media texts is the preferred reading.

28. Patricia Tjaden and Nancy Thoennes, "Prevalence, Incidence and Consequences of Violence Against Women: Findings from the National Violence Against Women Survey," National Institute of Justice Centers for Disease Control and Prevention, 1998, http://www.ncjrs.gov/pdffiles/172837.pdf.

29. Sarah E. Needleman, "Pay Gap Between Men and Women Remains a Reality in Work Force," CareerJournal.com, April 24, 2007, http://208.144.115.170/salaryhiring/hotissues/20070424-needleman.html.

30. See "Bush Administration Weakens Title IX," by the National Women's Law Center at http://www.nwlc.org/details.cfm?id=2198&section=newsroom, 2003.

31. See the Rockefeller Foundation / *Time* magazine poll in Nancy Gibbs, "What Women Want Now," *Time*, October 26, 2009, 31.

32. See the various essays that make this point in Anita Harris, ed., *All About the Girl* (New York: Routledge, 2004).

1. GET THE GIRLS

1. Tom Shales, "Fox Forgets the Zip in *Beverly Hills 90210*," *Washington Post*, October 4, 1990, D12.

2. Matt Roush, " 'Beverly': Not Totally Cool in High School," *USA Today*, October 4, 1990, 3D.

3. Jay Sharbutt, "New Fox Series Says Values Distorted in Beverly Hills," Associated Press, October 4, 1990.

4. "21 Injured as Teen Girls Rush 'Beverly Hills 90210' Actor," Associated Press, August 10, 1991.

5. Deborah Hastings, "*Beverly Hills, 90210* Is, Like, Unbelievably Popular," Associated Press, December 29, 1991; Barry Layne, "FBC's Ratings Keen Among Teens," *Hollywood Reporter*, December 31, 1991.

6. E. Graham McKinley, *Beverly Hills 90210: Television, Gender and Identity* (Philadelphia: University of Pennsylvania Press, 1997), 16.

7. Ibid., 1.

8. Transcript of Hill's testimony available at http://www.mith2.umd.edu/WomensStudies/GenderIssues/SexualHarassment/hill-thomas-testimony, October 11, 1991.

9. Chris Black, "Four Women, Including First Black, Elected to US Senate," *Boston Globe*, November 4, 1992, 1.

10. "The Decade of Women, 1992–2002," women in Congress, http://womenincongress.house.gov/essays/essay4/decade-women.html.

11. Mary Celeste Kearny, "The Changing Face of Teen Television, or Why We All Love Buffy," in *Undead TV: Critical Writings on Buffy the Vampire Slayer*, ed. Elana Levine and Lisa Parks (Durham, N.C.: Duke University Press, 2006).

12. Academics refer to this as "parasocial interactions." For an important overview see D. C. Giles, "Parasocial Interaction: A Review of the Literature and a Model for Future Research," *Media Psychology* 4 (2002): 279–305.

13. McKinley, who conducted focus groups with viewers, describes this as "playing pundit." McKinley, *Beverly Hills 90210*, 10.

14. Naomi R. Rockler, "From Magic Bullets to Shooting Blanks: Reality, Criticism and Beverly Hills 90210," *Western Journal of Communication* 63 (Winter 1999): 72–95.

15. Ibid.

16. As Roiphe wrote, in challenging statistics from the National Women's Study that one in eight American women have been raped at least once, and that the number was even higher for attempted rapes, "If I was really standing in the middle of an epidemic, a crisis, if 25 percent of my female friends were really being raped, wouldn't I know about it?" See Katha Pollitt, *Reasonable Creatures* (New York: Alfred A. Knopf, 1994), 164.

17. Darcy Haag Granello, "Using *Beverly Hills, 90210* to Explore Developmental Issues in Female Adolescents," *Youth and Society* 29 (September 1997): 37.

18. In 1992 Fox moved *90210* from its previous slot on Thursdays to a Wednesday slot at 8:00 P.M., followed by *Melrose Place*. *Melrose* became such a hit that in 1994 they moved it to Monday nights at 8:00 to serve as its prime-time lead-in show that night, paving the way for *Party of Five*.

19. Lisa de Moraes, "Ratings: *Melrose Place* to Be," *Hollywood Reporter*, April 22, 1994; Lisa de Moraes, "Kiss or No Kiss, *Melrose* Lifts Fox to Top Spot," *Hollywood Reporter*, May 20, 1994.

20. Cited in Robert Miklitsch, "Gen-X TV: Political-Libidinal Structures of Feeling in *Melrose Place*," *Journal of Film and Television* 55 (Spring 2003): 16.

21. "Interview: Heather Locklear," *Playboy*, October 1994, 136.

22. Robert Miklitsch, "Gen-X TV," 23.

23. Cited in Bonnie J. Dow, *Prime-Time Feminism: Television, Media Culture, and the Women's Movement Since 1970* (Philadelphia: University of Pennsylvania Press, 1996), 140. I rely heavily on Dow's sharp interpretation of this show.

24. Ibid., 143.

25. Claudia Collins, "Viewer Letters as Audience Research: The Case of *Murphy Brown*," *Journal of Broadcasting and Electronic Media* 41 (1997): 117–18.

26. Ibid., 123.

27. Ibid., 152.

28. I draw from Jimmy Draper's excellent senior honors thesis, "How to Suppress Women Rioting: The News Media Coverage of the Riot Grrrl Movement" (unpublished senior honors thesis, Arts and Ideas Program, Residential College, University of Michigan, 2000), chap. 2, p. 2.

29. Kearney, "The Changing Face of Teen Television," 60–61.

30. I draw here from Mary Celeste Kearney's fine book, *Girls Make Media* (New York: Routledge, 2006), 59.

31. Ibid., 60.

32. Draper, "How to Suppress Women Rioting," chap. 2.

33. Ibid.

34. Ibid.

35. Elizabeth Snead, "Feminist Riot Grrls Don't Just Wanna Have Fun," *USA Today*, August 7, 1992, 5D.

36. "Anti-Fashion Statements," *USA Today*, August 7, 1992, 5D.

37. Farai Chideya et al., "Revolution, Girl Style," *Newsweek*, November 23, 1992, 84–86.

38. Dan Auty, Justin Cawthorne, Chris Barrett, and Peter Dodd, *The 100 Best-Selling Albums of the '90s* (Phoenix, Ariz.: Amber Books, 2004).

39. Kara Jesella and Marisa Meltzer, *How Sassy Changed My Life: A Love Letter to the Greatest Teen Magazine of All Time* (New York: Farrar, Straus and Giroux, 2007).

40. Alex Ross, in his blurb for Jesella and Metzer, *How Sassy Changed My Life*.

41. Jesella and Meltzer, *How Sassy Changed My Life*, 4, 8.

42. Ibid., 8.

43. Ibid., 32, 95; "Petersen Snaps Up *Sassy*," *Folio*, November 15, 1994, 13; Farai Chideya, "Revolution, Girl Style," 84.

44. Jesella and Meltzer, *How Sassy Changed My Life*, 12.

45. Grace Kyung Won Hong, "I Hate My Body," *Sassy*, December 1990, 48–49.

46. Karen Catchpole, "Karen Tries to Get Thinner Thighs, Longer Hair, Bigger Breasts, Tanner Skin and a Boyfriend Through the Mail," *Sassy*, February 1991, 48–49.

47. Christina Kelly, "Why You Liked Yourself Better When You Were 11," *Sassy*, July 1991, 56.

48. Christina Kelly, "What Now?" *Sassy*, January 1994, 48–49.

49. Christina Kelly, "The Dirty, Scummy Truth About Spring Break (Or Where the Jerks Are)," *Sassy*, April 1989, 57, 83.

50. Most of the writers went and were known by their first names. Their bylines often listed only their first names. Margie and Mary Ann, "How to Make Him Want You . . . Bad," *Sassy*, March 1993, 82.

51. Kim, "6 Reasons You Don't Want to Be Popular," *Sassy*, September 1991, 62–63.

52. Fashion layout, "Holiday Party Dresses," *Sassy*, December 1991, 57–59.

53. "Listen Up," *Sassy*, January 1989, 39.

54. Jesella and Meltzer, *How Sassy Changed My Life*, 59.

55. Karen, Margie, Mary Kaye, and Mike, "9 Things About America That Make Us Want to Scream and Throw Stuff," *Sassy*, August 1991, 92.

56. Jodie Hargus, "How to Fight Sexism," *Sassy*, December 1991, 60–61.

57. Christina Kelly, "I Am Woman, Hear Me Roar," *Sassy*, June 1992, 60–63.

58. Christina Kelly, "The Iraq Thing," *Sassy*, February 1991, 74–75.

59. Jesella and Meltzer, *How Sassy Changed My Life*, 69.

60. Christina Kelly, "*Beverly Hills 90210* Indecently Exposed," *Sassy*, September 1991, 53–54.

61. "Annual Entertainment Poll," *Sassy*, January 1993, 53; January 1994, 68–69.

62. Jesella and Meltzer, *How Sassy Changed My Life*, 40–41.

63. This important point, made by Barbara Hudson, is cited in Kearney, *Girls Make Media*, 5–6.

2. CASTRATION ANXIETY

1. Marylou Tousignant and Carlos Sanchez, "Va. Woman Tells Police She Mutilated Husband After He Raped Her," *Washington Post*, June 24, 1993, D1.

2. Ibid.

3. Joe Treen, "Treachery in the Suburbs," *People Weekly*, June 29, 1992, 32.

4. Timothy Egan, "Police in Oregon Makes Arrests in Assault on Olympic Skater," *New York Times*, January 14, 1994, A1.

5. Timothy Egan, "A Hard Life Spent Searching for Money and a Gold Medal," *New York Times*, January 15, 1994, A1; Michael Janofsky, "Ex-Husband of Harding Arrested in Skating Attack," *New York Times*, January 20, 1994, A1.

6. *ABC World News Tonight*, February 11, 1993.

7. Andrew Sum et al., "The Growing Gender Gaps in College Enrollment and Degree Attainment in the U.S. and Their Potential Economic and Social Consequences," Center for Labor Market Studies, Northwestern University, 2003, http://www.emc.com/about/emc_philanthropy/roundtable/pdf/gender gaps_coll_enroll_plus.pdf.

8. Patricia Bliss, "Law School Enrollment and Employment for Women and People of Color," Minority Corporate Counsel Association, no date, http://www.mcca.com/index.cfm?fuseaction=page.viewPage&pageID=680.

9. Bill Hewitt, "Courting Trouble: A Defiant Joey Buttafuoco Is Indicted in the Statutory Rape of Amy Fisher," *People Weekly*, April 26, 1993, 122ff.

10. John T. McQuiston, "Girl, 17, Arraigned in Shooting of Woman," *New York Times*, May 24, 1992, M40.

11. Josh Barbanel, "17-Year-Old Is Charged in Shooting," *New York Times*, May 23, 1992, A28.

12. Rod Carveth, "Amy Fisher and the Ethics of 'Headline' Docudramas," *Journal of Popular Film and Television* 21 (September 22, 1993): 121.

13. Bob Kappstatter, "Tale of Lust, Vengeance Worth Millions," *Gazette* (Montreal), October 1, 1992, B5.

14. John T. McQuiston, "Lawyer Seeks Release of Girl in Shooting," *New York Times*, May 31, 1992, A35.

15. Joe Treen, "Sex, Lies and Videotapes," *People Weekly*, October 12, 1992, 104ff.

16. Paula Span, "Lolita's Hard Sell from the Cell; Studios and Publishers Pant for an Amy Fisher Deal," *Washington Post*, June 12, 1992, C1; Josh Barbanel of the *New York Times* reported on Naiburg's vibrating bed sales days in "A Morality Tale in Court and Tabloid," September 27, 1992, A38.

17. Span, "'Lolita's Hard Sell from the Cell."

18. John T. McQuiston, "Victim's Family Threatens Suit Against L.I. Girl," *New York Times*, June 11, 1992, B5.

19. Treen, "Sex, Lies and Videotapes."

20. Diana Jean Schemo, "Hidden and Haunted Behind the Headlines," *New York Times*, June 12, 1992, B1.

21. Treen, "Sex, Lies and Videotapes."

22. For a discussion of the conflation of these two categories in late-twentieth-century sex scandals, see Joshua Gamson, "Jessica Hahn, Media Whore: Sex Scandals and Female Publicity," *Critical Studies in Media Communication* 18 (June 2001): 157–73.

23. Bob Kappstatter, "Tale of Lust, Vengeance Worth Millions," *Gazette* (Montreal), October 1, 1992, B5.

24. Bill Carter, "Amy Fisher Story a Surprise Smash in 3 TV Movies," *New York Times*, January 5, 1993, C11.

25. Ibid.

26. Promotional lines cited in Carveth, "Amy Fisher and the Ethics of 'Headline' Docudramas."

27. Jeff Simon, "Random Notes on Amy Fisher's TV Trilogy of Sleaze," *Buffalo News*, January 10, 1993.

28. Carter, "Amy Fisher Story a Surprise Smash in 3 TV Movies."

29. "Younger Americans and Women Less Informed: One in Four Americans Follow National News Closely," Times Mirror News Interest Index: 1989–1995; released: December 28, 1995.

30. Hewitt, "Courting Trouble."

31. "Joey Buttafuoco," absoluteastronomy.com, www.absoluteastronomy .com/topics/Joey_Buttafuoco#encyclopedia, no date.

32. For an excellent analysis of the scandal, see Lorraine Delia Kenny, "Amy Fisher, My Story: Learning to Love the Unlovable," *Socialist Review* 24 (1994): 87.

33. Frank DeCaro, "Bobbitt Case Makes Half the Nation Extremely Jittery," *Washington Post*, November 17, 1993, D2.

34. Bill Hewitt, "Slice of Life," *People Weekly*, August 30, 1993, 57; Elizabeth Gleick, "Severance Pay: Amid Media Circus, the Bobbitts of Manassas Prepare for Her Day in Court," *People Weekly*, December 13, 1993, 92; Elizabeth Gleick, "Battle of the Bobbits," *People Weekly*, November 22, 1993, 57.

35. "Take These Jokes—Please," *People Weekly*, December 13, 1993, 95.

36. David A. Kaplan, "Bobbitt Fever," *Newsweek*, January 24, 1994, 52.

37. Andrea Sachs, "The Rise of the Penis," *Columbia Journalism Review*, March–April 1994, 7.

38. Kaplan, "Bobbitt Fever," 52.

39. Melissa Weininger, "The Trials of Lorena Bobbitt," no date, posted on

http://www.digitas.harvard.edu/~perspy/old/issues/2000/retro/lorena_bobbitt
.html.

40. Jerry Adler and Ellen Ladowsky, "Hanging by a Thread," *Newsweek*,
November 22, 1993, 50.

41. Cited in Sachs, "The Rise of the Penis."

42. Sheila Cavanaugh, "Upsetting Desires in the Classroom: School Sex
Scandals and the Pedagogy of the Femme Fatale," *Psychoanalysis, Culture and
Society* 9 (2004): 317.

43. Brian D. Johnson, "The Male Myth," *Maclean's*, January 31, 1994, 38ff.

44. "Clinton Taps Florida Prosecutor Reno to Head Justice," *All Things
Considered*, NPR, February 11, 1993; "Search for Attorney General Finally
Final," *Morning Edition*, NPR, February 12, 1993.

45. "Search for Attorney General Finally Final."

46. *ABC World News Tonight*, February 11, 1993.

47. "Clinton Taps Florida Prosecutor Reno to Head Justice."

48. David Kaplan with Bob Cohn and Spencer Reiss, "Janet Reno: 'Are You
Ready to Go,'" *Newsweek*, February 22, 1993, 26.

49. Elizabeth Gleick, "'General Janny Baby,'" *People Weekly*, March 29, 1993,
40–42.

50. Debra Gersh, "Reno Meets Press in Friendlier Confines; U.S. Attorney
General Addresses National Press Club Audience," *Editor and Publisher*, July
24, 1993, 17.

51. Joe Treen, "Zealot of God," *People Weekly*, March 15, 1993, 38ff.

52. Stephen Labaton, "Reno Sees Error in Move on Cult," *New York Times*,
April 20, 1993, A21.

53. Sam Howe Verhovek, "Decibels, Not Bullets, Bombard Texas Sect,"
New York Times, March 25, 1993, A16.

54. Laura Blumenfeld, "Janet Reno, in the Fires of Justice," *Washington Post*,
April 21, 1993, B1.

55. Judy Keen, "Reno Is Weathering the Storm," *USA Today*, April 21,
1993, 6A.

56. Stephen Labaton, "Reno Wins Praise at Senate Hearing," *New York
Times*, April 23, 1993, A20.

57. On the centrality of such sex-marking see the pathbreaking essay by
Marilyn Frye, "Sexism," in her book *The Politics of Reality: Essays in Feminist
Theory* (Trumansburg, N.Y.: Crossing Press, 1983).

58. This crucial term is from Frye, *The Politics of Reality*.

59. Frye, *The Politics of Reality*.

60. On the sexualization of Reno see Liza Mundy, "Why Janet Reno Fasci-
nates, Confounds and Even Terrifies America?" *Washington Post*, January 25,
1998, W06. Mundy may have read Frye's essay as well, as Mundy also makes

a point of how Reno is a "marked woman" by not taking on the trappings of femininity.

61. Lyn Mikel Brown, *Raising Their Voices: The Politics of Girls' Anger* (Cambridge, Mass.: Harvard University Press, 1998), 124.

3. WARRIOR WOMEN IN THONGS

1. Jennifer Steinhauer, "Pow! Slam! Thank You, Ma'am," *New York Times*, Week in Review, November 5, 2000, 5; Shawna Malcom, "They've Got the Power," *TV Guide*, June 23–29, 2001, 17.

2. Susan Hopkins, *Girl Heroes: The New Force in Popular Culture* (Annandale, N.S.W., Australia: Pluto Press, 2002).

3. A. Susan Owen, "Vampires, Postmodernity, and Postfeminism: Buffy the Vampire Slayer," *Journal of Popular Film and Television* 27 (Summer 1999): 24.

4. Cited in Dawn Heinecken, *The Warrior Women of Television* (New York: Pete Lang, 2003), 101.

5. Jennifer Pendleton, "A Place for the Spunky Gals," *Television Week*, November 10, 2003, 26.

6. I am indebted to my colleague Amanda Lotz for reminding me of this context.

7. "Sexual Harassment Charges," http://www.eeoc.gov/stats/harass-a.html. FY 1992–FY 1996, last modified, January 31, 2007.

8. http://www.rainn.org/statistics/index.html. (Data for rape notes 1991 and 1992 no longer in Web site.)

9. Heinecken, *The Warrior Women of Television*, 110.

10. Owen, "Vampires, Postmodernity, and Postfeminism."

11. Amanda Lotz emphasizes this point in her outstanding book *Redesigning Women: Television After the Network Era* (Urbana: University of Illinois Press, 2006).

12. Jennifer Weiner, "She's a Kick, in More Ways Than One," *Philadelphia Inquirer*, January 30, 1996, F01.

13. Jim Benson, "'Xena' Climbs Past 'Hercules,'" *Variety*, December 18–31, 1995, 35; Jim Benson, "'Xena's' Paradox: No. 1 Spot in Poor Syndie Week," *Daily Variety*, January 16, 1996, 20.

14. Jenny Hontz, "'Xena' Powers to Record Rating," *Daily Variety*, February 27, 1997, 5; and Jenny Hontz, "'Hercules,' 'Xena,' Tops in Top Markets," *Daily Variety*, February 4, 1997, 6.

15. Jenny Hontz, "'Xena' Hits a Season Zenith, Tops All Syndie Action Hours," *Daily Variety*, March 6, 1997, 7.

16. Elyce Rae Helford, "Feminism, Queer Studies, and the Sexual Politics of *Xena: Warrior Princess*," in *Fantasy Girls*, ed. E. R. Helford (Boston: Rowman & Littlefield, 2000), 136.

17. Ken Parish Perkins, "Fans from 6 to 60 Love Xena," *Fort Worth Star-Telegram*, February 15, 1997, C4.

18. William Grimes, "A Woman Wielding Many Weapons, Among Them a Sneer and a Stare," *New York Times*, May 19, 1996, sec. 12, 4.

19. Both quotations cited in Helford, "Feminism, Queer Studies, and the Sexual Politics of *Xena*," 138.

20. Grimes, "A Woman Wielding Many Weapons."

21. Shirley Knott, "Trendy TV: The X(ena)—philes, Xena's Tough, She's Funny and She Kicks Butt. What's Not to Like?" *Globe and Mail*, August 23, 1997, 9.

22. Helford, "Feminism, Queer Studies, and the Sexual Politics of *Xena*," 141.

23. Elizabeth Kastor, "Woman of Steel: Television's Warrior Xena Is a Superheroine with Broad Appeal," *Washington Post*, September 21, 1996, C01.

24. Heinecken, *The Warrior Women of Television*, 91.

25. Beth Braun, "The X-Files and Buffy the Vampire Slayer: The Ambiguity of Evil in Supernatural Representations," *Journal of Popular Film and Television* 28 (Summer 2000): 90.

26. Cited in Jessica Prata Miller, " 'The I in Team': Buffy and Feminist Ethics," in *Buffy the Vampire Slayer and Philosophy*, ed. James B. South (Chicago: Open Court, 2003), 35.

27. Owen, "Vampires, Postmodernity, and Postfeminism," 28.

28. Elizabeth Hills, "From 'Figurative Males' to Action Heroines: Further Thoughts on Active Women in the Cinema," *Screen* 40 (Spring 1999): 47–49.

29. Heinecken, *The Warrior Women of Television*, 108–10.

30. Ibid., 106.

31. Claudia Puig, "Box Office Soars on the Wings of 'Angels'; Divine Opening Gives Business a High Kick," *USA Today*, November 6, 2000, 1D.

32. Gina Arnold, "Girl Power," *Scotsman*, November 22, 2000, 10.

33. Carl Diorio, "No Kick for Slick Chicks," *Daily Variety*, June 30, 2003, 1.

34. David Hinckley, "Angelina's 'Lara' Raids Box Office," *Daily News*, June 18, 2001, 17.

35. Cited in the documentary *Lara Croft: Lethal and Loaded*, dir. Dev Varma, 2001.

36. Owen, "Vampires, Postmodernity, and Postfeminism," 24.

37. For a discussion of action films overturning these binaries see Hills, "From 'Figurative Males' to Action Heroines," 38–50.

4. THE NEW GIRLINESS

1. Nicholas Fonseca, "'Clueless' Is More," *Entertainment Weekly*, July 26, 2002, 72; Bernard Weinraub, "A Surprise Film Hit About Rich Teen-Age Girls," *New York Times*, July 24, 1995, C10.

2. Susan Faludi, *Backlash* (New York: Crown, 1991), 99–100.

3. This point was made by Laurie Ouellette in her excellent "Victims No More: Postfeminism, Television and Ally McBeal," *Communication Review* 5 (2002): 322.

4. Ouellette, "Victims No More," 316, 321.

5. The academic term for this is "essentialism."

6. John Gray, *Men Are from Mars, Women Are from Venus* (New York: HarperCollins, 1992), 16, 18–19, 33, 44.

7. Ellen Fein and Sherrie Schneider, *The Rules: Time-Tested Secrets for Capturing the Heart of Mr. Right* (New York: Warner Books, 1996), passim.

8. This point is made by Amanda D. Lotz, "In Ms. McBeal's Defense: Assessing *Ally McBeal* as a Feminist Text," in *Searching the Soul of Ally McBeal*, ed. Elwood Watson (Jefferson, N.C.: McFarland & Co., 2006), 143.

9. Tom Bierbaum, "Post-Globes Zeal for Fox's 'McBeal,'" *Variety*, January 26–February 1, 1998, 36.

10. Michael Epstein, "Breaking the Celluloid Ceiling: Ally McBeal and the Women Attorneys Who Paved Her Way," *Television Quarterly* 30 (1999): 28–39.

11. Lotz, "In Ms. McBeal's Defense," 139.

12. Jessica Lyn Van Slooten, "A Truth Universally (Un)acknowledged: *Ally McBeal, Bridget Jones's Diary* and the Conflict Between Romantic Love and Feminism," in *Searching the Soul of Ally McBeal*, 36–37.

13. Lotz, "In Ms. McBeal's Defense," 147–49.

14. For more on this see Jennifer Harris, "Worshipping at the Altar of Barry White: *Ally McBeal* and Racial and Sexual Politics in Crisis," in *Searching the Soul of Ally McBeal*, 160–75.

15. Lotz and Ouellette make this point as well. Lotz, "In Ms. McBeal's Defense," 150–51; Ouellette, "Victims No More," 329.

16. Cited in Lotz, "In Ms. McBeal's Defense," 152.

17. Helen Fielding, *Bridget Jones's Diary* (New York: Penguin, 1998), 15, 195, 24.

18. Joel E. Siegel, "Dear Diary," *Washington City Paper*, April 19, 2001, 45.

19. Andi Zeisler, "Bridget Jones's Diary," *Bitch*, October 31, 1998, 54.

20. Fielding, *Bridget Jones's Diary*, 36.

21. Ibid., 18.

22. Angela McRobbie, "Notes on Postfeminism and Popular Culture: Bridget Jones and the New Gender Regime," in *All About the Girl*, ed. Anita Harris (Cambridge, U.K.: Polity Press, 2007), 12.

5. YOU GO, GIRL

1. I am especially grateful to Robin Means Coleman and Catherine Squires for their comments on this chapter.

2. The term "Black Speak" is from Antonio Brown, "Performing 'Truth': Black Speech Acts," *African American Review* 36 (Summer 2002): 214.

3. Joan Morgan, *When Chickenheads Come Home to Roost* (New York: Simon & Schuster, 1999), 26.

4. Amy Caiazza et al., "The Status of Women in the States," Institute for Women's Policy Research, 2004, http://www.iwpr.org/pdf/R260.pdf.

5. "Health Status of African American Women," U.S. Department of Health & Human Services, 2005, http://www.omhrc.gove/templates/content .aspx?ID=3723.

6. "Women's Health USA 2005: Incarcerated Women," 2005, http://mchb .hrsa.gov/whusa_05/pages/0423iw.htm.

7. African American scholars who have documented how the media have elevated black women yet castigated them and, as Robin Means Coleman puts it, reproduced a "racist regime of representations" include Beretta E. Smith-Shomade, *Shaded Lives: African-American Women and Television* (New Brunswick, N.J.: Rutgers University Press, 2002), 6; Robin R. Means Coleman, *African American Viewers and the Black Situation Comedy: Situating Racial Humor* (New York: Garland, 2000), 107; see also Julianne Malveaux, *Sex, Lies and Stereotypes: Perspectives of a Mad Economist* (Los Angeles: Pines One, 1994); Bambi Haggins, *Laughing Mad: The Black Comic Persona in Post-Soul America* (New Brunswick, N.J.: Rutgers University Press); and Morgan, *When Chickenheads Come Home to Roost.*

8. For an excellent discussion of this struggle over defining "blackness" in the media see Herman Gray, *Watching Race: Television and the Struggle for Blackness* (Minneapolis: University of Minnesota Press, 2004).

9. For the paradox surrounding the demonization of the black "underclass" and the success of images about it, see S. Craig Watkins, *Representing: Hip Hop and the Production of Black Cinema* (Chicago: University of Chicago Press, 1998).

10. See Sut Jhally and Justin Lewis, *Enlightened Racism: The Cosby Show, Audiences, and the Myth of the American Dream* (Boulder, Colo.: Westview Press, 1992).

11. Layli Phillips et al., "Oppositional Consciousness Within an Oppositional Realm: The Case of Feminism and Womanism in Rap and Hip Hop, 1976–2004," *Journal of African American History* 90 (Summer 2005): 254.

12. S. Craig Watkins, *Hip Hop Matters* (Boston: Beacon Press, 2005), 216.

13. Tricia Rose, *Black Noise: Rap Music and Black Culture in Contemporary America* (Middletown, Conn.: Wesleyan University Press, 1994), 103–4.

14. Camille Jackson, "Essence Takes on Rap Music," January 20, 2005, http://www.tolerance.org/news/article_tol.jsp?id+1141.

15. Rose, *Black Noise*, 146–48.

16. Phillips et al., "Oppositional Consciousness Within an Oppositional Realm," 255.

17. Cited in Phillips et al., "Oppositional Consciousness Within an Oppositional Realm," 265.

18. Rose, *Black Noise*, 168.

19. Cited in Angie Colette Beatty, "What Is This Gangstressism in Popular Culture? Reading Rap Music as Legitimate Hustle and Analyzing the Role of Female Agency in Intrafemale Aggression" (unpublished doctoral thesis, University of Michigan, 2005), 49.

20. Elizabeth Kolbert, "The Media Business; TV Viewing and Selling, by Race," *New York Times*, April 5, 1993, D7.

21. Cited in Coleman, *African American Viewers and the Black Situation Comedy*, 111.

22. Anon., "How Blacks Differ from Whites in TV Show Choices," *Jet*, March 17, 1997, 54.

23. Alan Bash, "Competitive 'Living' Among 'Friends,'" *USA Today*, December 15, 1994, 3D.

24. Kristal Brent Zook, *Color by Fox: The Fox Network and the Revolution in Black Television* (New York: Oxford University Press, 1999), 102.

25. Bash, "Competitive 'Living' Among 'Friends,'" 3D.

26. Zook, *Color by Fox*, 67.

27. Lynn Elber, "TV Accused of Relegating Blacks to Low Comedy," Associated Press, May 20, 1994.

28. Smith-Shomade, *Shaded Lives*, 43.

29. Zook, *Color by Fox*, 68.

30. For a discussion of the complicated discursive spaces blacks must inhabit see Marcyliena Morgan, "Hip-Hop Women Shredding the Veil: Race and Class in Popular Feminist Identity," *South Atlantic Quarterly* 104 (Summer 2005): 425–44.

31. Smith-Shomade, *Shaded Lives*, 53.

32. Coleman, *African American Viewers and the Black Situation Comedy*, 202, 207.

33. Zook, *Color by Fox*, 54.

34. Ibid.

35. This point is especially emphasized by Zook.

36. Coleman, *African American Viewers and the Black Situation Comedy*, 170–71.

37. Zook, *Color by Fox*, 57.

38. Ibid., 63.

39. Ibid., 59.

40. Smith-Shomade, *Shaded Lives*, 68.

41. Costas Panagopoulos, "Obama Supporter Oprah Takes a Big Dive," *Politico*, April 7, 2008, http://www.politico.com/news/stories/0408/9427_Page2.html.

42. P. David Marshall, *Celebrity and Power: Fame in Contemporary Culture* (Minneapolis: University of Minnesota Press, 1997), 132, 134–35.

43. These insights come from my former Ph.D. student Antonio Brown, "Performing 'Truth': Black Speech Acts," *African American Review* 36 (Summer 2002): 213.

44. Kathleen Dixon, "The Dialogic Genres of Oprah Winfrey's 'Crying Shame,'" *Journal of Popular Culture* 35 (2001): 177.

45. Beretta E. Smith-Shomade makes this point as well in *Shaded Lives*, 176.

46. Antonio Brown cites this episode in particular in "Performing 'Truth,'" 221.

47. Smith-Shomade, *Shaded Lives*, 150.

48. See the cover of *O* for May 2008 for just one example.

49. Kathryn Lofton, "Practicing Oprah; or, the Prescriptive Compulsion of a Spiritual Capitalism," *Journal of Popular Culture* 39 (2006): 603.

50. Carroll J. Glynn et al., "When Oprah Intervenes: Political Correlates of Daytime Talk Show Viewing," *Journal of Broadcasting and Electronic Media* 51 (June 2007): 240–41.

51. See Jane Peck's book-length study of Oprah, *The Age of Oprah: Cultural Icon for the Neoliberal Era* (Boulder, Colo.: Paradigm, 2008), 9.

52. Lofton, "Practicing Oprah," 609–10.

53. Dana Cloud, "Hegemony or Concordance? The Rhetoric of Tokenism in 'Oprah' Winfrey's Rags-to-Riches Biography," *Critical Studies in Mass Communication* 13 (June 1996): 117.

54. This point is forcibly made by Jane Peck in *The Age of Oprah*, 38.

55. Elaine Lafferty, "Funny Starts Right Here," *Ms.*, Summer 2004, http://www.msmagazine.com/summer2004/wandasykes.asp; thanks to Robin Means Coleman for pointing out this quotation.

56. Benjamin Svetkey, Margeaux Watson, and Alynda Wheat, "Tyler Perry: The Controversy Over His Hit Movies," March 17, 2009, http://www.ew.com/ew/article/0,,20266223,00.html.

6. SEX "R" US

1. You can see all of these, courtesy of YouTube.

2. Helen A. S. Popkin, "Klein Gets the Message," *St. Petersburg Times*, August 30, 1995, 1D.

3. Brain McNair, *Striptease Culture: Sex, Media and the Democratisation* *of Desire* (London: Routledge, 2002); Pamela Paul, *Pornified: How Pornography Is Damaging Our Lives, Our Relationships, and Our Families* (New York: Henry Holt, 2005); Diane E. Levine and Jean Kilbourne, *So Sexy So Soon: The New Sexualized Childhood and What Parents Can Do to Protect Their Kids* (New York: Ballantine Books, 2008); M. Gigi Durham, *The Lolita Effect: The Media Sexualization of Young Girls and What We Can Do About It* (New York: Overlook Press, 2008).

4. The observation that American popular culture is simultaneously prudish and pornographic comes from Theodor Adorno and Max Horkheimer, "The Culture Industry: Enlightment as Mass Deception" in Max Horkheimer and Theodor W. Adorno, *Dialectic of Enlightenment*, trans. John Cumming (New York: Continuum, 1993).

5. See Rosalind Gill's brilliant discussion of this in *Gender and the Media* (Cambridge, U.K.: Polity Press, 2007), 90–91.

6. Gill analyzes these contradictory discourses about female sexuality in *Gender and the Media*, 194, 242–44.

7. Dean Chang et al., "Horrific End to Fairy Tale Life; Little Girl's Glittery Life, Violent Death Leave Nation Bewildered," *Daily News* (New York), January 5, 1997, 6.

8. Jerry Adler et al., "The Strange World of JonBenet," *Newsweek*, January 20, 1997, 43.

9. Keith J. Kelly, "Year of Living Successfully; Fuller Has *Cosmo* Covered Editorially & Financially," *Daily News* (New York), February 27, 1998, 42.

10. From the covers of the May, August, and November issues of *Cosmopolitan*, 1992.

11. From the covers and issues of *Cosmopolitan*, January, August, and November 1992.

12. From the covers and tables of contents of the January, May, August, and November 1997 issues of *Cosmopolitan*.

13. From the covers of the January, May, August, and November 2002 *Cosmo* issues.

14. "Get More *Cosmo*," *Cosmopolitan*, April 2008, 20.

15. Gill, *Gender and the Media*, 248.

16. "How to Be a Superhottie," *Cosmopolitan*, August 2006, 68.

17. All three articles are in the July 2007 issue of *Cosmopolitan*, 111, 116, 120.

18. "4 Reasons He's Not Talking," *Cosmopolitan*, July 2007, 56.

19. "Love and Lust," *Cosmopolitan*, April 2008, 137.

20. Myatt Murphy, "50 Things Guys Wish You Knew," *Cosmopolitan*, April 2008, 142.

21. Zoe Ruderman, "Cosmo Weekend," *Cosmopolitan*, April 2008, 240.

22. Brian O'Leary, "His Point of View," *Cosmopolitan*, April 2008, 76.

23. Murphy, "50 Things Guys Wish You Knew," 142.

24. Ibid., 145.

25. Peter Carlson, "If It Only Had a Brain; Maxim: Mindless Entertainment for Men," *Washington Post*, December 8, 1998, C1.

26. Richard Turner with Ted Gideonse, "Finding the Inner Swine," *Newsweek*, February 1, 1999, 52.

27. Alfred Lubrano, "On Fifth Anniversary, Maxim Still a Huge Hit with the Boys," *Philadelphia Inquirer*, April 2, 2002.

28. Turner with Gideonse, "Finding the Inner Swine," 52.

29. Peter Jackson et al., *Making Sense of Men's Magazines* (Cambridge, U.K.: Polity Press, 2001), 70–71.

30. Ibid., 69–70.

31. David Robbeson, "Saturday Night Special: Fun with Women," *Maxim*, April 2000, 136.

32. Ibid., 134; "Drive-Ins Live!" *Maxim*, June 2008, 82.

33. "30 Worst Albums of All Time!" *Maxim*, April 2000, 106–8.

34. "Fill Your Inner Emptiness with Material Goods," *Maxim*, June 2008, 52.

35. Lubrano, "On Fifth Anniversary, Maxim Still a Huge Hit with the Boys."

36. Gillian Telling, "Employee Benefits," *Maxim*, June 2008, 64.

37. Hayley Kaufman, "The Women of Maxim Behind the Racy Men's Magazine Is a Female Staff That Swears the Publication Makes Better Men," *Boston Globe*, April 11, 2002, C11.

38. Carol J. Pardun and Kathy Roberts Ford, "Sexual Content of Television Commercials Watched by Early Adolescents," in *Sex in Consumer Culture: The Erotic Content of Media and Marketing*, ed. Jacqueline Lambaise and Tom Reichere (Philadelphia: Lawrence Erlbaum Associates, 2005), 125.

39. Jillian Bailey, "The Home Front: Dysfunctional Family Hour," *Hollywood Reporter*, November 8, 1995.

40. Pardun and Ford, "Sexual Content of Television Commercials Watched by Early Adolescents," 126.

41. Jennifer Stevens Aubrey, "Does Television Exposure Influence College-Aged Women's Sexual Self-Concept?" *Media Psychology* 10 (June 2007): 160.

42. Dan Ronan, "TV's Family Hour Loaded with Sexual Content," CNN, December 12, 1996, citing a Kaiser Family Foundation study, http://www.cnn.com/US/9612/12/tv.sex.am/.

43. Ibid.

44. R. Ballie, "Study Shows a Significant Increase in Sexual Content on TV," Monitor on Psychology, May 2001, citing the research of Dale Kunkel, http://www.apa.org/monitor/may01/sexualtv.html.

45. Aubrey, "Does Television Exposure Influence College-Aged Women's Sexual Self-Concept?" 159.

46. Dale Kunkel et al., "Sexual Messages on Television: Comparing Findings from Three Studies," *Journal of Sex Research* 36 (August 1999): 235.

47. Monique Ward, "Talking About Sex: Common Themes About Sexuality in the Prime-Time Television Programs Children and Adolescents View Most," *Journal of Youth and Adolescence* 24 (October 1995): 595ff.

48. Jennifer Stevens Aubrey, "Sex and Punishment: An Examination of Sexual Consequences and the Sexual Double Standard in Teen Programming," *Sex Roles*, April 2004, 505ff.

49. Alex Kuczynski, "Noticed; In Offices, an Excuse to Mention S*x," *New York Times*, February 1, 1998, sec. 9, 1.

50. Kathleen Kenna, "From Prude to Lewd: America's New Obsession, Bill Clinton's Sex Life Has Become Talk of the U.S.," *Toronto Star*, January 31, 1998, A1.

51. Zell Miller, "A Deficit of Decency," Salon.com, February 13, 2004.

52. Lisa de Moraes, "CBS Gave 90 Million an Eyeful," *Washington Post*, February 3, 2004, C1.

53. Ibid.

54. Ann Oldenburg, "A Culture Clash . . . in a Nation a Flutter," *USA Today*, February 3, 2004, 1A.

55. Miller, "A Deficit of Decency."

56. Oldenburg, "A Culture Clash . . . in a Nation a Flutter."

57. Kimberle Williams Crenshaw, "Beyond Racism and Misogyny: Black Feminism and 2 Live Crew," in *Feminist Social Thought: A Reader*, ed. Diana T. Meyers (New York: Routledge, 1997), 254–55.

58. S. Craig Watkins, *Hip Hop Matters* (Boston: Beacon Press, 2005), 211, 217.

59. Ibid., 207.

60. Beretta E. Smith-Shomade, *Shaded Lives: African-American Women and Television* (New Brunswick, N.J.: Rutgers University Press, 2002), 81.

61. C. L. Keyes, *Rap Music and Street Consciousness* (Urbana: University of Illinois Press, 2002), 200.

62. Angie Colette Beatty, "What Is This Gangstressism in Popular Culture? Reading Rap Music as Legitimate Hustle and Analyzing the Role of Female Agency in Intrafemale Aggression" (unpublished doctoral dissertation, University of Michigan, 2005), 12.

63. Ibid., 46; Smith-Shomade, *Shaded Lives*, 103.

64. Watkins, *Hip Hop Matters*, 219.

65. Gina M. Wingood et al., "A Prospective Study of Exposure to Rap Music Videos and African American Female Adolescents' Health," *American Journal of Public Health* 93 (March 2003): 438.

66. Beatty, "What Is This Gangstressism in Popular Culture?" 12.

67. Dionne P. Stephens and April L. Few, "The Effects of Images of African

American Women in Hip Hop on Early Adolescents' Attitudes Toward Physical Attractiveness and Interpersonal Relationships," *Sex Roles*, February 2007, 251–64.

68. Rana A. Emerson, "'Where My Girls At?' Negotiating Black Womanhood in Music Videos," *Gender and Society* 16 (February 2002): 128.

69. M. Gigi Durham, *The Lolita Effect* (New York: Overlook Press, 2008), 69.

70. "The Supergirl Dilemma: Girls Grapple with the Mounting Pressure of Expectations," Girls Inc., 2006; available at http://www.girlsinc.org, 29, 17.

71. Jane D. Brown et al., "Sexy Media Matter: Exposure to Sexual Content in Music, Movies, Television, and Magazines Predicts Black and White Adolescents' Sexual Behavior," *Pediatrics* 117 (April 2006): 1018–19.

72. "Sex on TV 4," Kaiser Family Foundation, 2005, http://www.cnn.com/US/9612/12/tv.sex.am/.

73. Rebecca Wind, "One in Three Teens Get No Formal Education about Birth Control," November 28, 2006, www.guttmacher.org/media/nr/2006/11/28/index.html.

74. Chris McGreal, "Teen Pregnancy and Disease Rates Rose Sharply During Bush Years, Agency Finds," *Guardian*, July 20, 2009, http://www.guardian.co.uk/world/2009/jul/20/bush-teen-pregnancy-cdc-report.

75. Dr. Eileen L. Zurbriggen, chair, "Report of the APA Task Force on the Sexualization of Girls," American Psychological Association, 2007, 21.

76. Ibid., 30.

77. Ibid., 32.

78. Ward, "Talking About Sex."

7. REALITY BITES

1. Rick Kissell, "An Eye-land Paradise: CBS Sets Summer Record with Socko 'Survivor,'" *Daily Variety*, August 25, 2000, 1.

2. Wayne Friedman, "No Ad Immunity: Prices Triple for 'Survivor' Sequel; As Ratings Soar, CBS Hikes Rates to $14 Million for Series Sponsors," *Advertising Age*, August 28, 2000, 2.

3. "'Survivor' Winner Loses," *New York Times*, February 4, 2008, B2.

4. This point is made emphatically clear by Angela McRobbie, *The Aftermath of Feminism: Gender, Culture and Social Change* (London: Sage, 2009), 55.

5. George Bagley, "A Mixed Bag: Negotiating Claims in MTV's *The Real World*," *Journal of Film and Video* 53 (Summer 2001): 61–62, 69–73; Susan Murray and Laurie Ouellette, eds., "Introduction," in *Reality TV: Remaking Television Culture* (New York: New York University Press, 2004), 5.

6. Cited in Bagley, "A Mixed Bag," 66.

7. Annette Hill, *Reality TV: Audiences and Popular Factual Television* (London: Routledge, 2005), 179.

8. I chose those shows that had the highest ratings and/or created the most media buzz, and those, of course, that focused on female makeovers, women competing for men, and the like. Because many of these shows had great ratings their first season and then saw those ratings drop, sometimes considerably, I watched the first season and then compared it to a later (or several later) seasons, in part to track the devolution of the genre. Watching every single season of all these shows would have further rotted my brain and certainly crushed whatever remains of my spirit.

9. Edward Wyatt, "On Reality TV, Tired, Tipsy and Pushed to the Brink," *New York Times*, August 2, 2009, A1.

10. Laura S. Brown, "Outwit, Outlast, Out-Flirt? The Women of Reality TV," in *Featuring Females: Feminist Analyses of the Media*, ed. E. Cole and J. H. Daniel (Washington, D.C.: American Psychological Association, 2005), 72–73.

11. Steven Reiss and James Wiltz, "Why People Watch Reality TV," *Media Psychology* 6 (2004), 374.

12. Bagley, "A Mixed Bag," 64.

13. These are referred to by media scholars as "parasocial relationships." David C. Giles, "Parasocial Interaction: A Review of the Literature and a Model for Future Research," *Media Psychology* 4 (2002): 279–305.

14. Jennifer Maher, who was referring specifically to TLC's *A Dating Story* in "What Do Women Watch? Tuning In to the Compulsory Heterosexuality Channel," in Murray and Ouellette, "Introduction," *Reality TV: Remaking Television Culture*, 197.

15. Bill Carter, "'Survivor' Star: One Man Is an Island Villain," *New York Times*, August 16, 2000, E1.

16. Brown, "Outwit, Outlast, Out-Flirt?" 80.

17. Ibid., 77–78.

18. Ibid., 80.

19. Rachel E. Dubrofsky, "The Bachelor: Whiteness in the Harem," *Critical Studies in Media Communication* 23 (March 2006): 42.

20. Brown, "Outwit, Outlast, Out-Flirt?" 76.

21. Laurie A. Rudman and Eugene Borgida, "The Afterglow of Construct Accessibility: The Behavioral Consequences of Priming Men to View Women as Sexual Objects," *Journal of Experimental Social Psychology* 31 (1995): 513–14.

22. Danielle M. Stern, "MTV, Reality Television and the Commodification of Female Sexuality in *The Real World*," *Media Report to Women*, Spring 2005, 19.

23. Paul Davies et al., "Consuming Images: How Television Commercials That Elicit Stereotype Threat Can Restrain Women Academically and Professionally," *Personality and Social Psychology Bulletin*, December 2002, 1626.

8. LEAN AND MEAN

1. Jennifer Cognard-Black, "Extreme Makeover: Feminist Edition," *Ms.* 17 (Summer 2007): 48.

2. Anna Ayala, "10 Follies," *Advertising Age*, December 19, 2005, 4.

3. The sample in this study was quite small but compared women of different generations; the generational differences have been corroborated by other studies. See Marcene Goodman, "Culture, Cohort, and Cosmetic Surgery," *Journal of Women and Aging* 8 (1996): 67.

4. "The Supergirl Dilemma: Girls Grapple with the Mounting Pressure of Expectations," Girls Inc., 2006, available at www.girlsinc.org, 3, 12, 34–35.

5. Courtney E. Martin, *Perfect Girls, Starving Daughters* (New York: Free Press, 2007), 1.

6. The National Center on Addiction and Substance Abuse, Columbia University, *Women Under the Influence* (Baltimore: The Johns Hopkins University Press, 2006), 36.

7. Susan Bordo, *Unbearable Weight* (Berkeley: University of California Press, 1993), 208–9.

8. Angela McRobbie, *The Aftermath of Feminism: Gender, Culture and Social Change* (London: Sage, 2009), 60, 1.

9. Barbara Friedrickson and her colleagues have especially documented this. See Barbara Friedrickson et al., "That Swimsuit Becomes You: Sex Differences in Self-Objectification, Restrained Eating and Math Performance," *Journal of Personality and Social Psychology* 75 (1998): 269–84.

10. Yvonne Tasker and Diane Negra, "Introduction: Feminist Politics and Postfeminist Culture," in *Interrogating Postfeminism*, ed. Y. Tasker and D. Negra (Durham, N.C.: Duke University Press, 2007), 1–2.

11. See McRobbie's incredibly astute argument here in *The Aftermath of Feminism*, chap. 4, "Illegible Rage: Post-Feminist Disorders"; her analysis is much more complex and sophisticated than the one I offer here.

12. McRobbie, *The Aftermath of Feminism*, 104.

13. Ibid., 1.

14. "Pleasure Reading: Associations Between Young Women's Sexual Attitudes and Their Reading of Contemporary Women's Magazines," Janna L. Kim, L. Monique Ward, *Psychology of Women Quarterly* 28 (March 2004), 48.

15. Rick Kissell, "'Swan' on the Nose," *Daily Variety*, April 12, 2004, 6.

16. "Effects of Reality Television on Plastic Surgery," *Association of Operating Room Nurses Journal* 79 (June 2004): 1215.

17. George W. Weston, "T.V.'s Cosmetic and Plastic Surgery Shows," 2009, http://www.cosmeticsurgery.com/articles/archive/an~157/.

18. "Surgery; ASPS Study Proves Plastic Surgery Reality TV Shows Directly

Influence Patients to Have Surgery," *Surgery Litigation and Law Weekly*, August 10, 2007, 703.

19. "Women on 'Procedures,'" *Adweek*, February 2, 2004, 31.

20. "Surgical Technology; Study Shows Cosmetic Surgery on the Rise as Safety and Efficacy of Procedures Increase," *Medical Devices and Surgical Technology Week*, October 14, 2007, 77.

21. http://www.plasticsurgery.org/Media/stats/2008-surgeon-physician-fees-cosmetic-surgery-minimally-invasive-procedures.pdf, 2008.

22. "Quick Facts: Highlights of the ASAPS 2006 Statistics on Cosmetic Surgery," American Society for Aesthetic Plastic Surgery, 2006, www.surgery.org/download/2006. Facts.pdf.

23. Sooyoung Cho, "TV News Coverage of Plastic Surgery," *Journalism and Mass Communication Quarterly* 84 (Spring 2007): 81.

24. For a full discussion of the breast implant controversy see Marcia Angell, *Science on Trial: The Clash of Medical Evidence and the Law in the Breast Implant Case* (New York: W. W. Norton, 1997).

25. Jennifer Cognard-Black, "Extreme Makeover: Feminist Edition," *Ms.* 17 (Summer 2007): 48.

26. Kelly Jane Torrance, "Weighing In on This; Wispy Models Seen Harmful to the Culture," *Washington Times*, April 21, 2008, A2.

27. Eric Wilson, "Doctors Fault Designers' Stance over Thin Models," *New York Times*, January 9, 2007, C1.

28. Eric Wilson, "Amid Drug Use Reports, 2 More Brands Drop Kate Moss," *New York Times*, September 22, 2005, C3.

29. Nicole Lampert, "Dumped? Not Our Kate, Says Fashion Chiefs," *Daily Mail*, November 11, 2005, 27; Robyn Riley, "A Model Not to Be Followed," *Sunday Herald Sun*, April 16, 2006, 19.

30. Michelle Jeffers, "Behind Dove's 'Real Beauty,'" *Adweek*, September 12, 2005.

31. Jack Neff, "Unilever: Don't Let Beauty Get Too Real," *Advertising Age*, April 16, 2007, 1.

32. "U.S. Obesity Trends, Trends By State, 1985–2008," 2009, Centers for Disease Control and Prevention, http://www.cdc.gov/obesity/data/trends.html.

33. Suzanne Gleason, "Sudden Implant," *Vogue*, May 1997, 250–51.

34. "Lip Enhancement, Frequently Asked Questions," http:www.dermanetwork.org.

35. Gleason, "Sudden Implant," 251.

36. Anne Weintraub, "Plastic Surgery's Wild Kingdom," *Vogue*, May 1997, 252.

37. Lynn Snowden, "Face Forward," *Vogue*, August 2002, 256.

38. Helen Bransford, "Welcome to Your Facelift," *Vogue*, May 1997, 324.

39. Gleason, "Sudden Implant," 250.

40. Bransford, "Welcome to Your Facelift," 324.

41. Snowden, "Face Forward."

42. Jenny Bailly, "Risky Business," *Vogue*, May 2008, 284.

43. Ibid.

44. Bransford, "Welcome to Your Facelift," 322–24.

45. Ibid., 354.

46. Karen S. Schneider et al., "Facing Off Over Plastic Surgery," *People*, October 18, 2004, 60ff.

47. Ibid.

48. David B. Sawyer et al., "Cosmetic Breast Augmentation and Suicide," *American Journal of Psychiatry* (July 2007): 1006–14.

49. Cognard-Black, "Extreme Makeover: Feminist Edition," 47.

50. Plasticsurgery101.blogspot.com/2007/06/drive-thru-botox-andmarketing-of.html, dated 2007/06.

51. Laura Hurd Clarke et al., "Non-Surgical Cosmetic Procedures: Older Women's Perceptions and Experiences," *Journal of Women and Aging* 19 (2007): 69–70.

52. For an excellent critique of the media frenzy surrounding mean girls see Rachel Blustain, "The Mean Scene: Who Are These New Bad Girls?" *Lilith* 27 (Fall 2002): 10.

53. "Cyberbullying and Online Teens," 2007, http://www.pewinternet.org/.pdfs/PIP%20Cyberbullying%20Memo.pdf.

54. Erika D. Felix and Susan D. McMahon, "Gender and Multiple Forms of Peer Victimization: How Do They Influence Adolescent Psychosocial Adjustment?" *Violence and Victims* 21 (December 2006): 708–9.

55. Felix and McMahon, "Gender and Multiple Forms of Peer Victimization," 720.

56. "Comedy 'Mean Girls' Tops Box Office with $25 Million," *St. Petersburg Times*, May 3, 2004, 2B.

57. Blustain, "The Mean Scene," 10ff.

58. These points are made by Blustain, ibid.

59. Meg James, "'Gossip Girl' Fans Will Need Remote, Not Net," *Los Angeles Times*, April 18, 2008.

60. Bill Carter, "For CW, a New Plot: Improved Ratings," *New York Times*, October 25, 2008, C1.

9. RED CARPET MANIA

1. Jennifer Davies, "Gluttons for Gossip," *San Diego Union-Tribune*, September 4, 2005; Vanessa Grigoriadis, "The Tragedy of Britney Spears," *Rolling Stone*, February 21, 2008.

2. See John B. Thompson, *The Media and Modernity* (Stanford, Calif.: Stanford University Press, 1995), 208.

3. Nat Ives, "Guess Who's Not Getting Any Fatter! Celeb Mags Max Out," *Advertising Age,* April 9, 2007, 1.

4. Simon Dumenco, "The Media Guy: In the Celeb-azine Universe, Subtle Shades of Stupidity," *Advertising Age*, September 5, 2005, 24.

5. Circulation figures for these magazines in 2005 can be found at the Web site, Magazine Publishers of America, "Average Circulation for Top 100 ABC Magazines," 2005, http://www.magazine.org/CONSUMER_MARKETING/ CIRC_TRENDS/16117.aspx.

6. Ives, "Guess Who's Not Getting Any Fatter!" 1.

7. Richard Perez-Pena, "Celebrity Magazines Gain, but Not Industry Circulation," *New York Times*, August 14, 2007, C7.

8. Jennifer O. Cuaycong, "In Pursuit of Fame & Fortune," *Business World*, June 2, 2006, S3.

9. David Samuels, "Shooting Britney," *Atlantic*, April 2008, 43.

10. Richard Perez-Pena, "Celebrity Magazines Post a Downturn in Sales," *New York Times*, February 10, 2009, B5.

11. Chris Rojek coined the term "achievement famine" in *Celebrity* (London: Reaktion Books, 2001), 149.

12. Joke Hermes, "Reading Gossip Magazines: The Imagined Communities of 'Gossip' and 'Camp,'" in *The Celebrity Culture Reader*, ed. P. David Marshall (New York: Routledge, 2006), 298.

13. Ibid., 302.

14. For an excellent discussion of how women identify with stars, see Jackie Stacey, "Feminine Fascinations: A Question of Identification?" in *The Celebrity Culture Reader*, 252–85. Much of this discussion draws from her fine work on this topic.

15. Stacey, "Feminine Fascinations," 254.

16. Ibid., 253.

17. Samuels, "Shooting Britney," 44.

18. This notion of celebrity magazines constructing a "moral universe" comes from Hermes, "Reading Gossip Magazines," 293.

19. For a lacerating condemnation of the news media's obsession with triviality in the 1990s, see Frank Rich, *The Greatest Story Ever Sold* (New York: The Penguin Press, 2006).

20. Joli Jensen, "Fandom as Pathology," in *Adoring Audience: Fan Culture and Popular Media*, ed. Lisa A. Lewis (New York: Routledge, 1992), 9–11.

21. Samuels, "Shooting Britney," 38.

22. Ibid.

23. Lynn E. McCutcheon et al., *Celebrity Worshippers: Inside the Minds of Stargazers* (Baltimore: Publish America, 2004), 120, 136.

24. Thompson, *The Media and Modernity*, 223–24.

25. "Shocking Trend: Stars Flaunt Their Stick Figures," *In Touch*, December 19, 2005, 58–61.

26. "Bare Bones!" *Star*, August 12, 2006, 34–35.

27. "Stressed-Out Lindsay Is Down to 97 Pounds," *In Touch*, May 11, 2009, 34–35.

28. "Who Wore It Better?" *In Touch*, December 19, 2005, 96–97.

29. "Red-Carpet Ready?" *In Touch*, July 10, 2006, 58–59.

30. "Hot or Not?" *In Touch*, July 10, 2006, 52–53.

31. P. David Marshall, "Intimately Intertwined in the Most Public Way," in *The Celebrity Culture Reader*, 317.

32. "Ecofriendly Makeover," *Life & Style*, May 11, 2009, 68–69.

33. "The Feud's Back On!" *In Touch*, July 10, 2006, 17.

34. "What I've Kept Secret," *US Weekly*, October 2, 2006, 76.

35. "The Twins Made Me a Better Man," *In Touch*, May 11, 2009, 39–43.

36. "The Feud's Back On!" 18.

37. "Mom at Last," *Star*, May 11, 2009, 49–50.

38. "Is Their Age Difference Tearing Them Apart," *In Touch*, July 10, 2006, 22.

39. See the *Star*, July 10, 2006, 24–25, and August 28, 2006, 24–25.

40. "Only the Best Baby Presents for J.Lo," *National Enquirer*, February 18, 2008, 6.

41. Susan Bordo makes this point about slim people's attitudes toward the obese in *Unbearable Weight* (Berkeley: University of California Press, 1993), 203.

42. Hermes, "Reading Gossip Magazines," 304.

43. Samuels, "Shooting Britney," 40.

44. Hermes, "Reading Gossip Magazines," 299.

45. Ibid., 305, 296.

46. "Women on Film—Dr. Martha Lauzen's 2009 Celluloid Ceiling Report," http://awfj.org/2009/02/28/women-on-film-women-on-film-martha-lauzens-2009-celluloid-ceiling-report-jennifer-merin-reports/; www.alternet.org/movies/39478/.

10. WOMEN ON TOP . . . SORT OF

1. I wrote an article about this that got me into some trouble, "Why Women Hate Hillary," *In These Times*, May 2007. Available at http://www.inthesetimes.com/article/3129/why_women_hate_hillary.

2. Most of these men were white and working class, a distinction not always made in the news media. My thanks to Robin Means Coleman for pointing this out.

3. Howard Kurtz, "Hardbrawl; Candid Talker Chris Matthews Pulls No Punches," *Washington Post*, February 14, 2008, C1.

4. Howard Kurtz, "Chris Matthews Backs Off 'Nasty' Remark on Clinton," *Washington Post*, January 18, 2008, C1.

5. Jamison Foser, "Media Matters," February 8, 2008, http://mediamatters .org/columns/200802080011.

6. Tim Harper, "Women Supporters Blame Clinton's Imminent Defeat on Sexism," *Toronto Star*, May 23, 2008, AA1.

7. Katharine Q. Seelye and Julie Bosman, "Critics and News Executives Split Over Sexism in Clinton Coverage," *New York Times*, June 13, 2008, A1, A22.

8. *NBC News* Transcript, *Today Show*, December 13, 2007.

9. Harper, "Women Supporters Blame Clinton's Imminent Defeat on Sexism," AA1.

10. Featured on *ABC World News Tonight*, December 7, 1994.

11. Sam Stein, "Campbell Brown Rips McCain Camp's 'Sexist' Treatment of Palin," September 23, 2008, http://www.huffingtonpost.com/2008/09/23/ campbell-brown-rips-mccai_n_128782.html.

12. Lynne Duke, "To Do: Slipcover Oven, Embroil Self in Scandal," *Washington Post*, February 22, 2004, D1.

13. Ibid.

14. Maria Puente, "Stewart's Image Is Tarnished, But for How Long?" *USA Today*, March 8, 2004, 5D.

15. Duke, "To Do: Slipcover Oven, Embroil Self in Scandal," D1.

16. Greg Farrell, "Lie May Cost Stewart Her Freedom," *USA Today*, March 8, 2004, 1B.

17. Stephen Winzenburg, "Is Couric Ready for Prime-Time TV News?" *USA Today*, April 10, 2006, 15A.

18. Veronika Belenkaya et al., "Katie's 'Eye' Do to 15M. Men Left in Dust as She Flees NBC," *Daily News*, April 6, 2006, 7.

19. Gail Shister, "Couric Takes TV Out of 'The Dark Ages,'" *Philadelphia Inquirer*, April 6, 2006, A1.

20. Eric Deggans, "Can Katie Save Network News?" *St. Petersburg Times*, April 6, 2006, 1A.

21. Peter Johnson, "Couric Makes It Official; She'll Be Broadcast News' First Solo Female," *USA Today*, April 6, 2006, 1D.

22. Sally Quinn, "Anchor Job Has Chain Attached; Like Others Before Her, Katie Couric Is Tethered to a Double Standard," *Washington Post*, September 12, 2006, C1.

23. Tom Shales, "No News Not the Best News for Katie Couric's Debut," *Washington Post*, September 6, 2006, C1; Eric Deggans, "Couric Presents a Softer Vision," *St. Petersburg Times*, September 6, 2006, 1A.

24. Deggans, "Couric Presents a Softer Vision," 1A.

25. Rosalind Rossi, "The Woman Behind Obama," January 20, 2007, http://www.suntimes.com/news/politics/obama/221458,CST-NWS-mich21.article.

26. See, for example, Christi Parsons, "Michelle Obama's Conquest of Europe," April 5, 2009, http://www.latimes.com/news/nationworld/world/la-fg-michelle-obama5-2009apr05,0,6697503.story.

27. Dave Cook, "Michelle Obama Now More Popular Than Barack," *The Christian Science Monitor*, April 23, 2009, http://features.csmonitor.com/politics/2009/04/23/michelle-obama-now-more-popular-than-barack/.

28. Imaeyen Ibanga, "Obama's Choice to Bare Arms Causes Uproar," March 2, 2009, http://abcnews.go.com/GMA/story?id=6986019.

29. Jodi Kantor, "Michelle Obama Goes Sleeveless Again," February 25, 2009, http://thecaucus.blogs.nytimes.com/2009/02/25/michelle-obama-goes-sleeveless-again/.

30. Jacqueline Mroz, "Female Police Chiefs, a Novelty No More," April 6, 2008, http://www.nytimes.com/2008/04/06/nyregion/nyregionspecial2/06Rpolice.html.

31. See this and comparable data from Catalyst, at Catalyst.org. See for example, "Women CEOs and Heads of the Financial Post 500, http://www.catalyst.org/publication/271/women-ceos-and-heads-of-the-financial-post-500.

32. Timothy L. O'Brien, "Why Do So Few Women Reach the Top of Big Law Firms?" March 19, 2006, http://www.nytimes.com/2006/03/19/business/yourmoney/19law.html?ei=5090&en=7cd938ca277b02bb&ex=1300424400&partner=rssuserland&emc=rss&pagewanted=all.

33. Jacob Goldstein, "For Female Surgeons, Barriers Persist," April 16, 2007, http://blogs.wsj.com/health/2007/04/16/for-women-in-surgery-barriers-persist/.

34. I am especially indebted to my research assistant Catherine Hammond for her help with this chapter.

35. http://www.northwestern.edu/univ-relations/media_relations/releases/2003_08/leadership_text.html, citing a study by Alice Eagly et al. in *Psychological Bulletin* 129, no. 3 (2003).

36. For a more in-depth and intellectual analysis of this see Angela McRobbie, *The Aftermath of Feminism: Gender, Culture and Social Change* (London: Sage, 2009), chap. 4.

37. Eve Kosofsky Sedgwick, "The L Word: Novelty in Normalcy," *Chronicle of Higher Education*, January 16, 2004, B10.

38. Lisa Diamond, "'I'm Straight, but I Kissed a Girl': The Trouble with American Media Representations of Female-Female Sexuality," *Feminism & Psychology* 15, no. 1 (2005): 105.

39. Ibid., 106.

40. Kathy Belge, "A History of Lesbians on TV," http://lesbianlife.about.com/cs/subject1/a/lesbiansonTV.htm.

41. Yvonne Tasker and Diane Negra, eds., *Interrogating Postfeminism: Gender and the Politics of Popular Culture* (Durham, N.C.: Duke University Press, 2007), 21.

42. "Taking a Toll: The Effects of Recession on Women," April 18, 2008, http://kennedy.senate.gov/imo/media/doc/Taking%20a%20Toll—%20report%20on%20effects%20of%20recession%20on%20women1.pdf.

43. Heather Boushey, "Women Breadwinners, Men Unemployed," July 20, 2009, http://www.americanprogress.org/issues/2009/07/breadwin_women.html.

44. Catherine Rampell, "As Layoffs Surge, Women May Pass Men in Job Force," February 5, 2009, http://www.nytimes.com/2009/02/06/business/06women.html?pagewanted=1&_r=1.

45. See Susan J. Douglas and Meredith W. Michaels, *The Mommy Myth: The Idealization of Motherhood and How It Has Undermined Women* (New York: Free Press, 2004).

46. For a detailed statistical analysis, see Heather Boushey, "'Opting Out?' The Effect of Children on Women's Employment in the United States," *Feminist Economics* 14 (January 2008): 1–36.

EPILOGUE: THE F-WORD

1. "Women in National Parliaments," Interparliamentary Union, July 31, 2009, http://www.ipu.org/wmn-e/classif.htm.

2. April 16, 2009, http://www.nytimes.com/2008/10/16/health/16infant.html.

3. Martha Burk, "Paid Family Leave—It's About Time," July 18, 2007, http://www.msmagazine.com/radar/2007-07-18-familyleave.asp.

4. Carol Hollenshead, "Women and Poverty," http://www.umich.edu/~cew/aboutcew/womenpov.html.

5. Alexandra Cawthorne, "The Straight Facts on Women and Poverty," Center for American Progress, October 8, 2008, http://www.americanprogress.org/issues/2008/10/women_poverty.html.

6. Ibid.

7. Media Report to Women, February 2009, http://www.mediareportto women.com/statistics.htm.

8. "The Supergirl Dilemma: Girls Grapple with the Mounting Pressure of Expectations," Girls Inc., 2006.

9. The pioneering work on ambivalent sexism is by Peter Glick and Susan T. Fiske, who developed the "ambivalent sexism inventory" to assess attitudes toward women's roles. See Peter Glick and Susan T. Fiske, "The Ambivalent

Sexism Inventory: Differentiating Hostile and Benevolent Sexism," *Journal of Personality and Social Psychology* 70 (1996): 491–512, and their summary of ambivalent sexism at http://www.understandingprejudice.org/asi/faq/htm.

10. Thomas B. Edsall, "Obama Seeks to Kill Hedge Fund Tax Break," *Huffington Post*, February 26, 2009, http://www.huffingtonpost.com/2009/02/26/will-the-taxman-cometh_n_170082.html.

11. Anup Shah, "World Military Spending," Global Issues, March 1, 2009, http://www.globalissues.org/article/75/world-military-spending.

12. Barbara Ehrenreich, "A Homespun Safety Net," *New York Times*, July 12, 2009, The Week in Review, 9.

13. Jessica Valenti, *Full Frontal Feminism: A Young Woman's Guide to Why Feminism Matters* (Emeryville, Calif.: Seal Press, 2007), 15.

14. Heather Boushey and Ann O'Leary, eds., *The Shriver Report: A Woman's Nation Changes Everything* (Washington, D.C.: Center for American Progress, 2009).

ACKNOWLEDGMENTS

Whenever Terry McDonald, the dean of my college, sends an e-mail with the subject heading "exciting opportunity," the faculty know they are in for major administrative duties. Thus in 2004 did I become chair of my department, a position not known for cultivating a contemplative frame of mind or allowing time for writing anything other than e-mails and memos that one's colleagues would prefer to live without. So my first and greatest debt of gratitude is to Terry McDonald, who granted me a leave for a year so I could write this book. His ongoing support of my work in so many ways has been invaluable to me. I am also indebted to my friend and colleague Michael Traugott, who agreed to serve as chair while I was away, even though he had already put six years into that job himself. His legendary sense of civic duty helped make this book possible.

The idea for this book resulted from extended conversations—and debates—between my agent, Chris Calhoun, and me. I want to thank Chris for always having my best interests at heart, for insisting that I stay true to my voice, and for representing those interests so well to others. I am grateful for his fidelity to my work and to me.

I have been heavily influenced by several scholars, most especially Angela McRobbie, whose work on postfeminism has been pathbreaking, and whose brilliant insights I seek to bring to a larger audience. The work of Rosalind Gill and Amanda Lotz has been inspiring and thought-provoking, and it has redirected and refined my thinking. I also owe a deep and heartfelt thanks to Stuart Hall, who met with me early on in this project and, not surprisingly, cut right to the heart of the issues that I was confronting. My conversation with him changed the direction and framework of the book, and I am very much in his debt, as are all of us who do media studies.

I am also indebted to so many colleagues here at the University of Michigan. Phil Hallman, the incredibly generous and helpful librarian of the Donald Hall Collection in the Department of Screen Arts and Culture, enabled me to view any and every television show and film I needed, and if the collection didn't own it, he would order it for me. My smart, enterprising, and indefatigable research assistants—Megan Biddinger, Helen Ho, Jennifer Fogel, and Catherine Hammond—found whatever I needed, typically in record time, and also brought their own astute perspectives on gender and the media to bear on their research for me. My colleagues Amanda Lotz and Robin Means Coleman read portions of the draft manuscript and offered sharp, invaluable comments on what was right and what was wrong, as did Catherine Squires. Mary Kelley and Alvia Golden also read portions of the manuscript and offered crucial boosts at critical moments. Dara Greenwood constantly steered me toward articles I might find helpful and illuminating. And the ongoing conversations with and support of Sid Smith, Carroll Smith-Rosenberg, Sonya Rose, Paddy Scannell, Phil Deloria, Peggy Burns, Gabrielle Hecht, Paul Edwards, Mary Kelley, Phil Pochoda, and Rowell Huesmann have informed my work and kept me going. Thanks also to Melanie DeNardo and Maggie Richards for their promotional work on behalf of the book.

I am also grateful to Janice Radway, Andrea Press, Toby Miller, Susan Faludi, Katha Pollitt, and Joan Braderman for their work, their continually stimulating ideas, and their comradeship. I also want to thank the staff in the Department of Communication Studies, especially Dawn Viau, Jessica Brown, Cornelius Wright, and Chris Gale, who enabled me to juggle my schedule so that the book could be completed. And at Times Books, I'd like to thank Kira Peikoff for her tireless and enterprising work on finding just the right illustrations for the book.

About eighteen years ago, a young editor called me to talk about a possible book on the images of women in the media. This was my introduction to Paul Golob, and my life has not been the same since. As we worked together on *Where the Girls Are* (his terrific title, by the way), I was amazed at my good fortune in finding such an astute, meticulous, and professional editor who also had a great sense of humor. *Where the Girls Are* inaugurated my career as a writer for a broader audience; it paved the way for me to write other trade books as well. When I submitted the proposal for this book, the editor I most hoped to work with was Paul. I lucked out. And once again, the partnership with this amazing, incredibly smart, and, yes, fun editor has meant so much to me. Paul is always in your corner yet helps you see how your book could be better without ever, for a second, making you feel like another vision is being imposed on the manuscript. Because I owe so much to Paul, admire him so, and because he is, to me, the Platonic ideal of the editor, I dedicate this book to him.

I also dedicate it to my daughter Ella, and to her generation. Ella has opened my eyes to the cultural forces and media representations that surround her generation, and has shown me how she and others resist and succumb to the various blandishments of the mass media. So she has given me a perspective that I didn't have. As the daughter of a feminist (and a feminist father as well), and as a member of the girl power generation, Ella has been told she can do anything. And yet she has learned to appreciate all too well how her choices are constrained by unforgiving workplace schedules in some professions, the continued sexism of some men, and a government that has been, so far, too shortsighted to see how supporting women and families lifts everyone's boats. So my hope is that my smart, hardworking, accomplished, and funny daughter, with one of the best bullshit detectors I know, and her generation, will talk back to and resist the constraints that still hobble their hopes and ambitions.

And finally, my deepest thanks to T.R., who always listens to the ideas, the rants, the kvetching about impossible deadlines, who read portions of the manuscript, who puts up with a house and a schedule constantly on the verge of total entropy, and who always offers support, reassurance, and another glass of wine. You're in my heart, you're in my soul.

INDEX

ABOUT THE AUTHOR

SUSAN J. DOUGLAS is the author of *Where the Girls Are*, *The Mommy Myth*, and other works of cultural history and criticism. She is the Catherine Neafie Kellogg Professor of Communication Studies, Arthur F. Thurnau Professor and chair of the department at the University of Michigan, where she has taught since 1996. Her work has appeared in *The Nation*, *The Progressive*, *Ms.*, *The Village Voice*, and *In These Times*. She lives in Ann Arbor, Michigan, with her husband, T. R. Durham.